GRAMMAR
MASTER ②

WorldCom Edu

Grammar Master

구성과 활용법

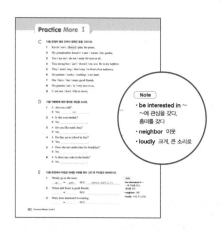
Point Check I

◆ **인칭대명사** : 사람, 동물, 사물의 이름을 대신하여 가리키는 말이다. 1, 2, 3인칭으로 구분되며, 문장에서의 역할에 따라 주격, 소유격, 목적격으로 사용된다.

◆ **be동사 (am, are, is)** : 주어의 상태를 나타내는 말이다.

◆ **일반동사** : 주어의 동작이나 상태를 나타내는 말이다.

1. 인칭대명사와 be동사

be동사는 주어의 인칭에 따라 그 형태가 'am, are, is'로 다르게 사용된다.

	단수형	be동사	복수형	be동사
1인칭	I	am	we	
2인칭	you	are	you	are
3인칭	he, she, it	is	they	

2. 인칭대명사와 일반동사

일반동사는 주어의 인칭에 따라 '동사원형' 또는 '동사원형+-s / -es'의 형태로 사용한다.

(1) 1, 2인칭 단수 / 복수, 3인칭 복수	I, you, we, they	동사원형 사용
(2) 3인칭 단수	he, she, it	동사원형+-s / -es
(3) 단수의 사람, 사물, 동물	Mary, a book, a dog	

3. Yes / No 의문문

Be동사 의문문 [Am / Are / Is + 인칭대명사~?]	일반동사 의문문 [Do(es) + 인칭대명사 + 동사원형~?]
• Are you a teacher? Yes, I am. / No, I'm not. (= No, I am not.)	• Does she teach English? Yes, she does. / No, she doesn't. (= No, she does not.)

4. There is… / There are… : ~이 있다

There is [셀 수 없는 명사, 셀 수 있는 명사 단수]	• There is an orange on the table. [셀 수 있는 명사 – 단수] • There is some salt in the bottle. [셀 수 없는 명사]
There are [셀 수 있는 명사 복수]	• There are many toys in the box. [셀 수 있는 명사 – 복수]

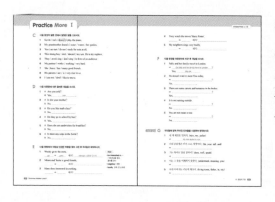

다양한 유형의 문제풀이!

앞서 학습한 내용들의 확실한 이해를 돕기
위한 다양한 유형과 난이도를 가진 문제
풀기 연습을 통해 문법에 대한 자신감을
높여 줄 수 있어요.

Lesson 1-1 문장의 종류

인칭대명사와 be동사

- 명사: 이름이 있는 사람, 동물, 사물을 말한다.
  ex) Susie, Tom, a cat, a book, Seoul, Korea
- 인칭대명사: 명사를 대신하여 나타내는 말을 가리킨다.

1. 인칭대명사와 be동사

	인칭대명사	be동사	줄임말		인칭대명사	be동사	줄임말
단수	I	am	I'm (= I am)	복수	we		we're (= we are)
	you	are	you're (= you are)		you	are	you're (= you are)
	he she it	is	he's (= he is) she's (= she is) it's (= it is)		they		they're (= they are)

2. be동사의 쓰임

(1) [be동사 + 명사] ~이다
- I **am Woody** from *Toy Story*.

(2) [be동사 + 형용사] ~이다
- She **is kind**.

(3) [be동사 + 형용사 + 명사] ~이다
- We **are good friends**.

(4) [be동사 + 전치사 + 장소] ~에 있다
- He **is in Seoul, Korea**.

Grammar Plus +

be동사 뒤에 오는 형용사, 명사 단어를 '보어' 라고 한다. be동사 뒤에 오는 이 단어들이 주어를 보충 설명하고 있기 때문이다.
I am an engineer. (I = an engineer)
➡ "내"가 "기술자"라는 것을 보충 설명해준다.

☆Check up!

Answer Keys p. 01

A 다음을 인칭대명사(I, you, we, they, he, she, it)로 바꾸어 쓰시오.

1	my cat	➡	it	2	Jack and me	➡
3	her brother	➡		4	our sisters	➡
5	Mary and you	➡		6	the oranges	➡
7	a short boy	➡		8	you and I	➡
9	this long ruler	➡		10	their cousins	➡

01. 문장의 기초 **011**

---

03 단계별 설명과 문제풀이!

많은 분량의 문법을 단계적으로 나누어 학습하는데 부담을 덜어 주었어요.

04 Grammar Plus +

본문에서 다루어진 핵심 문법사항보다 좀 더 심화된 내용을 살펴볼 수 있어요.

05 Check up

학습한 내용에 맞는 반복적인 문제풀이 연습을 통해 문법을 확실히 이해할 수 있도록 했어요.

내신대비를 위한 마지막 단계!

내신 최다 출제 유형

전국 중학교의 중간 / 기말고사 기출 문제들을 분석하여 가장 많이, 자주 출제되는 문제들의 유형을 파악하고 학습해요.

내신 대비 문제

해당 Chapter의 문법을 이용한 다양한 유형의 문제풀이로 내신에 완벽 대비할 수 있어요.

Grammar Master

Grammar Master Level 2

01

Chapter
문장의 기본

Point Check I

◆ **의문문:** 'Yes/No'로 답할 수 있는 의문문과 의문사를 사용하는 의문문으로 나뉜다.

◆ **Yes / No의문문:** be동사, 일반동사, 조동사를 사용한 의문문이다.

◆ **부가의문문:** 앞의 문장(주절)에서 말했던 내용을 한 번 더 확인하는 의문문이다.

◆ **선택의문문:** 둘 중 하나를 선택하도록 물어보는 의문문이다.

◆ **간접의문문:** 의문문이 문장 안으로 들어가 묻는 내용을 간접적으로 전달한다.

1. Yes / No의문문

(1) be동사의 의문문

- A   **Are they** dancers?
  B   Yes, they are. / No, they aren't.

(2) 일반동사의 의문문

- A   **Does he like** to play baseball?
  B   Yes, he does. / No, he doesn't.

(3) 조동사의 의문문

- A   **Will you go** to the swimming pool?
  B   Yes, we will. / No, we won't (will not).

(4) 부정의 의문문: '동사 + not'으로 시작하는 의문문을 말한다.

- A   **Aren't John and Mary** nice?
  B   Yes, they are. / No, they aren't.

2. 부가의문문

- Let's help the old people, **shall we**?
- Do not make a noise, **will you**?

3. 선택의문문

- A   **Which** subject does he like, English **or** music?
  B   English. / He likes English.
- A   **Do** you study math **or** social studies?
  B   Social studies. / I study social studies.

4. 간접의문문

- I don't know. + What does it mean?
  ➡ I don't know **what it means**.

의문문

Yes/No 의문문

> • Yes/No의문문은 크게 be동사, 일반동사, 조동사의 의문문으로 나눌 수 있다.
> • **be동사의 의문문**: be동사 + 주어~?
> • **일반동사의 의문문**: Do/Does + 주어 + 동사원형~?
> • **조동사의 의문문**: 조동사 + 주어 + 동사원형~?

1. be동사의 의문문

- **A** **Are you** a teacher?
  B Yes, I am./No, I'm not.

2. 일반동사의 의문문

- **A** **Do they like** to play soccer?
  B Yes, they do./No, they don't.
- **A** **Does he practice** the piano?
  B Yes, he does./No, he doesn't.

3. 조동사의 의문문

(1) 조동사: be동사 또는 일반동사를 도와주는 역할을 한다.
  ➡ can, will, may, must, have to, should, be going to

(2) 조동사의 의문문

- **A** **Will you** go to the party?
  B Yes, I will./No, I won't (will not).

4. 부정의 의문문: '동사+not'으로 시작하는 의문문을 말한다.

➡ 부정의문문에 대한 대답으로 부정을 뜻할 경우 'not'을, 그렇지 않을 경우 'yes'로 대답한다.

- **A** **Isn't Jenny** kind?
  B Yes, she is./No, she isn't.
- **A** **Don't you eat** vegetables?
  B Yes, I do./No, I don't.
- **A** **Can't he run** fast?
  B Yes, he can./No, he can't.

Answer Keys p. 01

A 보기 와 같이 주어진 문장을 의문문으로 바꾸시오.

> 보기
>
> Mike has a great jacket.
> ➡ Does Mike have a great jacket?

1 The girls aren't in the classroom.

➡ _____

2 Jane will pass the exam.

➡ _____

3 The giraffe's neck is long.

➡ _____

4 Students have to follow the rules.

➡ _____

5 John can speak Chinese.

➡ _____

6 Sally rides a bike.

➡ _____

7 He was angry with Jessica.

➡ _____

8 My father can't make cookies.

➡ _____

B 다음 의문문에 대한 대답을 빈칸에 알맞게 채우시오.

1 Can I use your umbrella? — Yes, _____you can._____

2 Did he bring his car? — No, _____

3 Was the picnic great? — Yes, _____

4 Didn't Tomas tell you something? — Yes, _____

5 Have you ever been to Japan? — No, _____

6 Can Jinju get there on time? — Yes, _____

7 Were they playing soccer yesterday? — No, _____

8 Can it be true? — Yes, _____

1-2 부가의문문과 선택의문문

- **부가의문문**: 평서문이나 명령문의 끝에 앞의 내용을 한 번 더 확인하는 의문문이다.
- **선택의문문**: A와 B중 어느 것을 고를지 묻는 의문문이다.

1. 부가의문문

⑴ 평서문: 부가의문문은 주절이 긍정이면 부정으로, 주절이 부정이면 긍정으로 묻는다.

be동사	You <u>aren't</u> angry, are you?
일반동사	People <u>love</u> that actor, don't they?
조동사	She <u>can</u> jump high, can't she?
완료시제	Harry <u>hasn't</u> lived here, has he?

➡ 완료시제는 과거보다 더 이전의 과거를 뜻하며 'have(has) + 과거분사'의 형식을 취한다.
완료시제의 부정형은 'have(has) **not** + 과거분사'의 형태이다.

⑵ 명령문: 긍정/부정에 상관없이 'will you'를 붙인다.

- Be careful wherever you go, **will you**?
- Don't be late again, **will you**?

⑶ Let's 명령문: 긍정/부정에 상관없이 'shall we'를 붙인다.

- Let's go on a picnic this Saturday, **shall we**?
- Let's not laugh at others, **shall we**?

Grammar Plus +

- 평서문에서 'I am not'은 'I'm not'이라고 표현한다.
- 부가의문문에서 '<u>I am</u>'의 부가의문문은 'aren't I'로 표현해 준다.
  I am smart and pretty, aren't I?

2. 선택의문문

- **A** **Which** will you eat, pizza **or** spaghetti?
  B Pizza. / I will eat pizza.

- **A** **Do** you want to go to New York **or** California?
  B California. / I want to go to California.

- **A** **Is** she French **or** German?
  B French. / She's French.

A 다음 문장의 빈칸에 알맞은 부가의문문을 쓰시오.

1 You ate lunch, ____*didn't you*____?

2 It isn't a good idea, _____?

3 Max could get first prize, _____?

4 They have not met before, _____?

5 Those guys live there, _____?

6 Let's have dinner tomorrow, _____?

7 Don't tell a lie again, _____?

8 This pie tastes bad, _____?

9 Sally has been to Japan, _____?

10 It's very cloudy today, _____?

B 괄호 안에서 알맞은 것을 고르시오.

1 Which chair is more comfortable, the former (or / and) the latter?

2 Is he American (or / to) Canadian?

3 Did she meet (Jack or Harry / Jack but Harry)?

4 Which shirt is more popular in LA, the blue one (with / or) the red one?

5 Do you want to go out with Sam (or not / not or)?

6 (Which / What) picture do you prefer, this one or that one?

7 (What / Which) scarf is beautiful, this one or that one?

8 Julia can't play with us, (does she / can she)?

9 You got a driver's license. You will drive a car, (will you / won't you)?

1-3 간접의문문

> • **간접의문문**: 의문문이 문장 안으로 들어가 의문의 내용을 간접적으로 전달한다.
> 이 의문문이 절을 만들면서 간접의문문이 된다.

1. 평서문 + 의문사 의문문: [의문사 + 주어 + 동사]

- I don't know. + What is this?

  ➡ I don't know **what this is**.
  ➡ 의문사가 문장으로 들어가 절이 될 때 주어와 동사의 자리가 바뀐다.

- Do you remember? + **Who** gave you water?

  ➡ Do you remember **who gave you water**?
  ➡ 의문사가 주어로 쓰인 경우에는 직접의문문의 어순을 그대로 사용한다.

2. 평서문 + Yes / No 의문문: [if(whether) + 주어 + 동사]

- I wonder. + Is he a new teacher?

  ➡ I wonder **if(whether) he is a new teacher**.
  ➡ 의문사가 없는 경우 if(whether)를 쓰며 '~인지 아닌지'로 해석한다.
    마찬가지로 주어와 동사의 자리도 바뀐다.

- I wonder. + Did they find a new route?

  ➡ I wonder if (whether) they found a new route.
  ➡ 조동사의 과거형은 본동사의 과거형으로 고쳐준다.

Grammar Plus +

- 'think, believe'와 같이 생각이나 추측을 나타내는 동사가 간접의문문의 주절에 있을 경우
  의문사는 문장의 맨 앞에 위치한다.
  Do you think? + What is he making now?

  ➡ What do you think he is making now?

Answer Keys p. 01

A 다음 문장에서 어법상 <u>어색한</u> 것을 찾아 바르게 고치시오.

1   Do they know where is Tommy?

         is Tommy ➡ *Tommy is*

2   Do you remember who cookies bought?

         ➡

3   I don't know what is his name.

         ➡

4   We don't know who the window broke.

         ➡

5   Max doesn't know what did she.

         ➡

6   Ask Helen why didn't she come to the party.

         ➡

B 다음 두 문장을 결합하여 간접의문문이 있는 문장을 만드시오.

1   I wonder. + Is Max a businessman?

➡   *I wonder if Max is a businessman.*

2   Let's ask Jim. + How did he find it?

➡

3   Please tell us. + How can we get to the station?

➡

4   Do you think? + How can she solve the problem?

➡

5   Do you believe? + Where did Sean get it?

➡

6   I wonder. + Do you love John?

➡

7   Please tell me. + Did she pass the exam?

➡

Practice More I

Answer Keys p. 01~02

A 다음 문장에서 어법상 <u>어색한</u> 것을 찾아 바르게 고치시오.

1 He couldn't know how old is the woman.

   <u>   is the woman   </u> ➡ <u>   the woman is   </u>

2 Whose subject do you like most?

   _____ ➡ _____

3 Hide your legs, can't you?

   _____ ➡ _____

4 Do you know where does he?

   _____ ➡ _____

5 What one is better for Nick, a novel or a magazine?

   _____ ➡ _____

6 He asked me that he could go hiking with Adam.

   _____ ➡ _____

7 Are they know what your hobby is?

   _____ ➡ _____

8 Make a chocolate cake only for John, won't you?

   _____ ➡ _____

9 I don't know what he is smart.

   _____ ➡ _____

10 Kate didn't tell her mom where was she.

   _____ ➡ _____

11 Do you think where I can find him?

   _____ ➡ _____

12 Thinking positive, and you can enjoy the present.

   _____ ➡ _____

13 Ask Timothy when leaves he.

   _____ ➡ _____

14 The press should be fair, isn't it?

   _____ ➡ _____

15 I can't find out where does Inho's car.

   _____ ➡ _____

Practice More I

B 다음 두 문장을 결합하여 간접의문문이 있는 문장을 만드시오.

1 I can't remember. + Who is James?

➡ *I can't remember who James is.*

2 Please tell me. + Why did Linda leave home?

➡ _____

3 Do you believe? + Who will gain the final victory?

➡ _____

4 Let's ask him. + How can we get to the station?

➡ _____

5 Peter wanted to know. + Was the book sold out?

➡ _____

6 I don't know. + Did Amy become a nurse?

➡ _____

7 Do you guess? + When will they come back?

➡ _____

8 Can you tell me? + What does that mean?

➡ _____

9 I wonder. + Did he break the window?

➡ _____

10 Do you know? + Who helped the old man last night?

➡ _____

11 I can't believe. + What did he say?

➡ _____

C 주어진 단어를 알맞은 형태로 바꾸어 문장을 완성하시오.

1 Julia forgot the boy's name, ____*didn't*____ she? (do)

2 I'm your best friend, _____? (be)

3 _____ book is this? (who)

4 Why didn't you _____ me yesterday? (help)

5　You look so tired, _____ you? (do)

6　Does the singer have an overseas performance schedule?
　　– No, he _____. (do)

7　Wrap this cake, _____ you? (will)

8　This song is great, _____ it? (be)

9　You are a good student, _____ you? (be)

10　He _____ go to the concert, did he? (do)

D　다음 단어들을 문법에 맞게 배열하여 문장을 완성하시오.

1　_____*When do you guess he will*_____ come back?
　　(do, guess, when, will, you, he)

2　They didn't know _____.
　　(is, when, Max's birthday)

3　_____?
　　(did, the key, where, find, you)

4　_____?
　　(don't, will, late, again, you, be)

5　_____, kimchi or bulgogi?
　　(to, want, which food, you, do, eat)

6　_____?
　　(did, night, what, last, do, you)

7　Mom wants to know _____
　　(be, what, want, to, I)

8　_____, will you?
　　(please, my dog, draw)

9　_____?
　　(do, is, what, day, know, today, you)

10　_____
　　(go, be, early, late, for, you, to, school, bed, or, will)

Point Check II

◆ **부사어 :** 부사처럼 쓰여 문장의 다른 요소들을 꾸며주는 역할을 함으로써 문장을 더욱 풍부하게 해준다.

◆ **1~5형식 문장의 동사 :** 목적어 여부에 따라 '자동사'와 '타동사'로 나뉘며, 각 문장의 형식에 따라 '완전/불완전 자동사', '완전/불완전 타동사'로 나뉜다.

1. 주어 : '~은, 는, 이, 가' 로 해석

- **The siblings** are very friendly to each other.
- **He** is a strong man.
- **Reading books** is very interesting.

2. 동사 : '~이다, ~하다' 로 해석

- He **goes** there tonight.
- They **are** so positive.
- We **will see** her next week.
- She **cooks** us warm chicken soup.
- Eventually, he **made** it successfuly.

3. 보어 : 주어나 목적어를 보충 설명

- Julia is **a pretty woman**. (주격보어 a pretty woman이 주어 Julia를 설명)
- He kept his desk **messy**. (목적격보어 messy가 목적어 his desk의 상태를 설명)
- I saw a man **singing** on the stage. (능동)
- The rumors made him **confused**. (수동)

4. 목적어 : 동사의 행위나 이유를 설명

- The wise man told **us** about the wisdom of life.
- My little brother enjoys **playing computer games**.

5. 부사어 : 동사, 형용사, 부사 및 문장 전체를 수식

- Wendy gets up early **in the morning**.
- She eats **very fast**.
- Animals make sounds **differently than** humans.

문장의 요소

주어

> • 주어: '~은, ~는, ~이, ~가'로 해석하며, 주어로 명사, 대명사, to부정사, 동명사 등이 올 수 있다.

1. 명사
• **My parents** always love me.

2. 대명사
• **She** is a graceful actress.

3. to부정사
• **To win the game** is not easy.
➡ to부정사는 'to + 동사원형'의 형태이며 항상 단수 취급을 해준다.

4. 동명사
• **Learning a musical instrument** is so exciting.
➡ 동명사가 주어로 사용될 때는 항상 단수 취급을 해준다.

5. 명사절
• **That you are honest** is certain.
= It is certain that you are honest. (가주어 it, 진주어 that절)

6. 비인칭 주어 it
• **It** is sunny today.

7. There + be동사 + 주어
• There are **many people** in the concert hall.
➡ 'There + be동사'는 '~이 있다'라는 뜻으로 하나의 동사로 취급한다.
한 개나 셀 수 없는 명사를 표현할 때는 'there is', 복수를 표현할 때는 'there are'를 사용한다.

Grammar Plus +

• **동격**: 주어, 보어, 목적어를 다시 한 번 설명해 주는 것으로 ',' (콤마)를 넣어서 표현해준다.
My little sister, Amy is very smart.

A 괄호 안에서 알맞은 것을 고르시오.

1 (I / My) bought a new car yesterday.

2 (Exercise / Exercising) regularly is important.

3 What I want to eat (is / are) a chocolate cake.

4 (It / That) is certain that it will rain tomorrow.

5 Many students (don't / doesn't) like to study math.

6 (There is / There are) many people in the park.

7 (It / That) is windy and rainy today.

8 Going hiking (is / are) exciting.

9 (This / It) is exactly 10 o'clock now.

10 (To keep a diary / Keep a diary) is good for you.

B 다음 문장에서 어법상 <u>어색한</u> 것을 찾아 바르게 고치시오.

1 This is difficult to understand the lecture.

This ➡ _It_

2 There was some students in the hall. _____ ➡ _____

3 Go hiking is my hobby. _____ ➡ _____

4 That's sunny and hot today. _____ ➡ _____

5 Many girls in the hall wears coats. _____ ➡ _____

6 Her comes to my house tonight. _____ ➡ _____

7 Taking a picture in the country are interesting.

_____ ➡ _____

8 It Helen is beautiful is certain. _____ ➡ _____

9 My wanted to buy a new pen. _____ ➡ _____

10 There is seven players on my team. _____ ➡ _____

동사

> - **동사**: '~이다', '~하다'의 뜻으로 주어의 동작이나 상태를 나타내는 말이다.
>   동사의 종류에 따라 문장의 형식이 달라진다.
> - **자동사**: 목적어를 필요로 하지 않는 동사이다.
> - **타동사**: 목적어를 필요로 하는 동사이다.

1. 완전자동사 : 동사만으로 완전한 뜻을 가진다.
- Harry **comes** in the afternoon.

2. 불완전자동사 : 동사 뒤에 보어가 나온다.
- Lucy **is** so intelligent.

3. 완전타동사 : 동사 뒤에 목적어가 나온다.
- I **will meet** them next week.

4. 수여동사 : '누구에게 무엇을 주다'라는 뜻을 가진 동사로 목적어가 두 개 나온다.
- She **sent** him an email.

5. 불완전타동사 : 동사 뒤에 목적어와 목적격보어가 나온다.
- Sometimes she **makes** me depressed.

☆Check up!

Answer Keys p. 02

A 괄호 안에서 알맞은 것을 고르시오.

1   Linda (wears / wearing) a black raincoat.

2   She (wants / want) to buy a new car.

3   The full moon (rise / rises) in the sky.

4   John didn't (study / to study) for mid-term exams.

5   I met (they / them) to complete a report.

6   He can (swim / swimming) in the sea.

7   Please (leave / to leave) her alone.

8   They (go / went) to the amusement park last week.

9   He found the box (empty / emptiness).

10 My mother made (he / him) a cheesecake.

Answer Keys p. 02

B 다음 문장에서 어법상 어색한 것을 찾아 바르게 고치시오.

1   I lose my bike on the way home.

_____lose_____ ➡ _____lost_____

2   He send an email last night.

_____ ➡ _____

3   He become a doctor.

_____ ➡ _____

4   They went shopping tomorrow.

_____ ➡ _____

5   John didn't said anything.

_____ ➡ _____

6   Tina making a cake last week.

_____ ➡ _____

7   She lived in Seoul when she is young.

_____ ➡ _____

8   Mom have me wake up early this morning.

_____ ➡ _____

9   Brian gave your some money.

_____ ➡ _____

10 We elected the leader Sally.

_____ ➡ _____

보어

> • **보어**: 불완전자동사와 함께 쓰이며, 주어와 목적어가 어떤 상태인지를 알려주는 역할을 한다.
> 보어로 명사나 형용사가 나온다.

1. 명사 보어: 주어나 목적어가 누구인지 알려주며, 주격보어, 목적격보어로 쓰인다.

- <u>She</u> is **a nice woman.** [주격보어 a nice woman이 주어 she를 설명]
- They called <u>me</u> **a chatterbox.** [목적격보어 a chatterbox가 목적어 me를 설명]

2. 형용사 보어: 주어나 목적어의 상태를 보충 설명한다.

- <u>Harris</u> looks very **happy** today. [주격보어 happy가 주어 Harris의 상태를 설명]
- My mother always keeps <u>our house</u> **clean.**
  [목적격보어 clean이 목적어 our house의 상태를 설명]

3. 현재분사/과거분사 보어: 현재분사와 과거분사가 형용사처럼 쓰여 보어의 역할을 한다.
현재분사는 능동을, 과거분사는 수동의 관계를 의미한다.

- The action movie is so **exciting.** [능동]
- Amy is **excited** at the news. [수동]

☆Check up!

Answer Keys p. 02

A 괄호 안에서 알맞은 것을 고르시오.

1   Listening to music makes me (comfortable / comfortably).

2   Susan usually keeps her hands (cleaned / clean).

3   I saw the boy (dancing / dance) on the stage.

4   You are a (nicely / nice) boy.

5   Joe makes me (sadness / sad).

6   We considered Linda (lovely / love).

7   The horror movie was (exciting / excited).

8   We saw the boys (playing / played) soccer in the field.

9   Today's breaking news is (surprising / surprised).

10   He found the story (boring / bored).

11   I was (confused / confusing) last night.

12   Your gentle smile makes me (happy / happily).

• **목적어**: '~을, ~를, ~에게'의 뜻으로 목적어로 명사, 목적격의 대명사, to부정사, 동명사, 명사절 (that절) 등이 온다.

1. 명사
• Jimmy bought **a new wallet** yesterday.

2. 대명사
• She thought **me** a genius.

3. to부정사
• You should try **to find the answer**.

4. 동명사
• I enjoy **listening to music**.

5. 명사절
• Everyone knows **that the moon changes regularly**.

☆Check up!

Answer Keys p. 02

A 괄호 안에서 알맞은 것을 고르시오.

1 The teacher told (me / I) about the test result.

2 Linda is looking for (him / his).

3 Thomas considered (she / her) a princess.

4 You have to try (to find / find) the nearest subway.

5 A woman is talking with (they / them).

6 My father enjoyed (cooking / cook) delicious food.

7 He thought (himself / he) handsome.

8 Jane believes that her mom loved (her / she).

9 Nick stopped (yelling / yelled) in front of the public.

10 James wants (to go / going) hiking with his son.

Lesson 1-8 부사어

- **부사어**: 부사처럼 쓰이며 동사, 형용사, 부사, 문장 전체를 꾸며준다.
  부사어에는 두 단어 이상의 부사, 접속사로 이루어진 부사(절)이 있으며, 부사어는 문장의 형식에 영향을 주지 않는다.

1. 동사 수식
- Johnny walks **slowly**.

2. 형용사 수식
- The perfume smells **very** good.

3. 부사 수식
- He spoke **very** fast in today's speech.

4. 전치사구의 동사 수식
- We got up **late** *in the afternoon*.

5. 부사절
- I helped an old lady **when she asked me to carry the heavy luggage**.

6. 문장 전체 수식
- **Fortunately**, she wasn't hurt at the accident.

Check up!

Answer Keys p. 03

A 다음 괄호 안에서 알맞은 것을 고르시오.

1 I could sleep ((well) / good) last night.
2 She is sleeping (peacefully / peace).
3 (Strangely / Strange), it started to rain.
4 He gets up early (in the morning. / on the morning).
5 I will drive (careful / carefully).
6 He worked too (hasty / hastily).
7 (Unluckily / Unlucky), he didn't come back home.
8 Miranda is talking too (fast / fastly).
9 It's a (specially / special) baked cake.
10 We left for Seoul (late, later)

> **Note**
> - **hastily** 급히, 경솔하게
> - **unfortunately** 불행하게도
> - **fortunately** 다행스럽게도
> - **specially** 특별히

Practice More Ⅱ

A 다음 문장에서 어법상 <u>어색한</u> 것을 찾아 바르게 고치시오.

1 Lily said that we should stop pollute.

<u>   pollute   </u> ➡ <u>   polluting   </u>

2 They will welcome to John with a glad heart.

_____ ➡ _____

3 Mrs. White wants meeting Sophia again.

_____ ➡ _____

4 Foreign names can be easy forgotten.

_____ ➡ _____

5 There are a lot of information about the test.

_____ ➡ _____

6 Watch horror movies reduces stress.

_____ ➡ _____

7 Did they allowed you to go to the concert?

_____ ➡ _____

8 He needs being quiet in the library.

_____ ➡ _____

B 주어진 단어를 빈칸에 들어갈 알맞은 형태로 바꾸어 문장을 완성하시오

1 There ____*are*____ many books on the table. (be)

2 Listen _____ and repeat. (careful)

3 The weather changed _____. (sudden)

4 _____ a book report is our homework today. (write)

5 Joan makes Linda _____ hard for tomorrow's exam. (study)

6 Johnny works hard until _____ at night. (lately)

7 When he _____ home, we started to have dinner. (arrive)

8 I could sleep _____ because I was really tired. (good)

9 She was _____ yesterday because no one celebrated her birthday. (disappoint)

10 Mr. Kim can make a pie _____. (quick)

11 Mina saw a man _____ a bike in the park. (ride)

12 My baby makes me _____. (laugh)

13 They planned to _____ Mt. Annapurna. (climb)

14 The game was _____ to play. (excited)

15 I found my wallet _____. (steal)

C 다음 괄호 안의 단어들을 문법에 맞게 배열하여 문장을 완성하시오.

1 Duri can't _____*receive her salary this month.*_____
(receive, this, her, month, salary)

2 My job _____
(novels, and, writing, poems, is)

3 _____
(was, at, he, the meeting, impolite)

4 They elected _____
(president, James, class)

5 It is important _____
(there, how, to, get, to, remember)

6 _____
(taste, coffee, bad, this, doesn't)

7 _____
(at, is, memorizing, good, am, what, I)

8 _____
(shocked, the, us, news)

9 Max _____
(diagnosed, lung, with, was, cancer)

10 _____
(fast, dog, running, my, is)

11 John _____
(her, anymore, love, doesn't)

12 You _____
(always, morning, exercise, every)

> **Note**
> • **be diagnosed with**
>   ~로 진단 받다
> • **lung cancer** 폐암

Point Check Ⅲ

◆ **완전자동사 :** '주어＋동사'의 1형식 문장을 만든다.

◆ **불완전자동사 :** '주어＋동사＋보어'의 2형식 문장을 만든다.

◆ **완전타동사 :** '주어＋동사＋목적어'의 3형식 문장을 만든다.

◆ **수여동사 :** '주어＋동사＋간접목적어＋직접목적어'의 4형식 문장을 만든다.

◆ **불완전타동사 :** '주어＋동사＋목적어＋목적격보어'의 5형식 문장을 만든다.

1. 완전자동사 : 동사만으로 완전한 문장이 된다.

- Kongji **lived** happily ever after.
- Little Mermaid **sleeps** on the beach.

2. 불완전자동사 : 보어가 있어야 완전한 문장이 된다.

- Her hobby **is** going fishing.
- My dream **was** to be a musician.

3. 완전타동사 : 목적어가 있어야 완전한 문장이 된다.

- Finally they **left** the city.
- She **says** that we have to study hard.

4. 수여동사 : 간접목적어와 직접목적어가 있어야 완전한 문장이 된다.

- She **gave** us some fried chicken.
- Mr. Baker **taught** us science at that time.

5. 불완전타동사 : 목적어와 목적격보어가 있어야 완전한 문장이 된다.

- The war **destroyed** everything.
- My mom **calls** him cuttie.

5형식 문장의 동사

1형식 동사_완전자동사

• 완전자동사: 동사만으로 완전한 뜻을 가지므로 보어나 목적어 없이도 문장이 완성되는 동사를 말한다. '주어 + 동사'의 1형식 문장을 만든다.

◆ 대표적인 1형식의 동사

왕래발착	go	come	leave	start	begin
	arrive				
발생	arise	occur	happen		
존재	be	exist	lie	live	

• The musical **starts** at 7:30.
• Something special will **happen** tonight.
• My cat **lies** on the couch every day.
• I **am** on top of the mountain.
• The princess **lived** happily with the prince.

Grammar Plus +

• 1형식은 '주어+동사'만으로도 완벽한 문장을 만들 수 있지만 부사어를 함께 사용해 문장의 내용을 보충하거나 풍부하게 만들어준다.
Tyler leaves tonight. ➡ 'tonight' – 부사
Tyler는 오늘 밤에 떠난다.
• 부사어: 부사: late, tonight, happily
　　　전치사구: in the morning, at that time (* 전치사구는 부사구에 포함된다.)
　　　부사구(전치사구를 제외한 '부사 + 부사'): very carefully, so fast

✭Check up!

Answer Keys p. 03

A 다음 우리말 해석에 맞게 문장을 완성하시오.

1 영어 수업은 3시에 시작한다.
➡ The English class ___begins___ at three.

2 갑자기 이상한 일이 일어났다.
➡ A strange thing _____ suddenly.

3 John의 부모님은 50년을 행복하게 사셨다.
➡ John's parents _____ happily for 50 years.

4 내일 몇 시쯤에 집에 올 거니?
➡ What time will you _____ home?

5 그녀는 작별 인사 없이 떠났다.
➡ She _____ without saying goodbye.

1-10 2형식 동사_불완전자동사

• **불완전자동사**: 보어가 있어야 완전한 문장을 만드는 동사로 2형식 문장을 만든다. 주어나 목적어가 누구인지 또는 어떤 상태인지를 알려주는 주격보어나 목적격보어와 함께 사용된다.

◈ **대표적인 2형식의 동사**

be동사	am, are, is			
감각동사	look	smell	taste	+형용사 (or 명사(절))
	feel	sound		
become 동사	come	go	get	
	grow	turn		
인식동사	seem / appear	prove		

• My hobby **is** <u>making model airplanes</u>.
• Jack and Tony **are** <u>my good friends</u>.
• My baby brother **looks** <u>hungry</u>.
• The artificial flower **appears** <u>to be real</u>.

Grammar Plus +

• 감각동사 뒤에는 형용사가 오지만 '감각동사+like'의 형태가 되면 뒤에 명사가 오며, 문장의 형식은 그대로 2형식이 된다.
sound like + 명사: ~처럼 들리다
That <u>sounds like a great idea</u>.

Check up!

Answer Keys p. 03

A 다음 괄호 안에서 알맞은 것을 고르시오.

1 John looks ((tired)/ tire) today.

2 The kimchi tasted (spicy / spice) to Jane.

3 My job is (writing / write) novels.

4 He keeps (talking / talk) on the phone with his girlfriend.

5 Mike (became / becoming) a politician.

6 The rumor about him was (proved / to prove) to be false.

7 The information was (to use / useful) to me.

8 The rumor seems to be (true / truth).

9 I think Amy's dream will (come / coming) true.

10 It smells like (chocolate / sweet).

1-11 3형식 동사_완전타동사

• 완전타동사: 목적어가 있어야 완전한 문장을 갖추며, '주어 + 동사 + 목적어'의 형태로 3형식 문장을 만든다.

◈ 주의해야 할 완전타동사

타동사	resemble lay approach say	reach enter mention	marry discuss explain	+ 목적어
타동사+부사	put on wake up take off	put off turn on	 turn off	
타동사	want hope refuse	wish decide agree	expect plan need	+to부정사
타동사	mind admit stop quit	enjoy practice deny avoid	give up dislike finish consider	+동명사
타동사	begin love	start hate	like continue	+동명사/to부정사

• My sister **resembles** my mom very much.
• You must **put on** a long skirt before you go into the temple.

• I **refused** to go back there.
• William **denied** eating the cake alone.
• We **think** that she is beautiful.

☆Check up!

Answer Keys p. 03

A 다음 문장에서 어법상 어색한 것을 찾아 바르게 고치시오.

1   I resemble like my mother very much.   *resemble like* ➡ *resemble*

2   He wants me doing my homework now.   _____ ➡ _____

3   Would you mind to turn off the radio?   _____ ➡ _____

4   They discussed about air pollution.   _____ ➡ _____

5   Lucas decided to wakes up early in the morning.   _____ ➡ _____

6   Linda and I entered into the room.   _____ ➡ _____

7   I plan traveling all around the world.   _____ ➡ _____

4형식 동사_수여동사

- **수여동사**: '누구에게 무엇을 주다'의 의미를 가진 동사로서 목적어(누구에게, 무엇을)가 두 개 오며,
  '주어 + 동사 + 간접목적어 + 직접목적어'의 형태로 4형식 문장을 만든다.

1. 단순 전달의 동사: ~에게 주다

동사	4형식	3형식으로 전환할 때
bring, give, lend, offer, pay, send, show, tell, teach	+ 간접목적어 + 직접목적어	+ 목적어 + to + 목적격

Jane **brings** me a glass of milk. [4형식]

➡ Jane **brings** a glass of milk to me. [3형식]

2. 이중 행위의 동사: ~을 해서 주다

동사	4형식	3형식으로 전환할 때
make, buy, cook, get, find	+ 간접목적어 + 직접목적어	+ 목적어 + for + 목적격

Mrs. Howard **makes** us pretty white dresses. [4형식]

➡ Mrs. Howard **makes** pretty white dresses for us. [3형식]

3. 질문 행위의 동사: ~을 묻다

동사	4형식	3형식으로 전환할 때
ask, inquire, require	+ 간접목적어 + 직접목적어	+ 목적어 + of + 목적격

Michael always **asks** his teacher weird questions. [4형식]

➡ Michael always **asks** weird questions of his teacher. [3형식]

Answer Keys p. 03~04

A 다음 4형식 문장을 3형식으로 바르게 고치시오.

1 Mr. Kim will make her a delicious cake.

➡ *Mr. Kim will make a delicious cake for her.*

2 The cook teaches me baking cookies.

➡ _____

3 He bought Jennifer a bunch of flowers.

➡ _____

4   My teacher told us the story of his first love.

➡ _____

5   She gave me difficult homework.

➡ _____

6   Eric got us some chocolate.

➡ _____

7   I cooked my father a pasta salad.

➡ _____

8   They showed us their new house.

➡ _____

9   Sandra requires him some information about the test.

➡ _____

10   Liam brought Angela a cup of coffee.

➡ _____

B   다음 3형식 문장을 4형식으로 바르게 고치시오.

1   I will lend my car to Inho next week.

➡ _____ *I will lend Inho my car next week.* _____

2   Jiho asked a favor of me.

➡ _____

3   The policeman found Linda's lost daughter for Linda.

➡ _____

4   She offered some new data to her employees.

➡ _____

5   I bought a robot for my son.

➡ _____

6   The detective asked many questions of her.

➡ _____

• **불완전타동사**: 목적어만으로는 완전한 문장이 될 수 없으므로 목적격보어가 와야 한다.
'주어 + 동사 + 목적어 + 목적격보어'의 형태로 5형식 문장을 만든다.

1. 동사에 따른 목적격보어의 형태

call, elect, make, name	+ 명사(목적격보어)
consider, find, keep, leave, make, think, turn	+ 형용사(목적격보어)

➡ 목적격보어가 명사일 때는 목적어가 누구(무엇)인지를, 형용사일 때는 목적어의 상태가 어떠한지를 말하는 것이다.

• Gijun **named** his cat Nyang.
　　　　　　 목적어　 목적격보어(명사) ➡ (his cat = Nyang : 고양이가 누구인지 설명)

• Jasmine **keeps** her mind calm.
　　　　　　　 목적어　　 목적격보어(형용사) ➡ (her mind = calm : 마음의 상태를 설명)

2. [주어 + 동사 + it + 목적격보어 + to부정사]의 형태

believe/find/make/think + it + 목적격보어 + to부정사

➡ 'it'은 가짜 목적어이고, 'to부정사'가 진짜 목적어이다.
5형식의 문장에서 to부정사가 목적어로 나올 때는 목적어 자리에 가목적어 it을 두고, 진목적어를 to부정사로 만든다.

• My sisters and I **make** it a rule to wash the dishes together.
　　　　　　　　　　　 가짜목적어　　　 진짜 목적어

Grammar Plus +

• 5형식에서의 본동사가 사역동사 또는 지각동사일 경우 목적격보어는 원형부정사(동사원형)가 나와야 한다.
- **사역동사**: have, let, make - '~하게 하다' 의 뜻을 가진다.
　Jane had me wash the dishes.
- **지각동사**: feel, see, hear, touch, watch 등
　Mr. Jackson watched her singing in the park.
➡ 목적어가 하고 있는 행동이 진행중임을 강조할 때는 목적격보어로 현재분사를 쓸 수 있다.

A 괄호 안에서 알맞은 것을 고르시오.

1 I think it is impossible ((to go) / going) hiking this week.

2 Helen thought his song was (fantastic / fantasy).

3 He keeps his room (clean / cleaning).

4 She found it difficult (to solve / solving) the problem.

5 I consider love (important / importantly).

6 Dorothy made her father (angry / angrily).

7 They elected her (to president / president) of their school.

8 Andrew named his son (Billy / a Billy).

9 We believe it the other creatures (to exist / existed) in the universe.

10 My father calls me (angel / an angel).

11 The earthquake (destroyed / destroy) our village.

12 Mr. Kim keeps the children (quietly / quiet).

13 Everybody thinks it is wrong (to jaywalk / jaywalking).

14 They thought the movie (interesting / interest).

Note
- **fantastic** 환상적인
- **exist** 존재하다
- **earthquake** 지진
- **destroy** 파괴하다
- **jaywalk** 무단횡단하다

Practice More Ⅲ

A   다음 문장에서 어법상 <u>어색한</u> 것을 찾아 바르게 고치시오.

1   Cindy called her husband a cowardly.

<u>　cowardly　</u> ➡ <u>　coward　</u>

2   I agreed your opinion.

<u>　　　　　</u> ➡ <u>　　　　　</u>

3   Father's advice was lead me in the right direction.

<u>　　　　　</u> ➡ <u>　　　　　</u>

4   The song made me happily.

<u>　　　　　</u> ➡ <u>　　　　　</u>

5   I think that her dream will come truly.

<u>　　　　　</u> ➡ <u>　　　　　</u>

6   The accident was happened suddenly.

<u>　　　　　</u> ➡ <u>　　　　　</u>

7   Minji will bring notebooks for Tom.

<u>　　　　　</u> ➡ <u>　　　　　</u>

8   He ran quick to arrive on time.

<u>　　　　　</u> ➡ <u>　　　　　</u>

9   She found the movie excite.

<u>　　　　　</u> ➡ <u>　　　　　</u>

10   I asked her sending an email then.

<u>　　　　　</u> ➡ <u>　　　　　</u>

11   Let me to know who Lily is.

<u>　　　　　</u> ➡ <u>　　　　　</u>

12   My parents allowed me cut my hair.

<u>　　　　　</u> ➡ <u>　　　　　</u>

13   I found the book easy.

<u>　　　　　</u> ➡ <u>　　　　　</u>

14   She made him peeling the apple.

<u>　　　　　</u> ➡ <u>　　　　　</u>

15   Dongjin thought her fool.

<u>　　　　　</u> ➡ <u>　　　　　</u>

B 주어진 단어를 알맞은 형태로 바꾸어 빈칸을 채우시오.

1 I don't want you ___to stand___ here. (stand)

2 Kate had her right leg _____. (break)

3 She let me _____ along the street. (walk)

4 Angela believed it impossible _____ the problem without hints. (solve)

5 The storm _____ the village. (devastate)

6 Mom always said that I should consider time _____. (importance)

7 Andy helped Jihyun _____ the project. (finish)

8 Staying all night makes you feel _____. (exhaust)

9 Group projects make people _____ with others. (cooperate)

10 Karen keeps _____ even though she had dinner. (eat)

11 Will you _____ off the radio, please? (turn)

12 Eventually, we gave up _____ a bookshelf. (make)

13 She cannot refuse _____ her coat to John. (loan)

14 Would you mind _____ the door? (close)

15 They decided _____ the house for their children. (buy)

Note

- **opinion** 의견
- **agree with**
  ~에 동의하다
- **advice** 충고
  (**advise** 충고하다)
- **peel** (껍질을) 벗기다
- **devastate** 황폐시키다
- **exhaust**
  지치다, 피곤하다
- **cooperate**
  협력하다, 협조하다
- **loan**
  (돈을)빌려주다, 대출하다

Practice More Ⅲ

Answer Keys p. 04

C 다음 우리말 해석에 맞게 주어진 단어를 이용하여 문장을 완성하시오.

1 Kate는 자기 아들을 위해 장갑을 만들어 주었다. (make, glove)
➡ Kate _____ *made the gloves for her son.* _____

2 창문을 열어도 괜찮을까요? (would, mind, open)
➡ _____

3 나의 남동생이 내게 어려운 질문을 했다. (ask, difficult)
➡ My brother _____

4 그녀는 자기의 엄마를 가장 많이 닮았다. (resemble, very much)
➡ She _____

5 Matthew는 겨울에 스케이트 타는 것을 즐긴다. (enjoy, skate)
➡ Matthew _____

6 그는 어제 Mary에게 자기의 자전거를 빌려주었다. (lent, bicycle)
➡ He _____

7 거리에서 고양이 한 마리가 그 개를 쫓아가고 있다. (chase after)
➡ _____ in the street.

8 Minsu는 자기 여동생에게 약간의 과자를 주었다. (give, cookie)
➡ Minsu _____

9 그들은 그 영화가 흥행이 실패할 것이라는 걸 알았다. (will be, a box-office, failure)
➡ They knew that _____

10 늦은 시간까지 일하는 것은 너를 피곤하게 만든다. (work late, tired)
➡ _____

11 부모님은 내게 늘 최선을 다하라고 말씀하신다. (tell, do one's best)
➡ My parents _____

Answer Keys p. 04

내신 최다 출제 유형

01 다음 밑줄 친 부분이 바르게 쓰인 것을 고르시오.

[출제 예상 85%]

① She has a puppy, <u>hasn't she</u>?
② Let's go swimming, <u>aren't we</u>?
③ He never goes out with his dog, <u>doesn't he</u>?
④ They have finished cleaning the house, <u>don't they</u>?
⑤ You read this story before, <u>didn't you</u>?

02 다음 밑줄 친 부분의 쓰임이 옳은 것을 고르시오.

[출제 예상 90%]

① She will help her mom <u>do</u> the dishes.
② We saw our teacher <u>to cross</u> the street.
③ I let my son <u>driving</u> my car this Friday.
④ My mom made me <u>cleaned</u> my room.
⑤ She refused <u>going to</u> alone.

03 다음 중 밑줄 친 부분이 <u>어색한</u> 것을 <u>모두</u> 고르시오.

[출제 예상 85%]

① My friend <u>bought</u> some sandwiches <u>to</u> me for lunch.
② She <u>made</u> special books <u>for</u> her kids.
③ Jennifer wants to <u>ask</u> a tricky question <u>of</u> me.
④ Can you <u>show</u> your album <u>to</u> me?
⑤ Mr. Han <u>teaches</u> world history <u>for</u> us.

04 다음 중 문장의 형식이 보기 와 같은 것을 고르시오.

[출제 예상 90%]

보기
> One of my friends showed me some coins from around the world.

① I bought a laptop computer yesterday.
② We bought our neighbors some rice cake.
③ Danny sent pop songs to his Korean friends.
④ Jack got an A on the mid-term test.
⑤ People elected him mayor.

05 다음 중 어법상 옳은 문장을 고르시오. [출제 예상 90%]

① What stupid you were!
② You have such a loud voice.
③ She is sure fooled us.
④ The cave was so nicely.
⑤ How a wonderful echo it is!

06 다음 밑줄 친 부분 중 잘못 쓰인 것 <u>두 개</u>를 고르시오.

[출제 예상 85%]

① Your brother isn't tall, <u>is he</u>?
② Let's go to the park, <u>will you</u>?
③ It will rain this afternoon, <u>won't it</u>?
④ Don't be late for school, <u>will you</u>?
⑤ Jenny made a fine chair and a table, <u>did she</u>?

[01~04] 다음 중 짝지어진 두 단어의 관계가 나머지 넷과 다른 것을 고르시오.

01
① thin – thinner
② teach – teacher
③ love – lover
④ run – runner
⑤ play – playcr

02
① succeed – success
② pollute – pollution
③ depart – departure
④ excite – excited
⑤ invent – invention

03
① happy – happiness
② bore – bored
③ long – length
④ beautiful – beauty
⑤ wide – width

04
① hunt – hunter
② dance – dancer
③ cook – cooker
④ sing – singer
⑤ teach – teacher

05 다음 괄호 안의 동사의 알맞은 형태가 바르게 짝지어진 것을 고르시오.

> • I told her (keep) waiting.
> • She'll let us (know) when it's ready.

① keep – know
② to keep – know
③ keeping – to know
④ to keep – to know
⑤ keep – to know

06 다음 중 어법상 어색한 것을 고르시오.

① I found the game interest.
② Jane always makes me angry.
③ This song makes me happy.
④ We thought him a great musician.
⑤ She made him a doctor.

[07~08] 다음의 질문에 대한 대답이 올바른 것을 고르시오.

07

> A Which do you want to play, the guitar or the drums?
> B _____.

① I want to do.
② I want to play the guitar.
③ Yes, I do.
④ No, they don't.
⑤ Yes, I like guitars.

08

> A Isn't Sally a model?
> B _____.

① She is a model.
② Yes, she is.
③ No, she is.
④ Yes, she isn't.
⑤ No, she is a model.

[09~10] 다음 빈칸에 공통으로 들어갈 알맞은 말을 고르시오.

09

- Let's _____ a cross stitching class.
- I _____ second prize in the running race.

① take   ② share   ③ be
④ make   ⑤ do

> **Note**   cross stitching class 십자수 수업

10

- What _____ of films do you like?
- It is very _____ of you to say so.

① nice   ② kind   ③ good
④ well   ⑤ bad

[11~12] 다음 두 문장을 한 문장으로 바르게 바꾼 것을 고르시오.

11

- I don't know.
- Who bought those roses?

① I didn't know who those roses buy.
② I don't know who did buy those roses.
③ I didn't know who buy those roses.
④ I don't know who those roses bought.
⑤ I don't know who bought those roses.

12

- Do you believe?
- What will happen to us?

① Do you believe what happen to us?
② Do you believe what will happen to us?
③ What do you believe happen to us?
④ What do you believe will happen to us?
⑤ What will happen to us do you believe?

[13~15] 다음 글을 읽고 물음에 답하시오.

A What did you do last weekend?
B I went to my grandparents' house. It is in the country.
A ⓐ _____ did you go there with?
B I went there with my brother. We went fishing and swimming. And we hiked a mountain.
A Oh, you had a great time, ⓑ _____?
B Yes. ⓒ 나중에 나와 함께 가볼래?

13 윗글 ⓐ에 들어갈 말로 바른 것을 고르시오.

① What   ② When   ③ Who
④ Where   ⑤ Why

14 윗글 ⓑ에 들어갈 알맞은 부가의문문을 고르시오.

① hadn't you   ② didn't you
③ did you   ④ have you
⑤ haven't you

15 윗글 ⓒ를 영어로 바르게 고친 것을 고르시오.

① Will you want to go to, too?
② Are you going to with me?
③ Why don't you go with me later?
④ Don't you going with me next time?
⑤ Do you go to there with me?

[16~18] 다음 중 어법상 어색한 문장을 고르시오.

16 ① Her idea didn't sound great.
② The sunflower smells sweetly.
③ Sammy looks sad.
④ Those cherries taste good.
⑤ This scarf feels smooth.

★★★
17 ① Ellen watched me cross the street.
② I felt the house shake.
③ I want you to get a good grade.
④ We heard the rain fell on the ground.
⑤ Did you see the pretty girl smile at me?

18 ① Mommy looks gloomy.
② They look like real things.
③ You look like your mother.
④ They look upset now.
⑤ She looks like pleased.

[19~20] 다음 중 어법상 옳은 문장을 모두 고르시오.

19 ① We found the quiz show interest.
② The snow made the world white.
③ My sister taught them English.
④ The doctor advised us jog every day.
⑤ Let me to introduce myself.

20 ① This book makes me happy.
② You made me an angry.
③ She makes Mrs. Grey busily.
④ James makes me sadly.
⑤ Make your parents glad.

[21~22] 다음 중 문장의 형식이 나머지 넷과 다른 것을 고르시오.

★★★
21 ① I found many people excited under the waterfall.
② The principal made the students clean the school.
③ My uncle bought me an electronic guitar.
④ She often calls me a little elf.
⑤ The tea helps us relax at night.

★★★
22 ① Leah's mom made dresses for her and her sister.
② Tell us what to bring to his party.
③ We must keep our promise.
④ Susan dropped my wallet somewhere.
⑤ He wrote a long letter to me.

[23~25] 다음 빈칸에 공통으로 들어갈 알맞은 단어를 고르시오.

23
> • We shouldn't give chocolate _____ the dogs.
> • I asked her _____ take the test again.

① of   ② at   ③ in
④ to   ⑤ for

24

> • Jenny's boyfriend bought perfume _____ her.
>
> • Can you get some ice water _____ me?

① for   ② to   ③ at
④ by   ⑤ of

25

> • James told me _____ call him anytime.
>
> • I gave my favorite skirt _____ my little sister.

① for   ② of   ③ by
④ with   ⑤ to

★★★
26 다음 밑줄 친 부분의 쓰임이 보기 와 같은 것을 고르시오.

> 보기
>
> They want me to tell the truth.

① Mary likes red.
② Jacky calls her a jelly fish.
③ The old man was so rude to us.
④ Sometimes my little brother asks me difficult questions.
⑤ Our teacher gave us some gifts.

27 다음 보기 의 밑줄 친 부분과 같은 뜻으로 쓰인 것을 고르시오.

> 보기
>
> Gina misses her family and friends.

① We cannot miss it.
② Jenny missed the bus, so she was late.
③ Greg missed his grandparents in Chicago.
④ Don't miss the train anymore. It's the last.
⑤ Some people miss breakfast.

Note   miss 그리워하다, 놓치다

[28~29] 다음 주어진 문장과 의미가 같은 것을 고르시오.

28

> People give the poor a big hand on a special day.

① People give a big hand for the poor on a special day.
② People give a big hand to them on a special day.
③ People give a big hand to the poor on a special day.
④ The poor give a big hand to people on a special day.
⑤ The poor give people a big hand on a special day.

Note   give a big hand 큰 도움을 주다

29

> He asked a hard question of the scholars.

① He asked of the scholars a hard question.

② He asked the scholars of a hard question.

③ He asked a hard question to the scholars.

④ He asked a hard question the scholars.

⑤ He asked the scholars a hard question.

(**Note**) scholar 학자

30 다음 중 밑줄 친 부분이 잘못 쓰인 것을 고르시오.

① The soup smells good.

② This chocolate cake tastes too sweet.

③ The bread feels hard.

④ That sounds gratefully.

⑤ The man looks nice.

31 다음 질문에 대해 가장 알맞은 대답을 보기 에서 고르시오.

보기
① Cream spaghetti.

② Jerry.

③ We picked them up on the seashore.

④ At Green Elementary School.

(1) How did you get those seashells?

(2) Where did she take a test?

(3) What did they have for lunch?

(4) Who do you like?

32 다음 중 어법상 알맞은 문장을 모두 고르시오.

① Miyoung didn't want me clean my room.

② The teacher advises me to stay more days.

③ I hope you to enjoy the party.

④ She will give it to my brother.

⑤ Do you want him comes back?

★★★
33 다음 중 어법상 어색한 문장을 모두 고르시오.

① My parents like I to play the violin for them.

② She hopes that I pass the examination.

③ I want draw pictures as well.

④ Mr. Jackson didn't want students to fail the test.

⑤ We always wish you will be happy.

34 다음 빈칸에 들어갈 단어가 알맞게 짝지어진 것을 고르시오.

> • Jack always shows a new magic trick _____ me.
>
> • Uncle Tim has cooked some Italian food _____ us.

① to − to   ② for − to   ③ for − for

④ for − with   ⑤ to − for

35 다음 빈칸에 들어갈 말로 알맞은 것을 고르시오.

> You were angry with me yesterday, _____?

① were you   ② weren't you

③ are you   ④ did you

⑤ didn't you

★★★
36 다음 우리말을 영어로 바르게 영작한 것을 <u>모두</u> 고르시오.

> 나는 그에게 처음으로 라면을 요리해 주었다.

① I cooked ramen for the first time to him.
② I cooked ramen to him for the first time.
③ I cooked him ramen for the first time.
④ I cooked him for ramen for the first time.
⑤ I cooked ramen for him for the first time.

★★★
37 다음 주어진 문장과 형식이 같은 것을 <u>모두</u> 고르시오.

> James believes it wise to think positively.

① Jenny makes pizza for us.
② We found it hard to make a difference.
③ I sometimes made clothes of dolls for my little sister.
④ They won't keep the rumor spreading.
⑤ He brought me some cookies.

◇◇◇◇◇◇◇◇◇ 서술형 평가 ◇◇◇◇◇◇◇◇◇

[38~39] 다음 글의 <u>어색한</u> 부분을 찾아 고쳐 쓰시오.
38

> I saw Camilla run in the morning. Her doctor advised her exercise regularly. So she often ran at the park in the morning.

_____ ➡ _____

39

> My friends said that I looked sadly. And they asked the reason. I got a bad score on the science test. So, my friends went out with me and made me feel better.

_____ ➡ _____

40 다음 밑줄 친 우리말을 올바르게 영작하시오.

> A You won't be angry again, will you?
> B <u>응, 안 그럴게</u>.

➡ _____

41 다음 주어진 문장에 대한 올바른 부가의문문을 쓰시오.

(1) Miran and Teddy are going to Tokyo, _____?

(2) Maria has already finished her work, _____?

(3) Let's join the meeting this afternoon, _____?

[42~43] 다음의 직접의문문의 문장들을 간접의문문으로 바꿔 쓰시오.

42 ★★★

I wonder.
Did she tell her secret to everyone?

➡ _____

43 ★★★

Does he think?
How can we translate it into Korean?

➡ _____

[44~45] 다음 괄호 안의 단어를 문맥에 맞게 고쳐 쓰시오.

44

Jack and Ashley denied _____ a book club. (join)

➡ _____

45

I think that Joshua dislike _____ dates with her. (have)

➡ _____

[46~47] 다음 우리말과 같은 뜻이 되도록 괄호 안의 단어를 알맞게 배열하시오.

46

모든 사람들은 그녀를 최고의 배우로 존경하기 시작했다.
(the / best / actress / respect / her / as)

➡ Everyone started to _____

_____

47

시청 근처에 꽃집이 있는지 없는지 말씀해 주시겠어요?
(can / shops / are / there / if / me / you / tell / flower)

➡ _____

near City Hall?

02
Chapter
동사의 시제

Point Check I

◆ **현재형 :** 현재의 사실, 반복적인 일상, 속담, 불변의 진리에 대해서 말할 때 사용한다.

◆ **과거형 :** 과거 어느 시점에 일어났던 사실이나 습관을 말할 때 사용한다.

◆ **현재진행형 :** 현재 일어나고 있는 일이나 가까운 미래를 말할 때 사용한다.

◆ **과거진행형 :** 과거의 어느 시점에서 일어나고 있었던 일에 대해서 말할 때 사용한다.

◆ **미래형 :** 미래에 예정되거나 계획된 일을 말할 때 사용한다.

1. 현재형과 과거형

	현재	과거
be동사	**[am/are/is]** • Anna is an engineer. • They are my classmates.	**[was, were]** • She was at the shopping mall. • They were my textbooks in elementary school.
일반동사	**[동사원형 + -s/-es]** • He goes to school every day. • Eric delivers milk in the morning.	**[동사원형 + -d/-ed, 또는 불규칙동사]** • I took a nap in the afternoon. • She did her homework yesterday.

2. 현재진행형 : [be동사 + 동사 -ing]

• We **are doing** homework together in the library.
• They **are having** a party now.

3. 과거진행형 : [was / were + 동사 -ing]

• I **was burning** my old clothes at that time.
• A **Were** they **playing** basketball together?
  B Yes, they were. / No, they weren't (were not).

4. 미래형

(1) will + 동사원형

• We **will** go to the art museum.

(2) be going to + 동사원형

• They **are going to** have a music concert.

현재형

• **현재형**: 현재의 습관, 사실, 진실, 속담 등을 말할 때 사용한다.

1. 일반동사 3인칭의 현재 단수형

대부분의 경우	동사원형 + -s	work − works grow - grows	say − says leave − leaves
'-o, -x, -s, -sh, -ch'로 끝나는 경우	동사원형 + -es	go − goes wash − washes	teach − teaches relax − relaxes
'자음 + y'로 끝나는 경우	y를 i로 고치고 -es	cry − cries try − tries	fly − flies study − studies

2. 현재형의 쓰임

(1) 현재의 사실, 상태, 습관, 반복적인 동작, 불변의 진리, 격언 등을 사용한다.

- Maria **is** an astronaut.
- Erica **works** at a publishing house.

(2) 시간과 조건의 부사절을 쓸 때 사용한다.

- I will talk to her when I **meet** her.
- Lucy will be angry if he **sings** with the band.

(3) '왕래발착의 동사 + 미래를 나타내는 부사(구)'의 형태가 되면 가까운 미래를 나타낸다.

- They **leave** for Hawaii tomorrow morning.

Grammar Plus +

• 왕오다 래가다 발출발하다 착도착하다: go, come, start, leave, arrive, reach, depart
Emma goes back to school tonight.

A 다음 주어진 동사들을 이용하여 현재 시제 문장을 완성하시오.

1   My brother _____*is*_____ an actor. (be)

2   Mr. Lee _____ up early in the morning. (get)

3   Water _____ at 100 degrees Celsius. (boil)

4   He _____ some chicken for his children. (order)

5   He _____ playing soccer every Saturday morning. (enjoy)

6   The baby _____ all day long. (cry)

7   Chris _____ around the city by bike. (travel)

8   My father _____ to church on Sundays. (go)

9   The concert _____ soon. (start)

10 Call me when she _____ home. (arrive)

B 다음 문장에서 어법상 <u>어색한</u> 것을 찾아 바르게 고치시오.

1   If it will snow, I will make a snowman with my dad.

_____*will snow*_____ ➡ _____*snows*_____

2   My sister leave LA next month.

_____ ➡ _____

3   Tom is baking bread until they come back home.

_____ ➡ _____

4   Let's go as soon as Alex will arrive.

_____ ➡ _____

5   I wonder if he becomes a doctor.

_____ ➡ _____

6   If it rains next week, I don't go on a picnic.

_____ ➡ _____

7   He fix the computer when he finishes his homework.

_____ ➡ _____

현재형과 현재진행형

> • 현재진행형: 현 시점에서 일어나고 있는 일이나 가까운 미래를 표현할 때 사용한다.
> 'be동사(am/are/is) + 동사원형-ing'의 형태로 '~하고 있는 중이다'로 해석한다.

1. 현재형

- Heaven **helps** those who help themselves.

- Just call me <u>when</u> you **arrive**.

2. 현재진행형

⑴ 현 시점에서 진행 중인 일에 대하여 표현

- He **is eating** a hamburger and drinking some coke <u>now</u>.

  ➡ 현재 진행되고 있는 일을 말할 때 부사 right now, now, at this time과 함께 쓰인다.

⑵ 미래를 나타내는 부사(구)와 함께 쓰여 가까운 미래를 표현

- Jack and Jill **are going** on their honeymoon <u>the day after tomorrow</u>.

Grammar Plus +

- 진행형을 만들 수 없는 동사
  ⓐ 지각: know 알다, understand 이해하다, remember 기억하다
  ⓑ 소유: have 가지다, belong to ~에 속하다, own 소유하다
  ⓒ 존재: be 있다, exist 존재하다
  ⓓ 감정: love 사랑하다, like 좋아하다, hate 싫어하다, prefer 더 좋아하다
  ⓔ 감각: see 보다, hear 듣다, smell 냄새나다, taste 맛이 나다
  ⓕ 기타: want 원하다, resemble 닮다, keep 유지하다, seem ~인 것 같다

##

Answer Keys p. 07

A 다음 괄호 안의 단어를 현재진행 시제에 맞게 바꾸어 쓰시오.

1 He ___*is playing*___ tennis with Jane. (play)

2 They _____ in the street. (dance)

3 My dog _____ on the sofa. (lie)

4 She _____ pictures in the park. (take)

5   I_____ lunch in the Mexican restaurant. (eat)

6   We _____ about the rumor. (talk)

7   The baby _____ in the room. (sleep)

8   Helen _____ a detective novel. (write)

9   She _____ to take a trip tomorrow night. (go)

10 _____ you _____ English? (study)

B 다음 문장에서 어법상 어색한 것을 찾아 바르게 고치시오.

1   I'm loving you.

     _____'m loving_____ ➡ _____love_____

2   She is owning her car.

     _____ ➡ _____

3   Jane is go to the beach right now.

     _____ ➡ _____

4   They are hating each other.

     _____ ➡ _____

5   The sun is rising in the east.

     _____ ➡ _____

6   Sujin is remembering John.

     _____ ➡ _____

7   They are belonging to Jim.

     _____ ➡ _____

8   I ate some apples now.

     _____ ➡ _____

9   Helen thinking about him.

     _____ ➡ _____

10 We are understanding the lecture.

     _____ ➡ _____

2-3 과거형

• **과거형**: 과거에 일어난 동작이나 상태, 역사적 사실처럼 과거에 이미 끝난 일을 표현한다.

1. be동사의 과거형

주어	현재형	과거형
I	am	was
you, we, they	are	were
he, she, it	is	was

2. 일반동사의 과거형 _ 규칙변화

대부분의 경우	동사원형 + -ed	brush − brushed	pull − pulled
-e로 끝나는 경우	동사원형 + -d	close − closed	use − used
'자음+y'로 끝나는 경우	y를 i로 고치고 -ed	reply − replied	deny − denied
'단모음+단자음'으로 끝나는 경우	자음을 한 번 더 쓰고 -ed	drop − dropped	stop − stopped

3. 일반동사의 과거형 _ 불규칙변화

원형	과거형	과거분사형	원형	과거형	과거분사형
be	was / were	been	bear	bore	born
beat	beat	beaten	become	became	become
begin	began	begun	blow	blew	blown
bring	brought	brought	build	built	built
buy	bought	bought	choose	chose	chosen
come	came	come	cost	cost	cost
cut	cut	cut	do	did	done
draw	drew	drawn	dream	dreamed / dreamt	dreamed / dreamt
drink	drank	drunk	drive	drove	driven
eat	ate	eaten	fall	fell	fallen
feel	felt	felt	fight	fought	fought
find	found	found	fly	flew	flown

원형	과거형	과거분사형	원형	과거형	과거분사형
forget	forgot	forgotten	get	got	got(ten)
give	gave	given	go	went	gone
grow	grew	grown	have	had	had
hear	heard	heard	hide	hid	hidden
hit	hit	hit	hold	held	held
hurt	hurt	hurt	keep	kept	kept
know	knew	known	lay	laid	laid
lead	led	led	leave	left	left
let	let	let	lie(눕다)	lay	lain
lose	lost	lost	make	made	made
mean	meant	meant	meet	met	met
overcome	overcame	overcome	pay	paid	paid
put	put	put	read	read	read
ride	rode	ridden	ring	rang	rung
rise	rose	risen	run	ran	run
say	said	said	see	saw	seen
sell	sold	sold	send	sent	sent
set	set	set	shut	shut	shut
sing	sang	sung	sink	sank (sunken)	sunk(sunken)
sit	sat	sat	sleep	slept	slept
smell	smelled / smelt	smelled / smelt	speak	spoke	spoken
spend	spent	spent	spread	spread	spread
stand	stood	stood	steal	stole	stolen
sweep	swept	swept	swim	swam	swum
take	took	taken	teach	taught	taught
tell	told	told	think	thought	thought
throw	threw	thrown	understand	understood	understood
wake	woke	woken	wear	wore	worn
win	won	won	write	wrote	written

Answer Keys p. 07~08

A 다음 빈칸에 과거, 과거분사형을 쓰시오.

1 tell – *told* – *told*

2 think – _____ – _____

3 begin – _____ – _____

4 mistake – _____ – _____

5 wind – _____ – _____

6 prove – _____ – _____

7 blow – _____ – _____

8 fly – _____ – _____

9 eat – _____ – _____

10 bring – _____ – _____

11 leave – _____ – _____

12 win – _____ – _____

13 ride – _____ – _____

14 see – _____ – _____

15 choose – _____ – _____

16 forget – _____ – _____

17 shake – _____ – _____

18 lose – _____ – _____

19 cut – _____ – _____

20 catch – _____ – _____

21 cast – _____ – _____

22 bend – _____ – _____

23 drive – _____ – _____

24 do – _____ – _____

25 feed – _____ – _____

26 show – _____ – _____

27 tear – _____ – _____

28 bleed – _____ – _____

29 bear – _____ – _____

30 dig – _____ – _____

31 build – _____ – _____

32 hang – _____ – _____

33 grow – _____ – _____

34 know – _____ – _____

35 feel – _____ – _____

36 hide – _____ – _____

37 lay – _____ – _____

38 make – _____ – _____

39 meet – _____ – _____

40 write – _____ – _____

41 read – _____ – _____

42 keep – _____ – _____

43 shoot – _____ – _____

44 stand – _____ – _____

45 teach – _____ – _____

46 pay – _____ – _____

47 sweep – _____ – _____

48 sell – _____ – _____

49 let – _____ – _____

50 overcome – _____ – _____

B 다음 주어진 단어를 과거형으로 알맞게 바꾸어 빈칸을 채우시오.

1   I ___danced___ with James at the last party. (dance)

2   They _____ this building in 2010. (build)

3   Linda _____ English to her daughter yesterday. (teach)

4   He _____ his old friend on the way home. (meet)

5   She _____ the robber last night. (catch)

6   Max was _____ in Italy. (bear)

7   We _____ that the English test was too difficult. (think)

8   He and I _____ kites last weekend. (fly)

9   They _____ next to her in the seminar at that time. (sit)

10   I _____ to bring an umbrella this morning. (forget)

과거형과 과거진행형

> • **과거진행형**: 과거 어느 시점에서 진행 중이었던 일에 대하여 나타낸다.
> 'be동사 과거(was / were) + 동사원형 -ing'의 형태로 '〜하고 있던 중이었다'로 해석한다.

1. **과거형**: 과거형은 단순한 과거의 일을 나타낼 때 사용한다.

   • I **took** <u>a shower</u> at home.

   • She **didn't** <u>understand</u> what he said.

   • **A** **Did** you <u>win</u> the game?
     B Yes, I did. / No, I didn't (did not).

   ➡ 일반동사 과거형의 부정문은 'did not + 동사원형'의 형태이고,
     의문문은 'Did + 주어 + 동사원형〜?'의 형태이다.

2. **과거진행형**: 'was / were + <u>동사원형 −ing</u>' 〜하고 있던 중이었다

   • Uncle Tom **was having** dinner when I came back home.

   • Wendy and Mina **weren't hiding**.

   • **A** **Was** he **studying** at that time?
     B Yes, he was. / No, he wasn't (was not).

   ➡ 과거진행형의 부정문은 'was / were not + 동사원형-ing'의 형태이고,
     의문문은 'Was / Were + 주어 + 동사원형-ing〜?'의 형태이다.
     과거진행형 의문문의 대답은 be동사 과거인 'was / were'로 대답한다.

☆Check up!

Answer Keys p. 08

A 다음 그림은 Max의 아침 일과를 다룬 것이다. 그림을 보고 과거진행 시제의 문장을 완성하시오.

1 He ___*was jogging*___ in the morning.

2 He _____ a shower.

3 He _____ breakfast with his family.

4 He _____ his room.

5 He _____ a book.

미래형

- **미래형**: 앞으로 하게 될 일이나 일어날 일에 대해 말할 때 사용한다.

  미래를 말할 때는 'will'과 'be going to'를 사용하며, 둘 다 '~할 것이다'라는 뜻을 가지고 있다. 모두 뒤에 동사원형이 나온다.

◈ will과 be going to

	will	be going to
미래에 대한 추측	~일 것이다 • It will snow tomorrow. • My art lesson will start at six.	~일 것이다 • 추측을 할 근거가 있을 만한 상황에서 사용한다. It is going to snow soon.
미래의 의지	~할 예정이다 • 즉석에서 결정할 때 사용한다. I'll go there again.	~할 예정이다 • 이미 계획되어진 일이나 하려고 생각했던 일을 말할 때 사용한다. I'm going to buy a new jacket tomorrow.

☆Check up!

Answer Keys p. 08

A 괄호 안의 동사에서 알맞은 것을 고르시오.

1 If you (will arrive / (arrive)) early, call Jack.

2 I (do / will do) something special for my son tomorrow.

3 Minji (are going to / is going to) visit Linda's house tonight.

4 When you (return / will return) to Korea, I will come to see you.

5 I (will visit / visit) John's house the day after tomorrow.

6 If you (don't / will not) hurry up, you will miss the train.

7 He (is going to travel / travel) all around the country next year.

8 She (buy / will buy) a new car next week.

9 We (will / are) meet again in the near future.

10 I'm not (going to play / playing) tennis after school.

Practice More I

Answer Keys p. 08

A 다음 괄호 안에서 알맞은 것을 고르시오.

1 The movie (start /(starts)) at 10 o'clock today.

2 He (came / comes) here last night.

3 In 2002, Korea (made / make) it to the semifinals of the World Cup.

4 I will buy some books when I (go / will go) to the bookstore.

5 Her sons (fought / fighted) each other yesterday.

6 I was (bore / born) in 2003.

7 If you (will want / want) more money, you have to work hard.

8 He (is leaving / was leave) the country next month.

9 Did you know the sun (rises / rose) in the east?

10 Tomorrow (is / is going to) my parents' wedding anniversary.

B 주어진 단어를 알맞은 형태로 바꾸어 문장을 완성하시오.

1 It _____is_____ hot in summer. So, I'm always worried what to wear. (be)

2 I will bring some DVDs before James _____. (arrive)

3 At that time, he _____ a photo with his girlfriend. (take)

4 Timothy _____ early in every morning. (get up)

5 He will help me as soon as he _____ his project. (finish)

6 I _____ TV just before. (watch)

7 My teacher explained that World War I _____ in 1914. (break out)

8 It _____ right now. (rain)

9 Five times seven _____ thirty-five. (equal)

10 When you _____ in Rome, do as the Romans _____. (be / do)

Answer Keys p. 08

C 다음 문장에서 어법상 <u>어색한</u> 것을 찾아 바르게 고치시오.

1 I like the proverb that no news be good news.

           ___*be*___ ➡ ___*is*___

2 Here come the bus.   _____ ➡ _____

3 The apple is smelling sweet. _____ ➡ _____

4 I am thinking John is rude.   _____ ➡ _____

5 If you will want to lose weight, just start exercising right now.

           _____ ➡ _____

6 The bag is belonging to our brand.

           _____ ➡ _____

7 I will make some cookies after I will finish my task.

           _____ ➡ _____

8 We having a great time together.

           _____ ➡ _____

9 Water freeze at zero degrees Celsius.

           _____ ➡ _____

D 다음 제시된 시제에 맞춰 주어진 단어를 이용하여 영작을 하시오.

1 play the piano, now (현재진행형)

   ➡ I _____ *am playing the piano now.* _____

2 write, a novel, three years ago (과거형)

   ➡ I _____

3 go, the concert, with Olivia, next week (미래형)

   ➡ Jiyoung _____

4 prepare for, the party, last night (과거진행형)

   ➡ We _____

5 draw, a portrait, for her, now. (현재진행형)

   ➡ James _____

6 wash, my dog, every evening (현재형)

   ➡ I _____

7 go hiking, to enjoy mountain, the (과거형)

   ➡ They _____

Point Check II

◆ **현재완료:** 과거에 시작한 일이 현재까지 계속 진행되고 있거나, 현재에 완료가 되는 표현을 말할 때 사용한다.

◆ **현재완료의 용법:** '완료, 결과, 경험, 계속'의 용법으로 구분하여 사용할 수 있다.

1. 현재완료의 형태: [have / has + 과거분사]

(1) **완료:** (벌써, 지금 막) ~했다
- The action star Robert Downey Jr. **has** just **left**.
- They **have** not **cleaned** their room yet.

(2) **결과:** ~해 버렸다 (그래서 현재는 ...하다)
- She **has gone** to New York.
- We **have** not **bought** the football tickets.

(3) **경험:** ~한 적이 있다
- Lucy **has sung** with the band several times.
- They **have** never **seen** such a beautiful view before.

(4) **계속:** ~해 오고 있다
- I **have studied** English since I was 10 years old.

2. 현재완료의 부정문: [주어 + have / has not + 과거분사]

- We **have not (haven't) been** to London.
- My little brother **has not (hasn't) broken** my toy robot.

3. 현재완료의 의문문: [Have / Has + 주어 + 과거분사~?]

- A **Have** they **lived** in New York before?
- B **Yes, they have. / No, they haven't.**

4. 과거완료

- She was so sad because she **had lost** her favorite bag.

◆ **현재완료와 과거완료**

had + 과거분사	have/has + 과거분사	will/be going to
과거완료	과거 현재	미래

Lesson 2-6 현재완료의 쓰임과 형태

- **현재완료**: 과거형과 비교하여 과거에 일어난 일이 현재까지 영향을 미칠 때 사용한다.
  'have / has + 과거분사(p.p.)'의 형태로 나타낸다.

◈ **현재완료의 형태**

형태	• 1, 2인칭 단수/복수: have + 과거분사(p.p.) • 3인칭 단수: has + 과거분사(p.p.)
의미	과거부터 일어난 일에 대한 '완료, 결과, 경험, 계속'을 표현
함께 쓰는 부사	already, just, ever, before, once

have / has + 과거분사

과거　　　　　　　　　　　　　　　　현재　　　　　　　　　　　　미래

- I **have been** to England <u>before</u>.

- Jenny **has** <u>already</u> **finished** her homework.

➡ 현재완료는 과거를 나타내지만, 과거를 나타내는 부사(구)와는 함께 사용할 수 없다. 하지만 'when'처럼 특정한 과거를 나타내는 부사절을 함께 쓸 때는 반드시 과거형만 사용한다.

Grammar Plus +

- **현재완료와 과거형**
  I **have lost** my cap. (→ 아직 찾지 못함)
  I **lost** my cap. (→ 찾았는지 아닌지 알 수 없음)

☆Check up!

Answer Keys p. 08

A 다음 주어진 단어를 이용하여 현재완료 시제의 문장을 완성하시오.

1 ___*Have*___ you ever ___*been*___ to France? (be)

2 Jane _____ her hometown. (forget)

3 Linda _____ in Seoul for seven years. (live)

4 I _____ my wallet. (lose)

5 Tommy _____ English since 2013. (study)

6 She _____ just _____ her homework. (finish)

7 Mr. Anderson _____ already _____ lunch. (eat)

8 James _____ never _____ such a big apple. (see)

9 _____ Jane _____ Nick before? (meet)

2-7 현재완료_완료

- **현재완료_완료**: '(벌써, 지금 막) ~했다'라는 뜻을 가지고 있으며, 과거부터 일어난 일이 현재에 막 끝난 경우에 사용한다.

- My family and I **have** just **arrived** at grandparents' house.
- He **has** not **brought** the food yet.

➡ 현재완료와 함께 쓰이는 부사 'already (이미, 벌써), just (지금 막)'는 긍정의 뜻을, 'yet (아직)'은 부정의 뜻을 가지고 있다.

Check up!

Answer Keys p. 09

A 다음 우리말 해석에 맞게 문장을 알맞게 완성하시오.

1 나는 이제 막 숙제를 마쳤다.
➡ _____ *I have just finished my homework.* _____

2 James는 아직 학교에 도착하지 못했다.
➡ _____

3 버스는 이미 떠났다.
➡ _____

4 그녀는 나에게 이제 막 이메일을 보냈다.
➡ _____

5 Linda는 아직 밥을 먹고 있니?
➡ _____

6 그는 이제 막 설거지를 마쳤다.
➡ _____

7 그들은 벌써 산을 올랐다.
➡ _____

8 제주도는 이미 유명한 관광명소가 되었다.
➡ _____

9 Brad는 벌써 자기 방을 치웠니?
➡ _____

10 그녀는 이제 막 50송이의 해바라기를 심었어.
➡ _____

2-8 현재완료_결과

- 현재완료_결과: '~해 버렸다 (그래서 현재 ...하다)'라는 뜻을 가지고 있으며, 과거에 일어난 일로 인해 현재의 결과가 나왔을 때 사용한다.

- Ian **has broken** my umbrella, <u>so I am wet.</u>
- My brother **has lost** his new smartphone. (→ 다시 찾지 못함)

★Check up!

Answer Keys p. 09

A 다음 문장을 우리말로 바르게 해석하시오.

1 I have lost my key.

➡ _____ *나는 내 키를 잃어버렸다.* _____

2 Jane has been to Rome.

➡ _____

3 She has bought this car.

➡ _____

4 I have broken my leg.

➡ _____

5 My father has gone home.

➡ _____

B 다음 두 문장을 한 문장으로 쓸 때 괄호 안의 단어를 사용하여 쓰시오.

1 Jack took my pencil. I don't have it.

➡ Jack _____*has taken*_____ my pencil. (take)

2 My T-shirt was dirty. The T-shirt is clean now.

➡ I _____ the T-shirt. (wash)

3 He told me something. I know everything.

➡ He _____ me everything. (tell)

4 He made a promise. He didn't get there.

➡ He _____ his promise. (forget)

5 Linda went to New York. Linda is still in New York.

➡ Linda _____ New York. (go)

현재완료 _ 경험

- **현재완료_경험**: '~한 적이 있다'라는 뜻을 가지고 있으며, 과거부터 현재까지의 경험을 나타낼 때 사용한다.

- Gina **has been** to Japan several times.

Grammar Plus +

- Elena **has gone** to China. [결과]
➡ 어떤 장소를 방문한 경험을 이야기할 때는 be동사의 과거분사형인 'been'을 써주고, 그 장소로 가고 없을 때는 'go'의 과거분사형인 'gone'을 써준다.

➡ '현재완료의 경험'을 나타낼 때는 부사 'ever, never, once, twice, ~times, before' 등을 함께 사용한다.

Check up!

Answer Keys p. 09

A 다음 우리말 해석에 맞게 빈칸을 알맞게 채우시오.

1 Jisu는 미국에 가본 적이 없다.

➡ Jisu ___*has never been*___ to America.

2 그는 이렇게 재미있는 영화를 본 적이 없었다.

➡ He _____ such an interesting movie.

3 너는 중국에 가본 적 있니?

➡ _____ you _____ to China?

4 Amy는 한국 음식을 먹어본 적이 없다.

➡ Amy _____ Korean food.

5 그들은 한 번 만난 적이 있다.

➡ They _____.

6 Jack은 자기의 가족들에 대해서 들은 적이 없다.

➡ Jack _____ about his family.

7 나는 전에 그녀를 본 적 있다.

➡ I _____ her _____.

8 나와 여동생은 그 박물관을 두 번 가봤다.

➡ My sister and I _____ to the museum _____.

9 Alex는 기린에 대한 책을 읽어 본 적이 없다.

➡ Alex _____ a book about giraffes.

현재완료_계속

- 현재완료_계속: '~해 오고 있다'라는 뜻을 가지고 있으며, 과거에 시작된 동작이 현재까지 계속 이어져 오는 것을 표현할 때 사용한다.

- Wendy **has worked** for this company for 15 years.

➡ '현재완료의 계속'을 표현할 때는 주로 부사 'for (~동안), since (~이후로)'와 함께 사용한다.

◈ for와 since의 쓰임

for + 시간의 길이	He has studied Chinese for <u>five years</u>.
since + 시작한 시점	She has studied Chinese since <u>last year</u>.

☆Check up!

Answer Keys p. 09

A   다음 빈칸에 for, since 중 알맞은 것을 쓰시오.

1   I have studied English _____*for*_____ 13 years.

2   Jane has worked at the company _____ 2013.

3   They have prepared for this party _____ three days.

4   He has lived in Brazil _____ then.

5   I have enjoyed playing baseball _____ 11 years.

6   John and Matthew have raised two pets _____
   they were young.

7   Peter has been sick _____ last Thursday.

8   My father has had the car _____ 15 years.

9   She has been famous _____ a long time.

10 They have been learning how to drive a car
   _____ yesterday.

11 Lisa has lived here _____ many years.

12 I have raised the cat _____ May.

13 Eunyoung has played the flute _____ a year.

14 Many students have entered the college _____ then.

15 My family has lived here _____ I was a baby.

2-11 현재완료의 부정문과 의문문

- 현재완료의 부정문: '주어 + have/has not + 과거분사'의 형태를 가진다.

- 현재완료의 의문문: 'Have/Has + 주어 + 과거분사~?'의 형태를 가진다.

1. 현재완료의 부정문: 주어 + have/has not + 과거분사

- We **have not (haven't) seen** the movie 'Home Alone.'

  ➡ 'have not'의 줄임말은 'haven't'이고, 'has not'의 줄임말은 'hasn't'이다.

2. 현재완료의 의문문: Have/Has + 주어 + 과거분사~?

- **A Have you** <u>ever</u> **seen** the Great Wall?

  B Yes, I have. / No, I haven't.

  ➡ 'have' 뒤에 바로 'not'이 붙는 경우와 'have'가 문장 맨 앞에서 의문문을 이끄는 경우에 대개 현재완료형의 문장이 사용된다.

Answer Keys p. 09

A 다음 문장에서 어법상 <u>어색한</u> 것을 찾아 바르게 고치시오.

1 I have finished not the project.

  <u>finished not</u> ➡ <u>not finished</u>

2 Do you have ever been to France?

  _____ ➡ _____

3 I haven't not read this novel. _____ ➡ _____

4 Have you not prepared for the party yet?

  _____ ➡ _____

5 Hasn't you eaten Mexican food before?

  _____ ➡ _____

6 We not have participated in the speaking contest.

  _____ ➡ _____

7 Has ever John seen the Eiffel tower?

  _____ ➡ _____

8 Eric hasn't meet the girl before.

  _____ ➡ _____

9 Have driven you a truck? _____ ➡ _____

10 I hasn't turned in my science report yet.

  _____ ➡ _____

현재완료와 과거형

- **현재완료** : 과거에 일어난 일이 현재까지 영향을 주는 것을 나타낸다.

- **과거형** : 과거의 습관, 반복적인 일이 과거 시점에서 끝난 것을 나타낸다.

현재완료	과거형
[완료] • Jenny has <u>already</u> washed the dishes. [결과] • Mina and Jinho have spent all the money, so they cannot buy anything. [경험] • My friend and I have read the book 'Chicken Soup for the Soul' <u>before</u>. [계속] • We have written the brochure for travelers <u>for four years</u>.	[과거의 사실, 상태, 동작] • He was very tired <u>last night</u>. [과거의 습관, 반복적 동작] • Wendy never ate breakfast <u>when she was in her 20s</u>.

✪Check up!

Answer Keys p. 10

A 다음 주어진 동사를 시제에 맞게 바꾸어 빈칸을 채우시오.

1 I _____visited_____ my grandfather two weeks ago. (visit)

2 Linda _____ in Italy since 2004. (live)

3 My dad _____ a new car last week. (buy)

4 I _____ never _____ that boy. (see)

5 Kate _____ the piano for six years. (play)

6 Jinsu and Jina _____ a baby last month. (have)

7 She _____ math since then. (teach)

8 When the bell _____, I came out of the door. (ring)

9 He _____ just _____ out with his friend. (go)

10 I_____ my room last night. (clean)

과거완료

> • 과거완료: 과거의 어느 시점을 기준으로 그 이전의 시점부터 과거의 그 시점까지 일어난 일을 나타내는 경우에 사용된다.

◈ 과거완료: [had + 과거분사]

had + 과거분사

```
├─────────────────────────────────────────────┤──────────────────────────────▶
과거완료                                        과거                          현재
```

• I appreciated her because she **had helped** me before.

• Minsu and Junho thought that Mr. Green **had taught** them well.

Check up!

Answer Keys p. 10

A 다음 주어진 동사를 알맞은 시제로 바꾸어 문장을 완성하시오.

1 He found that he ___had lost___ his bike. (lose)

2 The festival _____ when we arrived there. (end)

3 He _____ in Seoul before he moved here. (live)

4 Amy sent an email after she _____ the call. (got)

5 They _____ once, but they didn't remember each other. (meet)

6 Alex became a painter two years later after he _____ to Italy. (go)

7 Mom liked the dress that I _____ her last week. (buy)

8 Alice realized that she _____ a mistake. (make)

9 We couldn't solve the problem because we _____ the hint. (forget)

10 My father _____ usually _____ fishing before he got a new job. (go)

11 I met my old friend after I _____ my homework. (finish)

12 Sue _____ for her mom before she called. (wait)

Practice More II

A 괄호 안에서 문맥상 알맞은 시제를 고르시오.

1 Billy ((visited) / has visited) his uncle's house yesterday.

2 I (bought / have bought) a new car last night.

3 Mina (lose / has lost) her wallet recently.

4 I (ran / have run) there because I missed the train.

5 We (don't eat / have't eaten) anything since last night.

6 Heeyeon (was / have) born in LA.

7 They (have lived / lived) here for 40 years.

8 John (has finished / finished) his homework two hours ago.

9 I (went / have gone) to Osaka last Monday.

10 I (have heard / heard) about Jim many times before.

B 다음 문장에서 어법상 어색한 것을 찾아 바르게 고치시오.

1 I have lived in Egypt for I was young.

_____for_____ ➡ _____since_____

2 He have visited his grandfather recently.

_____ ➡ _____

3 They have known each other since six years.

_____ ➡ _____

4 We have seen the movie yesterday.

_____ ➡ _____

5 She had played the violin two weeks ago.

_____ ➡ _____

6 He studied baking for seven years.

_____ ➡ _____

7 I have lost my bag last night.

_____ ➡ _____

8 They never heard from John since 2014.

_____ ➡ _____

9 It has rained heavily yesterday.

_____ ➡ _____

10 Linda has finished her work thirty minutes ago.

_____ ➡ _____

11 He already has seen the drama.

_____ ➡ _____

12 Has he been late for the meeting yesterday?

_____ ➡ _____

13 He has just going to school. _____ ➡ _____

C 주어진 단어를 이용하여 우리말 해석과 일치하도록 문장을 완성하시오.

1 넌 시골에서 살아본 적이 있니? (live)
   ➡ ___*Have you ever lived*___ in the country?

2 그 의자는 부서져 버렸어. (break)
   ➡ The chair _____.

3 John은 일본에 가고 없다. (go)
   ➡ John _____.

4 네가 할 일은 다 했니? (do)
   ➡ _____ the work you need to do?

5 언제 그 가방을 샀니? (buy)
   ➡ When _____ the bag?

6 우리는 9시에 학교에 갔다. (go)
   ➡ We _____ at nine.

7 내 아들은 전에 치타를 본 적이 없다. (see)
   ➡ My son _____ a cheetah before.

8 나는 TV를 2001년부터 가지고 있다. (have)
   ➡ I _____.

9 그는 Sam을 오랫동안 알아 왔다. (know)
   ➡ He _____ Sam for a long time.

10 우리 어머니는 이 주전자를 7년째 쓰고 계신다. (use)
   ➡ My mom _____ this kettle _____.

11 그들은 영어를 10년간 공부하고 있다. (study)
   ➡ They _____ English _____.

12 Cindy는 5시간 동안 벽에 페인트를 칠하고 있다. (paint)

➡ Cindy _____ the wall _____ .

13 수 세기 동안 사람들은 이 식물을 약으로 사용해 왔다. (use)

➡ For centuries, people _____ this plant for medicine.

14 그는 어제부터 쭉 화가 나있다. (angry)

➡ He _____ since yesterday.

D 다음 두 문장을 한 문장으로 연결하시오.

1 She bought the bag three years ago. She still uses it.

➡ _____ *She has had the bag for three years.* _____

2 They went to my grandmother's house on Thursday. They still stay there.

➡ _____

3 They started to work here two months ago. They still work here.

➡ _____

4 My mom bought the dress last year. She still has it.

➡ _____

5 I began to teach students thirty years ago. I still teach students.

➡ _____

6 Yujin started to play soccer in 2011. Yujin still plays soccer.

➡ _____

7 He met Linda last May. They are still friends.

➡ _____

8 My dad bought the shirt twenty years ago. He still has it.

➡ _____

9 Tim lived in Gwangju as of two years ago. He still lives there.

➡ _____

10 James left Korea. He isn't here now.

➡ _____

내신 최다 출제 유형

01 다음 빈칸에 들어갈 말이 바르게 짝지어진 것을 고르시오.
[출제 예상 85%]

> (1) Jena _____ here when she was young.
> (2) Mina _____ Japanese for five years.
> (3) I _____ the TV drama for a month.

① came – studied – watched
② has come – studied – has watched
③ didn't come – has studied – watched
④ didn't came – studied – have watched
⑤ came – has studied – have watched

02 다음 밑줄 친 부분의 쓰임이 [보기]와 같은 것을 고르시오. [출제 예상 90%]

> [보기]
> Mirae has lived here for seven years.

① Sean has seen the view from Namsan once.
② I have never heard about his story.
③ We have been in Osaka since 2013.
④ Sunny has gone to America.
⑤ They have already left for Victoria, Canada.

03 다음 대화의 빈칸에 들어갈 말이 바르게 짝지어진 것을 고르시오. [출제 예상 80%]

> A Have you _____ Joy's uncle?
> B Yes, I _____ him yesterday.

① see – saw
② seen – seen
③ saw – seen
④ seen – saw
⑤ saw – saw

[04~05] 다음 글을 읽고 물음에 답하시오. [출제 예상 85%]

> A little boy and a little girl were playing on the escalator in the department store. They went up and down the escalator. Suddenly (A)it stopped, and a little girl ⓐ fall down on the escalator. And her finger ⓑ be bleeding and she needed a bandage. At that time, if the little boy hadn't cried out for help, what would happen to her?

04 윗글 ⓐ와 ⓑ의 형태를 알맞게 고쳐 쓰시오.

➡ ⓐ _____ , ⓑ _____

05 윗글의 (A)가 의미하는 것이 무엇인지 본문에서 찾아 그 단어를 쓰시오.

➡ (A) _____

06 다음 중 어법상 올바른 것을 고르시오. [출제 예상 90%]

① Jenny is hating hot weather.
② I am not believing your words.
③ They knows how to print yesterday.
④ We are liking to discuss the problems.
⑤ Children are running around at the playground.

07 다음 중 어법상 어색한 것을 고르시오. [출제 예상 90%]

① The doctor has given me some advice.
② The baby has just woken up and cried.
③ The heater hasn't worked last year.
④ His car is making a strange sound.
⑤ I have not decided where to go yet.

중간 기말고사 예상문제

[01~05] 다음 동사의 변화가 <u>잘못된</u> 것을 고르시오.

01
① bear – bore – born
② win – won – won
③ send – sended – sent
④ spend – spent – spent
⑤ run – ran – run

02
① plan – planned – planned
② take – took – taken
③ make – made – made
④ do – did – did
⑤ have – had – had

03
① hurt – hurt – hurt
② read – read – read
③ begin – began – begun
④ swim – swam – swum
⑤ come – came – came

04
① let – let – let
② write – wrote – writed
③ go – went – gone
④ choose – chose – chosen
⑤ fly – flew – flown

05
① leave – left – left
② hop – hopped – hopped
③ enjoy – enjoied – enjoied
④ lose – lost – lost
⑤ ride – rode – ridden

[06~08] 다음 빈칸에 들어갈 알맞은 단어를 고르시오.

06
> Jenny has already _____ most of her money to buy books.

① spend ② spent ③ be spent
④ spends ⑤ to spend

07
> _____ you ever heard a rumor about Harry?

① Had ② Has ③ Do
④ Did ⑤ Have

08
> Julie has _____ to China three times before.

① gone ② were ③ been
④ went ⑤ was

[09~10] 다음 문장의 밑줄 친 부분과 쓰임이 같은 것을 고르시오.

09
> She <u>has lived</u> in Canada since 2009.

① Kevin <u>has been</u> to Japan.
② I <u>have met</u> her before.
③ Mr. Chang <u>has studied</u> Korean for three years.
④ Jenny <u>has not read</u> the novel.
⑤ They <u>have not lost</u> their bags.

10

> Have you ever heard of the mysterious water in this town?

① We have been in China since 2010.
② Julia has just fallen her glasses.
③ We have never seen a rainbow.
④ They have gone to hospital.
⑤ They have lived here for five years.

[11~12] 다음 문장의 밑줄 친 부분의 쓰임이 잘못된 것을 고르시오.

11 ① Have you ever read a non-fiction novel?
② She had just seen the accident.
③ Have you ever became a teacher?
④ He has never sent a letter to him.
⑤ We have eaten Italian food before.

12 ① Jerry has studied Korean for two years.
② We have been sick since last week.
③ She has had this dress since 2014.
④ He has lived here for last month.
⑤ They have slept for seven hours.

[13~15] 다음 대화를 잘 읽고 물음에 답하시오.

> A Ching-Ching has already _____(A)_____ in Korea for three years.
> B I know. And she can speak Korean well.
> A You're right. But _____(B)_____ that she would leave for China the day after tomorrow?
> B No, _____(C)_____.
> (나는 전혀 그것에 대해 듣지 못했어.)

13 윗글의 (A)에 들어갈 알맞은 말을 고르시오.

① had   ② been   ③ gone
④ been to   ⑤ gone to

14 윗글의 (B)에 들어갈 알맞은 말을 고르시오.

① Have you ever
② Have you hear
③ Have you heard
④ Have you listen
⑤ Have you watched

15 윗글의 (C)를 영어로 바르게 영작한 것을 고르시오.

① I didn't have heard about it.
② I don't have heard about it.
③ I never have heard about it.
④ I have never heard about it.
⑤ I have heard never about it.

[16~17] 다음 중 어법상 올바른 문장을 모두 고르시오.

16 ① What will you do this weekend?
② I have took a shower.
③ Jade and you have to do this work by tomorrow.
④ We are going to study together yesterday.
⑤ She has watch the movie last month.

17
① They have gone to Beijing last summer.
② Hyera has worn glasses for three years.
③ When have you taught them?
④ They have been sad a week ago.
⑤ I met him yesterday.

[18~19] 다음 중 어법상 바르지 않은 것을 모두 고르시오.

18
① Have you ever hear about his news?
② We met Mr. Kan last year.
③ They have visited Tokyo last year.
④ We saw the movie last week.
⑤ Has she ever seen eagles?

19
① Will you join our book club?
② We're taking him to the hospital.
③ Jenny has played the piano since seven years.
④ I have saw this book before.
⑤ Julie's family has been here for a week.

★★★
20 다음 주어진 문장과 현재완료의 용법이 같은 것을 고르시오.

> We have been to France.

① My uncle has lost his watch.
② Have you seen this movie?
③ Have you finished your homework?
④ He has lived in this house since then.
⑤ Mr. Jackson has worked here for a year.

21 다음 중 빈칸에 들어갈 말로 맞지 않은 것을 고르시오.

> We are going to go to the camp
> _____.

① tonight   ② this Saturday
③ next weekend   ④ tomorrow
⑤ last Sunday

22 다음 중 대화가 어색한 것을 고르시오.

① A Have we met before?
  B Yes, we met last year.
② A Who has had lunch already?
  B We don't know.
③ A Have you done your work well?
  B Yes, I did.
④ A Have you ever thought about baking a cake?
  B Yes, I have.
⑤ A I have never been to China.
  B Really? I hope you will visit there someday.

23 다음 밑줄 친 부분 중 will과 바꿔 쓸 수 없는 문장을 고르시오.

① I am going to fly to Japan.
② They are going to go on a picnic.
③ Jessy is going to the traditional market.
④ I am going to ask her about this.
⑤ Madonna is going to go back to America.

★★★
24 다음 주어진 두 문장을 한 문장으로 바르게 표현한 것을 고르시오.

> · Peterson was interested in taking pictures when he was a kid.
> · He is still interested in taking pictures.

① Peterson has been interested in taking pictures when he is a kid.

② Peterson has interested in taking pictures since he was a kid.

③ Peterson has been interested in taking pictures since he was a kid.

④ Peterson interested in taking pictures since he was a kid.

⑤ Peterson has been interested in taking pictures for he was a kid.

[25~26] 다음 두 문장의 뜻이 같도록 빈칸에 알맞은 말을 고르시오.

25
> I forgot his email address, and still can't remember it.
> = I _____ his email address.

① have forgotten   ② had forgotten

③ has forgotten   ④ forgotten

⑤ forget

26
> Mrs. White bought a unique vase 20 years ago, and she still has it.
> = Mrs. White _____ a unique vase for 20 years.

① bought   ② have   ③ has have

④ has had   ⑤ had

★★★
27 다음 밑줄 친 부분 중 바르지 않은 것을 모두 고르시오.

> The first seed ① said, "I don't want to go out. I want to stay here." The second seed said, "But it's not winter any more. I ② want to see the bright sun." The first seed and the second seed ③ try to go out of the earth. Finally, they ④ grow and grow, and ⑤ opened their buds.

28 다음 우리말을 영어로 바르게 옮긴 것을 고르시오.

> 너는 이탈리아에서 젤라또를 먹어본 적 있니?

① Have you ever eat gelato in Italy?

② Did you ever eat gelato in Italy?

③ Have you ever eaten gelato in Italy?

④ Did you ever eaten gelato in Italy?

⑤ Have you ever ate gelato in Italy?

29 다음 빈칸에 들어갈 동사의 알맞은 형태를 고르시오.

> Their son _____ arrive here next Sunday.

① is being   ② is going

③ is going to   ④ was

⑤ will be

30 주어진 우리말에 맞게 빈칸에 들어갈 알맞은 말을 <u>모두</u> 고르시오.

> Jessica는 매주 목요일마다 노래 연습을 한다.
> = Jessica practices singing _____.

① on Thursdays ② next Thursday
③ last Thursday ④ every Thursday
⑤ on Thursday

◇◇◇◇◇◇◇◇◇ 서술형 평가 ◇◇◇◇◇◇◇◇◇

31 다음 주어진 문장과 같은 뜻이 되도록 빈칸에 알맞은 단어를 쓰시오.

> My sister and I will go camping this Saturday.
> = My sister and I _____ go camping this Saturday.

➡ _____

[32~33] 다음 괄호 안에 주어진 단어를 알맞은 형태로 고쳐 쓰시오.

32
> • We have just _____ making dresses. (finish)
> • She _____ to Hong Kong last month. (go)

➡ _____

33
> Marian has just _____ Christmas cards. (write)

➡ _____

[34~35] 주어진 우리말과 같은 뜻이 되도록 빈칸에 알맞은 말을 쓰시오.

34
> 세상에서 가장 큰 동물이 우리지역 동물원에 있는것을 들어본 적 있니?

➡ _____ _____ ever _____
that largest animal in the world is at our local Zoo?

35
> 이상한 소리를 들었을 때 나는 TV를 보고 있던 중이었다.

➡ I _____ _____ TV when I heard a strange sound.

[36~37] 다음 주어진 두 개의 문장을 하나로 바르게 고쳐 쓰시오.

36
> Danny started to visit the orphanage a month ago.
> He still visits there.

➡ _____

37

> They went to Thailand three weeks ago.
> They came back today.

➡ _____

[38~39] 다음 주어진 우리말에 맞게 괄호 안의 단어를
배열하여 문장을 완성하시오.

★★★
38

> Judy는 그녀의 친구들을 한 달 전 콘서트에
> 서 보았다.
> (Judy / ago / concert / saw / her friends
> / at / the / month / a)

➡ _____

39

> 그들은 10년 동안 축구를 해 왔다.
> (They / years / have / soccer / for /
> played / ten)

➡ _____

[40~41] 다음 그림을 보고 괄호 안의 단어를 사용하여
현재완료형 문장을 완성하시오.

40

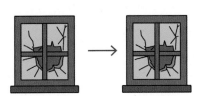

➡ The window_____ _____.
(break)

41

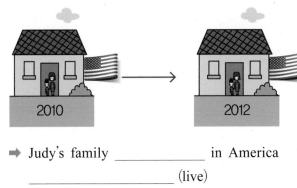

➡ Judy's family _____ in America
_____ (live)

★★★
42 다음 제시된 조건에 따라 우리말 문장들을 바르게
영작하여 쓰시오.

> 〈조건〉 (1) 단순과거 문장이 들어갈 것.
>   (2) 현재완료형 문장이 들어갈 것.
>   (3) 현재완료형과 함께 쓰이는 부사
>   (구)가 들어갈 것.

> Ron은 5년 전에 런던에서 살았다.
> 그는 3년 전에 한국으로 이사를 왔다.
> 그는 3년 동안 한국에서 살고 있다.

➡ _____
_____
_____

Note

03

Chapter
조동사

Point Check I

◆ **조동사:** be동사와 일반동사 앞에서 특정한 의미를 더해 주는 동사를 말한다.

조동사는 동사원형과 함께 쓰이며, 주어의 수와 인칭에 관계없이 언제나 같은 형태를 가진다.

1. 조동사의 종류

가능	can / be able to ~할 수 있다
추측	can 과연 ~일까, may / might ~일지도 모른다, must ~일지도 모른다, ~인 것이 틀림없다
허가/요청	can / may / might / will / would ~해도 된다(될까요?), ~해 주다(주겠어요?)
의무	should / ought to / have to / must ~해야 한다
충고/권유	should / had better ~하는 것이 낫다(좋겠다)

(1) **would / would like to**

- **Would you** mind opening the window?
- **Would** you **like to** drink some cold water?

(2) **can**

- **Can** she play the violin? [능력]
- You **can** eat chicken now. [허락]
- It **can** be true. [추측]
- **Can** you sing for me, please? [요청]

(3) **be able to**

- Tommy **is able to** earn enough money from his painting. [능력]

(4) **will**

- I **will** study hard to pass the exam. [미래]
- **Will** you have dinner with me? [요청]

(5) **be going to**

- They **are going to** have a vacation in New Zealand.

2. 조동사의 부정문 : [주어+조동사 + not + 동사원형]

- You **shouldn't (should not)** cheat in an exam.

3. 조동사의 의문문 : [조동사 + 주어 + 동사원형~?]

- A　**May** I go out for a walk?
- B　Yes, you may. / No, you may not.

3-1 조동사의 종류

> • **조동사**: 동사 앞에서 의무, 추측, 가능, 요청, 허가, 제안 등의 의미를 더해주는 동사로 조동사 뒤에는 동사원형이 나온다.

1. 조동사의 종류

의미 / 종류	can(=be able to)	may / might	will / would	should	have to	must
가능 ～할 수 있다						
추측 ～일지도 모른다 ～임에 틀림없다						
허가 / 요청 ～해도 된다 (될까요?) ～해 주다(주겠어요?)						
의무 ～해야 한다						
충고/권유 ～하는 것이 낫다						

2. 조동사의 부정문: [조동사 + not + 동사원형]

- You **may not** <u>go</u> there.
- Sammy **mustn't (must not)** <u>be</u> a very smart boy.
- It **can't** <u>be</u> a lie.

3. 조동사의 의문문: [조동사 + 주어 + 동사원형?]

- **Can** you <u>speak</u> Japanese?
- **May** I <u>speak</u> to Minsu?　(→ 전화상에서)
- **Should** we <u>wear</u> uniforms?

Answer Keys p. 13

A 우리말 해석에 맞게 알맞은 조동사와 주어진 단어를 이용하여 문장을 완성하시오.

Note
· **get off the grass**
잔디밭에 들어가지 않다

1 나는 올해 살을 뺄 것이다. (lose weight)

➡ I _____*will lose weight*_____ this year.

2 John은 다음 주에 패션쇼를 위해 미국에 갈지도 모른다. (for the fashion show)

➡ John _____ next week.

3 영어로 일기를 쓸 수 있니? (keep a diary)

➡ _____ you _____ in English?

4 사람들은 잔디밭에 들어가면 안 된다. (get off)

➡ People _____ the grass.

5 Tina는 내일 소풍을 위해 일찍 자는 것이 좋다. (go to bed)

➡ Tina _____ for tomorrow's picnic.

6 부탁 좀 들어주시겠어요? (a favor)

➡ _____ you do me _____?

7 내 여동생은 이 가방을 싫어할지도 모른다. (like)

➡ My sister _____ this bag.

8 Jimmy는 항상 서두르는 걸 보니 성격이 급한 것이 틀림없다. (hasty)

➡ Jimmy _____ because he always hurries.

9 우리 가족은 다음 달에 캐나다로 여행 갈 것이다. (go)

➡ My family _____ next month.

10 집으로 돌아왔을 때 손을 씻어야 한다. (wash)

➡ You _____ when you return home.

3-2   would / would like (to)

> • **would** : 'will'의 과거형으로 쓰이지만, 'Would you~?'의 형태로 '~하실 수 있나요?'라고
> 상대방에게 정중하게 요청할 때도 사용된다.
>
> • **would like (to)** : '~하고 싶다'라는 뜻으로 'would love (to)', 'want (to)'와 같은 말이다

1. would + 동사원형

- **Would you** <u>do</u> me a favor?
- **Would you** <u>explain</u> it one more time?

➡ 'Would you~?'의 바로 뒤나 문장의 맨 끝에 'please'를 붙이면 더욱 공손한 표현이 된다.

2. would like to ('d like to)

(1) **would like + 명사 (= want)**

- **Would** you **like** <u>some milk</u>? (= Do you **want** <u>some milk</u>?)
- I **would like** <u>some cookies</u>. (= I **want** <u>some cookies</u>.)

(= I'd like)

(2) **would like to + 동사원형 (= want to)**

- **Would** you **like to** <u>have</u> a date with Thomas?
  = **Do** you **want to** <u>have</u> a date with Thomas?

 **Check up!**

Answer Keys p. 13

A   다음 우리말 해석에 맞게 괄호 안에 알맞은 것을 고르시오.

1 달콤한 먹을 것을 좀 먹고 싶다.

➡ I (would / (would like)) something sweet to eat.

2 강아지를 키우고 싶나요?

➡ (Would you like / Would you) to raise a puppy?

3 나는 낚시하러 가고 싶다.

➡ I (would like / would like to) go fishing.

4 나와 함께 콘서트에 갈래요?

➡ (Would you like / Would you like to) go to the concert with me?

5 나는 낮잠을 자고 싶다.

➡ I (like to / would like to) take a nap.

6 설탕을 좀 건네주실래요?

➡ (Will / Would) you pass me the sugar, please?

7 너는 John과 축구를 하고 싶니?

➡ Would you like (to play / play) soccer with John?

3-3 can (1)

- **can**: 과거형은 could로, 능력을 나타내는 경우 'be able to'와 바꿔 쓸 수 있다.

1. 현재형: ~할 수 있다 (= am / are / is able to)

- My friend, Anna **can** dance ballet very well.
- They **cannot (can't)** go on a picnic.
- **A** **Can** you understand what I mean?
  B Yes, I can. / No, I can't.

2. 과거형: ~할 수 있었다 (= was / were able to)

- I **could** climb a tree very well.
- I **could not (couldn't)** write when I was very young.
- **A** **Could** he ride a bike when he was seven years old?
  B Yes, he could. / No, he couldn't.

 Check up!

Answer Keys p. 13

A 다음 두 문장의 의미가 같도록 빈칸에 알맞은 말을 넣으시오.

1 Helen can sing very well.
   ➡ Helen _____*is able to sing*_____ very well.

2 Semi could solve the problem easily.
   ➡ Semi _____ the problem easily.

3 I wasn't able to stop eating snack.
   ➡ I _____ eating snack.

4 We didn't know that we could win the game.
   ➡ We didn't know that we _____ the game.

5 Were you able to drive a car?
   ➡ _____ you _____ a car?

6 They are able to swim in the sea.
   ➡ They _____ in the sea.

7 I am not able to go to the concert with them.
   ➡ I _____ to the concert with them.

8 John couldn't read Korean when he was eight.
   ➡ John _____ Korean when he was eight.

can (2)

> • **can**: 추측, 허락, 요청 등의 의미를 가지고 있으며 'may'와 바꿔 쓸 수 있다.

1. 허락: ~해도 좋다

- **Can** I start now? = **Could** I start now? → 'can'보다 더 정중한 표현이 된다.

2. 추측

(1) ~일지도 모른다: 주로 주어는 사물이 되고, 'can' 다음에 'be동사'가 나온다.
- I know it **can** be real.

(2) 과연 ~일까?: 'Can+주어+be~?'처럼 의문문의 형태로 쓰이며, 'can' 다음에 'be동사'가 나온다.
- **Can** he be really silly?

(3) ~일 리가 없다: cannot의 형태로 다음에 주로 'be동사'가 나온다.
- It **cannot** be true.

3. 요청/허가: ~해 주다, ~해 주겠어요?

- **Can** you stop singing, please?
- = **Could** you stop singing, please?

4. 약한 금지: ~해서는 안 된다

- You **can't** walk along this way.

★Check up!

Answer Keys p. 13

A   다음 문장에서 어법상 <u>어색한</u> 것을 찾아 바르게 고치시오.

1   He can took a picture.   ___took___ ➡ ___take___

2   You are able to making cookies.

_____ ➡ _____

3   They can coming to my birthday party.

_____ ➡ _____

4   You cannot being silly.   _____ ➡ _____

5   He can passed the exam last week.

_____ ➡ _____

6   She can to learn how to bake bread.

_____ ➡ _____

7   Eric can teaches English.   _____ ➡ _____

3-5 be able to

- **be able to** : '~할 수 있다'의 뜻을 가지고 있으며 'can'을 대신해 사용될 수 있다.
  미래를 표현할 때는 'will be able to + 동사원형'의 형태를 사용해
  '~할 수 있을 것이다'라는 뜻을 가진다.

1. 현재형

(1) **긍정문** : [주어 + be able to + 동사원형]

- Jenny **is able to** swim very well.
  (= can)

(2) **부정문** : [주어 + be not able to + 동사원형]

- She **isn't able to** play the piano.
  (= cannot)

(3) **의문문** : [be + 주어 + able to + 동사원형~?]

- **A** **Is** he **able to** throw the ball?
  (= Can he)
- **B** Yes, he is. / No, he isn't.

2. 과거형

(1) **긍정문** : [주어 + was / were able to + 동사원형]

- Jenny and Dan **were able to** read books when they were young.
  (= could)

(2) **부정문** : [주어 + was / were not able to + 동사원형]

- He **wasn't able to** dance before.
  (= could not)

(3) **의문문** : [Was / Were + 주어 + able to + 동사원형~?]

- **A** **Were** they **able to** play soccer well?
  (= Could they)
- **B** Yes, they were. / No, they weren't.

3. 미래형

(1) **긍정문** : [주어 + will be able to + 동사원형]

- We **will be able to** win the game.

(2) **부정문** : [주어 + will not be able to + 동사원형]

- She **won't be able to** be a dentist.

(3) **의문문** : [Will + 주어 + be able to + 동사원형~?]

- **A** **Will** Sam **be able to** catch the train on time?
- **B** Yes, he will. / No, he won't.

A 다음 우리말 해석에 맞게 주어진 단어를 바르게 배열하시오.

1 그는 영어로 말을 잘할 수 있다.
(English, can, he, well, speak)
➡ _____He can speak English well._____

2 우리는 내일 너를 공항에 마중 나갈 수 있을 것이다.
(we, pick you up, at the airport, tomorrow, will be able to)
➡ _____

3 그녀는 하루에 커피 세 잔 이상을 마실 수 없다.
(she, drink, three cups of coffee, isn't able to, more than)
➡ _____ in a day.

4 그들은 제시간에 도착할 수 있을까?
(are, on time, able to, they, arrive)
➡ _____

5 그녀는 열심히 공부하기 때문에 의사가 될 수 있을 것이다.
(she, a doctor, will be able to, become)
➡ _____ because she
studies hard.

6 Andy는 스스로 중국어 공부를 할 수 있니?
(Andy, Chinese, is, himself, teach, able to)
➡ _____

7 그녀는 몇 년 전에는 관객 앞에서 춤을 출 수 없었다.
(she, in front of, the audience, not, was, able to, dance, a few, ago)
➡ _____

8 나는 아직도 자전거를 탈 수 없다. (I, still, able, to, ride, am, not, a, bike)
➡ _____

9 그는 다시는 그녀를 볼 수 없을 것이다. (he, again, her, see, be, to, able, won't)
➡ _____

10 그들은 그곳에 갈 수 없었다. (they, there, go, able, to, weren't)
➡ _____

3-6 will / be going to

- **will**: 미래에 대한 예정, 의지 또는 요청을 나타낼 때 사용한다.
- **be going to**: 가까운 미래의 예정이나 계획을 나타낼 때 사용한다.

1. will: ~할 것이다 [미래]

- I **will** go to Harvard University.
- He **will not (won't)** study for the final exam.
- **A** **Will** she be alone this weekend?
  B Yes, she will. / No, she won't.

2. will / would: ~해 주실래요? [요청]

- **Will** you come to my birthday party?
  = **Would** you come to my birthday party?

➡ will보다는 would가 더 정중한 표현이다. 문장의 끝에 please를 붙여주면 더욱 공손한 표현이 된다.

3. be going to: ~할 것이다 [미래]

- She **is going to** go to the concert.
- They **aren't going to** write letters about their mistakes.
- **A** **Is** Mary **going to** go shopping with you?
  B Yes, she is. / No, she isn't.

➡ 'will'과 'be going to' 뒤에는 반드시 동사원형이 온다. 이들 뒤에 be동사를 쓸 경우 'am/are/is'의 원형인 'be'를 사용한다.

 Check up!

Answer Keys p. 14

A 두 문장의 의미가 같도록 빈칸에 알맞은 말을 써 넣으시오.

1 I will read a newspaper every morning.
➡ I ___*am going to read*___ a newspaper every morning.

2 You will not go hiking next week.
➡ You _____ hiking next week.

3 She is going to knit a sweater for her father.
➡ She _____ a sweater for her father.

4 Will you take pictures for me?
➡ _____ you _____ for me?

5   Are they going to study English tonight?

➡ _____ they _____ English tonight?

6   I am going to eat dinner with her tomorrow.

➡ I _____ dinner with her tomorrow.

7   My daughter will go to kindergarten next year.

➡ My daughter _____ to kindergarten next year.

8   Will you make a dress for me?

➡ _____ you _____ a dress for me?

9   I will buy some flowers for my grandmother.

➡ I _____ some flowers for my grandmother.

10 They will eat pasta for lunch.

➡ They _____ pasta for lunch.

11 We will prepare for our graduation party this weekend.

➡ We _____ for our graduation party this weekend.

12 Will you turn down the volume for me?

➡ _____ you _____ for me?

Practice More I

A 주어진 두 문장이 서로 같은 뜻이 되도록 빈칸에 알맞은 말을 채우시오.

1 He can fix his car by himself.
→ He _____ *is able to fix* _____ his car by himself.

2 I am not able to tell you the truth.
→ I _____ you the truth.

3 They are going to travel to Europe this summer.
→ They _____ to Europe this summer.

4 We could stay at Susan's house for a few days.
→ We _____ at Susan's house for a few days.

5 James will play the piano for his wife tonight.
→ James _____ play the piano for his wife tonight.

6 She can speak French fluently because her best friend comes from France.
→ She _____ French fluently because her best friend comes from France.

7 I will visit my grandfather's house next week.
→ I _____ my grandfather's house next week.

8 You can't fly like a bird.
→ You _____ like a bird.

9 Will you cook dinner tonight?
→ _____ you _____ cook dinner tonight?

10 Can you lend me a pen to write with?
→ _____ you _____ lend me a pen to write with?

11 Am I able to try on this coat?
→ _____ I try on this coat?

12 She will go for a walk this afternoon.
→ She _____ go for a walk this afternoon.

13 James is not going to buy the car.
→ James _____ buy the car.

14 They couldn't go fishing because of the terrible storm.
→ They _____ fishing because of the terrible storm.

B 다음 문장에서 어법상 <u>어색한</u> 것을 찾아 바르게 고치시오.

1   She can makes her own necklace.

_____makes_____ ➡ _____make_____

2   Eric is go to write a detective novel next month.

_____ ➡ _____

3   Mother will bought some flowers to decorate her room.

_____ ➡ _____

4   She would to raise a dog. _____ ➡ _____

5   I was able to reading the book last week.

_____ ➡ _____

6   Can believe you the rumor?

_____ ➡ _____

7   I'm able not to swim in the sea.

_____ ➡ _____

8   Mason would like to flying a kite.

_____ ➡ _____

9   Could you mind if I turn it off?

_____ ➡ _____

10   They are going participated in the piano competition.

_____ ➡ _____

11   Sam and I not will go back to school.

_____ ➡ _____

12   They could enjoyed the folk music festival last Saturday.

_____ ➡ _____

13   We are going not to turn in the paper now.

_____ ➡ _____

14   Yuna being able to run faster than before.

_____ ➡ _____

Practice More Ⅰ

Answer Keys p. 14

C 우리말 해석에 맞게 문장을 완성하시오.

1 그들은 축구장에 갈 예정이다.
➡ _____ *They are going to go to the soccer stadium.* _____

2 나는 다음 주에 너를 만나고 싶다.
➡ I _____ next week.

3 그녀는 우리 팀의 경기를 보러 오지 않을 예정이다.
➡ She _____ our team's game.

4 우리는 아침에 샌드위치를 좀 먹을 것이다.
➡ We _____ for breakfast.

5 나는 매일 아침 조깅을 할 예정이었다.
➡ I _____ every morning.

6 내가 라디오를 켜도 되겠습니까?
➡ _____ the radio?

7 그는 젊었을 때 더 빠르게 뛸 수 있었다.
➡ _____ when he was young.

8 정말로 그 소문이 사실일까?
➡ _____

9 Daniel은 혼자 컴퓨터를 조립할 수 있다.
➡ _____

10 우리는 최선을 다했는데도 불구하고 그 경기를 이기지 못했다.
➡ Although we did our best, _____.

Point Check II

◆ **조동사:** be동사나 일반동사 앞에서 특정한 의미를 더해 주는 동사를 말한다.
조동사는 동사원형과 함께 쓰이고, 주어의 수와 인칭에 관계없이 항상 같은 형태를 가진다.

1. may / might

- You **may** leave now. [허락]
- It **may** rain tonight. [추측]
- I **may have taken** a nap. [과거의 추측]
- He **might be** a singer. [추측]

2. have to

- You **have to** be careful when you cross the street. [의무]
- She **doesn't have to** go to his party. [불필요]

3. must

- Teachers **must** teach students well. [의무]
- She **must be** angry with me. [추측]
- You **must not** waste the money. [금지]

4. should

- You **should** listen to the doctor. [당연]

5. had better

- We **had better** take a taxi. [권유, 제안]

6. ought to

- You **ought to** work hard at the company. [의무]
- We **ought not to** copy others' reports. [금지]

7. would

- They **would** often send me letters. [과거의 불규칙한 습관]

8. used to

- He **used to** go shopping every season. [과거의 규칙적인 습관]
- She **used to** wear glasses. [과거의 사실/상태]

3-7 may / might

- **may** : '〜해도 좋다'라는 허락의 의미와 '〜일지도 모른다'라는 불확실한 추측의 의미를 가지고 있다.
- **might** : '허락/요청'의 의미일 때는 'may'보다 정중한 표현이 되고, 추측의 의미일 때는 'may'보다 가능성이 더 낮다.

1. 허락

- You **may** use my computer in my seat.
- **May** I drink some water?

2. 추측

- It **may** snow a lot at midnight.
- The rumor **might not** be true.

➡ 'might'는 'may'의 과거형이지만 의미상의 차이가 거의 없이 사용된다.

Grammar Plus +

- **can vs. may**

can은 일상생활이나 친한 사람 사이에서 주로 사용되며, may는 보다 격식을 갖춘 장소나 낯선 사람에게 사용된다.

☆Check up!

Answer Keys p. 14

A 다음 문장에서 밑줄 친 may가 허락, 추측 중 어떤 뜻으로 쓰였는지 고르시오.

1 <u>May</u> I come in? [허락]

2 She <u>may</u> come back next week. _____

3 It <u>may</u> not be difficult to solve. _____

4 You <u>may</u> be able to take a picture here. _____

5 They <u>may</u> be sleepy. _____

6 It <u>may</u> be true. _____

7 <u>May</u> I send an email to Mr. Lee? _____

8 He <u>may</u> go to the gym for exercise. _____

9 You <u>may</u> drink and eat here. _____

10 She <u>may</u> not eat dinner for diet. _____

may have + 과거분사 / might be

- **may have + 과거분사**: '~이었을지도 모른다'라는 뜻으로 과거의 추측을 나타낼 때 사용된다.
- **might be**: '~일지도 모른다'라는 뜻으로 비교적 약한 추측을 나타낼 때 사용된다.
  이때 'might'는 'may'의 과거형이 아닌 보다 공손한 표현 또는 가능성이 더 약한 뜻으로 쓰인다.

1. may have + 과거분사

⑴ **긍정**: ~이었을지도 모른다, ~했을지도 모른다

- I **may have written** a letter at that time.

⑵ **부정**: [may not have+과거분사] ~하지 않았을지도 모른다

- You **may not have missed** the bus.

2. might be: 'may'보다 더 약한 추측을 나타내거나 불확실한 추측을 나타낸다.

⑴ **긍정**: (어쩌면) ~일지도 모른다

- He **might be** a famous tap dancer in his country.

⑵ **부정**: [might not be] (어쩌면) ~이 아닐지도 모른다

- They **might not be** professors of the university.

Answer Keys p. 14

A 다음 우리말 해석에 맞게 주어진 단어를 알맞게 배열하시오.

1 우리는 기차를 놓쳤을지도 모른다.

➡ We ___*may have missed*___ the train. (may, missed, have)

2 그들이 서로에게 거짓말을 안 했을지도 모른다.

(not, may, lied, have)

➡ They _____ each other.

3 그 당시에 그녀는 울고 있었을지도 모른다. (cried, have, may)

➡ She _____ at that time.

4 그는 어쩌면 요리사일지도 모른다. (be, might, a, chef)

➡ He _____.

5 그들은 3년 전에 이 영화를 봤을지도 모른다. (watched, may, have)

➡ They _____ this movie three years ago.

6 John은 배우가 아닐지도 모른다. (be, not, an, might, actor)

➡ John _____.

7 Sandra는 시험에 합격하지 않았을지도 모른다.

(might, passed, not, have, the, exam)

➡ Sandra _____.

have to / must

- **have to**: '~해야 한다'의 뜻으로 강한 의무를 나타낼 때 사용한다.
- **must**: '~해야 한다'의 뜻으로 쓰일 때는 강한 의무를, '~인 것이 틀림없다'의 뜻으로 쓰일 때는 강한 추측을 나타낸다.

1. have to

(1) **긍정문**: [= must] ~해야 한다

- We **have to** <u>be</u> quiet in the library. [현재]
- They **had to** <u>stand</u> in the right line. [과거]

➡ 'must'에는 과거형이 없기 때문에 'had to'로 나타낼 수 있다.

(2) **부정문**: [do / does not have to] ~할 필요가 없다

- She **doesn't have to** <u>study</u> French. [현재]
- They **didn't have to** <u>go</u> to the park. [과거]

➡ 'have to'의 과거 부정은 'do / does'를 'did'로 바꾸고 'not have to'를 붙인다.

➡ 'have to'의 부정은 'must not'과는 뜻이 다르기 때문에 대신해 쓸 수 없다.

(3) **의문문**: [Do / Does + 주어 + have to ~?] ~해야만 하니?

- **Do** you **have to** <u>go</u> there tonight?
- **Did** you **have to** <u>wait</u> long to ride the subway?

2. must

(1) **강한 추측**: [must be] ~인 것이 틀림없다, ~이 분명하다

- Those boys **must be** elementary school students.
- He **must be** proud of you.

(2) **의무**: [must + 동사원형] 반드시 ~해야만 한다

- We **must** <u>obey</u> the rules.
- You **must** <u>take</u> a shower before bed.
- **Must** I <u>study</u> for the entrance exam?

(3) **must not**: [강한 금지] 절대로 ~해서는 안 된다

- You **must not** <u>steal</u> other people's things.
  (= mustn't)

A 다음 문장에서 밑줄 친 must가 추측과 의무 중 어떤 의미로 쓰였는지 구분하시오.

1   Andy <u>must</u> turn in his homework by five.   ___[의무]___

2   She <u>must</u> be thirteen years old.   _____

3   People <u>must</u> fasten their seatbelt when they drive a car.

   _____

4   Linda <u>must</u> be very sad to hear the news.   _____

5   Mr. Lee thinks I <u>must</u> keep our promise.   _____

6   Jisun <u>must</u> attend the seminar because she is the speaker.

   _____

7   She <u>must</u> be proud of herself.   _____

8   I <u>must</u> exchange the broken chair tonight.   _____

B 주어진 우리말 해석에 맞게 단어들을 알맞게 이용하여 올바른 문장을 만드시오.

1   너는 내일 일찍 일어날 필요가 없다. (don't have to, get up)

   ➡ _____*You don't have to get up early tomorrow.*_____

2   학생들이 교복을 입어야만 하나요?
   (have to, wear, school uniforms)

   ➡ _____ students _____ school uniforms?

3   그는 그 비행기를 탈 필요가 없었다. (take the plane)

   ➡ He _____.

4   다른 사람들을 때려서는 안 된다. (hit, others)

   ➡ You _____.

5   Hana는 내일 밤 꼭 그 파티에 가야 하니? (have to, go to the party)

   ➡ _____ Hana _____ tomorrow night?

6   너는 시험에서 부정행위를 하면 안 된다. (cheat)

   ➡ You _____ on the test.

7   우리는 게임의 규칙을 따라야만 한다. (follow, the rule of the game)

   ➡ We _____.

8   도서관에서는 조용히 해야 한다. (be quiet)

   ➡ You _____ in the library.

should / had better

- **should**: 약한 의무나 당연히 해야 할 일 또는 조언을 할 때 사용한다.

- **had better**: 상대방에게 충고나 권유를 할 때 사용한다.

◈ **should / had better**

긍정	should + 동사원형	had better + 동사원형
부정	should not + 동사원형	had better not + 동사원형

1. should : ∼해야 한다 [의무/당연]

- If you are sick, you **should** go to the hospital.

- You **shouldn't (should not)** enter the grass.

2. had better : ∼하는 것이 낫다 [충고/권유]

- He **had better** take a test.

- You **had better not** swim in the river.

☆Check up!

Answer Keys p. 15

A 주어진 우리말에 맞게 단어들을 알맞게 배열하여 올바른 문장을 만드시오.

1 너는 쉬는 것이 좋겠다. 너무 피곤해 보여.

(take, had, a rest, better)

➡ You _____had better take a rest_____. You look so tired.

2 목표를 달성하고 싶다면 열심히 노력해야 한다.

(do, should, best, your)

➡ If you want to achieve your goal, you _____.

3 나는 책 세 권을 다음 주까지 읽어야 한다.

(should, next week, three books, by, read)

➡ I _____.

4 너는 일찍 집에 가는 것이 좋겠다. (go, early, had better, home)

➡ You _____.

5 Helen은 택시를 타는 것이 좋겠다. (take, had better, a taxi)

➡ Helen _____.

6 우리는 일을 미뤄서는 안 된다. (should, put off, not, work, our)

➡ We _____.

7 비가 많이 올 예정이므로 그들은 밖에 나가지 않아야 한다.
   (go, should, outside, not)
   ➡ They _____ because it is going to rain.

8 Sally는 TV 보는 것을 멈춰야만 한다. (stop, watching TV)
   ➡ Sally _____.

9 그는 다섯 접시 더 요리 하는 것이 좋겠다.
   (had better, five, cook, dishes)
   ➡ He _____ more.

10 사람들은 가난한 사람들을 도와야 한다. (help, the poor)
   ➡ People _____.

B 다음 문장에서 어법상 어색한 것을 찾아 바르게 고치시오.

1 She has better study hard for the final test.
   _____has_____ ➡ _____had_____

2 You had better to get up early tomorrow morning.
   _____ ➡ _____

3 They should picking the speaker up at the airport.
   _____ ➡ _____

4 Andrew had not better go to school on foot.
   _____ ➡ _____

5 Mrs. Brown not should act like that.
   _____ ➡ _____

6 I have better buy some pens to write with.
   _____ ➡ _____

7 The students should paying attention to the lecture.
   _____ ➡ _____

8 He had eat better not junk food to lose weight.
   _____ ➡ _____

9 Tim and I had better setting priority for our project.
   _____ ➡ _____

10 Should I to take the medicine?
   _____ ➡ _____

ought to

• **ought to** : '~해야 한다'의 뜻으로 'should'보다는 강하고, 'have to/must'보다는 약한 '의무'를 나타낼 때 사용한다. 부정문은 '금지'의 의미를 가진다.

1. **긍정문:** [ought to + 동사원형] ~해야 한다, ~하지 않으면 안 된다

   • We **ought to** help the people in trouble.

   • You **ought to** open the window because the smell is so bad.

2. **부정문:** [ought not to + 동사원형] ~해서는 안 된다

   • We **ought not to** make a prank call.

   • They **ought not to** drive too fast at the school zone.

 **Check up!**

Answer Keys p. 15

A 다음 우리말 해석에 맞게 주어진 단어를 알맞게 배열하시오.

1 Sam은 자기 동생을 혼자 집에 두어서는 안 된다.

(his brother, at home, ought, to, leave, not, alone)

➡ Sam _____ought not to leave his brother alone at home_____ .

2 어린이들은 폭력적인 것에 노출돼서는 안 된다.

(violent things, ought, to, be exposed, not to)

➡ Children _____ .

3 너는 고장 난 차를 고쳐야 한다. (ought, your broken car, fix, to)

➡ You _____ .

4 음주 운전을 해서는 안 된다. (people, drink and drive, ought, to, not)

➡ _____ .

5 John은 약속 장소에 제시간에 와야 한다.

(ought to, for, be on time, the appointment)

➡ John _____ .

6 그들은 여기서 사진을 찍어서는 안 된다.

(here, take, ought, to, a picture, not)

➡ They _____ .

7 Julian은 그 책을 읽고 독후감을 써야 한다.

(write, ought, a book report, to)

➡ Julian _____ after he reads the book.

would / used to

> • would / used to : 과거에 반복적으로 일어났던 일들에 대해 표현할 때 사용하며,
> '~하곤 했다'의 뜻으로 해석한다.

1. would : 'often, sometimes' 등과 함께 쓰여 '자주/가끔 ~하곤 했다'의 뜻으로 <u>과거의 불규칙한 습관</u>을 나타낸다.

- We **would** often <u>play</u> badminton at night.
- I **would** sometimes <u>call</u> him.

2. used to

⑴ 과거의 규칙적인 습관: 언제나 ~하곤 했다

- My family **used to** <u>take</u> a trip every summer.

⑵ 과거의 사실이나 상태: 전에는 ~이었다(있었다)

- There **used to** <u>be</u> a parking lot here.

➡ 'would / used to' 뒤에는 항상 동사원형이 온다.

☆Check up!

Answer Keys p. 15

A 밑줄 친 부분이 과거의 습관과 상태 중 어떤 의미로 쓰였는지 구분하시오.

1 There <u>used to</u> be a hospital around the corner.   [과거의 상태]

2 I <u>used to</u> go to church on Sundays.   _____

3 This room <u>used to</u> be a warehouse.   _____

4 She <u>used to</u> jog every day.   _____

5 He <u>used to</u> be my best friend.   _____

6 This building <u>used to</u> be a gym.   _____

7 Lily <u>used to</u> get up early in the morning.   _____

B 우리말 해석에 맞게 빈칸에 would와 used to 중 알맞은 말을 쓰시오.

1 아빠는 일요일 오후에 등산을 하곤 했다.

➡ Father _used to_ climb the mountain on Sunday afternoons.

2 그는 매일 아침마다 아침을 먹곤 했다. (지금은 아니다)

➡ He _____ eat breakfast every morning.

3 나는 종종 한강에서 연을 날리곤 했다.
➡ I _____ often fly a kite in Hangang River.

4 건너편에는 이탈리아 식당이 있었다. (지금은 없다)
➡ There _____ be an Italian restaurant across the way.

5 이 방은 전에 Tim의 방이었다.
➡ This room _____ be Tim's room.

6 여름에 John과 Lina는 가끔씩 록 페스티발에 가곤 했다.
➡ John and Lina _____ sometimes go to rock music festival in summer.

7 이 경기장은 전에 야구장이었다.
➡ This stadium _____ be a ballpark.

8 내 동생은 종종 밤새 컴퓨터 게임을 하곤 했다.
➡ My brother _____ often play the computer game all night.

9 우리 가족은 토요일 저녁마다 영화를 보곤 했다. (지금은 아니다)
➡ My family _____ watch movies every Saturday evening.

10 Mr. Lee는 종종 점심 식사 후 테니스를 치곤 했다.
➡ Mr. Lee _____ often play tennis after lunch.

3-13 조동사 do

• **조동사 do**: 일반동사의 의문문이나 부정문을 만들 때 쓰이고, 동사(구)를 강조할 때도 쓰인다.

1. 일반동사의 의문문과 부정문을 만들 때

• **Do** you remember me?

• He **doesn't** like to play sports.

2. 동사를 강조할 때

• She **does** <u>have</u> great memories about everything. ^(have 강조)

• Children **do** <u>like</u> pizza. ^(like 강조)

3. 동사(구)의 반복을 피하기 위한 '대동사 do'

• Do you like to write poems? Of course, I **do**.
_(like to write poems)

☆Check up!

Answer Keys p. 15

A 다음 밑줄 친 부분의 do가 대동사와 강조 중 어떤 의미로 쓰였는지 구분하시오.

1 I <u>do</u> fix my car by myself.   [강조]

2 He made a mistake and I <u>did</u>, too.   _____

3 I <u>do</u> love my parents.   _____

4 Do you want to eat more? Of course, I <u>do</u>. _____

5 Sam <u>does</u> hate bugs.   _____

B do를 알맞은 형태로 바꾸어 문장을 완성하시오.

1 I _____did_____ go to the hospital yesterday.

2 _____ she prepare for today's meal?

3 You _____ like to eat sweet things!

4 She _____ draw pictures well.

5 I wrote a letter to Tim, and Sally also _____.

6 _____ you know her name? – Yes, I do.

7 He _____ meet her yesterday because he was playing soccer.

8 They _____ enjoy the summer party last year.

Practice More II

A 주어진 문장들이 같은 뜻이 되도록 괄호 안에서 알맞은 것을 고르시오.

1 Every employee may use this program.
   ➡ Every employee ((can) / should) use this program.

2 Harry must attend the tomorrow's meeting.
   ➡ Harry (has to / should) attend the tomorrow's meeting.

3 I should clean my room before mom wakes up.
   ➡ I (ought to / am going to) clean my room before mom
   wakes up.

4 You have to take a rest. You look so tired.
   ➡ You (must / had better not) take a rest. You look so tired.

5 I need not buy new furniture anymore.
   ➡ I (don't have to / must not) buy new furniture anymore.

6 How about going fishing tomorrow?
   ➡ (Shall / Should) we go fishing tomorrow?

7 Jihoon, you had better change your hair color.
   ➡ Jihoon, you (should / should not) change your hair color.

8 The baby should not touch the dangerous things.
   ➡ The baby (had better / must not) touch the dangerous
   things.

9 She had better not buy the new house.
   ➡ She (should not / must) buy the new house.

10 Would you like to go hiking this weekend?
   ➡ (Shall we / Can we) go hiking this weekend?

B 다음 문장에서 어법상 <u>어색한</u> 것을 찾아 바르게 고치시오

1 I ought read the book because it is my homework.

   _____read_____ ➡ _____to read_____

2 You had better starting to exercise right now.

   _____ ➡ _____

3 We has to find the answer to solve the problem.

   _____ ➡ _____

4 Sam has to not have a meeting.

_____ ➡ _____

5 Linda must be fix the broken chair by herself.

_____ ➡ _____

6 She has to watch the documentary last night.

_____ ➡ _____

7 You had not better act like that.

_____ ➡ _____

8 Teenagers should not hitting weak students.

_____ ➡ _____

9 He oughts to eat fresh food to be healthy.

_____ ➡ _____

10 Does he has to finish the project by tomorrow?

_____ ➡ _____

C 각 대화를 읽고 괄호 안에서 알맞은 것을 고르시오.

1 A (Should / Would) you come to my house tomorrow?
   B I'm so sorry. I have homework to finish tomorrow.

2 A Do you (have to / had better) wait for your sister?
   B No, she already arrived home.

3 A (May / Shall) I close the door?
   B Sure, if you want.

4 A It (might / had better) be true.
   B Oh, no. I can't believe that rumor.

5 A Mom, (can / should) I eat chocolate cookies?
   B No. You (are going to / had better) make an appointment with dentist.

6 A Let's go to the movie tonight!
   B I'm so sorry. I have a headache. I (should / may) take a rest tonight.

Practice More II

Answer Keys p. 16

7 A Hey, Tim! (Can / Will) I borrow your skates?
   B Oh, sorry. They won't fit you.

8 A Must you buy this jacket?
   B Oh, I (don't have to / must not) buy it. I have other choice.

9 A (Can / Must) I borrow your note?
   B Sure. Here you are.

10 A (Would / May) I have something to drink?
   B Okay, wait a minute.

D 우리말 해석에 맞게 주어진 단어들을 알맞게 배열하여 문장을 완성하시오.

1 나는 Lina와 쇼핑을 가는 것이 좋을 것 같다.
   (had, Lina, go, I, with, better, shopping)
   ➡ _____ I had better go shopping with Lina. _____

2 그는 Jim의 영어 선생님이 분명해. (teacher, he, Jim's, must, English, be)
   ➡ _____

3 자기 소개를 해주시겠습니까? (would, yourself, introduce, you)
   ➡ _____

4 집으로 돌아가는 것은 3주 이상 걸릴 지 모른다.
   (returning, weeks, might, more than, three, home, take)
   ➡ _____

5 우리 집에는 정원에 분수가 있었다.
   (used, in the garden, house, fountain, my, have, to, a, I, in)
   ➡ _____

6 우리와 저녁을 함께 먹을래? (you, us, like, would, dinner, with, have, to)
   ➡ _____

7 John은 어렸을 때 축구 선수로 활동하곤 했다.
   (John, young, soccer, be, when, would, was, player, he, a)
   ➡ _____

내신 최다 출제 유형

01 다음 중 어법상 틀린 것을 고르시오. [출제 예상 90%]

① You should drive slowly here.
② Should we bring some bread and drinks?
③ Jackson should not eat and drinks in the library.
④ All students should listen carefully.
⑤ Shouldn't we draw a picture here?

02 다음 밑줄 친 부분 중 어법상 맞는 것을 고르시오.
[출제 예상 85%]

Sera ① doesn't has any clothes. But she ② can't go out shopping this Sunday. She ③ will buys some clothes on the Internet. She ④ need someone to help her. But her best friend, Gina ⑤ cann't help her, either.

03 다음 중 어법상 올바른 문장을 고르시오. [출제 예상 90%]

① The balloon may pops.
② If you have a headache, you can get some fresh air.
③ If you are thirsty, you may drinking as much water as you need.
④ It's raining, so you may uses an umbrella.
⑤ Jenny not may go to the party.

04 Choose the wrong sentence. [출제 예상 85%]

① He doesn't does his homework.
② We may go outside to play.
③ It might be snowy tonight.
④ I can help you if you want.
⑤ I ought to study hard for the test.

05 다음 밑줄 친 부분의 쓰임이 나머지 넷과 다른 것을 고르시오. [출제 예상 85%]

① Children do like hamburgers.
② I do have a lot of work to do.
③ Jerry and Sandra do love each other.
④ We have to do our homework first.
⑤ They do clean the house.

06 다음 밑줄 친 부분의 쓰임이 보기 와 같은 것을 고르시오. [출제 예상 85%]

보기

Dorothy must be happy. She won the first prize in the final exam.

① She must not bring a pet to the restaurant.
② They must get to the bus station in time.
③ We must finish the homework by tomorrow.
④ Tommy must not throw away garbage.
⑤ She must be more than fifteen years old.

07 Which one is grammatically correct? [출제 예상 85%]

① Would you like a coffees?
② She can drank two bottles of juice.
③ He can able to buy two pounds of meat.
④ I had better eat something warm.
⑤ You should taking some medicine.

[01~03] 다음 밑줄 친 부분과 바꿔 쓸 수 있는 단어를 고르시오.

01

> **A** <u>Can</u> I take your order?
> **B** Yes, two hamburgers, please.

① Am ② Do ③ Must
④ May ⑤ Will

02

> Maria can run fast now, but she <u>couldn't</u> run fast before.

① may not ② can't
③ could ④ wasn't
⑤ wasn't able to

03

> **A** You <u>must</u> not be late again.
> **B** I'm sorry.

① may ② should
③ will ④ are able to
⑤ need

[04~05] 다음 우리말에 맞게 빈칸에 들어갈 말로 알맞은 것을 고르시오.

04

> You _____ watch too much TV.
> (너는 너무 많이 TV를 보면 안 돼.)

① need not ② don't have to
③ must not ④ don't need to
⑤ have to not

05

> She _____ sick today.
> (그녀는 오늘 아픈 것이 틀림없다.)

① must be ② have to be
③ have to ④ must
⑤ may

[06~07] 다음 주어진 문장의 밑줄 친 부분과 뜻이 같은 것을 고르시오.

06

> She <u>must</u> be a foreigner.

① You <u>must</u> turn around.
② They <u>must</u> clean the house.
③ You stayed up late last night. You <u>must</u> be tired.
④ She <u>must</u> do her best.
⑤ You <u>must</u> change your clothes.

07

> I <u>do</u> have a lot of pictures of my childhood.

① She <u>doesn't</u> have anything to do.
② They smile as you <u>do</u>.
③ He <u>does</u> like her very much.
④ I don't have to <u>do</u> it.
⑤ <u>Does</u> she remember me?

08 다음 주어진 문장의 밑줄 친 부분과 다른 의미로 쓰인 것을 고르시오.

> You <u>must</u> be careful when you cross the road.

① He <u>must</u> be Judy's brother.
② Jade <u>must</u> get there on time.
③ We <u>must</u> study hard for the exam.
④ You <u>must</u> stop laughing at the others.
⑤ We <u>must</u> collect more information about it.

09 다음 중 어법상 올바른 문장을 고르시오.

① She'd not better go shopping today.
② You'd better to ask him.
③ They'd better to get his advise.
④ You'd better washing the dishes.
⑤ I'd better not eat too much.

10 다음 중 어법상 어색한 문장을 모두 고르시오.

① You didn't do well on the test.
② Paul didn't nothing for us.
③ Don't be late again.
④ She don't know about the news.
⑤ You didn't look good yesterday.

[11~13] 다음 빈칸에 들어갈 말로 알맞은 것을 고르시오.

11

> You _____ drink coffee a lot because you can't sleep well.

① must   ② can   ③ should not
④ could not   ⑤ may

12

> _____ she have to wear a raincoat when it rains?

① Do   ② Does   ③ Did
④ Should   ⑤ Must

13

> Don't you see the red light? We _____ cross when the light is red.

① must   ② should   ③ have to
④ must not   ⑤ don't have to

14 다음 문장에 이어지는 말로 가장 알맞은 것을 고르시오.

> Mrs. Smith doesn't look well today. _____.

① She must be happy.
② She must be hungry.
③ She must be sick.
④ She must be kind.
⑤ She must be smart.

15 다음 빈칸에 들어갈 말로 알맞지 않은 것을 고르시오.

> You _____ go to bed early if you don't want to miss the bus.

① must   ② have to   ③ should
④ need not   ⑤ had better

16 다음 밑줄 친 부분과 뜻이 다른 것을 고르시오.

> It <u>may</u> not be true.

① They <u>may</u> get lost.
② It <u>may</u> be cold there.
③ He <u>may</u> already know the answer.
④ You <u>may</u> go home now.
⑤ She <u>may</u> be Chinese.

17 다음 밑줄 친 부분과 바꿔 쓸 수 있는 단어를 고르시오.

> I'm very happy because I <u>can</u> do it better than before.

① am able to   ② will   ③ should
④ may   ⑤ must

★★★
18 다음 중 어법상 틀린 문장을 모두 고르시오.

① She would take a walk in the park before.
② You had better follow all the directions.
③ There would be a post office over there.
④ You had better not call her again.
⑤ The bottle used to be filled with cold water.

19 다음 질문에 대한 대답으로 바르지 않은 것을 모두 고르시오.

> A May I take a picture here?
> B _____

① Yes, you may.   ② No, you may not.
③ Yes, you can.   ④ No, you may.
⑤ No, you must not.

20 다음 대화의 빈칸에 들어갈 말로 알맞은 것을 고르시오.

> A Can I stand here?
> B No, _____.
>   Many people are in line.

① you should here
② you shouldn't stand here
③ you may stand here
④ you may
⑤ you don't have to

21 다음 밑줄 친 부분을 대신해 쓸 수 있는 말로 알맞은 것을 고르시오.

> A Who broke the window over there?
> B Minho and Suho <u>did</u>.

① has not broken
② broke the window
③ didn't break the window
④ break it
⑤ didn't break it

22 주어진 우리말을 영어로 올바르게 영작한 것을 고르시오.

> 너는 복도에서 뛰면 안 돼.

① You must not run in the hallway.
② You must run in the hallway.
③ You may run in the hallway.
④ You don't have to run in the hallway.
⑤ You should run in the hallway.

23 다음 빈칸에 들어갈 말이 알맞게 짝지어진 것을 고르시오.

> • It's cloudy. You _____ take an umbrella.
> • The elevator stopped suddenly. We _____ wait for an hour.

① had better − had to
② will − will
③ must − should
④ have to − must
⑤ had better − have to

24 다음 대화의 밑줄 친 부분을 바르게 고친 것을 고르시오.

> A Who is that girl next to the door?
> B Well, I don't know exactly. She <u>be</u> Juna's sister.

① may be   ② will be   ③ must be
④ should be   ⑤ had better be

25 다음 짝지어진 문장의 의미가 <u>다른</u> 것을 고르시오.

① After lunch she would take a nap.
  → After lunch she used to take a nap.
② We can remember his phone number.
  → We're able to remember his phone number.
③ You should be quiet in public places.
  → You ought to be quiet in public places.
④ You must not drive so fast.
  → You don't need to drive so fast.
⑤ Could you close the door?
  → Would you close the door?

26 다음 밑줄 친 부분과 쓰임이 같은 것을 고르시오.

> You <u>can</u> use my electronic dictionary.

① I <u>cannot</u> remember his email address.
② My cat <u>can</u> jump high.
③ <u>Can</u> I ask you some questions?
④ Lina <u>can</u> ride a bike well.
⑤ Thomas <u>can</u> write a diary in English.

[27~28] 다음 그림을 영어로 잘 표현한 문장을 고르시오.

27

① You don't have to wear a life jacket.
② You have to wear a swimsuit.
③ You have to wear a life jacket.
④ You must not wear a life jacket.
⑤ You cannot wear a swimsuit.

28

① You don't have to take your pet inside.
② You don't need to take your pet inside.
③ You need not take your pet inside.
④ You must not take your pet inside.
⑤ You not must take your pet inside.

29 다음 주어진 문장들이 서로 뜻이 같도록 할 때 빈칸에 알맞은 것을 고르시오.

> I ate too many chocolate bars, but I don't eat them anymore.
> = I _____ eat too much chocolate bars.

① could   ② should   ③ had to
④ might   ⑤ used to

30 다음 밑줄 친 부분 중 어법상 어색한 것을 고르시오.

① She wasn't able to ride a horse then.
② You shouldn't break the windows.
③ You had not better meet a bad man.
④ They used to go fishing.
⑤ You must not run in the narrow road.

◇◇◇◇◇◇◇◇◇◇ 서술형 평가 ◇◇◇◇◇◇◇◇◇◇

[31~32] 다음 주어진 문장과 뜻이 같도록 빈칸에 알맞은 말을 쓰시오.

31
> We're sure that Becky's mother is a hair designer.

➡ Becky's mother _____ _____ a hair designer.

32
> Ben and Jen often went camping on Saturdays, but they don't anymore.

➡ Ben and Jen _____ _____ _____ _____ on Saturdays.

[33~35] 다음 글을 읽고 물음에 답하시오.

> People had to go out to the market when they needed to buy something.
> But we _____ (A) _____ go out to buy things these days. (B) We can order things on the Internet.
> (C) It is easy and saves time.

33 윗글의 (A)에 알맞은 말을 쓰시오.

➡ _____

34 윗글의 밑줄 친 (B)와 같은 뜻이 되도록 빈칸에 알맞은 말을 쓰시오.

➡ We _____ _____ _____ order things on the Internet.

35 윗글의 (C)가 의미하는 것이 무엇인지 영어로 쓰시오. (단, 4개의 단어로 이루어져야 하며, 'shopping'이라는 단어가 들어가야 한다.)

➡ _____ _____ _____ _____

36 우리말과 같은 뜻이 되도록 빈칸에 알맞은 말을
써 넣으시오.

> Mary와 Jake는 그리스에 머물지도 모른다.

➡ Mary and Jake _____ stay in
Greece.

[37~38] 다음 주어진 단어를 알맞게 배열하여 문장을
완성하시오.

37

> When you are not happy now, you
> _____.
> (had better / something / interesting /
> find / to / do)

➡ _____

38

> _____ when you
> come back home. (your / should / first
> / hands / wash / you)

➡ _____

39 다음 대화를 읽고 밑줄 친 부분의 의미가 무엇인지
영어로 쓰시오. (단, 문장으로 써야 하며 세 단어로
이루어져야 한다.)

> A Harry, you don't like dogs, do you?
> B Actually, I didn't like them. But now,
> because of my little sisters, I do.

➡ _____

40 다음 밑줄 친 부분과 바꿔 쓸 수 있는 단어를
쓰시오. (단, 두 단어여야 한다.)

> You don't have to go to work tomorrow.
> It's a national holiday.

➡ _____

41 다음 문장의 괄호 안의 주어진 단어와 같은 뜻이
되는 단어를 쓰시오.

> A It's a little difficult to learn a foreign
> language, isn't it?
> B No, it isn't difficult at all. You
> _____ (= must) practice harder
> and harder.

➡ _____

[42~43] 다음 우리말에 맞게 괄호 안의 단어를 배열하
여 문장을 완성하시오.

★★★
42

> 우리는 오늘 밤 밖에 나가지 않는 것이 좋겠다.
> (We / tonight / had / not / better / out /
> go)

➡ _____

★★★
43

> 너는 만화책을 읽기 전에 숙제를 다 해야만
> 한다.
> (You / comic books / must / your /
> homework / finish / you / read / before)

➡ _____

Note

04

Chapter
명사, 관사와 대명사

Point Check I

◆ **명사:** 이름이 있는 모든 것(사람, 동물, 사물 등)을 말한다.

◆ **관사:** 정해지지 않은 것의 앞에는 부정관사 'a/an', 정해진 것의 앞에는 정관사 'the'가 붙는다.

1. 명사

(1) 명사의 종류

셀 수 있는 명사	보통명사, 집합명사	셀 수 없는 명사	물질명사, 고유명사, 추상명사

(2) 명사의 복수형

대부분의 명사	-s	ball – balls bottle – bottles
-s, -x, -ch, -sh, 자음+o	-es	bush – bushes bus – buses
자음+y	y를 i로 고치고 -es	dragonfly – dragonflies
f(e)	f(e)를 v로 고치고 -es	leaf – leaves

(3) 셀 수 없는 명사의 양 표현

a piece of 한 조각의	a glass of 한 잔의	a loaf of 한 덩어리의
a bottle of 한 병의	a slice of 한 조각의	a bar of 한 개의
a cup of 한 잔의	a bowl of 한 그릇의	a pound of 1파운드의

(4) 명사의 소유격

's를 붙이는 경우	-s로 끝나지 않는 단수/복수 명사	Tom's bag, people's right
'를 붙이는 경우	-s로 끝나는 복수 명사	animals' world
	신화에 나오는 이름, 유명한 인물	Venus' son
of + 명사	무생물의 소유격	buttons of the shirt

2. 관사

	① 하나의 (one)	④ 같은 (the same)
부정관사 a/an	② 어떤 (certain)	⑤ ～마다 (per)
	③ 약간 (some)	⑥ 대표 단수
정관사 the	① 서수, 최상급 앞	③ 악기 이름 앞
	② only, very, same 앞	④ 대표 단수

명사와 관사

명사의 종류

• **명사**: 세상에 이름이 있는 모든 것(사람, 동물, 사물 등)을 명사라고 한다.

1. 명사의 종류

대분류	소분류	의미		
셀 수 있는 명사 (가산 명사)	보통명사	셀 수 있는 일반적인 명사 girl　　　　window　　　　table　　　　flower		
	집합명사	사람이나 사물(동물)이 모인 집합을 나타내는 말		
		• 단수/복수 취급	• 항상 복수 취급	• 항상 단수 취급
		family class committee crowd	the police the public the press cattle	furniture jewelry machinery stationery
셀 수 없는 명사 (불가산 명사)	물질명사	일정하게 정해진 형태가 없는 명사 bread　　　silver　　　snow　　　water		
	고유명사	사람, 강, 산, 나라의 이름과 같이 일반적인 명사에 붙는 이름 Jenny　　　Han River　　　Mt. Everest		
	추상명사	사람의 생각으로 그려낼 수 있는 감정이나 개념을 나타내는 말		
		• 감정	• 생각	• 속성
		sadness happiness love joy	thought wisdom knowledge information	beauty ugliness youth success

☆Check up!

Answer Keys p. 18

A　괄호 안에서 알맞은 것을 고르시오

1　I brought three (cup / cups) for the picnic.

2　Do you want some (bread / breads)?

3　The (painter / painters) belong to our committee.

4 Wisdom (**is** / are) as important as knowledge.

5 Our team (are / **is**) happy to win the English speaking contest.

6 There are many (person / **people**) who participated in the safety seminar.

7 Jenny (**likes** / like) to eat sweet things, so I bought a cheesecake for her.

8 I think your (**baby** / babies) looks happy.

9 Would you please pass me the (**salt** / salts)?

10 Our family (**is** / are) going to go hiking next week.

Note
- **belong to**
  ~소유이다, ~에 속하다
- **committee** 위원회
- **wisdom** 지혜
- **knowledge** 지식

B 다음 문장에서 어법상 <u>어색한</u> 것을 찾아 바르게 고치시오.

1 My brother are sad because he lost his wallet.

    _____are_____ ➡ _____is_____

2 I need some papers to write a letter.

    _____ ➡ _____

3 Father caught many fishes in the river.

    _____ ➡ _____

4 There are an accident at the corner.

    _____ ➡ _____

5 Some person like to eat chocolate.

    _____ ➡ _____

6 The movie directed by Tim were released in 1955.

    _____ ➡ _____

7 My family live in Seoul.   _____ ➡ _____

8 There are much shoes on the shelf.

    _____ ➡ _____

9 His parents is pleased with the news.

    _____ ➡ _____

Note
- **accident** 사고
- **be released in**
  ~에 상영되다
- **be pleased with**
  ~에 기뻐하다

10 I spend many money to buy clothes.

    _____ ➡ _____

4 - 2 명사의 복수형

· **명사의 복수형**: 셀 수 있는 명사가 한 개일 때는 명사 앞에 'a/an'이 붙고, 여러 개를 나타낼 때는 명사 뒤에 '-s/-es'가 붙는다.

1. 규칙 변화_복수형

대부분의 경우	-s	shoe – shoes bike – bikes	friend – friends place – places
-s, -x, -ch, -sh로 끝나는 경우	-es	bus – buses fox – foxes	match – matches dish – dishes
'자음＋y'로 끝나는 경우	y를 i로 고치고 -es	baby – babies city – cities	diary – diaries country – countries
'모음＋y'로 끝나는 경우	-s	day – days boy – boys	way – ways key – keys
f(e)로 끝나는 경우	f를 v로 고치고 -es	life – lives leaf – leaves	knife – knives wolf – wolves
		〈예외〉 roof – roofs belief – beliefs	safe – safes chief – chiefs
-o로 끝나는 경우	-es	potato – potatoes hero – heroes	tomato – tomatoes mosquito – mosquitoes
		〈예외〉 radio – radios kangaroo – kangaroos	zoo – zoos piano – pianos

2. 불규칙변화_복수형

goose – geese	foot – feet	tooth – teeth
man – men	woman – women	fish – fish/fishes
sheep – sheep	deer – deer	mouse – mice
child – children	ox – oxen	

➡ 일반적으로 'fish'의 복수형은 'fish'를 사용한다. 하지만 그 종류가 여러가지임을 나타낼 때는 'fishes'를 사용한다. 이와 같은 경우의 단어들로는 'food – foods', 'fruit – fruits'가 있다.

A 다음 괄호 안에서 알맞은 것을 고르시오.

1 The ((man) / men) wearing a red shirt is my father.

2 There are many (tomatos / tomatoes) in the basket.

3 We took many (pictures / picture) in LA.

4 There are lots of (foxs / foxes) in the zoo.

5 The (boys / boy) is my nephew.

6 Lots of big (companys / companies) produce smart devices.

7 In our basement, there are a few (mice / mouses).

8 Andy's room is filled with many (toys / toyes).

9 There are few (leaves / leafs) on the branch.

B 다음 문장에서 어법상 <u>어색한</u> 것을 찾아 바르게 고치시오.

1 I saw some monkeies in the zoo.

<u>　monkeies　</u> ➡ <u>　monkeys　</u>

2 A lot of child don't like to study math.

<u>　　　　　</u> ➡ <u>　　　　　</u>

3 They took a lot of photoes in the park.

<u>　　　　　</u> ➡ <u>　　　　　</u>

4 Some person are afraid of a death.

<u>　　　　　</u> ➡ <u>　　　　　</u>

5 My son has lost two front teeths last week.

<u>　　　　　</u> ➡ <u>　　　　　</u>

6 Do you have knifes?

<u>　　　　　</u> ➡ <u>　　　　　</u>

7 Lily brought three dishes and four cup.

<u>　　　　　</u> ➡ <u>　　　　　</u>

8 There were gooses on the farm.

<u>　　　　　</u> ➡ <u>　　　　　</u>

9 Our teacher gave us some potatos for lunch.

<u>　　　　　</u> ➡ <u>　　　　　</u>

관사의 쓰임

> • 관사: 정해지지 않은 것에 쓰이는 부정관사 'a/an'과 정해진 것에 쓰이는 정관사 'the'가 있다.
> 'a/an'은 셀 수 있는 명사가 한 개 있을 경우에 '하나'의 뜻으로, 'the'는 정해진 것이나
> 세상에 하나뿐인 것을 가리킬 때 쓰인다.

1. 부정관사 a/an: 단어의 첫 소리가 모음일 경우 'an'을, 자음일 경우 'a'를 붙인다.

a baseball	**a** lady	**a** bear
an apple	**an** elephant	**an** igloo

• My friend gave me **an** apple and said sorry.

• They eat out once **a** week.
  (= per ~마다)

Grammar Plus +

• 'university, uniform, unicorn'은 첫 글자가 모음이지만,
발음이 반자음으로 시작하기 때문에 'a'를 붙인다.

• 'honest, honor'의 경우에는 첫 글자가 자음이지만,
발음이 모음으로 시작하기 때문에 'an'을 붙인다. ➡ 모음: a, e, i, o, u

2. 정관사 the: 셀 수 있는 명사와 셀 수 없는 명사에 상관없이 문맥상 가리키는 것을 알 수 있는 경우에 쓴다.

• A monkey climbed a tree. **The** monkey jumped down on me. [앞 명사의 반복]

• Can you close **the** window, please? [서로 알고 있는 것]

• Sara got **the** first prize. [서수, 최상급, only, same 앞]

• Mercury is the first planet to **the** sun. [유일한 것의 앞]

3. 관사를 사용하지 않는 경우

• Jenny and my brother had dinner together last night. [식사명]

• I enjoy playing tennis every afternoon. [운동명]

• She goes to work by subway. [by + 교통수단]

• My parents go to church on Sundays. [장소, 건물이 원래의 목적으로 이용될 때]

• History is her favorite subject. [과목명]

• Mars is the 7th largest planet in the solar system. [행성명]

A 다음 빈칸에 알맞은 답을 쓰시오.

1   Sara is ____an____ honest girl.

2   Would you mind if I opened _____ window?

3   I bought _____ shirt to wear at my sister's wedding.

4   _____ movie I saw last night was 'Cold Eyes.'

5   Cindy used to live in _____ apartment.

6   Joe is _____ smartest boy in our class.

7   It takes _____ hour to get to the park.

8   _____ earth is the only planet where creatures live.

9   They usually meet three times _____ month.

10 Look at a girl dancing on the stage. _____ girl is just ten years old!

B 다음 문장에서 어법상 <u>어색한</u> 것을 찾아 바르게 고치시오.

1   I like the her hat.   ____the her____ ➡ ____her____

2   He likes to play the baseball with his friends.
                                _____ ➡ _____

3   A book on the table is mine. _____ ➡ _____

4   We went to the park by the bus.
                                _____ ➡ _____

5   Nick could play a flute when he was thirteen.
                                _____ ➡ _____

6   Did you eat a breakfast yesterday?
                                _____ ➡ _____

7   Selena goes to church to meet her teacher.
                                _____ ➡ _____

8   He goes to a gym every day.
                                _____ ➡ _____

9   Studying a science is difficult.
                                _____ ➡ _____

10 An woman talking with Sam is my aunt.
                                _____ ➡ _____

셀 수 없는 명사의 양 표현

• 셀 수 없는 명사는 모양이 뚜렷하지 않거나 없고, 알갱이가 너무 작아 한두 개로 셀 수 없는 것들이다. 그래서 이들을 담는 그릇이나 세는 단위를 이용하여 양을 나타낸다.

◈ 셀 수 없는 명사의 단위

단수	복수	명사
a piece of	two pieces of	bread, cake, cheese, cloth, furniture
a bottle of	two bottles of	beer, ink, juice, water
a cup of	two cups of	coffee, tea
a glass of	two glasses of	water, milk, juice
a slice of	two slices of	cheese, pizza, meat
a pound of	two pounds of	sugar, meat, beef, pork
a bar of	two bars of	soap, chocolate, gold
a bowl of	two bowls of	soup, rice
a sheet of	two sheets of	paper, plastic
a loaf of	two loaves of	bread
a spoon(ful) of	two spoon(fuls) of	sugar, salt, yogurt
a bunch of	two bunches of	flowers, grapes

• a piece of paper
• a bottle of water
• a cup of tea
• a glass of milk
• a slice of cheese
• a pound of meat

• two bars of chocolate
• three bowls of soup
• four sheets of paper
• five loaves of bread
• six spoon(fuls) of salt
• seven bunches of grapes

Answer Keys p. 18

A　괄호 안에서 알맞은 것을 고르시오.

1　Jessica buys (a piece of / (a pound of)) meat.

2　They ate (two cups of / two cup of) coffee.

3　He ordered five (bowls / bowl) of soup.

4　Albert bought a (pound / bottle) of ink at the shop.

5　Mike has three (slices / bars) of cheese.

6　My mom buys two (pounds of / bunches of) meat every Friday.

7　Mom added (a spoonful of / a loaf of) sugar into the soup.

8　Every morning my father reads (a slice of / a sheet of) newspaper.

9　He gave me (a bar of / a loaf of) soap.

B　다음 문장에서 어법상 <u>어색한</u> 것을 찾아 바르게 고치시오.

1　John drinks three cups of coffees everyday.

　　　　　　　　　　coffees ➡ *coffee*

2　They ordered four bottle of water.

　　　　　　　　　　＿＿＿＿ ➡ ＿＿＿＿

3　I had a cup of soup for breakfast.

　　　　　　　　　　＿＿＿＿ ➡ ＿＿＿＿

4　A hungry man ate 20 sheets of pizza.

　　　　　　　　　　＿＿＿＿ ➡ ＿＿＿＿

5　Please add a spoonfuls of salt to the pot.

　　　　　　　　　　＿＿＿＿ ➡ ＿＿＿＿

6　Ann received three pounds of gold from her father.

　　　　　　　　　　＿＿＿＿ ➡ ＿＿＿＿

7　I ordered two bunches of juice.

　　　　　　　　　　＿＿＿＿ ➡ ＿＿＿＿

8　After jogging, he drank three bars of water.

　　　　　　　　　　＿＿＿＿ ➡ ＿＿＿＿

주의해야 할 명사의 단수/복수

• 셀 수 있는 대부분의 명사는 뒤에 '-s/-es'를 붙여서 복수를 나타낸다. 그러나, 단수처럼 보이지만 복수로 쓰이고, 복수처럼 보이지만 단수로 쓰이는 명사들도 있다.

1. 쌍으로 이루어진 명사: 항상 복수형으로 쓰인다.

- glasses
- gloves
- jeans
- pants
- scissors
- shoes
- socks

2. 자체에 복수의 뜻을 지닌 명사

- people
- police
- cattle

3. 단수와 복수의 형태가 같은 명사

- deer – deer
- fish – fish
- sheep – sheep

4. 복수의 형태지만 단수 취급하는 명사

(1) 학문명	economics	mathematics	politics	physics
(2) 국가명	the United States of America		the Philippines	
(3) 기타	checkers	darts	customs	news

5. 단수와 복수의 의미가 서로 다른 명사

- arm – arms 팔 – 무기
- air – airs 공기 – 태도, 분위기
- manner – manners 방법 – 예절
- force – forces 힘 – 군대
- wood – woods 나무 – 숲
- custom – customs 관습 – 관세, 세관

☆Check up!

Answer Keys p. 19

A 괄호 안에서 알맞은 것을 고르시오.

1 Economics (is / are) too complicated to study.

2 Did you buy (glasses / glass) last week?

3 There are many (fish / fishes) in the lake.

4 Some people (think / thinks) reading books is a good habit.

5 There are (cattle / cattles) on the farm.

6 His death (are / is) shocking news today.

7 Britain (is / are) famous for fog and rain.

8 Darts (are / is) the most favorite activity in our class.

9 I received nice (pant / pants) for my birthday present.

10 She bought a pair of (gloves / glove) for exercise.

4 - 6 명사의 소유격

• **명사의 소유격**: 일반 명사의 소유를 표현한다.
'∼의'라는 뜻을 나타내기 위해 명사 뒤에 '-s'를 붙이거나 'of + 명사'로 나타낸다.

1. 명사의 소유격: ['s] / [']

['s]를 **붙이는 경우**	(1) -s로 끝나지 않은 단수 명사	
	• the book's thickness 그 책의 두께	• an ant's behavior 개미의 행동
	(2) -s로 끝나지 않은 복수 명사	
	• deer's horn 사슴들의 뿔	• young people's future 젊은이들의 미래
[']를 **붙이는 경우**	(1) -s로 끝나는 복수 명사	
	• my friends' dream 내 친구들의 꿈	• the girls' high school 여자 고등학교
	(2) 신화에 나오는 인물이나 예전의 인물	
	• Venus' beauty 비너스의 아름다움	
	• Achilles' heel 아킬레스건	• Aristoteles' ideas 아리스토텔레스의 사상

➡ 일반적인 사람의 이름이 '-s'로 끝나는 경우에는 ['s]가 붙는다

• James's life 제임스의 삶　　　　　　　　　• Jones's way 존스의 길

2. 무생물의 소유격: [of + 명사]

• the shape **of** the moons 달의 모양　　　　• wheels **of** the train 기차의 바퀴들
• the size **of** Jupiter (= Jupiter's size) 목성의 크기

➡ 행성명의 경우에는 ['s]도 함께 사용할 수 있다.
➡ 행성명 앞에는 관사를 쓰지 않는다.

> ### Grammar Plus +
>
> • '시간, 가격, 거리, 중량'을 나타내는 명사는 ['s], [']를 사용한다.
> yesterday's news 어제 소식　　　　　　ten dollars' value 10달러의 가치
> one hour's meeting 한 시간의 회의

3. 집, 상점, 교회 등을 나타내는 명사가 소유격 뒤에 올 때 생략 가능

• My sister will go to the hairdresser's (shop).

4. 복합어의 경우 맨 뒤에 ['s]를 붙임

• her father-in-law's book
• his mother-in-law's dress

5. 기타

• Anya's and Joseph's violin [Anya와 Joseph의 각자 소유]
• Anya and Joseph's violin [Anya와 Joseph의 공동 소유]

Answer Keys p. 19

A 다음에 주어진 단어를 이용하여 표현을 완성하시오.

1 cat, Sam, white ➡ _____Sam's white cat_____

2 Mira, book, English ➡ _____

3 butterfly, wings ➡ _____

4 this house, the owner ➡ _____

5 Helen, smile, beautiful ➡ _____

6 tail, the dog, black ➡ _____

7 the bottle, the top ➡ _____

8 bathroom, the women ➡ _____

9 yesterday, weather ➡ _____

10 the ball, the shape ➡ _____

B 다음 문장에서 어법상 어색한 것을 찾아 바르게 고치시오.

1 She can remember her daughter cute smile.

_____daughter_____ ➡ _____daughter's_____

2 My parents's wedding anniversary is next week.

_____ ➡ _____

3 She was satisfied with the test's result.

_____ ➡ _____

4 The blanket of Tim is black.

_____ ➡ _____

5 The news of today is so shocking.

_____ ➡ _____

6 I'm interested in reading Dickens's novel.

_____ ➡ _____

7 This is not a my bag. _____ ➡ _____

8 Poems of Kate moved me.

_____ ➡ _____

9 Mike drew his friends's faces on the canvas.

_____ ➡ _____

명사의 동격

- **명사의 동격**: 명사나 대명사를 보충 설명하거나 강조하기 위해 그 뒤에 다른 명사(구, 절)를 함께 쓰는데 이들의 관계를 동격이라 한다.
- '콤마(,), that, of'를 사용해 동격의 관계를 나타낸다.

1. 콤마(,)를 사용한 동격

- I like Jasmine, that cute girl next to the fence. (Jasmine = that cute girl)
- That man is my uncle, Jack. (my uncle = Jack)

2. that을 사용한 동격

- She knows the truth **that** Tom saved his money all. (the truth = Tom saved his money all)
- He has a dream **that** he wants to be a vet. (dream = he wants to be a vet)

3. of를 사용한 동격

- There is no food **of** eating full in Africa. (food = eating full)
- We were glad at the news **of** your passing the university entrance exam.
(the news = your passing the university entrance exam)

☆Check up!

Answer Keys p. 19

A 빈칸에 of, (,), that 중에서 알맞은 것을 쓰시오.

1   I know the fact ___*that*___ the sun rises in the east.

2   Sally _____ my sister _____ is reading a book on the sofa.

3   The news _____ his coming back home surprised mom.

4   Jane knows _____ she wants to become a doctor.

5   Our coach was satisfied with the result _____ the game.

6   The idea _____ we should plant some trees in the garden makes sense.

7   I missed Ann _____ my best friend.

8   John has the idea _____ going on a picnic this weekend.

Practice More Ⅰ

Answer Keys p. 19~20

A 각 명사의 복수형을 쓰시오.

1　company　➡　_companies_
2　child　➡　_____
3　tooth　➡　_____
4　deer　➡　_____
5　city　➡　_____
6　leaf　➡　_____
7　mouse　➡　_____
8　ox　➡　_____
9　goose　➡　_____
10　man　➡　_____

B 괄호 안에서 알맞은 것을 고르시오.

1　The cattle (is / are) running on the field.
2　She could play (the flute / flute) when she was young.
3　James bought two loaves of (bread / salt) last night.
4　There (were / was) lots of fish in the lake.
5　I have been to Japan by (the airplane / airplane).
6　He used to meet Maria once (a / the) week.
7　I love (children's smile / children's smiles) at all times.
8　Korea (have / has) many beautiful historic sites.
9　They usually go to (the school / school) to play basketball.
10　The building is 100 (meter / meters) high.

C 다음 보기 에서 알맞은 것을 찾아 빈칸에 쓰시오.

보기
| the | 's | X | a | an |

1　Andrea is _the_ tallest girl in our class.
2　My hobby is playing _____ tennis.
3　She eats bulgogi three times _____ week.

4   James should go to _____ bed early.

5   I bought _____ apple for my sister.

6   All of the doctors takes _____ Hippocratic oath.

7   I really envied James_____ success.

8   _____ second biggest planet in the solar system is _____ Saturn.

9   My wife wore my mother-in-law_____ wedding dress.

10 Kevin was _____ last runner in the race.

D   주어진 단어와 단위 명사를 이용하여 문장을 완성하시오.

1   I bought three _____*pieces of cake*_____ yesterday. (cake)

2   We need at least two _____. (chocolate)

3   Tim had a _____ for dinner. (bread)

4   There are four _____ in the box. (milk)

5   Why don't we make two _____ for dinner? (soup)

6   The dogs ate a _____. (meat)

7   Mom put a _____ and two _____ in the bowl. (salt / cheese)

8   I need three _____ to write on. (paper)

9   I bought two _____ at the store. (soap)

E   다음 문장에서 어법상 어색한 것을 찾아 바르게 고치시오.

1   We can't find many information about professor Lee.

　　　　　　　　　　　　_____*many*_____ ➡ _____*much*_____

2   I saw two deers on the farm.

　　　　　　　　　　　　_____ ➡ _____

3   He can't remember Toms' real name.

　　　　　　　　　　　　_____ ➡ _____

4   John needs much moneys to buy the car.

　　　　　　　　　　　　_____ ➡ _____

5 The woman ordered three cookie and a glass of juice.

_____ ➡ _____

6 I caught many fishes in the lake.

_____ ➡ _____

7 Do you like this pant? I think they're good to you.

_____ ➡ _____

8 Mike is a smartest boy in the class.

_____ ➡ _____

9 I want to take an economy class.

_____ ➡ _____

10 Daniel saw two womans dancing in the street.

_____ ➡ _____

11 We go to the church on Sundays.

_____ ➡ _____

12 Some people think they are heros.

_____ ➡ _____

F 다음의 우리말에 맞게 빈칸에 알맞은 말을 쓰시오.

1 Terry와 Jenny는 그들의 조부모님 댁에 다녀왔다.
➡ Terry and Jenny have been to their ___grandparents' (house)___.

2 Helen의 드레스와 Nami의 드레스는 똑같다.
➡ _____ are the same.

3 소녀들은 새의 날개를 닮은 얼음을 조각했다.
➡ The girls sculptured the ice like the _____.

4 물리학은 너무 어려워서 혼자서 공부할 수 없다.
➡ _____ too difficult to study alone.

5 그녀는 목이 말라서 세 잔의 얼음 물을 한 번에 마셨다.
➡ She was thirsty, so she drank _____ at once.

6 그는 단 음식을 너무 좋아해서 음식에 다섯 스푼의 설탕을 넣었다.
➡ He liked sweet food so much, so he put _____ in the food.

Point Check Ⅱ

◆ **대명사:** 사람이나 사물을 대신해서 가리키는 말로 인칭대명사, 소유대명사, 지시대명사, 재귀대명사, 부정대명사기 있다.

◆ **재귀대명사:** '~ 자신(oneself)'을 표현하는 말을 가리킨다.

◆ **지시대명사:** 정해진 사람이나 사물을 가리킬 때 사용하며, 'this(these), that(those)'이 있다.

◆ **의문대명사:** 의문사를 이용하여 사람이나 사물에 대해 물어볼 때 사용한다.

1. 대명사의 종류

수	인칭	인칭대명사			소유대명사	재귀대명사
		주격	소유격	목적격		
단수	1인칭	I	my	me	mine	myself
	2인칭	you	your	you	yours	yourself
	3인칭	he	his	him	his	himself
		she	her	her	hers	herself
		it	its	it	–	itself
복수	1인칭	we	our	us	ours	ourselves
	2인칭	you	your	your	yours	yourselves
	3인칭	they	their	them	theirs	themselves

2. 지시대명사

this	이것, 이 사람	that	저것, 저 사람
these	이것들, 이 사람들	those	저것들, 저 사람들

3. 의문대명사

who	누가 (주격)	whose	누구의, 누구의 것 (소유격)	who(m)	누구를 (목적격)
which	어느 것, 어느 사람	what	무엇		

4. 'It'의 여러 가지 쓰임

- That ice sculpture is great. **It** looks like a diamond. [명사의 반복] (It = That ice sculpture)

- **It** is sunny today. [비인칭주어_날씨]

- **It** is important that you know yourself well. [가주어 it] (It = that you know yourself well.)

대명사

대명사의 종류

• 대명사: 사람이나 사물을 대신해서 가리키는 말이다. 대명사에는 인칭대명사, 소유대명사, 재귀대명사, 지시대명사, 부정대명사가 있다.

1. 인칭 / 소유 / 재귀대명사

수	인칭	인칭대명사			소유대명사	재귀대명사
		주격	소유격	목적격		
단수	1인칭	I	my	me	mine	myself
	2인칭	you	your	you	yours	yourself
	3인칭	he	his	him	his	himself
		she	her	her	hers	herself
		it	its	it	−	itself
복수	1인칭	we	our	us	ours	ourselves
	2인칭	you	your	your	yours	yourselves
	3인칭	they	their	them	theirs	themselves

2. 지시 / 부정 / 의문대명사

대명사	종류	
지시대명사	this, these, that, those, it, they	정해진 사람이나 사물을 가리킬 때 사용한다.
부정대명사	one, another, other, some, any, all, both, either, neither, each, non, nothing, some, any, -body, -one, -thing	정해지지 않은 사람이나 사물을 가리킬 때 사용한다.
의문대명사	who, whose, whom, what, which, how	사람이나 사물에 대해 물어볼 때 사용한다.

Grammar Plus +

• 그 외의 대명사
  ① 관계대명사: who, whose, whom, which, that, what
  ② 복합관계대명사: whoever, whosever, whomever, whichever, whatever, however
    ➡ 관계대명사는 두 개의 문장을 하나로 이어주는 역할을 하며, 관계대명사가 있는 문장은 앞(뒤) 문장의 주어, 보어, 목적어를 수식한다.

Answer Keys p. 20

A 다음 〈보기〉에서 알맞은 것을 골라 빈칸에 써 넣으시오.

> 보기
>
> | his | her | our | yours | myself |
> |-----|-----|-----|-------|--------|
> | both | which | who | what | either |

1 Inho did ____his____ best to win the game.

2 _____ of them passed the exam.

3 _____ vacation plan is to go to Jeju Island.

4 Mary bought some flowers for _____ mom.

5 Let me introduce _____ .

6 My bike is as new as _____ .

7 _____ one do you like, the blue one or the red one?

8 _____ Amy or Linda can go to Japan.

9 _____ I want to do is to take a break.

10 He is the boy _____ got first place in the speaking contest.

B 다음 문장에서 어법상 어색한 것을 찾아 바르게 고치시오.

1 He didn't teach I English.   _____ ➡ _____

2 I think she should take care of she.   _____ ➡ _____

3 Either you nor I was wrong.   _____ ➡ _____

4 This book is as thick as him.   _____ ➡ _____

5 Your car is nice. It's color is great.   _____ ➡ _____

6 Jack and I finished the project by ours.

_____ ➡ _____

7 I can't eat some more.   _____ ➡ _____

8 Maria cooks the royal court cuisine she.

_____ ➡ _____

9 Narcissus loves herself.   _____ ➡ _____

10 There people are fans of Tom Cruise.

_____ ➡ _____

> **Note**
>
> • **do one's best**
>   최선을 다하다
>
> • **take care of**
>   ～을 돌보다
>
> • **royal court cuisine**
>   궁중요리
>
> • **Narcissus** 나르시스
>   (그리스 신화의 등장인물)

재귀대명사

• 재귀대명사: '~자신'을 표현하는 말을 나타낸다. 주어와 목적어가 같을 때 '자기 자신'의 의미로는 목적어 자리에 쓰이고, 주어, 보어, 목적어를 강조할 때는 '직접'의 뜻으로 쓰인다.

◈ **재귀대명사 형태:** oneself (selves) ~자신(들)

단수	I – myself	you – yourself	he – himself	she – herself	it – itself
복수	we – ourselves	you – yourselves	they – themselves		

1. 재귀용법: 주어와 목적어의 대상이 같을 때 사용

• I believe **myself** all the time. (I = myself)

• They are very proud of **themselves**. (they = themselves)

➡ 이때 인칭대명사의 목적격은 사용할 수 없다.

She looks at **herself** in the mirror. (O) ➡ She looks her in the mirror. (X)

2. 강조용법: 주어, 보어, 목적어를 강조할 때 사용하며 생략 가능

• He **(himself)** fixed the broken radio.

= He fixed the broken radio **(himself)**.

• You'd better do your homework **(yourself)**.

3. 재귀대명사 숙어

• enjoy oneself 즐기다

• by oneself 홀로, 혼자 힘으로

• help oneself 마음껏 먹다

• of itself 저절로

• say(talk) to oneself 혼잣말하다

• for oneself 혼자 힘으로

• make oneself at home 편히 쉬다

• in itself 본질적으로, 원래

Grammar Plus +

• 장소나 위치를 나타내는 전치사 뒤에는 재귀대명사를 쓰지 않는다.

Jerry saw a man next to him taking pictures of the city. (himself X)

A 다음 문장에서 생략 가능한 재귀대명사를 찾아 쓰시오. (없으면 X 표시를 하시오.)

1 She prepared for the party by herself.   (X   )

2 He himself will finish the homework.   (   )

3 I made a lot of food. Help yourself!   (   )

4 Mr. Kim took this picture himself.   (   )

5 She used to talk to herself.   (   )

6 They want to meet Mary herself.   (   )

7 They had better go back home themselves.   (   )

8 Tommy and I want to make ourselves at home.   (   )

9 I am enjoying myself on vacation.   (   )

10 You tried to repair the computer yourself.   (   )

B 다음 빈칸에 알맞은 말을 쓰시오.

1 She made the red dress for ___herself___.

2 I used to talk to _____ when I was alone.

3 Tim usually likes making _____ at home.

4 The window opened by _____.

5 They prepared for the seminar _____.

6 There is lots of food. Help _____!

7 Her hobby is to draw _____.

8 Don't be ashamed of _____.

9 Jessica finally found _____ famous.

10 Father used to tell me that enjoying _____ is important.

지시대명사

> • 지시대명사: 정해진 사람이나 사물을 가리키는 대명사를 말한다.
> 'this, these, that, those'가 있으며, 3인칭에 해당하고 말하는 사람과의
> 거리에 따라 구분하여 쓴다.

1. 'This/That'의 쓰임

	가까이 있는 사람이나 사물	멀리 있는 사람이나 사물
단수	**this** 이것, 이 사람 • This is my favorite book. • This is my teacher, Mr. Black.	**that** 저것, 저 사람 • That is dirty • That is my sister, Anna.
복수	**these** 이것들, 이 사람들 • These are my new pens. • These are my sister and brother.	**those** 저것들, 저 사람들 • Those are toy cars. • Those are new students.

2. 지시대명사의 다른 쓰임

앞의 명사를 대신하여 사용	that, those	• The history of China is longer than that of Japan. 　　　　　　　　　　　　　　　　　　　　(= the history) • The buildings of this city are older than those of London. 　　　　　　　　　　　　　　　　　　　　　　(= the buildings)
전화상에서의 사용	this, that	• Hello, this is Gijun. Is this (that) Jane?
특정한 사람이나 사물을 가리킬 때 사용	it, they	• I am singing a song. It is sung by Mariah Carey. 　　　　　　　　　　　　　(It = a song) • I watched a lot of people in a 2002 World Cup video. 　They were all cheering. (They = people)

Grammar Plus +

> • **those**: 'who'와 함께 쓰여 '~하는 사람들'이라고 해석한다.
>
> Heaven helps those who help themselves. [속담]
>
> • 지시형용사
>
> 'this (these) / that (those) + 명사'의 관계가 될 때는 '지시형용사'라고 한다.
>
> this (이~): this doll (이 인형), these (이 ~들): these people (이 사람들)
>
> that (저~): that boy (저 소년), those (저~들): those buildings (저 건물들)

A 괄호 안에서 알맞은 말을 고르시오.

1   I like to read books. ((It)/ This) makes me happy.

2   (These / That) are Sam's documents.

3   Those (who / which) exercise regularly are usually healthy.

4   Hello, (this / that) is Olivia speaking.

5   Tom's car is as old as (these / that) of Mike.

6   (This / Those) is for you.

7   (These / That) cars are awesome.

8   (Those / This) who like classical music would like him.

9   Is (that / those) your computer?

10 I know the people standing next to Sam. (They / These) are Sam's family.

B 다음 우리말 해석에 맞게 문장을 완성하시오.

1   저 꽃병은 Ted에 의해 깨졌다.
    ➡ _____*That vase was broken by Ted*_____ .

2   저 남자는 잘생겼다.
    ➡ _____ .

3   이것은 내가 가장 좋아하는 만화영화 'Magic Kaito'이다.
    ➡ _____ .

4   이 소녀는 내 친구 Linda이다.
    ➡ _____ .

5   저 귀여운 아기들을 봐!
    ➡ _____ !

6   겨울밤의 길이는 여름밤의 길이보다 길다.
    ➡ _____ .

7   그들은 교복을 입고 있다.
    ➡ _____ .

Lesson 4-11 의문대명사

> • 의문대명사 : 의문사를 이용하여 사람이나 사물을 가리키며 물어볼 때 사용한다.
> 의문대명사에는 'who(사람), what(사물, 동물), which(선택)'가 있다

1. Who : 사람을 가리킬 때 사용한다.

Who	주격 (누가)	• **A** Who cleaned the house? **B** I did. (= I cleaned the house.)
Whose	소유격 (누구의, 누구의 것)	• **A** Whose <u>dictionary</u> is this? =Whose is this dictionary? **B** It's Jerry's. (=It's Jerry's dictionary.)
Who(m)	목적격 (누구를)	• **A** Who(m) did she send an email to? =To whom did she send an email? (→ 전치사를 앞으로 보내는 경우 'who'를 쓸 수 없다.) **B** To Jenny. (=She sent an email to Jenny.)

2. Which/What : 사람, 사물, 동물을 가리킬 때 사용한다.

Which	둘 중 선택의 범위가 주어졌을 때 사용	• Which is faster, a train or an airplane? • Which do you like better, pizza or spaghetti?
What	동물, 사물, 사람의 직업이나 신분을 나타 낼 때 사용	• **A** What will she buy? **B** She'll buy a pair of shoes.

Grammar Plus +

• **의문형용사 What / Which**

➡ 명사를 수식하는 의문 형용사로도 쓰인다.

• What <u>color</u> do you like best?

• Which <u>camera</u> is yours?

Answer Keys p. 20

A 각 문장의 빈칸에 [보기]에서 알맞은 단어를 찾아 써 넣으시오.

(목적격일 때 생략하지 말고 원래 형태의 단어로 쓰시오.)

> **[보기]**
>
> what   which   who   whose   whom

1 _____Who_____ is your math teacher?

2 _____ did the woman say to you?

3 _____ phone number did you get?

4 With _____ are they going there?

5 _____ will you invite to the party?

6 _____ does your mother do?

7 _____ part did you study, Part 1 or Part 2?

8 _____ did the teacher try to talk to?

9 _____ smartphone is that?

10 _____ is cheaper, milk or juice?

B 우리말과 일치하도록 괄호 안의 단어를 바르게 배열하시오.

1 그들은 어떤 맛을 원하니?

(want, do, they, flavor, which)

➡ _____ Which flavor do they want? _____

2 너는 런던과 맨체스터 중 어느 도시를 방문하기를 원하니?

(which, Manchester, or, you, city, do, want, London, to, visit)

➡ _____

3 그녀는 어떤 무늬를 좋아하니?

(patterns, does, what, she, like)

➡ _____

4 그는 누구와 이야기 중이니?

(is, who, he, with, talking)

➡ _____

5 누구의 그림이 더 아름답니?

(picture, is, more, whose, beautiful)

➡ _____

'it'의 여러 가지 쓰임

> • it : 주로 단수의 사물을 가리키는 대명사로 사용되지만, 진짜 주어와 진짜 목적어를 대신하는 가주어와 가목적어로도 사용된다. 시간, 날씨, 날짜 등을 나타낼 때는 뜻이 없는 주어로 사용된다.

1. 대명사 it : 정해진 사물을 가리키기도 하고, 앞의 반복되는 문장이나 명사를 대신하기도 한다.

- The book is very thick. Did you read **it** all? (it = the book)

- I want to be rich. But **it** is not easy. (it = to be rich)

2. 비인칭주어 it : 특별한 뜻을 가지지 않기 때문에 해석되지 않는다.

날씨	• It will be rainy and chilly tomorrow.	날짜	• It is July 7th.
거리	• It is 15 miles to the shopping mall.	온도	• It is 22 degrees Celsius outside.
시간	• It is 3 o'clock now.	계절	• It is summer in Canada now.
요일	• It is Friday today.	명암	• It is so dark inside.

3. 가주어 / 가목적어 it

(1) **가주어** : to부정사, 동명사, that절이 주어인 경우 대신 사용하는 가짜 주어이다.

- **It** is very sad that you lied again. (It = that you lied again)

- **It** is important to teach children. (It = to teach children)

(2) **가목적어** : to부정사, that절 등이 목적어인 경우 대신 사용하는 가짜 목적어이다.
동사로 'make, think, believe, find, consider' 등이 주로 쓰인다.

- I think **it** helpful to exercise every day. (it = to exercise every day)

4. It is... that~ : 강조구문으로 주어, 보어, 목적어, 부사어를 강조한다.

- I met aunt Emily at the theater.

  ➡ It was **I** that (who) met aunt Emily at the theater. [주어 강조]
  It was **aunt Emily** that (who) I met at the theater. [목적어 강조]
  It was **at the theater** that (where) I met aunt Emily. [부사어 강조]

  ➡ 'that' 대신 주어, 목적어, 부사어에 따라 who(사람), which(사물), where(장소), when(시간) 등으로 나타낼 수 있다.

A 다음 문장에서 어법상 <u>어색한</u> 것을 찾아 바르게 고치시오.

1 There was a book on the table. I should read that by tomorrow.

　　　　　　　　　　　that ➡ *it*

2 This is not difficult for Helen to solve the problem.

　　　　　　　　　　➡

3 What do you like better, this one or that one?

　　　　　　　　　　➡

4 Which kind of fruit does she like? 　　　　➡

5 I think that is impossible to go to America this year.

　　　　　　　　　　➡

6 It are my friend who bought the car for me.

　　　　　　　　　　➡

7 People want to be happy. However, that's not easy.

　　　　　　　　　　➡

8 The chair is too weak. Could you exchange them?

　　　　　　　　　　➡

B 다음 우리말에 맞게 괄호에 주어진 단어를 이용하여 영작하시오.

1 그녀가 겨울에 돌아올 것은 확실하다.
　　(it, certain, she, come back, in winter)
　➡　　　*It is certain that she will come back in winter.*

2 다음 주에 비가 내릴 예정이다. (it, rain)
　➡

3 Goeun은 우리의 목표를 달성할 수 있게 해주었다.
　　(made, possible, to achieve)
　➡ Goeun

4 내가 지난주에 샀던 가방이 바로 그 가방이었다.
　　(it, the bag, that, bought)
　➡

5 Jenny는 오늘 오후에 어떤 수업이 있니?
　　(afternoon, have, classes, what, does, this, Jenny)
　➡

Practice More II

Answer Keys p. 21

A 다음 문장에서 어법상 어색한 것을 찾아 바르게 고치시오.

1 Tim and Jane had a baby last week. They love our baby.

   _____our_____ ➡ _____their_____

2 Did you enjoy your at the party? _____ ➡ _____

3 This is too difficult for me to understand the lecture.

   _____ ➡ _____

4 She is always kind to other people around herself.

   _____ ➡ _____

5 The door closed by it. _____ ➡ _____

6 That who exercise regularly are active and healthy.

   _____ ➡ _____

7 This is my car. I bought these last week.

   _____ ➡ _____

8 When you walk alone at night, you'd better look after you.

   _____ ➡ _____

9 Look at the hat. It's very nice. Which hat is it?

   _____ ➡ _____

B 다음 빈칸에 알맞은 대명사를 쓰시오.

> A Cindy, could you introduce ___yourself___ to everyone?
>
> B Ok. Hello, my name is Cindy. I'm fifteen years old. I have two sisters and _____ of them are high school students. _____ people said _____ are like twins. I have some close friends. Sujin, _____ of them, is my best friend. I like _____ because she always thinks positively and she's kind. In addition, her grade is better than _____. So, there are many things I learn from _____. I want to keep _____ friendship everlasting.

Practice More Ⅱ

Answer Keys p. 21

C 다음 괄호 안에서 알맞은 것을 고르시오.

1 Help (yourself / yours)! I prepared a lot of food for you.

2 William's coat is awesome! Where did he buy (it / one)?

3 Sometimes, my sister fixes her watch by (her / herself).

4 I think Helen doesn't have to look down on (herself / that).

5 (Those / That) movie will be released next Friday.

6 How long have you been in (this / that) country?

7 (It / That) is raining cats and dogs.

> **Note**
> - **lecture** 강의
> - **regularly** 정기적으로
> - **look after**
>   ~을 돌보다, 지키다
> - **awesome** 굉장한, 멋진

D 다음 우리말 해석과 같은 뜻이 되도록 주어진 단어를 알맞게 배열하시오.

1 그녀는 스스로 자동차를 고칠 수 없었다.
   (herself, couldn't, the car, by, fix)
   ➡ She _____ *couldn't fix the car by herself* _____.

2 그녀에게 밤새 영화를 보는 것은 힘들었다.
   (was, the movie, watch, hard, for, it, all night, to, her)
   ➡ _____.

3 그들은 스스로를 자랑스러워했다.
   (of, were, they, themselves, proud)
   ➡ _____.

4 저 박스들은 나의 것이 아니다. (those, are, boxes, mine, not)
   ➡ _____.

5 파리는 날씨가 덥고 습하다. (and, hot, humid, is, it, Paris, in)
   ➡ _____.

6 나는 그 셔츠가 싫지만 내 딸이 그것을 좋아한다.
   (I, it, but, like, my daughter, don't, likes, the shirt)
   ➡ _____.

7 어젯 밤 내가 본 것은 가로등이었다.
   (a, night, it, I, streetlamp, was, that, last, saw)
   ➡ _____.

8 John의 도움으로 우리는 그 세미나를 성공적으로 개최할 수 있었다.
   (John's help, successfully, hold, made, us, the seminar, to, for, possible, it)
   ➡ _____.

> **Note**
> - **fix** 고치다, 수리하다
>   (= repair)
> - **all night** 밤새
> - **be proud of** ~을 자랑
>   스러워하다
> - **humid** 습한
> - **increase** 증가하다

◆ **부정대명사 :** 정해지지 않은 사람이나 사물을 가리키는 대명사를 가리킨다.

1. one : 앞에 나온 명사와 같은 종류의 것을 가리킬 때 사용하며 복수형은 'ones'로 나타낸다.
- I needed a watch. So my father bought me **one**. (one = a watch)

2. some : '약간, 조금'의 뜻으로 긍정문, 제안의 의문문에 쓰인다.
- They have **some** carrots and tomatoes.
- Do you want **some** cookies?

3. any : '약간, 조금'의 뜻으로 부정문, 의문문에 쓰인다.
- Sara has some money, but I don't have **any** money.
- Does he have **any** paper?

4. another : '또 다른 하나, 하나 더'라는 뜻을 가진다.
- I drank a bottle of water but I'm still thirsty. Can you give me **another**?

5. other : '다른 사람, 다른 것'의 뜻을 가진다.
- Mary has two teddy bears. One is brown, and the **other** is white.

6. both : '양쪽, 둘 다'의 뜻을 가지며, 두 개의 대상을 의미하고, 복수로 취급한다.
- Mr. Wang has two porcelain dolls. **Both** were made in China.

7. all : '모두, 모든 것'의 뜻을 가진다.
- **All** of the fans want to meet the actor.

8. each : '각각, 각자'의 뜻을 가지며 항상 단수로 취급한다.
- **Each** of people has their own character.

9. every : '모두, 모든'의 뜻을 가지지만 단수로 취급한다.
- **Every** kid likes to play with toy cars.

10. either : '둘 중 어느 하나, 각각'의 뜻을 가지며 단수로 취급한다.
- You have to choose **either** sandwiches or hamburgers.

11. neither : '둘 중 어느 것도 아니다'의 뜻으로 부정의 의미로 쓰이며, 단수로 취급한다.
- We want to buy **neither** of them.

4-13 부정대명사_one / some / any

- **부정대명사**: 정해지지 않은 사람이나 사물을 가리키는 대명사를 가리킨다.
- **one**: 'one'은 정해지지 않은 '하나'를 가리키거나, 앞의 명사의 중복을 피하기 위하여 사용된다.
- **some, any**: 'some'은 긍정문에, 'any'는 주로 부정문, 의문문에 쓰인다.

1. one (ones)

앞의 명사와 종류는 같지만 대상이 다른 경우	• **A** Would you like a sandwich?　**B** No thanks. I already ate one. ➡ 샌드위치를 의미하지만 질문자가 말하는 샌드위치가 아닌 것을 의미하므로 'one'을 사용한다. • **A** Where did you get that rose?　**B** Jinsu gave it to me. ➡ 질문자가 말한 그 장미 꽃(the rose)를 의미하므로 'it'을 사용한다.
정해지지 않은 사람이나 사물을 가리키는 경우	• I used up all the ink, so I bought a new one. [정해지지 않은 사물] • I want to buy notebooks. I need new ones. [정해지지 않은 사물] • There are tall models in the gym. I know one of them. [정해지지 않은 사람]

2. some과 any

some	• 주로 긍정문에 쓰인다. • 'some (of)' 다음에는 셀 수 없는 명사와 셀 수 있는 명사 둘 다 사용 • Some of the mountains are disappearing. • He spent some money to buy books.
any	• 주로 부정문, 의문문에 쓰인다. • Jena doesn't have any good friends. • Do you have any ideas?

Grammar Plus +

- **some**: 주로 긍정문에 사용되지만, '제안, 권유, 부탁'의 의문문에서 사용된다.
  Would you bring me some cake?
- **any**: 'any'가 긍정문에 쓰일 경우 'every'보다 강한 뜻이 되며 '어떤 것이든지'로 해석된다.
  The monster can eat any of those things.

A 괄호 안에서 알맞은 것을 고르시오.

1 Do you like the bag? − No, I don't like (one / **it**).

2 Do you want (some / any) sandwiches?

3 Would you get me (any / some) stamps?

4 Which (one / it) do you prefer?

5 (Any / Some) of the lakes are polluted.

6 Jessica didn't have (some / any) friends to talk with.

7 (Some / Any) people said success is not our goal.

8 Amy didn't want (anything / something) to eat. She was full.

9 (One / that) should be satisfied with what he or she has.

10 He is (one / ones) of the people who got an A on the test.

B 우리말 해석에 맞게 보기 에서 알맞은 단어를 골라 문장을 완성하시오.

> 보기
>
> somebody   something   anyone   anything

1 Paul의 제안에 반대하시는 분 계신가요?
➡ Is there ___*anyone*___ who objects to Paul's proposal?

2 나는 다른 것을 둘러보고 싶다.
➡ I want to browse for _____ else.

3 어떤 사람이라도 우리 야구 동호회에 들어올 수 있다.
➡ _____ can join our baseball team.

4 따뜻한 마실 만한 것 좀 줄까?
➡ Would you like _____ hot to drink?

5 어떤 것이라도 원하는 것이 있다면 언제든지 전화하세요.
➡ If there is _____ you want, call me anytime.

6 내 코트 보신 분 있나요?
➡ Did _____ see my coat?

7 오늘 아침에 이상한 일이 일어났다.
➡ _____ strange happened this morning.

4-14 부정대명사 _ another / other (1)

- **another**: 정해지지 않는 사람이나 사물을 가리키며, '또 다른 하나'로 해석한다.
- **other**: 'one'이나 'some'과 짝을 이루어 'one~, the other(s)', 'some~, (the) others'로 사용된다.

1. another: 이미 언급한 것 외에 다른 하나를 가리킨다.

- This shirt is too small for me. Show me **another**.
- Sara was talking with **another** boy. [another+단수명사: 형용사의 형태로 사용]

2. other: 불특정한 사람이나 사물을 가리키며 '다른 ~'라고 해석한다.

- Mom always says that we have to help **others**.

3. one, another, the other: 셋 이상의 명사들을 하나씩 나열할 때 사용한다.

- There are three colors. **One** is red, **another** is green, and **the other** is black.

4. one another: 셋 이상일 때 사용하며 '서로서로'의 뜻을 가진다.

- They enjoy playing tennis against **one another** after school.

➡ 'each other'는 둘일 때 사용한다.
   We played a chess game against **each other**.

 **Check up!**

Answer Keys p. 21

A 괄호 안에 주어진 말 중 알맞은 것을 고르시오.

1   This watermelon is so sweet. Can I have (other / (another))?

2   I need (another / other) chance to take the exam.

3   Does he have (other / another) shirts to wear?

4   I have two friends. One has blond hair, and (the other / other) has black hair.

5   Mary wants to know what (another / other) people like.

6   I think we should be honest to (another / others).

7   We should help (other / another) people.

8   Could you show me (another / other)?

9   Don't mind what (others / the other) say about it.

10   Some girls like singing and (others / another) like dancing.

11   I have two dogs. One is white and (the other / other) is brown.

4-15 부정대명사 _ another / other (2)

1. one과 the other(s)

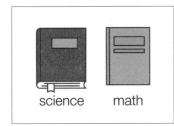
science   math

(1) **[one~, the other]** 하나는~, 다른 하나는

- Jerry has two books. **One** is a science book and **the other** is a math book.

(2) **[one~, another~, the other]** 하나는~, 다른 하나는~, 또 다른 하나는

- I have three baskets. **One** has oranges, **another** has apples, and **the other** has cherries.

(3) **[one~, another~, the others]** 하나는~, 다른 하나는~, 나머지들은

- There are five jack-o-lanterns. **One** is for my brother, **another** is for my sister and **the others** are just for me.

2. some과 (the) others

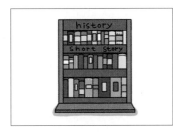

(1) **[some~, others]** 어떤 것들은~, 또 어떤 것들은

- Tom has a lot of novels. **Some** are short novels and **others** are historical novels.

(2) **[some~, the others]** 일부는~, 나머지들은

- I bought a box of apples. **Some** were fresh, but **the others** were rotten.

A 괄호 안에서 알맞은 말을 고르시오.

1 I have three dogs. One is big and ((the others) / others) are small.

2 Some people like to eat carrots. but (others / other) really hate them.

3 There are two girls. One is my sister and (the other / another) is my friend.

4 I buy six cookies. (One / Some) are chocolate and the others are blueberry.

5 Some students wear red shirts and (other / the other) students wear blue shirts.

6 She has two books. One is a romance novel and (the other / other) is a poem.

7 Some people are great but (others / the others) are useless.

8 Linda made three dresses. One is red and (another / the others) are white.

9 Kate has four pens. One is green and (the other / another) is red and (the other / the others) are blue.

B 다음 우리말에 맞게 빈칸에 알맞은 말을 쓰시오.

1 카네이션 세 송이가 있다. 하나는 아빠의 것이고, 다른 하나는 엄마의 것이고, 나머지 하나는 할머니의 것이다.
  ➡ There are ___three___ carnations. ___One___ is for my dad, ___another___ is for my mom, and ___the other___ is for my grandmother.

2 Kate에게는 두 명의 가장 친한 친구가 있다. 한 명은 나이가 어리고, 다른 한 명은 나이가 많다.
  ➡ Kate has two best friends. _____ is younger _____ _____ is older than Kate.

3 Ben이 말했다. 한 개는 James의 것, 다른 한 개는 Kelly의 것, 그럼 나머지들은 누구의 것이지?
  ➡ Ben said, "_____ is for James, another is for Kelly, _____ whose are _____?"

Lesson 4-16 부정대명사 _ both / all

- **both** : '양쪽, 둘 다'의 뜻을 가진다. 'of'가 함께 올 경우 뒤에 관사나 소유격이 온다.
- **all** : '모든, 모두'의 뜻을 가진다. 'of'가 함께 올 경우 뒤에 관사나 소유격이 온다.

1. both

(1) [both + 복수명사 + 복수동사]

- **Both** <u>dresses</u> <u>are</u> old-fashioned.

(2) [both (of) + 관사/소유격 + 복수명사 + 복수동사]

- **Both (of)** the <u>hats</u> <u>are</u> too big.

(3) [both A and B] A와 B 둘 다

- Maria chose **both apples and oranges**.

2. all

(1) [all + 복수명사 + 복수동사]

- **All** <u>students</u> <u>are</u> quiet in the hall.

(2) [all (of) + 관사/소유격 + 복수명사 + 복수동사]

- **All (of) the** <u>mice</u> <u>are</u> running away.

(3) [all (of) + 관사/소유격 + 단수명사 + 단수동사]

- **All (of)** the <u>water</u> in the bucket <u>is</u> on the floor.

3. both와 all의 부정 : 'not'과 함께 쓰여 일부를 부정하는 부분 부정이 된다.

- **Not all** the development is good.
- She does**n't** like **both of** the subjects.

> **Grammar Plus +**
>
> - **all** : 'all'이 명사로 사람을 나타낼 때는 복수로 취급하고, 사물이나 상황을 나타낼 경우 단수로 취급한다.
> - **All** <u>were</u> happy with the news. [All = 사람]
> - **All** I want <u>is</u> only the newest model of Gundam. [All = 물건]

A 괄호 안에서 알맞은 것을 고르시오.

1 (Every / (All)) the people should participate in the seminar this weekend.

2 All we need (is / are) time for rest.

3 I didn't like to eat (both / all) carrots and spinach.

4 All of the books written by James (get / gets) the prize.

5 Both hats (is / are) very nice. I want to buy them.

6 (All of / Both of) the information is useful.

7 (All not / Not all) sports players do their best.

8 All that glitters (are / is) not gold.

9 (Both / all) the pasta and salad were really delicious.

10 (Every / All) the boys were swimming in the pool.

B 다음 문장에서 어법상 <u>어색한</u> 것을 찾아 바르게 고치시오.

1 John is both handsome but kind.   _but_   ➡   _and_

2 All I want are to be loved.   _____ ➡ _____

3 All of the information were useless.

   _____ ➡ _____

4 Both of them is raising dogs.   _____ ➡ _____

5 All was sad to hear the news.   _____ ➡ _____

6 Sam didn't play both the games.   _____ ➡ _____

7 Both you or your sister will pass the exam.

   _____ ➡ _____

8 All of food that Jane prepared is really delicious.

   _____ ➡ _____

9 Both he and Jane will gets married today.

   _____ ➡ _____

10 All not technologies are profitable.

   _____ ➡ _____

4-17 부정대명사 _ each / every

- **each** : '각자, 각기, 각각의'의 뜻으로 명사를 수식하며 단수로 취급한다.
- **every** : '모든'의 뜻으로 해석하지만 단수로 취급한다.

1. each

(1) [**each** + 단수명사 + 단수동사]

- **Each** <u>person</u> <u>has</u> a unique personality.

(2) [**each of** + 복수명사 + 단수동사]

- **Each of** <u>the countries</u> <u>has</u> a different culture.

2. every

(1) [**every** + 단수명사 + 단수동사]

- **Every** <u>picture</u> <u>has</u> its own color.

(2) ~마다, 매~

- Sara and her family go skiing **every** winter.

(3) **every의 부정:** 'not'과 함께 쓰여 일부를 부정하는 부분 부정이 된다.

- **Not every** man likes baseball.

 **Check up!**

Answer Keys p. 22

A 괄호 안에서 알맞은 것을 고르시오.

1 (Each of / Each) my friends has a different job.

2 Although they are twins, (each of / each) them has different taste.

3 (All / Every) person has their own names.

4 (Everyone not / Not everyone) succeeds in the business world.

5 (Every / Each) of the rooms has a variety of furniture.

6 Every type of clothing (was / were) sold at the bazaar last week.

7 Each of the (actor / actors) did their best to make a great movie.

8 My family goes hiking (all / every) summer.

9 Each person (buy / buys) different souvenirs.

10 Each (students / student) chooses what to do over winter vacation.

4-18 부정대명사 _ either / neither

- **either**: '둘 중 어느 하나, 각각'의 의미로 단수로 취급한다.
- **neither**: '둘 중 어느 것도 ~이 아닌'의 뜻으로 부정을 의미하고 단수로 취급한다.

1. either

(1) 둘 중 어느 하나, 각각

- **Either** of you two <u>has</u> to wash the dishes. [둘 중 하나, 단수 취급]
- Jenny and Sam don't want to eat **either of** them. [둘 다]
  (= Jenny and Sam want to eat **neither** of them.)

  ➡ 'neither'는 자체에 부정을 의미하며, 'not either'와 바꿔 쓸 수 있다.

(2) [either A or B] A나 B 둘 중 하나

- **Either** Jack **or** Maria <u>has</u> to help me.

  ➡ 'either A or B'의 동사는 <u>두 번째 주어에 맞춘다.</u>

2. neither

(1) 둘 중 어느 것도 ~이 아닌

- **Neither** of the movies <u>was</u> wonderful. [단수 취급]

(2) [neither A nor B] A도 B도 ~아닌

- **Neither** Jenny **nor** I <u>want</u> any coffee.

  ➡ 'neither A nor B'의 동사는 <u>두 번째 주어에 맞춘다.</u>

3. either의 부정과 neither

(1) **either**의 부정: '역시, 또한'의 뜻을 가진다. (too는 긍정문에 쓰인다.)

- I <u>don't</u> like to play sports, and Jenny <u>doesn't</u>, **either**.

(2) **neither**: '또한 ~아닌'의 뜻을 가진다.

- I don't want any water, and **neither** does Jack. [또한 ~아니다]

  = I don't want any water, **nor** does Jack. ['nor'가 접속사이므로 'and'는 불필요]

  = I don't want any water, **and** Jack doesn't, **either**. ['not either'로 바꿀 수 있음]

Answer Keys p. 22

A 괄호 안에서 알맞은 것을 고르시오.

1 Both of you two (has / (have)) to eat vegetables for health.

2 Sam wanted to be either a singer (or / nor) a composer.

3 Neither he nor I (eat / eats) pasta.

4 I don't like Billy, and Jane doesn't, (either / neither).

5 John doesn't want to meet (either / neither) of them.

6 I can play neither baseball (nor / or) soccer.

7 Neither of the books (was / wasn't) interesting.

8 Either James or you should (makes / make) some food.

9 I don't eat anymore, (or / nor) does my brother.

10 Neither of the TV programs (is / are) funny.

B 다음 우리말에 맞게 빈칸에 알맞은 말을 쓰시오.

1 너나 내가 결승에서 이기게 될 것이다.
   ➡ ____Either____ you ____or____ I will win the final.

2 너는 숙제를 끝낼 수 없고 나 역시 할 수 없다.
   ➡ You can't finish the homework, and _____ I.

3 James는 수영하는 것을 좋아하지 않고 Jack 역시 좋아하지 않는다.
   ➡ James _____ swimming, and Jack doesn't,
   _____.

4 Peter와 Melisa, 그들 중 누구도 그것을 읽고 싶어 하지 않는다.
   ➡ _____ Peter _____ Melisa want to read it.

5 나의 아버지는 그것들을 다 보고 싶어 하지 않으신다.
   ➡ My father doesn't want to watch _____.

6 그 가수들 중 어느 한 명이라도 아니?
   ➡ Do you know _____ the singers?

Practice More Ⅲ

A 다음 문장에서 어법상 <u>어색한</u> 것을 찾아 바르게 고치시오.

1 This skirt is too long. Can you show me another it?

<u> it </u> ➡ <u> one </u>

2 I have another questions.

_____ ➡ _____

3 Jin has two pens. One is red and other is blue.

_____ ➡ _____

4 Some of the movie are violent and cruel.

_____ ➡ _____

5 I don't eat sweet anything anymore.

_____ ➡ _____

6 Either of you two are Korean.

_____ ➡ _____

7 Do you want any more?

_____ ➡ _____

8 Emily is one of the most beautiful girl.

_____ ➡ _____

9 Some of the information are false.

_____ ➡ _____

10 James didn't have nothing to talk about.

_____ ➡ _____

11 All we need are money.

_____ ➡ _____

12 She lost her wallet, but she got one back.

_____ ➡ _____

13 I don't have some friends to talk with.

_____ ➡ _____

B 빈칸에 알맞은 대명사를 쓰시오.

1 Is there _anything_ else she needs help with?

2 I have two dogs. _____ is big and _____ is small.

3 _____ of the water is too dirty.

4 Sandra didn't have _____ funny stories to tell me.

5 I don't like this chair. Show me _____.

6 _____ girls like listening to music and _____ girls like reading books.

7 They are different from _____ other.

8 _____ student should study hard to pass the exam.

9 _____ John nor I have anything to do.

10 There is _____ on my shoulder! What is it?

11 They couldn't buy the car because _____ of them had enough money.

12 I want to drink _____ hot. It's very cold today.

13 _____ she and I like dancing.

14 He is _____ of the people who solves the problems.

15 Do you like the book? — Yes, I like _____.

C 괄호 안에서 알맞은 것을 찾으시오.

1 Why are the white (one / ⟨ones⟩) cheaper?

2 All the babies (was / were) sleeping in the room.

3 Some of the women (is / are) enjoying the concert.

4 I don't think they know each (other / another) well.

5 (Every / Both) boys are kind and handsome.

6 My daughter wanted to be either a teacher (or / nor) a dancer.

7 I will not go there, and neither (will my sister / my sister will).

8 Sujin knows (something / nothing) about that theory. I should help her.

Practice More Ⅲ

Answer Keys p. 22~23

D 다음 우리말과 뜻이 같도록 주어진 단어를 사용하여 문장을 완성하시오.

1 Tim과 James 둘 중 아무도 도착하지 않았다.
(neither, has, arrived, yet)

➡ _____*Neither Tim nor James has arrived yet*_____.

2 나는 그 둘 중 하나는 이길 수 있다. (win, either)

➡ _____.

3 Sam의 이야기 중 어느 것도 놀라운 것이 없었다. (neither, amazing)

➡ _____.

4 몇몇 사람들은 조깅을 하고 있고 나머지 사람들은 배드민턴을 치고 있다. (some, jog, others, play badminton)

➡ _____.

5 그녀는 요즘 어떤 문제도 없다. (any problems, these days)

➡ _____.

6 나는 다른 사람들이 어떻게 생각하는지 알고 싶다.
(know, other people, think)

➡ _____.

7 집에 오는 길에 자전거를 잃어버려서 새 것을 하나 사야 한다.
(lost, on the way, new, one)

➡ _____.

Answer Keys p. 23

내신 최다 출제 유형

01 다음 빈칸에 공통으로 들어갈 알맞은 단어를 고르시오. [출제 예상 95%]

> • _____ of the languages are difficult to learn.
> • _____ the boys and the girls enjoyed themselves at the party.

① One   ② It   ③ All
④ Each   ⑤ Every

02 다음 밑줄 친 부분의 쓰임이 보기 와 다른 것을 고르시오. [출제 예상 80%]

> 보기
> Jeremy's uncle painted the wall himself.

① Did you see the actor himself?
② She herself called her friends this afternoon.
③ The man had to support his family himself.
④ We made the plan ourselves.
⑤ Mary drew herself many pictures.

03 다음 중 빈칸에 들어갈 말이 바르게 짝지어진 것을 고르시오. [출제 예상 85%]

> There are three wonderful mountains in Korea : _____ is Mt. Hallasan, _____ is Mt. Sŏraksan, and _____ is Mt. Jirisan.

① one − the second − another
② one − another − the other
③ one − other − another
④ one − other − the other
⑤ one − another − other

04 다음 밑줄 친 부분 중 생략할 수 있는 것을 고르시오. [출제 예상 85%]

① Danny was proud of himself.
② We enjoyed ourselves at the parade.
③ Henry tried to make spaghetti himself.
④ They solved the puzzle for themselves.
⑤ She looked at herself in the mirror.

05 다음 중 어법상 어색한 것을 고르시오. [출제 예상 90%]

① Give me two sheets of paper.
② There are three cups of tea.
③ Would you like a glass of milk?
④ He wants to eat two loaves of bread.
⑤ We want to buy two pairs of jean.

[01~02] 다음 중 단수와 복수의 연결이 올바른 것을 고르시오.

01
① hero – heros   ② knife – knives
③ roof – rooves   ④ tomato – tomatos
⑤ piano – pianoes

02
① kangaroo – kangarooes
② dish – dishies
③ city – citys
④ mosquito – mosquitoes
⑤ leaf – leafes

[03~04] 다음 빈칸에 들어갈 알맞은 단어를 고르시오.

03
> They did _____ best to solve the problems.

① her   ② them   ③ their
④ his   ⑤ its

04
> There are _____ on the farm.

① several benchs   ② two mouses
③ four donkeys   ④ some monkies
⑤ five pigges

05 다음 중 밑줄 친 부분의 쓰임이 나머지 넷과 다른 것을 고르시오.
① It is Tuesday.
② It is very cold to drink.
③ It will be sunny tomorrow.
④ It is twelve o'clock.
⑤ It takes about two hours.

[06~07] 다음 밑줄 친 부분과 용법이 같은 것을 고르시오.

06 ★★★
> Sally introduced herself in Chinese.

① Why don't we try it ourselves?
② The club members made the logo themselves.
③ She looked at herself for a long time.
④ My mother designed this building herself.
⑤ We painted the fence ourselves.

07
> It is still hot out there.

① It is on the bookshelf.
② It is an old-fashioned dress.
③ She doesn't want to buy it.
④ It is sunny and warm.
⑤ I'll do it for you.

[08~10] 다음 중 어법상 잘못된 문장을 고르시오.

08
① There are two glasses of juice.
② I have five bars of chocolate.
③ There is a pairs of glasses.
④ She cuts a slice of bread.
⑤ He puts three teaspoonfuls of salt.

09
① All the seats are taken.
② Each of the boys have his own computer.
③ They are not for sale.
④ We arrived in Seoul about three p.m.
⑤ They are going to Europe.

10 ① What's the title of the movie?

② Do you know the owner of this purse?

③ She stayed at her parents'.

④ We went to a girls' middle school.

⑤ That is watch of Kate's.

[11~13] 다음 문장 중 어법상 올바른 것을 고르시오.

11 ① Are they football players, too?

② She has a three cats.

③ My uncle is a very tall.

④ Is that your a bag?

⑤ Can you play flute?

12 ① Does Jinsu sad?

② Giwon is a radio reporter.

③ Today is a first day of school.

④ She looked a very smart.

⑤ Our teacher was homeroom teacher.

13 ① Can you pass me the peppers, please?

② We want to have a bottles of water.

③ Dongsu has meats for dinner every night.

④ My brother and sister drink milk every day.

⑤ She drinks two cups of coffees every day.

[14~15] 다음 문장의 빈칸에 공통으로 들어갈 알맞은 단어를 고르시오.

14

• I need _____ drink a glass of water.

• She has a plan _____ learn Japanese.

① to   ② of   ③ for

④ at   ⑤ that

15

• _____ kind of dress do you want to buy?

• _____ do you think of Mr. Brown?

① Which   ② When   ③ What

④ How   ⑤ Whom

16 다음 중 밑줄 친 부분을 생략할 수 있는 것을 고르시오.

① He solved the problem for <u>himself</u>.

② She said to <u>herself</u>, "Should I do?"

③ Mom is sick, so I prepare breakfast by <u>myself</u>.

④ You have to do that <u>yourself</u>.

⑤ Mary always thinks of <u>herself</u>.

[17~18] 다음 글을 읽고 밑줄 친 부분의 쓰임이 어색한 것을 고르시오.

17

Jennifer can't ① <u>sees</u> well, so she ② <u>needs</u> help at school. Her ③ <u>42-year-old</u> mother ④ <u>comes</u> to school with her every morning. And all her friends in the class are ⑤ <u>kind</u> to her.

18

When Mrs. Smith came into ① the classroom, she was angry. ② Students were making ③ noisy a lot. ④ Some were playing ⑤ games, and some were drawing on the board.

[19~21] 다음 문장의 빈칸에 들어갈 단어가 바르게 짝 지어진 것을 고르시오.

19

_____ of her friends like Asian food, but _____ of them don't.

① Some − some   ② All − some
③ Any − some   ④ Most − some
⑤ More − some

20

I have two hamsters. _____ is white and _____ is black.

① One − two   ② One − the other
③ One − others   ④ Other − one
⑤ One − other

21

There are three oranges. One of them is for Jenny, _____ is for Lina, and _____ is for me.

① one − the other
② another − others
③ another − the other
④ other − the others
⑤ other − other

[22~23] 다음 보기의 밑줄 친 부분과 용법이 같은 것을 고르시오.

22

Changsu told his friends the news that he would have a party this Saturday.

① I think that is a bad accident.
② June has a girl friend that is a dancer.
③ We know that she is unkind.
④ Junho thinks that is a good gift.
⑤ They knew the news that their teacher would leave.

23

It is exciting to learn about new things.

① It is not easy to speak a foreign language fluently.
② It is 500 meters to the school.
③ It is in the basket in front of the door.
④ It is very windy and stormy.
⑤ It is going to stop raining tonight.

24 다음 중 어법상 어색한 것을 모두 고르시오.

① Some of my friends are African.
② All her money was gone.
③ Both bowls is very dirty.
④ Every woman wants to be pretty.
⑤ Each team have 11 players.

★★★
25 다음 중 밑줄 친 부분이 올바른 것을 <u>모두</u> 고르시오.

① We're going on a trip next Monday, so I can't see you <u>that</u> week.

② <u>Those</u> who are standing there are waiting for the train.

③ The climate of Canada is milder than <u>this</u> of England.

④ <u>These</u> book is about the classic paintings.

⑤ We have a lot of pollution <u>those</u> days.

[26~27] 다음 주어진 우리말을 영어로 바르게 옮긴 것을 고르시오.

★★★
26
> 나는 그들이 자동차 경주에서 우승했다는 소식을 들었다.

① I hear the news that they won a car race.

② I heard that they win a car race.

③ I hear that they won a car race.

④ I heard the news that won a car race.

⑤ I heard the news that they won a car race.

★★★
27
> 너희 둘 중 하나는 집 청소를 해야 한다.

① Both of you two has to clean the house.

② Either of you two has to clean the house.

③ Neither of you two has to clean the house.

④ Either of you two have to clean the house.

⑤ Neither of you two have to clean the house.

28 다음 문장 중 the가 들어가기 알맞은 것을 고르시오.

① We went to Busan by _____ train.

② I don't like to listen to _____ rock music.

③ _____ sun rises in the east.

④ My favorite subject is _____ English.

⑤ Did you have _____ breakfast this morning?

★★★
29 다음 중 어법상 옳은 문장을 <u>모두</u> 고르시오.

① Neither of the movie were nice.

② Either Jerry or Tina has to help mom.

③ Neither you nor your brother didn't homework.

④ Each person has five blue jades.

⑤ Every pictures is beautiful.

30 다음 주어진 문장을 우리말로 잘 나타낸 것을 고르시오.

> Not every man likes slim and pretty women.

① 모든 남자들은 날씬하고 예쁜 여자들을 좋아한다.

② 날씬하고 예쁜 여자들은 남자들이 모두 좋아하는 것은 아니다.

③ 날씬하고 예쁜 여자들은 모든 남자들을 좋아하지 않는다.

④ 모든 남자들이 날씬하고 예쁜 여자들을 좋아하는 것은 아니다.

⑤ 모든 남자들은 날씬하고 예쁜 여자들을 좋아하지 않는다.

31 ★★★ 다음 밑줄 친 우리말 해석이 바르지 <u>못한</u> 것을 고르시오.

① They <u>enjoyed themselves</u> at the water festival. (즐겁게 보냈다)
② We were very hungry, so we <u>helped ourselves</u>. (마음껏 먹었다)
③ I just wanted to make some food <u>for myself</u>. (나 자신을 위해)
④ The window closed <u>of itself</u>. (저절로)
⑤ Sherry <u>prides herself on</u> her success.
(~에 대해 자부심을 느끼다)

32 다음 밑줄 친 부분이 바르게 쓰인 것을 고르시오.

① Two days later, <u>his</u> got a written claim for damages.
② Take good care of <u>yourself</u>.
③ She came back to <u>her's</u> house.
④ How <u>does</u> astronauts wash in space?
⑤ All the people like <u>herself</u> a lot.

> Note a written claim for damages 손해 배상 청구서

33 다음 중 밑줄 친 부분의 쓰임이 <u>어색한</u> 것을 고르시오.

① I had two dreams. One was to walk, and <u>the other</u> was to play baseball.
② Jackson has three goats. One is small, another is middle, and <u>the other</u> is big.
③ I didn't want this. Bring me <u>another</u>, please.
④ He bought a big car and she bought a small <u>ones</u>.
⑤ I met many people. Some were kind, and <u>others</u> were not.

34 다음 중 관사 a(n)의 쓰임이 나머지 넷과 <u>다른</u> 것을 고르시오.

① <u>An</u> orange fell down.
② Mia gave me <u>an</u> apple and said sorry.
③ <u>A</u> dog is very friendly.
④ She has <u>a</u> nickname, Kitty.
⑤ Mr. Black is <u>a</u> writer.

◇◇◇◇◇◇◇◇◇ 서술형 평가 ◇◇◇◇◇◇◇◇◇

[35~36] 다음 글을 읽고 <u>틀린</u> 곳을 찾아 고쳐 쓰시오.

35
> A How many childs do you want to have?
> B I want to have two daughters and two sons.

_____ ➡ _____

36
> Annie is one of the most diligent student in the class.

_____ ➡ _____

[37~38] 다음 각 문장의 빈칸에 들어갈 알맞은 말을 보기 에서 골라 쓰시오. (필요할 경우 단어를 변형시키시오.)

37
> 보기
> glass of piece of cup of pair of

(1) Jack was so thirsty. So he drank three _____ water.
(2) Mrs. Jake ordered a _____ black tea.
(3) I got five _____ socks as Christmas gifts.

38

보기

whose	what	which

(1) _____ computer is better?

(2) I like this report. _____ idea was it?

39 다음 빈칸에 공통으로 들어갈 단어를 쓰시오.

- I found _____ in the old pictures.
- I was invited to the Easter festival and I enjoyed _____.

➡ _____

[40~41] 다음 빈칸에 들어갈 알맞은 의문대명사를 쓰고, 우리말로 해석하시오.

★★★
40

With _____ should I discuss what to do for him?

➡ _____

➡ _____

41

_____ dress are you wearing tonight, a red one or a pink one?

➡ _____

➡ _____

[42~43] 다음 글의 밑줄 친 부분의 용법이 무엇인지 쓰고, 그와 같은 용법의 문장을 쓰시오.

42

Is it raining and the wind is blowing hard outside?

➡ (_____)

_____

★★★
43

Mark decided to go there himself.

➡ (_____)

_____

[44~45] 다음 괄호 안의 단어를 우리말에 맞게 알맞게 배열하여 문장을 완성하시오.

44

그는 소금 한 스푼과 설탕 두 스푼을 넣었다.
(He / in / sugar / salt / a spoonful of / two spoonfuls of / put / and)

➡ _____

45

그에게는 배불리 먹을 음식이 없다.
(there is / no / of / with / full / food / eating/ him)

➡ _____

Note

05

Chapter
수동태

◆ **수동태 :** 어떤 일이 어떻게 발생되거나 일어나게 됐는지에 초점이 맞춰진 문장을 말한다.
　　　　'be동사+과거분사'의 형태를 가진다.

1. 수동태 문장 만들기

① 능동태의 동사가 현재형 ⇒ be동사(am/are/is)+과거분사
② 능동태의 동사가 과거형 ⇒ be동사(was/were)+과거분사
③ 능동태의 불특정 주어 ⇒ 'by+행위자'는 생략 가능

　　Thomas respects Einstein. [능동태]
　　➡ Einstein **is respected** by Thomas. [수동태]

2. 수동태의 종류

동명사의 수동태 [being+과거분사]	• Sandra hates being treated like a boy.
진행형의 수동태 [be being+과거분사]	• They are listening to classical music. ➡ Classical music is being listened to by them.
조동사의 수동태 [조동사+be+과거분사]	• We will hold a garage sale this Saturday. ➡ A garage sale will be held this Saturday by us.
to부정사의 수동태 [to+be+과거분사]	• The project doesn't need to be finished by Sammy.
현재완료의 수동태 [have/has+been+과거분사]	• We have planted some flowers. ➡ Some flowers have been planted by us.
과거완료의 수동태 [had+been+과거분사]	• I had believed his lies. ➡ His lies had been believed by me.

3. 4형식 문장의 수동태

• Rachel gave us some muffins. [능동태]
　　　　　　　간목　　직목
➡ ① We **were given** some muffins by Rachel. [간접목적어의 수동태]
　② Some muffins **were given** to us by Rachel. [직접목적어의 수동태]

4. 5형식 문장의 수동태

• People **called** her a little princess.
➡ She **was called** a little princess by people. [목적격보어가 명사]

5-1 수동태 문장 만들기

> • **수동태**: 어떤 일이 어떻게 발생하거나 일어나게 되었는지에 초점이 맞춰진 문장을 말한다.
> 사물이 스스로 행동할 수 없기 때문에 수동태 문장을 사용할 때가 많다.

1. 수동태 만들기

능동태		수동태
주어		by 목적격
동사	➡	be동사 + 과거분사
목적어		주어

[능동태] People **called** John a musician of genius.

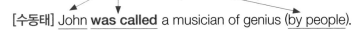

[수동태] John **was called** a musician of genius (by people).

➡ ① 능동태의 동사가 현재형이면 be동사는 주어의 인칭에 따라 'am, are, is' 중 하나를 선택한다.

② 능동태의 동사가 과거형이면 be동사는 주어의 인칭에 따라 'was, were' 중 하나를 선택한다.

③ 능동태의 주어가 'people'처럼 누구나 알거나, 'somebody'처럼 말하지 않아도 되는 경우, 즉 불특정한 주어가 수동태에서 'by + 행위자'가 되면 생략이 가능하다.

2. 수동태의 쓰임

(1) 주어가 행위를 당하는 대상일 경우

- Many people **use** smartphones. [능동태_현재]

 = Smartphones **are used** by many people. [수동태_현재]

- Poet Yoon Dong-ju **wrote** many great poems. [능동태_과거]

 = Many great poems **were written** by poet Yoon Dong-ju. [수동태_과거]

(2) 어떤 사건이 일어난 것을 중심으로 전달하는 경우

- Someone **broke** my car's rearview mirrors last night. [능동태_과거]

 = My car's rearview mirrors **were broken** last night. [수동태_과거]

Grammar Plus +

- **수동태로 쓰일 수 없는 동사**
 ① 목적어가 없는 자동사: happen, appear, arrive, get up 등
 ② 일부 타동사: have, resemble, fit 등

Answer Keys p. 25

A 다음 주어진 동사들을 능동태나 수동태 중 알맞은 형태로 바꾸어 쓰시오.
(수동태의 be동사는 과거형으로 표현하시오.)

1   The village <u> *was destroyed* </u> by the storm. (destroy)

2   Bell _____ the telephone. (invent)

3   The zebra _____ by a lion. (catch)

4   We _____ by John to the concert. (invite)

5   All the troubles _____ by him. (cause)

6   That movie _____ in 1998. (release)

7   These cookies _____ by Mrs. White. (make)

8   They _____ all night. (dance)

9   My bike _____ by John. (fix)

10 The film 'Old boy' _____ by Mr. Park. (direct)

B 다음 능동태 문장을 수동태 문장으로 전환하시오.

1   Susan washed her dog.
➡ _____ *Her dog was washed by Susan.* _____

2   Harry wrote the book.
➡ _____

3   She found the cave in 1989.
➡ _____

4   Emma buys some pants and glasses.
➡ _____

5   Mr. Han holds the flower festival every year.
➡ _____

6   I hung the picture on the wall.
➡ _____

7   He invited Helen to his graduation party.
➡ _____

8   The postman delivers a letter.
➡ _____

5-2 동명사/진행형의 수동태

> • **동명사의 수동태**: 동사 뒤에 'ing'가 붙어 동명사가 되는 것처럼, be동사에 'ing'가 붙어
> 'being + 과거분사'의 형태가 된다.
>
> • **진행형의 수동태**: be동사의 진행형 'be동사 + being'에 '과거분사'가 붙어
> 'be동사 + being + 과거분사'의 형태가 된다.

1. 동명사의 수동태: [being + 과거분사] ~되기

- We entered the concert <u>without</u> **being invited**.
- I <u>enjoy</u> **being asked** personal questions.

2. 진행형의 수동태: [be being + 과거분사] ~되고 있는 중이다

- Jane **is fixing** the radio <u>now</u>.

  = The radio **is being fixed** <u>now</u> by Jane.

- They **were playing** the violins at that time.

  = The violins **were being played** at that time **(by them)**.

  ➡ 'they'는 일반적인 사람들을 가리키므로 생략이 가능하다.

☆Check up!

Answer Keys p. 25

A   다음 주어진 동사들을 알맞은 동명사의 형태로 빈칸에 쓰시오.

1   Because of ___being bitten___ by a dog, she could not walk. (bite)

2   Max enjoyed his picture _____ . (take)

3   Hana attended the seminar without _____. (invite)

4   She doesn't like _____. She wants to do everything
on her own. (order)

5   I don't like _____ like a child. (treat)

B   다음 주어진 동사들을 알맞은 진행형의 형태로 빈칸에 쓰시오.

1   The car ___is being fixed___ by John. (fix)

2   A new version of the vaccine _____ by him.
(develop)

3   Smith's birthday party _____ by his parents. (prepare)

4   The cake _____ by mom. (make)

5   The broken chair _____ by Tim. (exchange)

6   The area _____ by janitors. (clean)

조동사 / to부정사의 수동태

- **조동사의 수동태:** 조동사 다음에 be동사와 과거분사를 사용하여 '조동사 + be + 과거분사'의 형태로 나타낸다.
- **to부정사의 수동태:** 'to부정사' 다음에 be동사와 과거분사를 사용해서 'to be + 과거분사'의 형태로 나타낸다.

1. 조동사의 수동태: [조동사 + be + 과거분사]

- Jack **will play** the cello tonight.

  = The cello **will be played** by Jack tonight.

- The students **must keep** the rules.

  = The rules **must be kept** by the students.

2. to부정사의 수동태: [to be + 과거분사]

- Helen is going **to sing** a song on the stage.

  = A song is going **to be sung** on the stage by Helen.

Grammar Plus +

- **수동태 + to부정사**

be expected to ~할 것으로 기대되다	be required to ~하라는 요구를 받다
be told to ~하라는 말을 듣다	be allowed to ~하도록 허락받다
be ordered to ~하라는 명령을 받다	be intended to ~하도록 의도되다
be forced to ~하라는 강요를 받다	be designed to ~하도록 계획되다
be advised to ~하라는 충고를 듣다	be meant to 꼭 ~하기로 되어있다
be asked to ~하라는 부탁을 받다	be bound to 꼭 ~하기로 되어있다

Check up!

Answer Keys p. 25

A 다음 우리말 해석과 뜻이 같도록 주어진 단어를 to 부정사의 알맞은 형태로 쓰시오.

1 그 드레스는 Jane에 의해 만들어질 예정이다. (make)
➡ The dress ___*is going to be made*___ by Jane.

2 Harry는 그것에 대해 비난 받아 마땅하다. (blame)
➡ Harry is _____ for it.

3 그 연극은 많은 사람들이 볼 것으로 기대된다. (see)
➡ The play _____ by many people.

4 그 건물 안에서는 사진 촬영이 금지된다. (take)

➡ Visitors _____ pictures in the building.

5 학생들은 그 규칙을 따르도록 명령을 받는다. (follow)

➡ The students _____ the rule.

6 이 편지는 꼭 태우기로 되어 있었다. (burn)

➡ This letter was meant _____ .

7 그 과제는 영어 선생님께 제출되어야 한다. (turn in)

➡ The homework _____ to my English teacher.

8 그 도시는 그 말을 보호하기로 부탁 받았다. (protect)

➡ The city _____ the horse.

9 직원들은 새 교육 프로그램에 참석하라는 말을 들었다. (attend)

➡ Employees _____ the new education program.

B 다음 능동태 문장을 수동태로 전환하시오.

1 Alex should not forget the promise.

➡ _____ *The promise should not be forgotten by Alex.* _____

2 Helen has to clean her room.

➡ _____

3 He may paint the picture.

➡ _____

4 The teacher should praise the students.

➡ _____

5 The storm may destroy our house.

➡ _____

6 Jane will lend her book to me.

➡ _____

7 The actors will perform the play.

➡ _____

8 The organization has to develop a new version of the design.

➡ _____

9 They should not touch the statue.

➡ _____

10 You must not steal other people's stuff.

➡ _____

5-4 완료형의 수동태

- **현재완료의 수동태**: 현재완료의 형태 'have/has been' 다음에 과거분사를 붙여 'have / has been + 과거분사'로 나타낸다.

- **과거완료의 수동태**: 과거완료의 형태 'had been' 다음에 과거분사를 붙여 'had been + 과거분사'로 나타낸다.

1. 현재완료의 수동태: [have/has been + 과거분사]

- I **have read** a short story by Tolstoy.

  = A short story by Tolstoy **has been read** by me.

2. 과거완료의 수동태: [had been + 과거분사]

- Jack **had made** some cheese in spring.

  = Some cheese **had been made** in spring by Jack.

- The company **had employed** Jenny and Tony.

  = Jenny and Tony **had been employed** by the company.

Grammar Plus +

- **완료형 수동태의 부정**
① 현재완료 수동태의 부정: [have/has not been + 과거분사]
  Mike **has not been invited to** the party.
② 과거완료 수동태의 부정: [had not been + 과거분사]
  The pool **had not been used** in the school by students.

Answer Keys p. 25

A 괄호 안에 주어진 말 중 알맞은 것을 고르시오.

1   The flower pot has been (carry / carried) by the girl.

2   This store has already (open / opened) early in the morning.

3   The plates (have not been / have been not) broken by Angela.

4   The warehouse (has been burned / have been burned) by fire.

5   Chinese Literature has (accepted / been accepted) as a new major by the university.

B 다음 문장이 능동태이면 수동태로, 수동태이면 능동태로 바꾸어 빈칸을 완성 하시오.

1   I have used this computer since 2013.
   ➡ This computer _____*has been used*_____ since 2013 by me.

2   The doctor had cured Lina.
   ➡ Lina _____ by the doctor.

3   The volunteers have helped the handicapped.
   ➡ The handicapped _____ by the volunteers.

4   I had done it.
   ➡ It _____ by me.

5   The air has been seriously polluted by people.
   ➡ People _____ the air.

6   The test has been postponed by the teacher.
   ➡ The teacher _____ the test.

7   Mary had thrown the garbage in the garden.
   ➡ The garbage _____ in the garden by Mary.

8   Sam and his father have built a cabin.
   ➡ A cabin _____ by Sam and his father.

9   Miranda had not bought the long coat.
   ➡ The long coat _____ by Miranda.

10   The teacher had not given homework this weekend.
   ➡ Homework _____ this weekend by the teacher.

5-5 4형식 문장의 수동태

• 4형식 문장의 수동태: '주어＋동사＋간접목적어＋직접목적어'로 이루어진 4형식 문장은 목적어가
두 개이기 때문에 수동태 문장을 두 개 만들 수 있다.

1. 4형식 문장의 수동태 만들기

• Sam gave me a diamond ring last Christmas. [능동태]
간목   직목

= ① I **was given** a diamond ring last Christmas by Sam. [간접목적어의 수동태]

  ② A diamond ring **was given** to me last Christmas by Sam. [직접목적어의 수동태]

➡ 수동태에서 직접목적어가 주어가 될 때는 간접목적어 앞에 'to, for, of'와 같은 전치사를 붙여준다.

2. 직접목적어를 수동태의 주어로 하는 동사

| buy | make | sell | write | cook | bring | throw | lend | read |

• He **will buy** me a new smartphone.

= A new smartphone **will be bought for me** by him.

Grammar Plus +

• **for**를 쓰는 동사: buy, cook, find, get, make
• **to**를 쓰는 동사: give, send, teach, tell
• **of**를 쓰는 동사: ask, require

 **Check up!**

Answer Keys p. 26

A   다음 주어진 문장을 직접목적어를 주어로 하여 수동태 문장으로 바꿔 쓰시오.

1 Mommy makes me some sandwiches.

  ➡   *Some sandwiches are made for me by mommy.*

2 Jeff bought me a new bag.

  ➡

3 Karen sent him a new shirt.

  ➡

4 Mr. Wang teaches us Chinese.

  ➡

B   다음 문장을 간접목적어와 직접목적어를 주어로 하는 수동태 문장으로 바꾸어 쓰시오.

1   He sends Mina an email.

➡ _____ *An email is sent to Mina by him.*

2   John showed me his new movie.

➡ _____

➡ _____

3   Anna cooked me a delicious pasta on our anniversary.

➡ _____

4   Tim didn't give her a new shirt.

➡ _____

➡ _____

5   Mr. Smith taught Hana how to make cookies.

➡ _____

➡ _____

6   Mom told me Sally's favorite movie.

➡ _____

➡ _____

7   Sam bought his girlfriend blue shoes yesterday.

➡ _____

8   Their teacher didn't return the answer sheets to the students.

➡ _____

➡ _____

9   Thomas lent his friends the rooms.

➡ _____

10   That boy didn't bring me the key.

➡ _____

5형식 문장의 수동태

• **5형식 문장의 수동태**: 목적격보어가 명사나 형용사인 5형식의 경우 'be동사 + 과거분사' 뒤에 'by + 목적격'을 이어서 써 준다.

1. 5형식 문장의 수동태

- People **call** him Timmy.
  = He is **called** Timmy by people. [목적격보어가 명사]
- The movie **made** us sad.
  = We **were made** sad by the movie. [목적격보어가 형용사]

2. 사역동사의 수동태: 'make, have, let' 중 'make'만 수동태로 쓰일 수 있다.

- Jane **made** him reply to the mail. [능동태]
  = He **was made** to reply to the mail by Jane. [수동태]
  ➡ 사역동사의 목적격보어로 쓰인 <u>원형부정사는 수동태 문장에서 'to부정사'로 바뀐다.</u>

3. 지각동사의 수동태: see, watch, hear, feel

- I **heard** her sing opera at the park. [능동태]
  = • She **was heard** to sing opera at the park. [수동태_to부정사]
    • She **was heard** singing opera at the park. [수동태_현재분사]
  ➡ 지각동사의 목적격보어로 쓰인 <u>원형부정사는 수동태 문장에서 'to부정사' 또는 '현재분사'로 바뀐다.</u>

Check up!

Answer Keys p. 26

A 다음 우리말과 뜻이 괄호 안의 말을 이용하여 빈칸에 알맞은 말을 쓰시오.

1 그녀는 의사에게서 쉬라는 충고를 들었다.
➡ She ___*was advised*___ to get some rest by the doctor.

2 그 강아지는 그에 의해 '나나'라고 이름 지어졌다.
➡ The puppy _____ Nana by him.

3 나는 친구들로 인해 행복해졌다.
➡ I _____ happy by my friends.

4 그는 형으로부터 수학을 가르침 받았다.
➡ He _____ math by his brother.

B 다음 5형식 문장을 수동태로 바꾸시오.

1 I saw the dog running down the street.

➡ *The dog was seen running down the street by me.*

2 Their teacher expected them to pass the exam.

➡ _____

3 Sue always keeps her clothes cleaned.

➡ _____

4 They called their baby Jake.

➡ _____

5 Father allowed me to go hiking with my friends.

➡ _____

6 People think Tina is a beautiful girl.

➡ _____

7 The team elected James a chief coach.

➡ _____

8 I found the medicine useless.

➡ _____

9 They warned her not to put anything on the table.

➡ _____

10 My teacher made me get a good grade.

➡ _____

Practice More I

A 다음 문장에서 어법상 <u>어색한</u> 것을 찾아 바르게 고치시오.

1 She was disappeared last night.

was disappeared ➡ disappeared

2 The dress is belonged to Helen.

_____ ➡ _____

3 I enjoyed be treated like a queen.

_____ ➡ _____

4 He was leave behind.

_____ ➡ _____

5 The information collected by mom.

_____ ➡ _____

6 The building is be using as a movie theater.

_____ ➡ _____

7 Tim should blame because he acted very rudely to her.

_____ ➡ _____

8 We were asked to being forgiven for the last accident.

_____ ➡ _____

9 The accident was happened yesterday.

_____ ➡ _____

10 My son can speak English without being teaching.

_____ ➡ _____

11 The new edition of the book will be publishing next week.

_____ ➡ _____

12 Jeju Island visited by many Chinese tourists.

_____ ➡ _____

13 The book was readed by many children.

_____ ➡ _____

14 Metal is to be using in building bridges.

_____ ➡ _____

15 He elected class president last week.

_____ ➡ _____

B 빈칸에 알맞은 전치사를 쓰시오.

1   The photo was shown ___to___ us by Lily.

2   A bunch of flowers was given _____ her by Jason.

3   The white hat was bought _____ Minji by him.

4   The questions were asked _____ Helen by me.

5   The portrait was drawn _____ me by James.

6   This letter was written _____ him by Mr. Kim.

7   The birthday cake was made _____ his daughter by Nick.

C 다음 문장을 간접목적어 또는 직접목적어를 주어로 하는 수동태 문장으로 바꾸시오.

1   I fed my dogs a delicious meal.
   ➡ _____ *My dogs were fed a delicious meal.* _____
   ➡ _____ *A delicious meal was fed to my dogs.* _____

2   He took care of his baby.
   ➡ _____

3   Somebody gave her a beautiful brooch.
   ➡ _____
   ➡ _____

4   I heard John sing a song with his brother.
   ➡ _____

5   The teacher made us quiet.
   ➡ _____

6   The researchers used the data to solve the problem.
   ➡ _____

7   Her father encourages Jina to become a musician.
   ➡ _____

8   Linda gave me the letter on our wedding anniversary.
   ➡ _____
   ➡ _____

9   Helen made her husband his white shirt.
   ➡ _____

10 Mom reads me the poem.

➡ _____

11 The doctor sent her a subscription.

➡ _____

D 우리말 해석에 맞게 주어진 단어를 이용하여 문장을 완성하시오.

1 그 그림은 그녀에게 팔려야 한다. (sell)

➡ The picture ____should be sold____ to her.

2 그 영화는 다음 주말에 개봉될 것이다. (release)

➡ The movie _____ next weekend.

3 재미있는 책을 아빠가 내게 사주셨다. (buy)

➡ An interesting book _____ by dad.

4 그 곡은 미국에서 녹음되었다. (record)

➡ The song _____ in America.

5 공장 폐기물로 인해 강이 오염될 것이다. (pollute)

➡ The river _____ by factory waste.

6 매력적인 광고로 인해 사람들은 그 물건을 사게 되었다.
(entice, buy)

➡ People _____ the product by the attractive
advertisement.

7 그들에 의해 많은 종류의 음식들이 사람들에게 배달될 수 있다.
(deliver, people)

➡ All kinds of food _____ by them.

8 나는 누군가에 의해 미행당했다. (follow)

➡ I _____ by somebody.

9 컵을 테이블 위에 올려놓아서는 안 된다. (put)

➡ The cup _____ on the table.

10 모든 사람들이 그 소문을 들어왔다. (hear)

➡ The rumor _____ by everyone.

11 그 음악은 Amy에 의해서 작곡되지 않았다. (compose)

➡ The music _____ by Amy.

Note

- **be released** 개봉되다 상영되다
- **record** 녹음하다
- **pollute** 오염되다
- **factory** 공장
- **entice** 부추기다, 유혹이다
- **attractive** 매력적인
- **advertisement** 광고
- **all kinds of** 온갖 모든 종류의, 많은,
- **deliver** 배달하다
- **compose** 작곡하다

Point Check Ⅱ

◆ **동사구의 수동태 :** 동사구가 수동태로 나올 경우 함께 묶어서 써야 한다.

◆ **be used to :** '～으로 사용되다'의 뜻을 가지고 있으며, 'to' 다음에 (동)명사가 올 경우 '～에 익숙하다'의
뜻으로 사용된다.

1. 자주 쓰이는 동사구

ask for	～을 요청하다	bring up	～을 기르다
catch up with	～을 따라잡다	laugh at	～을 비웃다
look after	～을 돌보다	look down on	～을 멸시하다
look up to	～을 존경하다	make use of	～을 이용하다
put off	～을 미루다	run over	～을 치다

2. be used to

be used to +동사원형	～하는 데 쓰이다 (수동태)
be used to +(동)명사	～하는 데 익숙하다
used to +동사원형	과거에 ～하곤 했다 (지금은 하지 않음), 과거에 ～이 있었다 (지금은 없음)
would +동사원형	과거에 ～하곤 했다 (지금은 하는지 안 하는지 모름)

3. 'by' 이외의 전치사를 사용하는 수동태

수동태 + 전치사 at		수동태 + 전치사 of/from	
• be disappointed at	～에 실망하다	• be made of	～로 만들어지다 (재료의 성질 변화가 없음)
• be excited at	～에 흥분하다	• be made from	～로 만들어지다 (재료가 화학적으로 변함)
수동태 + 전치사 with		기타	
• be filled with	～로 가득 차다	• be interested in	～에 관심 있다
• be satisfied with	～에 만족하다	• be involved in	～에 연루되다, 관여하다
• be covered with	～로 덮이다	• be known as	～로 알려지다
• be pleased with	～에 기뻐하다	• be married to	～와 결혼하다

5-7 동사구의 수동태

• **동사구의 수동태**: 동사구를 수동태로 만들 경우 함께 묶어서 써야 한다.
수동태가 될 때는 맨 앞의 동사를 'be동사 + 과거분사'의 형태로 만든다.

1. 수동태에 자주 쓰이는 동사구

• ask for	~을 요청하다	• bring up	~을 기르다
• catch up with	~을 따라 잡다	• laugh at	~을 비웃다
• look after	~을 돌보다	• look down on	~을 멸시하다
• look up to	~을 존경하다	• make use of	~을 이용하다
• run over	~을 치다	• take care of	~을 돌보다
• put off	~을 미루다	• turn on	~을 켜다

• Someone **asked for** me a help crossing the crosswalk.

= I **was asked for** a help crossing the crosswalk.

➡ 'someone'은 불특정한 사람을 의미하므로 생략이 가능하다.

• Anna **puts off** doing homework for the day.

= Doing homework **is put off** by Anna for the day.

☆Check up!

Answer Keys p. 27

A 다음 능동태 문장을 수동태로 전환하시오.

1 He laughed at my clothes.

➡ _____ *My clothes were laughed at by him.* _____

2 His mother couldn't catch up with Tom.

➡ _____

3 Many people look up to the president.

➡ _____

4 Brad turned off the radio at night.

➡ _____

5 The car ran over the dog on the street.

➡ _____

6 Harry took care of the orphans.

➡ _____

7 Some people make use of the park as a gym.

➡ _____

Grammar Plus +

• 수동태로 사용하지
않는 동사
① 목적어가 없는 자동사
appear, exist,
happen, look, smell
② 상태나 상호 관계를
나타내는 타동사
fit, have, meet,
resemble

5-8 be used to의 수동태

· be used to: '~으로 사용되다'의 뜻을 가지고 있으며, 'to' 다음에 (동)명사가 올 경우 '~에 익숙하다'의 뜻으로 사용된다.

◈ be used to의 쓰임

be used to +동사원형	~하는 데 쓰이다 (수동태)
be used to + (동)명사	~하는 데 익숙하다
used to + 동사원형	과거에 ~하곤 했다 (지금은 하지 않음), 과거에 ~이 있었다 (지금은 없음)
would + 동사원형	과거에 ~하곤 했다 (지금은 하는지 안 하는지 모름)

· This feather pen **is used to** <u>write</u> letters.
· Sam **is used to** <u>fishing</u> in the river.
· Sara **used to** <u>take</u> trips alone. (→ 지금은 다니지 않음)
· Jason **would** <u>write</u> in his diary every night. (→ 지금도 쓰고 있는지 아닌지 모름)

Answer Keys p. 27

A 우리말 해석에 맞게 다음 빈칸을 알맞게 채우시오.

1 이 숟가락은 수프를 먹을 때 쓰인다.
➡ This spoon _____ *is used to* _____ eat soup.

2 그들은 밤에 운동하는 데 익숙하다.
➡ They _____ at night.

3 코너에 약국이 있었지만 지금은 없다.
➡ There _____ a pharmacy around the corner.

4 소금은 음식의 간을 맞추는 데 사용된다.
➡ Salt _____ a dish.

5 나는 제빵을 배웠지만 지금은 아니다.
➡ I _____ breadmaking.

6 매일 밤마다 Sara는 스트레칭을 하곤 했다.
➡ Sara _____ every night.

7 그는 혼자 공부하는 데 익숙하다.
➡ He _____ alone.

8 우리 가족은 교회에 다녔지만 지금은 아니다.
➡ My family _____ to church.

Note
· **pharmacy** 약국
· **season** 양념하다
· **breadmaking** 제빵
· **alone** 혼자서

5-9 'by' 이외의 전치사를 사용하는 수동태

- 일반적으로 수동태의 행위자는 'by + 행위자'로 나타내지만 by 대신 다른 전치사가 쓰이는 경우가 있다.

◈ **by** 이외의 전치사를 사용하는 수동태

수동태 + 전치사 at		수동태 + 전치사 of/from	
• be surprised at	~에 놀라다	• be tired of	~에 싫증나다
• be shocked at	~에 충격을 받다	• be composed of	~로 구성되다
• be disappointed at	~에 실망하다	• be made of	~로 만들어지다 (재료의 성질 변화가 없음)
• be excited at	~에 흥분하다	• be made from	~로 만들어지다 (재료가 화학적으로 변함)
수동태 + 전치사 with		기타	
• be filled with	~로 가득 차다	• be interested in	~에 관심 있다
• be satisfied with	~에 만족하다	• be involved in	~에 연루되다, 관여하다
• be covered with	~로 덮이다	• be known as	~로 알려지다
• be pleased with	~에 기뻐하다	• be married to	~와 결혼하다

☆Check up!

Answer Keys p. 27

A 다음 주어진 단어를 알맞게 고쳐 빈칸을 완성하시오.

1 I _____was surprised at_____ the news yesterday. (surprise)

2 People _____ the accident. (shock)

3 Helen _____ studying. (tired)

4 I _____ knitting sweaters. (interest)

5 The ground _____ snow. (cover)

6 She _____ the result of the game. (excite)

7 This coin _____ gold. (make)

8 Mother _____ the present. (please)

9 These shoes _____ rubber. (make)

10 The cup _____ orange juice. (fill)

Grammar Plus +

- [be known + 전치사]
  ➡ 뒤에 오는 전치사에 따라 뜻이 달라진다.
- be known for (업적) ~로 유명하다
- be known as (신분) ~로 알려져 있다
- be known to (대상) ~에게 알려져 있다

Practice More II

Answer Keys p. 28

A 다음 빈칸에 알맞은 전치사를 쓰시오.

1 I am interested ____*in*____ dancing.

2 They were shocked _____ the accident.

3 Mom was satisfied _____ my test result.

4 Harry was tired _____ reading books.

5 The cake is made _____ chocolate.

6 All the people were surprised _____ her performance.

7 Helen was married _____ her childhood friend.

8 The table was covered _____ a white tablecloth.

9 The rice cake is made _____ rice.

10 The bottle is filled _____ wine.

B 다음 문장에서 어법상 <u>어색한</u> 것을 찾아 바르게 고치시오.

1 The air conditioner is used keeping the room cool.

___*keeping*___ ➡ ___*to keep*___

2 She was used to cry a lot when she was a baby.

_____ ➡ _____

3 There used to being a school here. _____ ➡ _____

4 People laughed up the boy. _____ ➡ _____

5 She is used to got up early. _____ ➡ _____

6 Linda was resembled her mother. _____ ➡ _____

7 He was used to write in a diary every night.

_____ ➡ _____

8 I don't use to exercising regularly. _____ ➡ _____

9 He was become an actor. _____ ➡ _____

10 She has seeing to shine her ring. _____ ➡ _____

11 Inho is expected getting an A on the test.

_____ ➡ _____

12 Some books were given for her by Tom.

_____ ➡ _____

Practice More II

C 다음 주어진 단어를 활용하여 문장을 완성하시오.

1 These days she ___is interested in___ playing tennis. (interest)

2 He _____ the library as a meeting place.
(make use of)

3 She is used to _____ Korean food. (make)

4 I used _____ in England. (live)

5 Hana is not used to _____ long distance. (drive)

6 SNS is used _____ much information these days.
(spread)

7 I was _____ on the project by Tom. (catch up)

8 She was _____ by him. (look at)

Note
- **night view** 야경
- **chemical weapon**
  화학무기
- **attack** 공격하다
- **traffic safety** 교통 안전
- **director** 감독
- **solar energy**
  태양열 에너지

D 다음 우리말 해석에 맞게 주어진 단어를 바르게 배열하시오.

1 그 지붕은 눈으로 뒤덮여 있었다.

(the, snow, was, with, roof, covered)

➡ _____ The roof was covered with snow. _____

2 아이들은 아이스 스케이팅에 신났다.

(children, skating, were, at, ice, excited)

➡ _____

3 남산 타워는 야경으로 유명하다.

(view, Namsan Tower, for, is, its, known, night)

➡ _____

4 그는 친절하고 아름다운 여자와 결혼했다.

(kind, woman, he, to, married, beautiful, was, a)

➡ _____

5 화학 무기는 옆 나라를 공격하는 데 쓰였다.

(chemical, country, were, attack, weapons, neighboring, to,
the, used)

➡ _____

6 그 규칙은 교통 안전을 가르치기 위해 만들어졌다.

(rule, safety, the, to, made, was, teach, traffic)

➡ _____

7 그 선수들은 대중들에게 환영 받는다.

(the players, by, are, the crowd, welcomed)

➡ _____

8 감독은 나의 연기에 만족했다.

(the director, satisfied, my, was, with, acting)

➡ _____

9 그 문제를 해결하기 위해 태양열 에너지가 사용될 것이다.

(Solar energy, to, the problem, will, be used, solve)

➡ _____

10 Helen은 내게 어려운 질문들을 하곤 했다.

(Helen, questions, were, some, me, difficult, asked, by, of)

➡ _____

E 다음 문장을 우리말을 참고하여 주어진 말로 시작하는 수동태의 문장으로 바꿔 쓰시오.

1 Mrs. Dickens gave the students some cookies.

➡ Some cookies _____were given to the students by Mrs. Dickens_____.

➡ 약간의 쿠키들이 Mrs. Dickens에 의해 그녀의 학생들에게 주어졌다.

2 Jerry handed Anna a bunch of files in his office.

➡ Anna _____.

➡ Anna는 Jerry에 의해 그의 사무실에서 한 묶음의 서류를 건네받았다.

3 They made me pay the fine yesterday.

➡ I _____.

➡ 나는 어제 (그들에 의해) 벌금을 물었다.

4 I let her go on a picnic yesterday.

➡ She _____.

➡ 그녀는 어제 나에게 소풍가는 것을 허락 받았다.

5 I heard Jeff laugh behind the door.

➡ Jeff _____.

➡ Jeff가 문 뒤에서 웃는 것이 내게 들렸다.

내신 최다 출제 유형

01 다음 중 어법상 **틀린** 문장을 고르시오. [출제 예상 90%]

① I was disappointed at the story.
② Some street trees were run over during the car accident.
③ I was met Dorothy in Manhattan last year.
④ The children are taken care of by me.
⑤ My brother and sister were brought up by my grandmother.

02 다음 중 어법상 옳은 것을 고르시오. [출제 예상 90%]

① The file will be attached Jack.
② The washing machine is used by Jamie.
③ I wasn't invite to her birthday party.
④ Danny is calling a little piggy by people.
⑤ The light bulb is invent by Edison.

03 다음 밑줄 친 부분 중 생략할 수 있는 것을 고르시오. [출제 예상 80%]

① English is spoken by people in Canada and America.
② The Christmas tree was decorated by children.
③ The building was destroyed by an earthquake.
④ The system was renewed by the engineer.
⑤ The actress is looked up to by many Koreans.

04 다음 우리말과 뜻이 같도록 할 때 빈칸에 들어갈 알맞은 말을 고르시오. [출제 예상 90%]

> 그 대통령은 사람들로부터 존경을 받았습니까?
> ➡ _____ the president _____ by people?

① Did − respect
② Was − respect
③ Have − respected
④ Has − respected
⑤ Was − respected

05 다음 주어진 문장을 수동태로 바르게 전환된 것을 고르시오. [출제 예상 90%]

> They will not forget the scenery Mt. Rocky.

① The scenery on Mt. Rocky will be forgotten.
② The scenery on Mt. Rocky will forgotten.
③ The scenery on Mt. Rocky will not forgotten.
④ The scenery on Mt. Rocky will not be forgotten.
⑤ The scenery on Mt. Rocky will not been forgotten.

[01~02] 다음 빈칸에 들어갈 단어로 알맞은 것을 고르시오.

01

A	Where are the berries?
B	They _____ kept in the refrigerator.

① is   ② are   ③ be

④ was   ⑤ were

02

A	Is Jerry _____ in playing the drums?
B	Yes, he likes it so much.

① interest   ② interesting

③ be interest   ④ to interest

⑤ interested

[03~05] 다음 괄호 안에 주어진 단어의 형태를 알맞게 고친 것을 고르시오.

03

The swimming center (lock) during the winter season.

① locked   ② is locking

③ is locked   ④ to locking

⑤ be locked

04

My sneakers (wash) by my mom last Sunday.

① washed   ② was washed

③ were washed   ④ is washing

⑤ are washing

05

My birthday party (will hold) next Saturday.

① will held   ② will be held

③ will be hold   ④ will hold

⑤ will be holding

[06~07] 다음 중 어법상 어색한 문장을 모두 고르시오.

★★★
06 ① The girl was teached by her teacher.

② A lot of fish were killed by the tsunami.

③ The book was wrote by a famous writer.

④ Smartphones are used by many people.

⑤ The blue sweater was knitted by Jane.

★★★
07 ① This is our new house.

② The photo took last week.

③ There is a famous picture on the wall.

④ He was call Tim.

⑤ This postcard was sent by his son.

[08~09] 다음 중 밑줄 친 부분의 쓰임이 어색한 것을 고르시오. (답이 여러 개 일 수도 있음)

08 ① This cake was baked by my dad.

② That house was built by my grandfather.

③ This car was bought by Tommy.

④ The table was making in England.

⑤ That shirt was washed by her sister.

09 ① Jenny's flower garden is ruined.
② Most people were chose by the director.
③ All the pets have been washed.
④ Her family is loved by their neighbors.
⑤ The lake is surround by many trees.

10 다음 중 빈칸에 들어갈 단어가 나머지 넷과 <u>다른</u> 것을 고르시오.

① This was written _____ my friends, Julie and Molly.
② These books were collected _____ Mr. Brown.
③ My glasses were broken _____ the baby.
④ We are interested _____ the hip-hop music.
⑤ The house with the red roof was sold _____ the young couple.

[11~12] 다음 빈칸에 알맞은 형태를 고르시오.

11
The pumpkin pie is _____ by my grandmother.

① cook ② cooked ③ cooks
④ cooking ⑤ is cooking

12
We were _____ to the music concert by our teacher.

① bring ② bringing ③ brings
④ brought ⑤ to bring

[13~14] 다음 주어진 문장과 뜻이 같은 것을 고르시오.

13
She didn't write this book.

① This book is not written by her.
② This book wasn't written by her.
③ This book is written by her.
④ This book was written by her.
⑤ This book weren't written by her.

14
Maria keeps her room clean.

① She was kept her room clean.
② She is kept her room clean.
③ Her room is kept clean by Maria.
④ Her room was kept clean by Maria.
⑤ Her room kept clean by Maria.

[15~16] 다음 중 어법상 올바른 문장을 <u>모두</u> 고르시오.
★★★
15 ① The sports car is belonged to my father.
② The puzzle book was given to me by my dad.
③ Hellen was bought a doll by her uncle.
④ The Japanese food was cooked for me by my sister.
⑤ The shelf is made with steel.

★★★

16 ① They were given some hard work by their boss.
② The room was keep quiet by the old gentleman.
③ Lots of leaves were raked by my sister.
④ Mr. Simpson was elect mayor.
⑤ Our house needs to be painting.

17 다음 단어의 밑줄 친 부분의 형태를 바르게 고친 것을 고르시오.

> If you <u>interest</u> playing a musical instrument, you may go to Mrs. White.

① interested
② is interested
③ are interested
④ are interested in
⑤ are interesting in

18 다음 글의 내용 중 어법상 잘못된 것을 고르시오.

> Last night, it ① <u>snowed heavily</u>. The road is ② <u>covered by</u> snow. We ③ <u>have to</u> ④ <u>be careful</u> when we ⑤ <u>walk</u> on the street.

★★★

19 다음 중 문장의 전환이 어색한 것을 고르시오.

① Ron baked this bread.
 → This bread was baked by Ron.
② Molly sent an email to us.
 → An email is sent to us by Molly.
③ People speak English in Canada.
 → English is spoken in Canada.
④ Mom will clean the house this weekend.
 → The house will be cleaned by mom this weekend.
⑤ My big brother made the pencil case.
 → The pencil case was made by my big brother.

[20~21] 다음 주어진 문장을 능동태로 바르게 바꾼 것을 고르시오.

20
> The pearl necklace was bought by a young man.

① A young man buys the pearl necklace.
② A young man bought the pearl necklace.
③ A young man is bought the pearl necklace.
④ A young man was bought the pearl necklace.
⑤ A young man is buy the pearl necklace.

21
> Hunguel was invented by King Sejong in 1443.

① King Sejong invents Hunguel in 1443.
② King Sejong is invents Hunguel in 1443.
③ King Sejong invent Hunguel in 1443.
④ King Sejong was invented Hunguel in 1443.
⑤ King Sejong invented Hunguel in 1443.

[22~23] 다음 주어진 문장을 수동태로 바르게 바꾼 것을 고르시오.

22

She raised three cats and two dogs.

① Three cats and two dogs are raised by her.
② Three cats and two dogs is raised by her.
③ Three cats and two dogs were raised by her.
④ Three cats and two dogs was raised by her.
⑤ Three cats and two dogs raised by her.

23

An old man cleans the park every morning.

① The park is cleaned by an old man every morning.
② The park was cleaned by an old man every morning.
③ The park cleaned by an old man every morning.
④ The park is cleaning by an old man every morning.
⑤ The park was cleaning by an old man every morning.

[24~25] 다음 중 어법상 맞지 않은 것을 고르시오.

24
① Jack's car was washed by him.
② The roses will be sent by Jacky.
③ We were made be happy by the news.
④ The news was reported yesterday.
⑤ Many fish will be caught by me.

25
① We were surprised at the music.
② The actress is known to everyone.
③ My mom was pleased with the gift.
④ Harry was worried about the test.
⑤ I was satisfied to the result.

★★★
26 다음 밑줄 친 부분 중 생략이 가능한 것을 고르시오.

① Tommy was introduced to us by Sena.
② The model is loved by teenagers.
③ Your pen was found by my brother.
④ This robot is made in Korea by them.
⑤ The bus was driven by the guard.

[27~28] 다음 우리말과 같은 뜻이 되도록 할 때 빈칸에 알맞은 단어를 고르시오.

27

태훈은 나에게 생일 선물로 손수건을 주었다.
➡ A handkerchief _____ me for my birthday by Taehun.

① were gave   ② were given to
③ has given   ④ given to
⑤ was given to

28

Jenny와 그녀의 친구들은 많은 가난한 아이들을 돕는다.
➡ Many poor kids _____ by Jenny and her friends.

① were helped   ② was helped
③ are helped   ④ is helped
⑤ have helped

[29~30] 다음 문장의 빈칸에 공통으로 들어갈 알맞은
단어를 고르시오.

29

- This report is composed _____ nine themes.
- The books are made _____ paper.

① is ② with ③ of
④ for ⑤ by

30

- Sue was very shocked _____ the large hurricane.
- I am so disappointed _____ his rude behavior.

① of ② at ③ for
④ to ⑤ with

◇◇◇◇◇◇◇◇◇ 서술형 평가 ◇◇◇◇◇◇◇◇◇

[31~32] 다음 우리말과 같은 뜻이 되도록 빈칸에 알맞은
말을 쓰시오.

31

이 요구르트는 우유로 만들어졌다.
➡ This yogurt is _____ _____ milk.

➡ _____

32

이 바구니는 블루베리로 가득 차 있다.
➡ This basket _____ _____ _____ blueberries.

➡ _____

[33~34] 다음 문장을 수동태로 바꿀 때 빈칸에 들어갈
알맞은 말을 쓰시오.

33

Our class recycles plastic bags and bottles.
= Plastic bags and bottles _____ _____ by our class.

➡ _____

34

Henry has watered his grandparents' garden.
= His grandparents' garden _____ _____ _____ by Henry.

➡ _____

35 다음 괄호 안의 단어를 이용하여 문장을 완성하시오.

(1) French _____ _____ in Canada. (use)
(2) The Olympics _____ _____ every four years. (hold)

Answer Keys p. 28~29

[36~37] 다음 대화의 밑줄 친 부분을 알맞은 형태로 고쳐 쓰시오.

36

A Who sculpted the Statue of David?
B It sculpted by Michelangelo.

➡ _____

37

A Where will the toy boxes be carried?
B They will carried to the big toy market.

➡ _____

[38~40] 다음 질문에 맞게 괄호 안의 단어를 배열하여 알맞은 대답을 완성하시오.

★★★
38

A Who broke your umbrella?
B (Jamie / broken / umbrella / was / my / by)

➡ _____

★★★
39

A What was the bracelet made of?
B (the / jade / green and pink / was / bracelet / made / of / beads)

➡ _____

40

A Who cleaned the garden?
B (cleaned / was / by / the / garden / me)

➡ _____

[41~43] 다음 주어진 문장을 지시어대로 바꿔서 다시 쓰시오.

★★★
41

Uncle Jack sent me a postcard with sunflowers printed on it.

➡ [수동태의 부정문]

_____

_____

★★★
42

Orange juice is prepared every morning by her mom.

➡ [능동태의 의문문]

_____

_____

43

My father made me a desk when I was young.

➡ [수동태의 평서문]

_____

06

Chapter
부정사

Point Check I

◆ **부정사 :** 'to+동사원형'을 'to부정사'라고 하고, 동사원형만 있는 것을 '원형부정사'라고 한다.

◆ **명사적 용법 :** 명사처럼 쓰여 문장에서 주어, 목적어, 보어 역할을 한다.

◆ **형용사적 용법 :** 문장에서 형용사처럼 쓰이며 명사, 대명사를 꾸며주는 역할을 한다.

1. 부정사의 형태 : to부정사 - [to + 동사원형]
원형부정사 - [동사원형]

2. 부정사의 명사적 역할

명사적 용법	예문
주어 역할 [~하는 것은]	• To travel makes you with a broad outlook on life. [주어]
목적어 역할 [~하는 것을, ~하기를]	• Tom managed to find a good job. [목적어]
보어 역할 [~하기, ~하는 것]	• She hopes that everyone is to be happy. [보어]
의문사 + to부정사	• We didn't know who(m) to go with. [주로 동사 뒤에서 동사의 목적어로 쓰인다.] = We didn't know who we should go with.

3. 의문사 + to부정사

what+to부정사 (무엇을 ~할지)	who(m)+to부정사 (누구와 ~할지)
where+to부정사 (어디에서 ~할지)	how+to부정사 (어떻게 ~할지)
when+to부정사 (언제 ~할지)	

4. 부정사의 형용사적 역할

형용사적 용법 [~할, ~하는]	예문
명사 수식	• Students have a lot of work to do.
대명사 수식	• I just want something to drink.
전치사의 목적어일 경우	• Jacky needs some paper to write on.

6-1 부정사의 형태와 역할

> • **부정사**: 동사원형 앞에 to를 붙이면 'to부정사', to가 없으면 '원형부정사'라고 한다.
> 명사처럼 쓰여 주어, 목적어, 보어 역할을 하기도 하며, 형용사, 부사처럼 쓰이기도 한다.

1. 부정사의 형태: [to + 동사원형]
　　　　　　　　　　[동사원형]

2. 부정사의 역할

(1) **명사적 쓰임**: 주어, 목적어, 보어 역할

　• **To eat** vegetables is good for your health.
　　주어 역할 (~하는 것은)

(2) **형용사적 쓰임**: 명사, 대명사를 수식

　• The best way **to move** heavy things is using a cart.
　　　　　명사 수식 (→ The best way)

(3) **부사적 쓰임**: 동사, 형용사, 부사, 문장 전체를 수식

　• I usually go to the bookstore **to search** for the new ones.
　　　　　　　동사 수식 (→ go)

Grammar Plus +

• **to부정사와 전치사 to 구분하기**
- to부정사: [to + 동사원형] '~하는 것, ~할, ~하기 위하여, ~해서, ~한다면' 등으로 해석
- 전치사: [to + 명사(동명사)] '~로, ~까지, ~에게, ~을, ~보다' 등으로 해석

 Check up!

Answer Keys p. 30

A 다음 괄호 안에서 알맞은 것을 고르시오.

1　(To be / be) a writer, I should read many books.

2　She wants (to go / go) hiking with her friends.

3　Mom and I have (buy / to buy) some bread for lunch.

4　We need some paper (write / to write) on.

5　My favorite activity is (to play / play) baseball.

6　He decided (goes / to go) to school by bus.

7　Sam's wish is (meet / to meet) his teacher again.

8　He bought a house (to live in / live in).

9　Lily planned (does / to do) exercise regularly.

10　It is impossible (to fly / fly) like a bird.

부정사의 명사적 용법 (1)_주어/보어 역할

- **부정사의 명사적 용법**: 명사처럼 쓰여서 주어, 목적어, 보어 역할을 하는 것을 말한다.
- 명사로 쓰였을 때 '~하는 것, ~하기'로 해석한다.

1. 주어 역할의 to부정사

- **To sleep** well is very important.
  = It is very important **to sleep** well.
  ➡ to부정사가 주어가 될 때 주로 문장의 뒤에 쓰고, 주어 자리에 it을 사용한다.
  이 때의 it을 가짜주어라고 하고 해석하지 않으며, to부정사를 진짜주어라고 한다.

2. 주격보어 역할의 to부정사

- Monica's dream is **to become** a famous opera singer.
  주격보어 (~이 되는 것 → 주어를 보충)

3. to부정사의 의미상의 주어: 의미상의 주어란 to부정사의 주어를 의미한다.

(1) [for + 목적격]

- It is difficult **for him** to understand this theory.

(2) [of + 목적격]

kind, nice, careful, careless, foolish, stupid, wise, honest, selfish, rude...	사람의 성격, 성질을 나타내는 형용사가 올 때는 to부정사의 의미상 주어를 'of + 목적격' 형태로 한다.

- It was wise **of you to say** so.
- It is selfish **of her to do** such a thing.

Answer Keys p. 30

A 보기와 같이 다음 문장을 바꾸어 쓰시오.

보기
To eat healthy food is important.
→ It is important to eat healthy food.

1 To get up early is usually hard.
➡ _____

2 To go hiking with friends is really fun.
➡ _____

3 To go out alone at night is dangerous.

➡ _____

4 To rest is necessary.

➡ _____

5 To watch horror movies is exciting.

➡ _____

B 다음 주어진 단어를 의미상의 주어로 두고 of, for를 이용하여 문장을 다시 쓰시오.

1 It is easy to understand this lecture. (I)

➡ *It is easy for me to understand this lecture.*

2 It is difficult to learn French. (Helen)

➡ _____

3 It was nice to visit his grandmother once a week. (he)

➡ _____

4 It is necessary to talk with my family. (I)

➡ _____

5 It is wise to make a priority list. (you)

➡ _____

6 It is interesting to ride a bike along the river. (Mike)

➡ _____

7 It is kind to help the poor. (they)

➡ _____

8 It is useful to study Korean history. (I)

➡ _____

6-3 부정사의 명사적 용법 (2)_목적어 역할

- **부정사의 목적어 역할:** 동사 뒤에서 동사의 목적어로 쓰이며 '~하기를, ~하는 것을'이라고 해석한다. 목적어로 to부정사만 갖는 동사와 목적어로 to부정사와 동명사 모두를 갖는 동사가 있다.

1. to부정사만을 목적어로 하는 동사

want, hope, agree, choose, decide, expect, plan, promise, fail,

learn, manage, mean, need, pretend, refuse, tend, would like

- They want **to buy** some game items.
- Thomas would like **to climb** Mt. Olympus.

2. to부정사와 동명사 모두를 목적어로 하는 동사

like, love, hate, begin, start, continue

- Tom likes **to play** soccer.
  = Tom likes **playing** soccer.
- She started **to roll** over the grass.
  = She started **rolling** over the grass.

★Check up!

Answer Keys p. 30

A 다음 빈칸에 알맞은 동사 형태를 모두 써서 문장을 완성하시오.

1 I want _____to be_____ an actor in the future. (be)

2 They pretend _____ me. (know)

3 He planned to go to America _____ English. (study)

4 We decide _____ the English speaking contest. (participate in)

5 He likes _____ shirts. (buy)

6 I would like _____ if you can come to my birthday party. (know)

7 Susan wishes _____ weight. (lose)

8 Professor Lee was expected _____ the seminar last week. (attend)

9 Mom promised _____ the dress for the graduation party. (make)

의문사 + to부정사

• **의문사 + to부정사**: 부정사의 명사적 용법 중 하나로, 주로 동사 뒤에서 동사의 목적어로 쓰이며, '의문사 + 주어 + should + 동사원형'의 형태로 바꿔 쓸 수 있다.

1. **의문사 + to부정사**: 명사처럼 쓰여 주어, 보어, 목적어 역할을 한다.

• **what + to부정사**	무엇을 ~할지	• **who(m) + to부정사**	누구와 ~할지
• **where + to부정사**	어디에서 ~할지	• **how + to부정사**	어떻게 ~할지
• **when + to부정사**	언제 ~할지		

- I have no idea **what to buy**.
- They searched the Internet **where to eat**.
- Jessy doesn't know **how to go** there.

2. [**의문사 + 주어 + should + 동사원형**]으로 바꿔 쓸 수 있다.

- We don't know <u>what to do</u>.
  = We don't know **what we should do**.
- People have to learn <u>what to do</u> in an emergency.
  = People have to learn **what they should do** in an emergency.

Grammar Plus +

- '의문사 + to부정사'의 형태가 오는 동사들: know, show, tell, talk about, learn, teach, explain...

Check up!

Answer Keys p. 30

A 다음 주어진 문장과 같은 의미가 되도록 빈칸을 채워 문장을 완성하시오.

1 I don't know where to go.
➡ I don't know _____*where I should go*_____.

2 Bob wanted to learn how to make a chocolate cookie.
➡ Bob wanted to learn _____.

3 The professor explained how we should protect the environment.
➡ The professor explained _____.

4 We don't know whom to teach us English.
➡ We don't know _____.

5 Sophia didn't tell us when to leave.
➡ Sophia didn't tell us _____.

6 She couldn't decide what to buy.

➡ She couldn't decide _____.

7 Mom taught me how I should use the microwave.

➡ Mom taught me _____.

8 Alex wants to learn how he should drive a car.

➡ Alex wants to learn _____.

9 Sam explained to me what I should do first.

➡ Sam explained to me _____.

10 I'm worried about when to start the project.

➡ I'm worried about _____ the project.

B 우리말과 같은 뜻이 되도록 보기 에서 알맞은 단어를 골라 빈칸을 채우시오.
(의문사＋to부정사 구문을 사용하시오.)

보기
bring / distinguish / attract / finish / do

1 네가 무엇을 할지 모르겠다면 너의 친구들에게 물어봐라.

➡ If you don't know ____*what to do*____, just ask your friends.

2 너는 그 쌍둥이들을 구별하는 방법을 알고 있니?

➡ Do you know _____ the twins?

3 그가 너에게 파티에 어떤 것을 가져올지 말해 주었니?

➡ Did he tell you _____ at the party?

4 그녀는 우리들의 관심을 끄는 방법을 알고 있다.

➡ She knows _____ our attention.

5 보고서를 언제 끝낼지 알려주세요.

➡ Please tell me _____ the report.

6-5 부정사의 형용사적 용법

> • **부정사의 형용사적 용법**: 형용사처럼 쓰여서 명사, 대명사를 꾸며주는 역할을 한다. '～할, ～하는' 이라는 뜻을 가지며, 반드시 꾸며주는 명사의 뒤에 위치해야 한다.

1. 명사를 수식

- Children, it's time **to go** to bed.
  (→ time)
- She had a lot of homework **to do**.
  (→ homework)

2. -thing, -one, -body로 끝나는 대명사를 수식

- They wanted something warm **to drink**.
  (→ something)
- She doesn't need anyone glad **to meet**.
  (→ anyone)

➡ -thing, -one, -body로 끝나는 부정대명사를 수식할 때는 '**부정대명사 + 형용사 + to부정사**'의 형태를 사용한다.

3. 전치사의 목적어일 경우

- He needs a pen **to write with**.
  (→ a pen)
- Many young people want to own a house **to live in**.
  (→ a house)

➡ to부정사가 수식하는 명사가 전치사의 목적어일 경우에는 전치사를 빠뜨리지 않도록 주의한다.

 **Check up!**

Answer Keys p. 30~31

A 우리말과 같은 뜻이 되도록 빈칸에 알맞은 말을 쓰시오.

1 저 나이 든 신사분에게 앉을 의자를 주는 게 어떠니?
➡ Why don't you give that old gentleman ___a chair to sit on___?

2 그는 우리에게 연습을 할 수 있는 약간의 기회를 주었다.
➡ He gave us some _____.

3 Sally는 함께 놀 친구들이 정말 필요하다.
➡ Sally really needs _____.

4 그들에게 쓸 종이를 좀 주거라.
➡ Give them some _____.

Answer Keys p. 30~31

5 그 아이들은 읽을 책이 아주 많이 필요하다.

➡ The children need a lot of _____.

6 나는 함께 살 친구를 찾고 있다.

➡ I'm looking for a _____.

7 Min은 자동차를 사려고 저축한다.

➡ Min is saving money _____.

8 Jacky는 파산했다. 그는 살 집이 없다.

➡ Jacky is bankrupt. He doesn't have _____.

B 다음 주어진 단어들을 알맞게 배열하여 문장을 완성하시오.

1 John has _____*many friends to talk with*_____.
(talk, to, many, with, friends)

2 I have _____.
(take care of, dogs, to, three)

3 Lisa, _____. (it's, to, time, get up)

4 Does she have _____?
(time, help, to, me, enough)

5 Mijin bought _____.
(to, something, drink)

6 I have _____.
(with, no one, go, to, fishing, me)

7 John was looking for _____.
(somebody, the work, to, volunteer, for)

8 Do you have money _____?
(to, some, buy, bread)

9 Kate has _____.
(work, much, do, to)

10 Helen needs _____.
(something, to relieve, interesting, stress, her, do, to)

Practice More Ⅰ

Answer Keys p. 31

A 괄호 안에서 알맞은 것을 고르시오.

1 It is kind (of / for) him to help the poor.

2 It was difficult (for / of) Sam to understand the history lecture.

3 It was happy (of / to) meet James again.

4 It is important (for / of) them to remember what to do next.

5 It is nice (for / of) you to act like that.

6 These pants were too small (of / for) her to wear.

7 These questions were so easy (for / of) Ann to answer.

8 It is so smart (for / of) him to solve the problem.

9 That's very stupid (of / for) me to make the same mistake.

10 It is good (for / of) you to get up early.

B 다음 주어진 해석과 일치하도록 문장을 완성하시오.

1 I bought some pens ___to write with___. (쓸 펜)

2 Sam's dream is to have a house _____. (살 집)

3 She has many friends _____. (얘기할 친구)

4 Mr. Lee told me that he needs a chair _____. (앉을 의자)

5 My daughter is looking for a spoon _____. (가지고 먹을 스푼)

6 Some people think that having a religion _____ is important. (의지할 종교)

7 I need some paper _____. (쓸 종이)

8 Give me some topics _____. (쓸 주제)

C 다음 문장에서 어법상 어색한 부분을 찾아 바르게 고치시오.

1 Tell the truth is important   ___Tell___ ➡ ___To tell___

2 Her hobby is take photos.   _____ ➡ _____

3 They want to climbing that mountain.

                              _____ ➡ _____

Practice More I

4   It is hard of him to buy that car.   _____ ➡ _____

5   I need a chair to sitting on.   _____ ➡ _____

6   Jimmy has lots of work doing.   _____ ➡ _____

7   My dream is be a math teacher.   _____ ➡ _____

8   We went to the library study for the exam.

                                          _____ ➡ _____

9   It is brave for her to save that girl.

                                            _____ ➡ _____

10   Mr. Han bought a house to live with.

                                            _____ ➡ _____

D   주어진 두 문장의 의미가 같도록 빈칸을 채우시오.

1   The boy began running away.

    ➡ The boy began _____*to run away*_____.

2   They told me the way to assemble the machine.

    ➡ They told me _____ the machine.

3   It is hard for me to decide when to stop.

    ➡ It is hard for me to decide _____.

4   Alex doesn't know where he should go during summer vacation.

    ➡ Alex doesn't know _____ during summer vacation.

5   To study all night makes me tired.

    ➡ It _____ all night.

6   I like to eat something spicy when I am upset.

    ➡ I like _____ when I am upset.

7   Let him know what to do first.

    ➡ Let him know _____ first.

8   To keep pets is not easy.

    ➡ _____

9   Linda started to play tennis with her mother.

    ➡ Linda _____ with her mother.

E 우리말 해석과 일치하도록 주어진 단어를 알맞게 배열하여 문장을 완성하시오.

1 그녀는 끝내야 할 프로젝트가 있다. (finish, a project, to)

➡ She has _____*a project to*_____ finish.

2 나와 Cindy는 이번 겨울방학에 스키를 배우기로 계획했다.
   (how to ski, to, this, learn, winter vacation)

➡ Cindy and I planned _____.

3 밤에 잠이 안 올 때 따뜻한 우유 한 잔을 마시는 것은 도움이 된다.
   (it, a cup of warm milk, drink, to, helpful, is)

➡ _____ if you cannot sleep at night.

4 목표를 달성하는 가장 좋은 방법은 최선을 다하는 것이다.
   (way, your goal, best, achieve, the, to)

➡ _____ is to do your best.

5 너의 나쁜 습관을 고치는 것은 매우 중요하다.
   (important, your, very, to, break, it, bad, is, habit)

➡ _____.

6 학교에 가장 빨리 가는 방법은 버스를 타는 것이다.
   (the, to school, go, way, to, fastest)

➡ _____ is to take the bus.

7 TV 볼륨을 너무 크게 하는 것은 좋지 않다.
   (to, so, up, the TV volume, high, turn)

➡ It is not good for you _____.

8 그들이 그런 행동을 한 것은 잘못된 것이다.
   (act, it, that, wrong, for, is, them, like, to)

➡ _____.

9 Amy는 더는 군것질을 하지 않기로 결심했다.
   (anymore, not, decided, have, to, snacks)

➡ Amy _____.

10 나는 그녀에게 해야 할 중요할 말이 있다.
   (I, tell, something, her, important, have, to)

➡ _____.

Point Check II

◆ **부정사 :** 'to + 동사원형'을 'to부정사'라고 하고, 동사원형만을 사용할 경우 '원형부정사'라고 한다.

◆ **부사적 용법 :** 문장 안에서 부사처럼 쓰이며 동사, 형용사, 다른 부사, 그리고 문장 전체를 수식한다.

1. 부정사의 부사적 용법

부사 역할	예문
목적, 의도 〜하기 위해서(= in order to)	• They went to London to watch the soccer games. 　=They went to London in order to watch the soccer games.
감정 〜해서, 〜하기 되어	• I am so happy to get a new laptop computer.
판단 〜하는 것을 보니	• He must be a doctor to examine the patients.
결과 〜해서(결국) ...되다	• I grew up to be a famous cook.
조건 〜한다면 (= if)	• To buy these drinks, you will get one more. 　= If you buy these drinks, you will get one more.

2. 목적격보어로 쓰이는 to부정사 (5형식 문장)

동사 + 목적어 + <u>to부정사</u>		동사 + 목적어 + <u>원형부정사</u>	
want, ask, tell, allow, get advise, expect 등	+to부정사	사역동사: have, let, make 지각동사: hear, feel, see, watch, notice 등	+ 원형부정사
• Mr. Smith <u>expected</u> them to have a great time.		• She <u>had</u> me boil the water. ➡ 원형부정사(동사원형)는 오직 사역동사와 지각동사 　만의 목적격보어 역할을 한다.	

부정사의 부사적 용법 (1)

> • **부정사의 부사적 용법**: 문장 안에서 부사처럼 쓰여 동사, 형용사, 다른 부사 또는 문장 전체를 수식하면서 문장을 더욱 자세히 설명하는 것을 말한다.
>
> • to부정사가 부사처럼 쓰일 때는 '왜 ~하는지, ~하기 위해서, ~해서'라는 뜻으로 해석한다.

1. '~하기 위해서'의 뜻으로 목적이나 의도를 나타낼 경우 'in order to'로 바꿔 쓸 수 있다.

- We are going to London **to visit** our aunt and uncle next week.

  = We are going to London **in order to visit** our aunt and uncle next week.

- A man built a house **to accept** people in need.

  = A man built a house **in order to accept** people in need.

2. 'for + 명사'를 대신 사용해서 목적과 의도를 표현할 수 있다.

- She prayed for a long time **to save** a poor man.

  = She prayed for a long time **for a poor man**.

- I decided to study hard **to become** a great inventor.

  = I decided to study hard **for a great inventor**.

 Check up!

Answer Keys p. 31

A 다음 두 문장이 같은 뜻이 되도록 빈칸을 채우시오.

1 He started to pack up in order to go hiking tomorrow.

➡ He started _to pack up to go hiking_ tomorrow.

2 I went to LA to meet my cousin.

➡ I went to LA _____ my cousin.

3 Mr. Lee visited city hall in order to issue documents.

➡ Mr. Lee visited city hall _____ some documents.

4 Jim and Hana went downtown to watch a romantic movie.

➡ Jim and Hana went downtown _____ a romantic movie.

5 John studied all night in the library in order to pass the exam.

➡ John studied all night in the library _____.

6 I want to save money to buy a new car.

➡ I want to save money _____ a new car.

Answer Keys p. 31

B 빈칸에 to나 for 중 알맞은 것을 쓰시오.

1   He donated all of his money ____for____ poor people.

2   I did my best _____ get first prize.

3   Let's go out _____ dinner tonight.

4   John wrote the letter _____ thank Jane for the nice present.

5   The volunteers gathered _____ help the victims.

6   I went to the library _____ find some books written by O. Henry.

7   Mark bought some dyes _____ dying a curtain.

8   They got up early _____ clean the whole house.

6-7 부정사의 부사적 용법 (2)

• to부정사가 부사처럼 쓰일 때 '왜 ~하는지, ~하기 위해서, ~해서'라는 뜻으로 해석한다.

1. 감정의 원인: 감정을 나타내는 형용사 뒤에 올 때는 '~해서, ~하게 되어'로 해석

sorry happy glad sad pleased surprised disappointed excited

• They are <u>glad</u> **to take** the train on time.
• I'm <u>disappointed</u> **to break** our plans.

2. 판단의 근거: ~하는 것을 보니

• She must be very sick **to take** a day off.

3. 결과: ~해서 (결국) ...되다, 하지만 ~하게 되다

• He grew up **to be** a famous dancer in the world.
• She ran fast to school only **to be** late.

4. 조건: ~한다면 (가정법의 if절처럼 쓰이는 to부정사)

• **To understand** the truth, you will like him.
  = **If you understand** the truth, you will like him.
  ➡ to부정사가 조건으로 쓰이면 반드시 주절 조동사 'will, shall, can, may, would, should, could' 가 온다. 이러한 문장을 'if'절로 바꾸어 사용하기 때문에 '조건'이라고 한다.

☆Check up!

Answer Keys p. 31~32

A 다음 두 문장을 to부정사를 이용하여 한 문장으로 연결하시오.

1 I am so tired. I can't go to the party .

➡ *I am so tired to go to the party.*

2 Helen practiced soccer everyday. She became a great soccer player.

➡ _____

3 You must be diligent. You always arrive at the office early.

➡ _____

4 She stopped eating junk food. She wants to lose weight.

➡ _____

Answer Keys p. 31~32

5 Mary was sad. Mary failed the interview.

➡ _____

6 I was frightened. I saw a black cat at midnight.

➡ _____

7 We were hungry. We didn't eat lunch.

➡ _____

8 John was smart. He solve the difficult problem easily.

➡ _____

9 I got an A on the math test. I was happy.

➡ _____

10 Jennifer went to a shopping mall. She buys new pants.

➡ _____

B 다음 문장을 우리말로 해석하시오.

1 I was so happy to participate in the global volunteering.

➡ _____ *나는 해외 봉사에 참여하게 돼서 너무 행복했다.* _____

2 If you lose weight, you will be healthier.

➡ _____

3 He grew up to be a famous artist in Italy.

➡ _____

4 He must be tired to walk so weakly.

➡ _____

5 We're sorry to hear the terrible news.

➡ _____

6 To know the importance of this English test, you will study hard.

➡ _____

자주 쓰이는 부정사 표현

1. too... to~: 너무 ...해서 ~하지 못하다

- Jenny is **too** young **to** write the alphabet.

  = Jenny is **so** young **that** she **can't** write the alphabet.

  ➡ 'too... to~'는 'so that cannot'으로 바꿔 쓸 수 있다.

2. ...enough to~: ~하기에 충분히 ...하다

- Anna is smart **enough to** understand the problem.

  = Anna is **so** smart **that** she **can** understand the problem.

  ➡ '..enough to~'는 'so that can'으로 바꿔 쓸 수 있다.

3. in order (not) to~, so as (not) to~: ~하기 위하여 (~하지 않기 위하여)

- We got up early **in order to**(so as to) arrive at the airport on time.
- I prepared very hard **in order not to**(so as not to) fail the interview.

Answer Keys p. 32

A 다음 문장에서 어법상 <u>어색한</u> 것을 찾아 바르게 고치시오.

1   The woman is to weak to participate in the triathlon.

<u>   to weak   </u> ➡ <u>   too weak   </u>

2   I'm enough strong to move the box.

<u>   </u> ➡ <u>   </u>

3   She made a cake in order to sold it at Tim's charity sale.

<u>   </u> ➡ <u>   </u>

4   We studied hard in not order to fail the exam.

<u>   </u> ➡ <u>   </u>

5   She is so lazy that she can exercise regularly.

<u>   </u> ➡ <u>   </u>

6   Joe is too tiring to do his homework.

<u>   </u> ➡ <u>   </u>

7   Park is too sadly to write the letter.

<u>   </u> ➡ <u>   </u>

B   다음 두 문장의 의미가 같도록 빈칸에 알맞은 말을 쓰시오.

1   My sister was so young that she couldn't go to the concert.
➡ My sister was ___*too*___ young ___*to go*___ to the concert.

2   Tim is too tired to play soccer.
➡ Tim is _____ tired _____ he _____ play soccer.

3   He practiced hard enough to join the baseball club.
➡ He practiced _____ hard _____ he _____ the
baseball club.

4   John went to the grocery store to buy some fruit.
➡ John went to the grocery store _____ some fruit.

5   Youngmin is so skillful that he can fix the car by himself.
➡ Youngmin is _____ the car by himself.

6   I studied hard in order not to fail the exam.
➡ I studied hard _____ the exam.

7   Mom is too old to knit the sweater.
➡ Mom is _____ old _____ she _____ the sweater.

8   I ran so fast that I could arrive on time.
➡ I ran _____ on time.

9   Sara will go to Paris to study art.
➡ Sara will go to Paris _____ art.

10   Tim and Jack practice soccer in order not to lose the game.
➡ Tim and Jack practice soccer _____ the game.

6-9 목적격보어로 쓰이는 부정사

- **목적격보어의 부정사**: 5형식 문장에서 목적어 다음에 to부정사가 오면 목적어의 의미를 보충 설명하는 목적격보어가 된다.
- 동사에 따라 to가 없는 동사원형, 즉 원형부정사만을 쓰기도 한다.

1. 동사 + 목적어 + to부정사 : 다음의 동사들은 to부정사를 목적격보어로 사용한다.

> want, ask, tell, allow, advise, expect, get, order, would like

- My parents allowed me **to attend** the prom.
  목적어   목적격보어
- The principal told us **to enjoy** the school life.
  목적어 목적격보어

2. 동사 + 목적어 + 원형부정사 : 다음의 동사들은 원형부정사를 목적격보어로 사용한다.

사역동사	'~을 누구에게 시키다'의 뜻을 가진 동사	have, let, make
지각동사	'보다, 듣다, 느끼다'처럼 눈으로 보거나 듣고, 느끼는 감각을 나타내는 동사	hear, feel, see, watch, notice, listen to, observe, look at

- Sam **had** his sister **water** the flowers.
  목적어   목적격보어 (원형부정사 사용)
- Mary **looked at** me play the drum.
  목적어 목적격보어 (원형부정사 사용)

3. help + 목적어 + to부정사/원형부정사

'help'는 목적격보어로 to부정사와 원형부정사 모두 쓸 수 있다.

- The book **helped** me to **think** positively.
  = The book **helped** me **think** positively.

 **Check up!**

Answer Keys p. 32

A 다음 괄호 안에서 알맞은 것을 고르시오.

1 Mom allowed me (to go / going) to LA during summer vacation.

2 Teacher had us (clean / to clean) our classroom.

3 The guide helped me (deciding / to decide) where to go.

4 I can hear my sister (to sing / sing) in her room.

5   Tom asked her not (to go out / going out) at night.

6   Jane expected her sons (become / to become) a baseball player.

7   Many people watch her (dance / to dance) on the stage.

8   Would he let her (stay up / to stay up) late?

9   He got me (to fix / fixing) his watch.

10 I can see a boy (stand / to stand) in the doorway.

B   다음 우리말 해석에 맞게 주어진 단어를 이용하여 문장을 완성하시오.

1   그는 내가 John을 만나기를 기대했다.
    (expected, me, John, to, he, meet)
    ➡ _____ *He expected me to meet John.* _____

2   Jane은 엄마에게 새로운 차를 사달라고 요청했다.
    (Jane, a new car, to, her mom, buy, asked)
    ➡ _____

3   그들은 우리가 그들 정원에서 파티를 열 것을 허락해주었다.
    (allowed, hold, they, to, in their garden, the party, us)
    ➡ _____

4   Mike는 Ted가 그의 셔츠를 입고 있는 것을 알아차렸다.
    (Mike, his shirt, Ted, noticed, wearing)
    ➡ _____

5   언제 Eric이 떠나는지 나에게 알려주세요.
    (Eric, will, when, let, leave, know, please, me)
    ➡ _____

6   그녀는 남편이 전등을 고치는 것을 도왔다.
    (the light, her husband, helped, she, fix)
    ➡ _____

7   Tim은 나에게 우리의 여름방학 일정을 확인하게 했다.
    (Tim, me, schedule, made, our summer vacation, check)
    ➡ _____

6-10 원형부정사

> • **원형부정사**: 사역동사와 지각동사의 목적격보어 역할을 한다.

1. 사역동사: have, make, let

- Edison's mother **made** him **become** a great inventer.
- Sumin **helped** an old man **(to) go** to the post office.
- ➡ 'help'는 목적격보어로 to부정사와 원형부정사 모두 사용할 수 있다.

2. 지각동사: see, watch, hear, feel

- I **saw** the police officer **run** after the thief.
- He **felt** the mood of the room **change**.
  - ➡ 지각동사의 목적어의 동작이 <u>진행 중임을 강조할 때</u>는 현재분사형을 사용하기도 한다.
- She **heard** Jason **shouting** in the hall.

Answer Keys p. 32

A 다음 주어진 단어를 이용하여 문장을 완성하시오.

1 Cindy didn't help her mom _(to) do_ the dishes. (do)

2 I saw the tower _____. (shake)

3 Hana's mom made her _____ a famous architect. (become)

4 She got her son _____ a diary every day. (write)

5 We could hear the baby _____. (cry)

6 Mom let me _____ to the gym to exercise. (go)

7 I watched my son _____ the flowers. (water)

8 I helped Jina _____ the exam. (pass)

9 She saw the dog _____ down the street. (run)

10 They helped the old woman _____ the cart. (move)

Practice More Ⅱ

Answer Keys p. 32~33

A   다음 중 to부정사의 용법이 같은 문장끼리 연결하시오.

1   I was happy to see you again.

2   Harry took a taxi not to be late.

3   Philip grew up to be a movie star.

4   The water in this bottle is cold to drink.

ⓐ She was shocked to know her grade.

ⓑ Sam woke up to find himself famous.

ⓒ This dictionary is comfortable to use.

ⓓ You have to go to sleep now to get up early.

B   괄호 안에서 알맞은 것을 고르시오.

1   I heard the baby (cry / to cry).

2   Tim let her (clean / to clean) her room.

3   Linda expects me (to buy / buy) that necklace.

4   Jenny is (too / to) young to watch the movie.

5   Tim helped his son (making / to make) a wooden table.

6   You are (enough smart / smart enough) to pass the exam.

7   John worked hard in order (succeeding / to succeed).

8   It's very rude (of / for) her not to say sorry to him.

9   I was so disappointed (losing / to lose) the game.

10   They had Tom (doing / do) his homework.

C 주어진 단어를 알맞게 배열하시오.

1 (it, too, wear, is, to, small).

➡ _____ *It is too small to wear.* _____

2 (hot, it, swim, in the sea, enough, is, to)

➡ _____

3 (ran, the, catch, I, train, to)

➡ _____

4 (went, our, the museum, do, to, homework, to)

➡ We _____

5 (let, the watch, how, me, fix, know, to)

➡ Mr. Park _____

6 (they, dance, saw, the boy)

➡ _____ on the stage.

7 (saved, John's, to, I, album, money, buy)

➡ _____

8 (made, when, the letter, it, cry, read, me, I)

➡ _____

9 (Joe, to, stupid, the rumor, was, believe, enough)

➡ _____

10 (was, his, it, remember, easy, Mina, to, name, for)

➡ _____

D 다음 문장에서 어법상 어색한 것을 찾아 바르게 고치시오.

1 I want you come early. ___come___ ➡ ___to come___

2 He is enough strong to move the box.

_____ ➡ _____

3 It is to late to meet Jane. _____ ➡ _____

4 I asked her buying a new jacket.

_____ ➡ _____

5   The boy is too tired to doing his homework.

　　　　　　　　　　＿＿＿＿＿＿＿ ➡ ＿＿＿＿＿＿＿

6   Inho heard the baby cried.　＿＿＿＿＿＿＿ ➡ ＿＿＿＿＿＿＿

7   Let me to know how to get an A on the test.

　　　　　　　　　　　　　　　 ➡ ＿＿＿＿＿＿＿

8   It was difficult of me to answer the question.

　　　　　　　　　　＿＿＿＿＿＿＿ ➡ ＿＿＿＿＿＿＿

9   She ordered Jack sitting down.

　　　　　　　　　　＿＿＿＿＿＿＿ ➡ ＿＿＿＿＿＿＿

10 Peter told me listening to the music.

　　　　　　　　　　＿＿＿＿＿＿＿ ➡ ＿＿＿＿＿＿＿

E   다음 우리말 해석에 맞게 주어진 단어를 이용하여 문장을 완성하시오.

1   나는 혼자 여행을 다닐 만큼 나이가 들었다. (enough to)
➡ ＿＿＿＿＿＿I'm old enough to travel alone.＿＿＿＿＿＿

2   Judy는 그 강의를 이해하기가 어려웠다.
(difficult, to understand, lecture)
➡ ＿＿＿＿＿＿＿＿＿＿＿＿＿＿＿＿＿＿＿

3   그녀는 그 램프를 사기 위해 상점에 갔다. (store, to buy)
➡ ＿＿＿＿＿＿＿＿＿＿＿＿＿＿＿＿＿＿＿

4   의자가 너무 낡아서 앉을 수 없었다. (too~to, sit on)
➡ ＿＿＿＿＿＿＿＿＿＿＿＿＿＿＿＿＿＿＿

5   엄마가 나에게 방 청소를 시켰다. (had, clean)
➡ ＿＿＿＿＿＿＿＿＿＿＿＿＿＿＿＿＿＿＿

6   나는 약속을 잊지 않기 위해 메모를 해 두었다.
(in order to, not, appointment)
➡ ＿＿＿＿＿＿＿＿＿＿＿＿＿＿＿＿＿＿＿

7   그 영화는 너무 폭력적이어서 아이들이 볼 수 없다.
(too, violent, for children)
➡ ＿＿＿＿＿＿＿＿＿＿＿＿＿＿＿＿＿＿＿

Answer Keys p. 33

내신 최다 출제 유형

01 다음 밑줄 친 부분 중 어법상 바르지 <u>않은</u> 것을 고르시오   [출제 예상 90%]

① The way <u>to get</u> to City Hall is not far.
② She has many friends <u>to help</u> her.
③ It's time <u>to go</u> to bed.
④ We have a house <u>to live</u>.
⑤ Andy doesn't have friends <u>to play with</u>.

02 다음 빈칸에 들어갈 말이 알맞게 짝지어진 것을 고르시오.   [출제 예상 80%]

- It was stupid _____ him to let them play outside.
- It's not difficult _____ me to run fast.

① of – of   ② for – for   ③ of – for
④ for – of   ⑤ for – to

03 다음 중 밑줄 친 부분의 쓰임이 나머지 넷과 <u>다른</u> 것을 고르시오.   [출제 예상 90%]

① We need chairs <u>to sit</u> on.
② Can I have some water <u>to drink</u>?
③ She needs someone <u>to help</u> her.
④ I am going out <u>to play</u> basketball.
⑤ They need some food <u>to eat</u>.

04 다음 주어진 문장의 밑줄 친 부분과 쓰임이 같은 것을 <u>모두</u> 고르시오.   [출제 예상 85%]

I went to the flower shop <u>to buy</u> some carnations for mom.

① Janet has many things <u>to buy</u> for the party.
② She wants <u>to be</u> a dancer.
③ We'll go to England <u>to visit</u> our uncle and aunt.
④ <u>To get</u> a good job is working diligently.
⑤ I'm so glad <u>to see</u> you again.

05 Which has a <u>different</u> usage from the others?   [출제 예상 90%]

① The only way <u>to have</u> friends is to be honest.
② He has a good room <u>to study</u> in.
③ I turned on the computer <u>to check</u> my email.
④ This is the best way <u>to get</u> there.
⑤ Do you have something interesting <u>to read</u>?

06 Choose the one which has the same usage as 'to study.'   [출제 예상 90%]

Marian went to the library <u>to study</u> for the exam.

① We have no money <u>to give</u> them.
② My dream is <u>to be</u> a lawyer.
③ We do our best <u>to solve</u> the problem.
④ They are planning <u>to go</u> to the prom.
⑤ It is exciting <u>to go</u> to a concert.

Note   **prom** 졸업 댄스파티

[01~05] 다음 빈칸에 들어갈 말로 알맞은 것을 고르시오.

01

> Dad told us _____ watching TV.

① stopping ② stop ③ stopped
④ to stop ⑤ stops

02

> Please let me _____ her phone number.

① know ② knew ③ knowing
④ to know ⑤ knows

03

> The blue dress made me _____ better.

① looked ② looking ③ look
④ to look ⑤ looks

04

> We are ready _____ the sea.

① take ② took ③ taking
④ to take ⑤ taken

Note   take the sea 승선하다

05

> She did a lot of research _____ a good place to travel.

① choose ② chose ③ chosing
④ chooses ⑤ to choose

[06~08] 다음 주어진 문장의 밑줄 친 부분과 용법이 같은 것을 고르시오.

06

> I study English to read books in English.

① She needs something to eat.
② It is exciting to play the drum.
③ I want to be a scientist.
④ He is going to school to study.
⑤ Mina likes to take care of pets.

07

> There is a good way to protect the mountain.

① We have a puppy to play with.
② He decided to study hard.
③ Jinny wants to get a good job.
④ Some men came to clean the building.
⑤ We hope to meet the celebrity.

Note   celebrity 유명인사, 명사

08

> My dad has some books to buy.

① We wish to travel around the world.
② I went to the cafe to see the events.
③ It's fun to study foreign languages.
④ Give her something to drink.
⑤ James hopes to meet her at the party.

[09~10] 다음 문장의 빈칸에 공통으로 들어갈 알맞은 단어를 고르시오.

09
- It is rude _____ them not to say a word.
- It is very kind _____ you to help us.

① for   ② at   ③ to
④ on   ⑤ of

10
- We'd love _____ watch soccer games.
- Anna is expecting _____ go shopping with her boyfriend.

① of   ② for   ③ to
④ with   ⑤ at

[11~12] 다음 중 어법상 어색한 문장을 고르시오.
★★★
11
① James is planning to take a trip to Germany.
② There are a lot of places to visit in Korea.
③ What should I do sing well?
④ Would you like to have some cookies?
⑤ She was never late for school.

★★★
12
① We are so tired to go there.
② That room is large enough for us to use it.
③ Harry is smart enough to understand it.
④ She is rich enough to buy the house.
⑤ The file is too big to send by email.

[13~15] 다음 중 밑줄 친 부분의 쓰임이 나머지 넷과 다른 것을 고르시오.

13
① They tried hard to help the poor.
② Miran had to work hard to support her family.
③ To save money, I usually take the bus.
④ I worked hard to pass the exam.
⑤ To see is to believe.

14
① She begins to clean the room.
② Marian has no time to waste playing with friends.
③ Would you like to have tea with me?
④ It is not easy to follow the rules.
⑤ The players want to play for a stronger team.

★★★
15
① They studied hard to pass the exam.
② We went to England to study English.
③ She wanted to meet him.
④ We went to the market to buy some vegetables.
⑤ She cleaned the oven to bake a brownie.

[16~17] 다음 중 빈칸에 들어갈 단어가 나머지와 다른 것을 고르시오.

16
① It's important _____ me to do my best.
② It's hard _____ her to tell them the truth.
③ It's not easy _____ her to live by herself.
④ It's very nice _____ you to take care of your little brothers.
⑤ It's too heavy _____ me to carry.

17
① It was selfish _____ her to have all dresses.
② It is possible _____ him to disappear suddenly.
③ It was stupid _____ me to act like that.
④ It is kind _____ them to find a lost kid's parents.
⑤ It is silly _____ him to make the same mistake.

[18~20] 다음 중 어법상 바르게 쓰인 문장을 고르시오. (답이 두 개일 경우 모두 표시하시오.)

18
① Dad wanted me to clean my room.
② He wants Jenny staying home.
③ Our teacher wanted everyone be on time.
④ Mary wanted he to play the piano for me.
⑤ Does he want us leaving?

★★★
19
① We are watching water to change into ice.
② She felt someone touch her shoulder.
③ They were listening to the singer to sing a theme song on the stage.
④ I am watching her going out of the house.
⑤ I heard someone to call my name.

★★★
20
① Kelly helped the children doing their homework.
② Our parents let us going out to play.
③ She had the waiter set the table.
④ She let him to see the movie.
⑤ I made my sister cleaning her room.

21 다음 주어진 문장의 밑줄 친 it과 쓰임이 같은 것을 고르시오.

> It is very good to go to bed early at night.

① It is snowing now.
② It's February 14th.
③ What is it?
④ We bought it yesterday.
⑤ It is exciting to play squash tennis.

[22~23] 다음 글에서 어법상 어색한 것을 고르시오.

22

> ① That was a great opportunity ② for ③ me ④ to succeed ⑤ as a writer.

23

> ① It is necessary ② for people ③ to memorizing expressions ④ in Spanish ⑤ to speak well.

24 다음 중 빈칸에 to를 쓸 수 없는 문장을 고르시오.

① I am looking for friends who would like _____ share things.
② We need _____ warm place located in Moscow.
③ They planned _____ hold festivals for children.
④ We want _____ learn the guitar.
⑤ Willy managed _____ defend the Universiade.

Note   **Universiade** 국제 학생 경기 대회 (**World University Games**)

25 다음 문장을 영어로 바르게 옮긴 것을 고르시오.

> 나는 자원봉사를 하기 위해 양로원을 갔다.

① I went to asylum the aged to do volunteer work.
② I went to an asylum the aged do volunteer work.
③ I went to an asylum the aged do volunteer working.
④ I went to an asylum the aged to do volunteer work.
⑤ I went to asylum the aged to doing volunteer work.

Note an asylum the aged 양로원

[26~27] 다음 문장의 빈칸에 들어갈 알맞은 표현을 고르시오.

26

> We're sure where to go.
> = We're sure _____.

① where should we go
② where we should go
③ should we go to where
④ we should to go
⑤ where for we to go

27

> Jessy hasn't decided what she should wear at the party.
> = Jessy hasn't decided _____ at the party.

① to wear   ② what wear
③ what   ④ wear to do
⑤ what to wear

[28~29] 다음 주어진 문장을 to부정사를 이용하여 바르게 쓴 것을 고르시오.

★★★
28

> Mr. Black is so strict that others can't say, "No."

① He is too strict not to say, "No."
② He is too strict to say, "No."
③ He is too strict to not say, "No."
④ He is strict enough to say, "No."
⑤ He is enough strict to say, "No."

★★★
29

> children enjoy Songpyeon because it is so delicious.

① Songpyeon is delicious for the children to enjoy.
② Songpyeon is delicious enough to children to enjoy.
③ Songpyeon is delicious enough for the children can enjoy.
④ Songpyeon is delicious enough for the children to enjoy.
⑤ Songpyeon is delicious enough the children enjoying.

30 다음 빈칸에 들어갈 말이 나머지 넷과 다른 것을 고르시오.

① Jimmy was _____ busy to stop by me.
② He is fast _____ to be a soccer player.
③ She is _____ diligent to get up late.
④ Saran ran _____ fast to be followed by others.
⑤ I am _____ sleepy to focus on his work.

31 다음 중 어법상 옳지 <u>않은</u> 것을 <u>모두</u> 고르시오.

① Jeremy continued listening to music.
② Helen wanted buy a new pair of mittens.
③ She decided leaving school.
④ She promised to be here tomorrow.
⑤ We began attending the meeting.

32 다음 문장의 빈칸에 들어갈 말로 알맞은 것을 고르시오.

> Jacky and Max are going to be all right. Tell their teachers _____ about them.

① worry　　　　② to worry
③ not worry　　④ to not worry
⑤ not to worry

★★★
33 다음 중 어법상 바른 문장을 <u>모두</u> 고르시오.

① I haven't decided when to start yet.
② We don't know where meet them.
③ Jason is sure how to get there.
④ Whom go with is the matter.
⑤ Mrs. White seems to know what to doing.

[34~35] 다음 문장의 빈칸에 들어갈 알맞은 말을 고르시오.

34
> A I don't know _____ to do for them.
> B Then, you should surf the Internet first.

① that　　　② why　　　③ what
④ how　　　⑤ where

35
> We don't know _____ play chess. Can you tell us the rules?

① what to　　② how to　　③ where to
④ why to　　⑤ when to

◇◇◇◇◇◇◇◇◇ **서술형 평가** ◇◇◇◇◇◇◇◇◇

[36~37] 주어진 두 문장의 뜻이 같도록 빈칸에 들어갈 알맞은 말을 쓰시오.

36
> To read and write French is not easy.
> = _____ is not easy to read and write French.

➡ _____

37
> Jamie wanted to buy some fruit, so she went to the market.
> = Jamie went to the market _____ some fruit.

➡ _____

[38~39] 주어진 우리말과 같은 뜻이 되도록 괄호 안의 단어를 바르게 배열하여 문장을 완성하시오.

38
> 여행 가방은 그녀가 들기에 너무 무거웠다.
> ➡ The suitcase was (too / lift / for / to / her / heavy).

➡ _____

39

그들은 하늘을 날고 싶어 한다.

➡ They (sky / to / in / like / fly / the / would).

➡ _____

[40~41] 다음 괄호 안의 단어를 알맞게 배열하여 문장을 완성하시오.

40

The park keeper (people / to / keep / told / away) the grass.

➡ _____

(Note)   park keeper 공원 관리인
keep away 떨어지다, 가까지 하지 않다.

41

I'm sorry. I (didn't / make / you / mean / to / angry).

➡ _____

[42~43] 주어진 우리말에 맞게 지시어를 따라 올바른 문장으로 영작하시오.

★★★
42

그 농부는 그들에게 약간의 블루베리를 딸 수 있도록 허락했다.

〈조건〉 'the farmer, allow, blueberries, pick'을 포함한 to부정사 문장으로 만드시오.

➡ _____

★★★
43

나는 무슨 말을 해야 할지 모르겠다.

〈조건〉 to부정사와 의문사를 넣어서 7단어 이내로 문장을 만드시오.

➡ _____

[44~45] 다음 그림의 주어진 상황에 맞는 문장을 영어로 쓰시오.

★★★
44

(too / Alex/ small / put / to / on / for / is)

➡ This shirt _____ .

★★★
45

(the barbell / lift / strong / is / enough / to)

➡ The man _____ .

Note

07
Chapter
동명사

Point Check I

◆ **동명사:** '동사＋ing'의 형태로 명사 역할을 한다.
'～함, ～하기'의 뜻을 가지며, 문장에서 주어, 보어, 목적어의 역할을 한다.

1. 동명사의 형태: [동사원형 + ing]

2. 동명사의 역할

주어 역할 [～하는 것은]	• Cooking Korean food is not easy. = It is not easy to cook Korean food. ➡ 동명사 문장은 'It ～ to부정사' 용법으로 전환할 수 있다.
보어 역할[～하기, ～하는 것]	• Tommy's hobby is solving riddles.
목적어 역할[～하는 것을, ～하기를]	• He imagines being a movie star.

3. 동명사를 목적어로 쓰는 동사

enjoy	즐기다	mind	신경을 쓰다	keep	유지하다	finish	끝내다
practice	연습하다	deny	부정하다	imagine	상상하다	quit	그만두다

4. 동명사와 to부정사의 사용에 따라 의미가 달라지는 동사들

try＋동명사	• (시험 삼아) ～해 보다	forget＋동명사	• ～한 것을 잊다 (이미 완료된 행동)
try＋to부정사	• ～하려고 노력하다, 애쓰다	forget＋to부정사	• ～할 것을 잊다 (완료되지 않은 것)
remember＋동명사	• ～한 것을 기억하다 (이미 완료된 행동)	stop＋동명사	• ～하는 것을 멈추다
remember＋to부정사	• ～할 것을 기억하다 (완료되지 않은 것)	stop＋to부정사	• ～하기 위해 멈추다

5. 동명사의 의미상의 주어와 생략

의미상의 주어	동명사의 의미상의 주어는 소유격 또는 목적격 인칭 대명사가 온다.
	• Jerry was sure of her breaking the vase.
의미상의 주어 생략하기	의미상의 주어가 문장의 주어, 목적어와 같을 때, 또는 의미상 주어가 불특정한 일반인일 때 생략할 수 있다.
	• They are afraid of (their / them) bungee jumping. [의미상의 주어＝문장 주어]

동명사의 쓰임

- **동명사**: 동사로 만든 명사의 형태를 말한다.
  동사의 끝에 'ing'를 붙여서 만들며, '~함, ~하기'로 해석한다. 명사처럼 문장의 주어, 보어, 목적어로 쓰이기도 하며, 동사의 성질도 지니고 있으므로 뒤에 목적어나 보어를 가질 수도 있다.

1. 동명사의 형태: [동사원형＋ing] ~하기, ~함

2. 주어로 쓰이는 동명사

- **Playing** musical instruments is very interesting.

  = **It**'s very interesting **to play** musical instruments.

  ➡ • 동명사의 주어는 부정사처럼 단수 취급해 준다.
  • 동명사가 주어로 쓰여진 문장은 'It ~ to부정사'의 문장으로 바꾸어 쓸 수 있으며, 이때 'it'은 가짜 주어이고, to부정사가 진짜 주어이다.

3. 보어로 쓰이는 동명사

- Mike's hobby is **collecting** miniature cars.

  = Mike's hobby is **to collect** miniature cars.

  ➡ 동명사는 'to부정사'의 문장으로 바꾸어 쓸 수 있다.

4. 목적어로 쓰이는 동명사

- Lee continues **learning** magic tricks.

  = Lee continues **to learn** magic tricks.

5. 동명사의 부정형: [not (never)＋동명사]

- I imagined **not flying** into the sky. [동명사 이하를 부정]
- I **didn't imagine flying** into the sky. [동사 이하를 부정]

Answer Keys p. 35

A 괄호 안에서 알맞은 것을 고르시오.

1 (Making / Make) a new friend is fun.

2 (Exercise / Exercising) regularly is important.

3 Seeing is (belief / believing).

4 Her hobby is (play / playing) the violin.

5 You are good at (speaking / speak) English very well.

6 Shouting aloud on top of the mountain (relieves / relieve) the stress.

7 My sister's dream is (being / be) a nurse.

8   His job is (making / makes) movies.

9   It is very difficult (solve / solving) the problem without hints.

10 His wish is (travel / traveling) all around the world next year.

B   다음 문장에서 어법상 <u>어색한</u> 것을 찾아 바르게 고치시오.

1   Ride a bike without a helmet is dangerous.

_____Ride_____ ➡ _____Riding_____

2   His goal is travel abroad this year.

_____ ➡ _____

3   James enjoys to go skiing with his family.

_____ ➡ _____

4   I really feel like get away from everyday life.

_____ ➡ _____

5   Nick's dream is be a policeman.

_____ ➡ _____

6   My hobby is knit sweaters.

_____ ➡ _____

7   I denied accepting not her proposal.

_____ ➡ _____

8   Exercising not regularly makes us fat.

_____ ➡ _____

9   Working everyday make me exhausted.

_____ ➡ _____

10 My bad habit is often act thoughtlessly.

_____ ➡ _____

11 Setting priorities are really important.

_____ ➡ _____

12 Play alone feels lonely.

_____ ➡ _____

13 Sammy's wish is not get a low score on the test.

_____ ➡ _____

동명사를 목적어로 쓰는 동사

• 동명사가 동사 뒤에서 목적어의 역할을 하며 '~하기를, ~하는 것을'이라고 해석하며, 동명사만을 목적어로 취하는 동사들이 있다.

1. 동명사가 목적어로 오는 동사

enjoy	mind	finish	stop	keep	practice	give up
deny	imagine	quit	suggest	dislike	put off	

• Jerry **practices** folk **dancing** every Sunday.

• When do you **finish cooking** dinner?

• Do you **mind going** up the stairs?

Grammar Plus +

• **to** 부정사만을 목적어로 갖는 동사

want, hope, expect, decide, need, plan, promise, refuse, learn, agree, wish, would like

Check up!

Answer Keys p. 35

A 괄호 안의 동사를 알맞은 형태로 바꾸어 빈칸에 쓰시오.

1 Please let me know if Jim stops _____playing_____ the computer game. (play)

2 Charley eventually gave up _____ an actor. (be)

3 He doesn't mind _____ our travel plans. (change)

4 Did she finish _____ her house? (clean)

5 Linda suggested _____ out tonight. (eat)

6 Can you imagine _____ like a bird? (fly)

7 She denied _____ to the library yesterday. (go)

8 Mom dislikes me _____ in my room. (litter)

9 Sam and I practiced _____ soccer everyday. (play)

10 They put off _____ hiking. (go)

11 David suggests _____ in the countryside. (live)

12 Selena quit _____ the math class. (take)

> **Note**
>
> • **litter** 어지르다

7-3 동명사와 to부정사의 동사

· **동명사와 to부정사의 동사**: 일부 동사는 목적어로 동명사와 to부정사를 둘 다 사용할 수 있다.
둘을 모두 사용했을 때 동사의 뜻이 같은 것도 있고, 다른 것도 있다.

1. 의미에 변화가 없는 동사

like	love	hate	begin	start	continue	intend

· Jerry and Maria **like to play** tennis after school.

= Jerry and Maria **like playing** tennis after school.

· The man **loves to write** poems to his lover.

The man **loves writing** poems to his lover.

2. 의미가 각각 다른 동사

try	+동명사	(시험 삼아) ~해 보다	· I tried taking the TOFEL exam.
	+to부정사	~하려고 노력하다 애쓰다	· I tried to take the TOFEL exam.
remember	+동명사	~한 것을 기억하다 (이미 완료된 행동)	· She remembered reading a book to kids.
	+to부정사	~할 것을 기억하다 (완료되지 않은 것)	· She remembered to read a book to kids.
forget	+동명사	~한 것을 잊다 (이미 완료된 행동)	· He forgot drying the laundry.
	+to부정사	~할 것을 잊다 (완료되지 않은 것)	· He forgot to dry the laundry.
stop	+동명사	~하는 것을 멈추다	· We stopped talking with them.
	+to부정사	~하기 위해 멈추다	· We stopped to talk with them.

A 다음 괄호에서 알맞은 것을 <u>모두</u> 찾으시오.

1 I like (to make / making) new friends.

2 Do you remember (visiting / to visit) your grandparents' house last week?

3 You should stop (to talk / talking) about my personal life.

4 Jane starts (to jog / jogging) every morning.

5 He forgot (to lock / locking) the door, so he returned home quickly.

6 I tried (to get / getting) a good result on the graduation test.

7 We hate (to spend / spending) a lot of money on parties.

8 They stopped (to buy / buying) something to drink on the way home.

9 She tried (changing / to changing) her hair color.

10 They continued (to work / working) until midnight.

B 다음 문장을 우리말로 해석하시오.

1 They stopped fighting.
   ➡ _____그들은 싸움을 멈췄다._____

2 John forgot to close the window before he left.
   ➡ _____

3 Emma remembered to proctor the English exam.
   ➡ _____

4 Helen tried calling him.
   ➡ _____

5 You should try to do your best.
   ➡ _____

Note
• **proctor** 시험 감독하다

7-4 동명사의 의미상의 주어와 부정

• **동명사의 의미상의 주어**: 문장의 주어와 동명사의 주어가 다를 경우 동명사의 주어는 소유격이나 목적격을 쓰고, 주어가 같을 경우 동명사의 주어는 생략한다.

1. 동명사의 의미상의 주어

➡ 동사의 성질을 가지고 있으므로 이에 대한 행위의 주어를 의미상의 주어라 한다.

• Monica is sure of **my / me** teaching English well. (문장의 주어: Monica, teaching의 주어: my / me)

2. 동명사의 의미상 주어의 생략

(1) 동명사의 의미상의 주어와 <u>문장의 주어가 같을</u> 때

• He is proud of **passing** the exam.

(2) 동명사의 의미상 주어가 <u>목적어와 같을</u> 때

• Jessy thanks them for **helping** her.

(3) 동명사의 의미상 주어가 <u>불특정한 일반인일</u> 때

• **Speaking** other languages well is not easy.

Check up!

Answer Keys p. 35

A 다음 문장에서 밑줄 친 동명사의 의미상의 주어를 찾아 쓰시오.

1 Do you mind my(me) <u>playing</u> the piano at night? ___my(me)___

2 She dislikes Jimmy's <u>spending</u> money on clothes. _____

3 I thank him for <u>helping</u> me. _____

4 They aren't used to her <u>talking</u> like that. _____

B 다음 문장에서 어법상 <u>어색한</u> 것을 찾아 바르게 고치시오.

1 He doesn't mind Lina's to ask for a favor.

___to ask___ ➡ ___asking___

2 She is sure of he preparing a surprise party.

_____ ➡ _____

3 Yohan apologizes for not come early.

_____ ➡ _____

4 Kate is proud of her danced in front of an audience.

_____ ➡ _____

Practice More I

Answer Keys p. 35~36

A 다음 밑줄 친 부분을 바르게 고치시오.

1 <u>Be</u> quiet in the library is necessary.

➡ _____*Being*_____

2 My hobby was <u>assembled</u> the parts of the machine.

➡ _____

3 He enjoyed <u>to bake</u> bread for his family.

➡ _____

4 I think <u>tell</u> the truth is important.

➡ _____

5 He avoided <u>to wear</u> the same clothes.

➡ _____

6 You should finish <u>to write</u> the book.

➡ _____

7 <u>Swim</u> in the sea requires practice.

➡ _____

8 He didn't mind <u>ask</u> for his test result.

➡ _____

9 They're worried about <u>to prepare</u> for the seminar.

➡ _____

10 I gave up <u>participated</u> in the contest.

➡ _____

B 두 문장의 뜻이 같도록 빈칸에 알맞은 말을 쓰시오.

1 She was surprised that she heard the news.
➡ She was surprised at ____*hearing*____ about the news.

2 I was shocked that he had an accident on the way to school.
➡ I was shocked at _____ an accident on the way to school.

3 Tim was so proud that he passed the exam.
➡ Tim was so proud of _____ the exam.

4 They were worried that I couldn't attend the seminar.

➡ They were worried about _____ the seminar.

5 Do you mind if I open the window?

➡ Do you mind _____ the window?

6 He is sure that you didn't turn in your homework.

➡ He is sure of your _____ your homework.

7 I apologized because I told a lie.

➡ I apologizied for _____ a lie.

C 다음 문장에서 어법상 어색한 것을 찾아 바르게 고치시오.

1 They enjoyed dance all night.

_____dance_____ ➡ _____dancing_____

2 What about to go shopping?

_____ ➡ _____

3 She remembered to buy a gift last night.

_____ ➡ _____

4 Are they interested in study science?

_____ ➡ _____

5 We are sure she becoming an actress in the future.

_____ ➡ _____

6 They continued talk about the rumor.

_____ ➡ _____

7 I forget telling everyone about the notice.

_____ ➡ _____

8 Mother was angry at I for not cleaning my room.

_____ ➡ _____

9 Keep to go! You will arrive at the finish line soon!

_____ ➡ _____

10 John denied make the same mistake again.

_____ ➡ _____

서술형 연습 **D**   다음 우리말 해석에 주어진 단어를 알맞게 배열하시오.

1 그녀의 직업은 학생들에게 수학을 가르치는 일이다.
(Her, students, job, to, is math teaching)

➡ _____ *Her job is teaching math to students.* _____

2 규칙적으로 운동하는 것은 나를 건강하게 한다.
(Exercising, healthy, regularly, me, makes)

➡ _____

3 나는 그녀가 그렇게 행동하는 것을 참을 수 없다.
(her, like that, I, acting, stand, can't)

➡ _____

4 한 남자가 길을 물어보기 위해 걸음을 멈추었다.
(a, for, man, walking, to, stopped, ask, directions)

➡ _____

5 그들은 Tim이 시험에 합격하기를 기대하고 있다.
(passing, are, the exam, looking forward to, Tim's, they)

➡ _____

6 그의 취미는 정물화를 그리는 것이다.
(His hobby, painting, is, still‒lifes)

➡ _____

7 나는 그 영화를 만드는 것을 연기해야 했다.
(had to, put off, the, I, movie, making)

➡ _____

8 단지 보는 것만으로도 많은 것을 배울 수 있다.
(you, watching, just, can, by, a lot, learn)

➡ _____

9 나는 시험 삼아 새로운 오븐을 사 보았다.
(new oven, a, buying, tried, I)

➡ _____

10 우리가 이 전화기를 좀 써도 될까요?
(Do, this phone, mind, you, us, using)

➡ _____

Point Check II

◆ 오랫동안 사용해 오던 것이 그대로 규칙으로 굳어져 버린 표현들이 있으며, 이들 뒤에는 반드시 '동명사'를 사용해 준다.

◈ 동명사의 숙어 표현

1	be excited about -ing	~에 대해 흥분하다
2	be good at -ing	~을 잘하다
3	be interested in -ing	~에 관심 있다
4	be responsible for -ing	~에 책임이 있다
5	be surprised at -ing	~에 대해 놀라다
6	be tired of -ing	~을 지겨워하다
7	be worried about -ing	~에 대해 걱정하다
8	feel like -ing	~하고 싶다
9	look forward to -ing	~을 고대하다
10	on -ing	~하자마자
11	thank ... for -ing	~에 대해 ...에게 감사하다
12	object to -ing	~에 반대하다
13	keep (prevent / stop) A from -ing	A가 ~하는 것을 막다 (못하게 하다)
14	be used to -ing	~하는 데 익숙하다
15	be busy -ing	~하느라 바쁘다
16	be worth -ing	~할 만한 가치가 있다
17	cannot help -ing = cannot but+동사원형	~하지 않을 수 없다
18	go -ing	~하러 가다
19	have trouble (in) -ing	~하는 데 어려움을 겪다
20	How / What about -ing? = What do you say to -ing?	~하는 게 어때?
21	It's no use -ing	~해 봐야 소용없다
22	need -ing = need to be + 과거분사	~할 필요가 있다
23	spend + ... (in) -ing	~하느라 ... 을 소비하다
24	There is no -ing = It is impossible to + 동사원형	~하는 것은 불가능하다

7-5 동명사의 숙어 표현 (1)

1	be excited about -ing ~에 대해 흥분하다
	• They were really excited about riding a roller coaster.

2	be good at -ing ~을 잘하다
	• I am good at singing songs.

3	be interested in -ing ~에 관심있다
	• Is she interested in solving difficult math problems?

4	be responsible for -ing ~에 책임이 있다
	• You are responsible for building this house.

5	be surprised at -ing ~에 대해 놀라다
	• We were surprised at him showing up at the party.

6	be tired of -ing ~을 지겨워하다
	• I am really tired of reading the same book over and over again.

7	be worried about -ing ~에 대해 걱정하다
	• Jack is worried about going to work.

8	feel like -ing ~하고 싶다
	• He didn't feel like being with her any more.

9	look forward to -ing ~을 고대하다
	• She's looking forward to meeting the actor. → 여기서 쓰인 'to'는 전치사이다.

10	on -ing ~하자마자
	• On leaving there, it started raining.

11	thank ...for -ing ~에 대해 ...에게 감사하다
	• Thank you for teaching us well.

12	object to -ing ~에 반대하다
	• They objected to going hiking on the mountain.

13	keep (prevent / stop) A from -ing A가 ~하는 것을 막다 (못하게 하다)
	• The man prevented people from cutting trees.

14	be used to -ing ~하는 데 익숙하다
	• He is used to waiting for someone.

Answer Keys p. 36

A 괄호 안의 단어와 알맞은 전치사를 이용하여 문장을 완성하시오.

1 I'm excited __about going__ to the concert with him. (go)

2 Sam is interested _____. (cook)

3 My sister and I are used _____ at night. (study)

4 Sally is looking forward _____ the seminar. (attend)

5 My father is worried _____ a lot tonight. (rain)

6 Hyuk is good _____ French. (speak)

7 Thank you _____ us to your wedding anniversary party. (invite)

8 I feel _____ more. (eat)

9 The rule prevented us _____ in the hallway. (run)

10 On _____ his homework, he played the computer game. (finish)

11 They are surprised _____ him on TV. (see)

12 Father objected _____ us his old photos. (show)

13 Jane is responsible _____ too much money on the party. (spend)

14 I am used _____ a newspaper at breakfast. (read)

15 They are looking forward to _____ him again. (see)

동명사의 숙어 표현 (2)

1	be busy -ing ～하느라 바쁘다
	· I was busy cleaning my room.
2	be worth -ing ～할 만한 가치가 있다
	· Niagara Falls is worth watching.
3	cannot help -ing＝cannot but＋동사원형 ～하지 않을 수 없다
	· She cannot help worrying about her son's wound.
4	go -ing ～하러 가다
	· Tom and Mary will go shopping tomorrow.
5	have trouble (difficulty, a hard time) (in) -ing ～하는 데 어려움을 겪다
	· I had difficulty making understand her.
6	How / What about -ing?＝What do you say to -ing? ～하는게 어때?
	· How about eating out tonight?＝What do you say to eating out tonight?
7	It's no use -ing ～해 봐야 소용없다
	· It's no use regretting your mistake.
8	need -ing＝need to be＋과거분사 (～가 되어질) 필요가 있다 (수동의 의미)
	· You need going to the doctor.
9	spend＋시간(돈) (in) -ing ～하느라 …을 소비하다
	· Jack spent a lot of money buying a sports car.
10	There is no -ing＝It is impossible to＋동사원형 ～하는 것은 불가능하다
	· There is no building a big house without money.

☆Check up!

Answer Keys p. 36

A 다음 문장에서 어법상 어색한 것을 찾아 바르게 고치시오.

1 My watch needs repair. _____repair_____ ➡ _____repairing_____

2 Her books are worth to read. _____ ➡ _____

3 Mary has trouble solved this problem.

   _____ ➡ _____

4 There is passing the exam without studying hard.

   _____ ➡ _____

5 How about to develop new vaccine?

   _____ ➡ _____

Practice More II

A 다음 문장에서 어법상 <u>어색한</u> 것을 찾아 바르게 고치시오.

1 They are really excited to go hiking next week.

            <u> *to go* </u> ➡ <u> *about going* </u>

2 I'm so tired to study English.   <u>   </u> ➡ <u>   </u>

3 The storm kept us from go on a picnic last week.

            <u>   </u> ➡ <u>   </u>

4 He couldn't but buying this car.   <u>   </u> ➡ <u>   </u>

5 Your room needs to be cleaning.   <u>   </u> ➡ <u>   </u>

6 Tim is used to jog every morning.   <u>   </u> ➡ <u>   </u>

7 It's not use regretting the past.   <u>   </u> ➡ <u>   </u>

8 I feel like to eat something sweet.   <u>   </u> ➡ <u>   </u>

9 We are responsible about happening the accident.

            <u>   </u> ➡ <u>   </u>

10 I'm looking forward to see you again.

            <u>   </u> ➡ <u>   </u>

11 In finishing the project, he started playing the computer game.

            <u>   </u> ➡ <u>   </u>

12 They objected to buy the house.   <u>   </u> ➡ <u>   </u>

13 She was good to playing tennis.   <u>   </u> ➡ <u>   </u>

14 He was sorry for broken window.   <u>   </u> ➡ <u>   </u>

15 She was worried about take the English exam.

            <u>   </u> ➡ <u>   </u>

B 다음 두 문장이 같은 뜻이 되도록 빈칸을 알맞게 채우시오.

1 The window needs exchanging.

  ➡ The window needs <u> *to be exchanged* </u>.

2 Sam cannot help crying because Sally left without saying goodbye.

  ➡ Sam <u>   </u> because Sally left without saying goodbye.

3 How about knitting a sweater for him?

➡ What do you say _____ a sweater for him?

4 Linda had trouble baking a cake.

➡ Linda had a hard time _____ a cake.

5 How about going to an amusement park this weekend?

➡ Let's _____ this weekend!

➡ Shall we _____ this weekend?

➡ What do you say _____ this weekend?

C 우리말 해석에 맞도록 주어진 단어를 이용하여 문장을 완성하시오.

1 사람들은 바다에서 수영을 하느라 바빴다. (busy, swim)

➡ _____ *People were busy swimming in the sea.* _____

2 그녀에게 이 드레스를 팔아봤자 소용이 없다. (sell, dress)

➡ _____

3 우리들은 그녀에게 답장이 오기를 기대하고 있다.
(receive, a reply)

➡ _____

4 방에 들어오자마자 아기가 우는 소리가 들렸다.
(enter, hear, crying)

➡ _____

5 겨울 방학 때 유럽 여행을 가는 것이 어때?
(travel, winter vacation)

➡ _____

6 John을 말려봐야 소용없다. (try to, stop)

➡ _____

7 사람들은 그를 보고 웃지 않을 수 없었다. (laugh at)

➡ _____

8 Mike는 그 책을 구하느라 어려움을 겪고 있다. (find, the book)

➡ _____

9 우리 가족은 어디로 휴가를 떠날지에 대해 얘기하면서 아주 많은
시간을 소비했다.

(too much time, talk about, where, holiday)

➡ _____

10 그가 왜 이 집에 이사 오는 것을 거절했니? (move, this house)

➡ _____

서술형 연습 D 주어진 단어를 알맞게 배열하여 문장을 완성하시오.

1 (on, homework, my, finishing), I started to cook.

➡ _____*On finishing my homework*_____, I started to cook.

2 (our child, how about, for, writing, a fairy tale)?

➡ _____

3 I (trouble, names, had, all the students', remembering).

➡ I _____

4 My father (kept, my friends, from, with, to, the concert, going, me)

➡ My father _____

5 (that, it, no, house, use, is, buying)

➡ _____

6 (to, objected, her, suggestion, accepting, I)

➡ _____

7 (laziness, from, her, exercising, her, prevented, regularly).

➡ _____

8 (do, a party, to, for, you, making, what, say, dress, Amy)?

➡ _____

9 John (not, a suit, used, is, wearing, to)

➡ John _____

10 Mrs. Kim (worth, by, being, is, everyone, honored)

➡ Mrs. Kim _____

내신 최다 출제 유형

01 다음 중 어법상 바르지 <u>않은</u> 것을 고르시오.

[출제 예상 90%]

① I can't learn English without making mistakes.
② Sara is not good at playing the guitar.
③ You don't enjoy watching TV, do you?
④ His hobby is collecting stamps.
⑤ Eat too many sweets is not good for your health.

02 다음 밑줄 친 부분의 쓰임이 보기 와 <u>다른</u> 것을 고르시오.

[출제 예상 90%]

보기
Emma has finished <u>washing</u> the dishes.

① The most important thing is <u>staying</u> healthy.
② He practiced <u>playing</u> the drum a lot.
③ <u>Reading</u> helps you become smart.
④ Tony is interested in <u>collecting</u> toy cars.
⑤ We are <u>swimming</u> and splashing.

03 다음 주어진 우리말과 같은 뜻이 되도록 할 때 빈칸에 알맞은 말을 고르시오.

[출제 예상 85%]

그 소식을 듣자마자 나의 조카는 웃기 시작했다.
➡ On _____ the news, my nephew began to laugh.

① listen   ② hear   ③ hearing
④ heard   ⑤ listened

04 다음 중 어법상 <u>어색한</u> 것을 <u>모두</u> 고르시오.

[출제 예상 90%]

① Tommy and Sam left Korea without saying goodbye.
② We're looking forward to meet the actress.
③ She was busy doing her homework.
④ I gave up exercise every morning.
⑤ He wasn't used to carrying the boxes.

05 다음 중 밑줄 친 부분이 바르게 쓰인 것을 고르시오.

[출제 예상 90%]

① Does she mind <u>give</u> you a hand with this piano?
② Sometimes I want <u>to say</u> nothing.
③ She likes <u>eat</u> ice cream after dinner.
④ My father finished <u>to remodeling</u> the kitchen.
⑤ I planned <u>visiting</u> my grandmother's house.

06 다음 중 어법상 올바른 문장을 <u>모두</u> 고르시오.

[출제 예상 85%]

① Rebeca's dream is to become a hair designer.
② Jack hopes visiting her cousin next month.
③ They are looking forward to travel to Liverpool.
④ Would you mind to take a picture, please?
⑤ Martin went playing football with his friends.

[01~03] 다음 대화의 빈칸에 들어갈 알맞은 말을 고르시오.

01

> A Would you mind _____ down the volume a little?
> B Of course not.

① turn   ② to turn   ③ turning
④ turned   ⑤ turns

02

> A What does Emily do on weekends?
> B She enjoys _____ rafting.

① go   ② going   ③ to go
④ went   ⑤ goes

03

> A Hi, there. How have you been?
> B Very good. I was looking forward _____ you.

① see   ② seeing   ③ to see
④ sees   ⑤ to seeing

04 ★★★ 다음 중 어법상 올바른 문장을 <u>모두</u> 고르시오.

① She doesn't feel like to talk to us.
② I want changing the schedule.
③ We decided taking the subway to the gym.
④ They denied stealing the money.
⑤ Would you mind turning off the radio?

05 다음 밑줄 친 부분의 쓰임이 나머지 넷과 <u>다른</u> 것을 고르시오.

① Jenny's hobby is playing badminton.
② Benny is reading a book now.
③ She stopped crying.
④ We enjoy jogging every morning.
⑤ Hansu likes taking pictures.

06 ★★★ 다음 밑줄 친 부분의 쓰임이 <u>잘못된</u> 것을 고르시오.

① Jason and Lina love writing letters.
② They finished having lunch.
③ I practiced to play the drum.
④ He likes to go skating.
⑤ Eddie wants to be an engineer.

07 다음 빈칸에 들어갈 말이 알맞게 짝지어진 것을 고르시오.

> _____ English TV programs _____ you improve your English.

① To watch − help
② Watching − helps
③ Watching − to help
④ To watch − to help
⑤ Watching − helping

[08~09] 다음 우리말을 영어로 바르게 옮긴 것을 고르시오.

★★★
08

영어로 일기를 쓰는 것은 어렵다.

① Keeping a diary in English is difficult.
② Keeping diary in English is difficult.
③ Keeping a diary is difficult in English.
④ In English keeping a diary is difficult.
⑤ Keeping an English diary is difficult.

★★★
09

집에서 새싹을 기르는 것이 유행이 되었다.

① Raising a sprouts has become popular.
② Raising sprouts in the house have become popular.
③ Raising sprouts in the house has become popular.
④ To raise sprouts in the house have becoming popular.
⑤ Raise sprouts in the house has become popular.

10 다음 문장의 <u>틀린</u> 부분을 바르게 고친 것을 고르시오.

Exercise regularly is very good for our health.

① Exercise → Exercising
② regularly → regular
③ is → are
④ good → well
⑤ health → healthy

11 다음의 두 문장이 같은 뜻이 되도록 빈칸에 알맞은 말을 고르시오.

Donna plays the cello very well.
= Donna is good _____ playing the cello.

① of   ② for   ③ to
④ at   ⑤ in

12 다음 문장 중 어법상 <u>틀린</u> 것을 <u>모두</u> 고르시오.

① My mom denied watching the magic show.
② Jinny is talking about her problems.
③ Jerry is tired of wake his sister up every morning.
④ Why don't you go home with me?
⑤ We're planning to having a surprise party for him.

[13~15] 다음 문장의 빈칸에 들어갈 알맞은 말을 고르시오.

13

They thanked me for _____ in their band.

① my join   ② I joined
③ I joining   ④ my joining
⑤ me joins

14

Josh couldn't help _____ about his friends.

① worrying   ② to worry
③ worried   ④ worries
⑤ worry

15

He is sorry for _____ us all the way.

① not help ② not helping
③ not to helping ④ helping not
⑤ to help not

[16~18] 다음 주어진 문장의 밑줄 친 부분과 쓰임이 다른 것을 고르시오.

16

What about <u>meeting</u> at the subway station?

① She's interested in <u>baking</u> cookies.
② Joshua will start <u>swimming</u> this Saturday.
③ They are <u>assembling</u> the model airplane.
④ His hobby is <u>climbing</u> mountains.
⑤ My sister loves <u>making</u> food.

17

<u>Having</u> breakfast is good for your health.

① You can solve it by <u>asking</u> your teacher for help.
② This movie is really <u>interesting</u>.
③ Gina's hobby is <u>cooking</u> Japanese food.
④ How about <u>having</u> dinner together?
⑤ My violin <u>playing</u> is not as good as hers.

18

Dave just finished <u>doing</u> his report.

① What about <u>joining</u> the reading club with me?
② They are looking forward to <u>eating</u> Thai food.
③ <u>Seeing</u> is believing.
④ I watched them <u>singing</u> on the stage.
⑤ <u>Smoking</u> inside is very bad for everyone.

[19~21] 다음 중 어법상 틀린 문장을 고르시오.

19 ① I like reading all kinds of books.
② Please stop making noise.
③ I enjoy taking a walk in the afternoon.
④ Would you mind my turning on the light?
⑤ Your friends don't want hearing an interesting story.

20 ① What do you say to swim in the river?
② Jane's father stopped smoking last month.
③ We'll try bungee jumping.
④ Sally is looking forward to his coming back.
⑤ Jenny avoided answering Tommy's question.

Note bungee jump 명 번지점프 통 번지점프를 하다

21
① On hearing the news, everyone was worried about it.
② They went shopping after lunch.
③ My baby sister began cry again.
④ This house is worth buying.
⑤ We were busy preparing for the trip.

[22~23] 다음 글의 빈칸에 들어갈 알맞은 말이 바르게 짝지어진 것을 고르시오.

22
Gloria was really excited about _____ with a foreign company. She went abroad and enjoyed _____ there.

① worked − work
② working − working
③ work − working
④ to work − work
⑤ working − worked

Note company 친구(들), 회사

23
The old woman had a habit of _____ in thought. She often walked silently without _____ anything.

① be lost − say
② be lost − saying
③ be lost − said
④ being lost − saying
⑤ being lost − to say

[24~25] 다음 우리말에 맞게 빈칸에 들어갈 알맞은 표현을 고르시오.

24
농구를 하는 것은 항상 재미있다.
➡ _____ is always exciting.

① Playing basketball
② Play basketball
③ Played basketball
④ Basketball play
⑤ Basketball to play

25
너는 그녀에게 내일 전화해야 하는 것을 기억해야 한다.
➡ You should _____ her tomorrow.

① remembering call
② remembered call
③ remember calling
④ remember call
⑤ remember to call

[26~27] 다음 문장의 밑줄 친 부분 중 잘못된 것을 고르시오.

26
① Playing tennis ② are fun, so ③ my sister and I enjoy ④ playing tennis every ⑤ night.

27
① Thank you for ② show ③ me the way ④ to the ⑤ art gallery.

[28~29] 다음 중 어법상 옳은 문장을 고르시오.

28
① He doesn't feel like to be here.
② I am interested in read a science fiction novel.
③ We're looking forward to taking a trip to Australia.
④ She was surprised at her to get first prize.
⑤ Molly is good at sings.

29
① They can't avoid going to meet her.
② On to leave, he called me.
③ The nation prevented people from hunt the animals.
④ Kelly is used to fix the broken things.
⑤ Marian objected to climb the tree.

[30~31] 다음 주어진 문장의 밑줄 친 부분과 쓰임이 같은 것을 고르시오.

★★★
30

> Larry enjoys singing songs in front of people.

① We started cooking pizza.
② Her hobby is collecting coins.
③ Rachel's goal is becoming a movie star.
④ I heard her shouting at something.
⑤ Sleeping too much is not good.

★★★
31

> Learning to love others is good for you.

① I began talking with a reporter.
② He gave up studying for the science test.
③ Playing computer games reduces his stress.
④ They like dancing so much.
⑤ Mandy finished doing her work.

★★★
32 다음 짝지어진 문장들 중 의미가 서로 다른 것을 고르시오.

① We love to meet our old friends.
   = We love meeting our old friends.
② They began to search for a lost necklace.
   = They began searching for a lost necklace.
③ Wei remembers to repair her radio.
   = Wei remembers repairing her radio.
④ Junho continues to write letters.
   = Junho continues writing letters.
⑤ They began to run.
   = They began running.

◇◇◇◇◇◇◇◇◇ 서술형 평가 ◇◇◇◇◇◇◇◇◇

[33~34] 다음의 우리말과 같은 뜻이 되도록 빈칸에 알맞은 말을 쓰시오.

33

> Sandy는 나의 편지에 답장을 해야 할 것을 잊었다.
> ➡ Sandy forgot _____ my letter.

➡ _____

34 아침에 일찍 일어나는 것은 좋은 습관이다.
(동명사)

➡ _____ up early in the morning is a good habit.

➡ _____

[35~36] 다음 문장에서 <u>틀린</u> 곳을 찾아 바르게 고쳐 쓰시오.

35 Email is a way of send messages to other countries.

➡ _____

36 It was sunny this morning. I thought of take a walk with my kid.

➡ _____

[37~39] 다음 괄호 안의 단어를 바르게 배열하여 문장을 쓰시오.

★★★
37 (problem / kind / of / discussing / worth / that / is)

➡ _____

★★★
38 (dangerous / walking / at / can / alone / night / be)

➡ _____

★★★
39 (I / too / small / skirt / but / wearing / tried / was / it / the)

➡ _____

[40~42] 다음 두 문장이 같은 뜻이 되도록 문장을 완성 하시오.

40 It is not bad to learn from your mistakes.

➡ _____

is not bad.

41 If you meet Ellen, you have to ask for her email address.

➡ Don't forget _____

42 We remember that we met him last year.

➡ We remember _____

Note

08
Chapter
분사

Point Check I

◆ **분사:** '동사원형＋ing' 또는 '동사원형＋ed'의 형태를 하고 있다.
명사를 수식하거나 주어와 목적어의 상태를 설명하는 형용사의 역할을 한다.

1. 현재분사와 과거분사

	현재분사	과거분사
형태	동사원형＋ing ～하고 있는 (진행)/～하게 하는 (능동)	동사원형＋ed, 불규칙 과거분사 ～한 (완료)/～된, ～해진 (수동)

- Jane is **baking** some bread. [baking-현재분사_진행]
- Jane watched an **interesting** movie. [interesting-현재분사_능동]
- Jimmy cleaned his **messed**-up room. [messed-과거분사_완료]
- Jimmy likes to eat **boiled** eggs. [boiled-과거분사_수동]

2. 형용사 용법의 분사 : 명사를 수식하거나 보어의 역할을 한다.

명사 수식	명사 앞	• The singing <u>bird</u> is in my cage. [singing → bird 수식]
	명사 뒤	• <u>The girl</u> wearing a yellow skirt is my best friend. [wearing a yellow skirt → the girl 수식]
보어 역할	주격보어	• <u>Tommy</u> is singing in front of people. [singing → Tommy의 상태를 설명]
	목적격보어	• They looked around the <u>room</u> cleaned. [cleaned → room의 상태를 설명]

3. 현재분사와 동명사 : [동사원형 + ing]

	현재분사	동명사
역할	형용사로서 명사를 수식하거나 보어의 역할을 한다.	명사로서 주어나 보어로 쓰이며, 동사나 전치사의 목적어 역할을 한다.
쓰임	상태, 동작 ～하는, ～하고 있는 • The crying boy is my little brother. 진행 ～하고 있는 중 • I am cooking Italian food.	목적, 용도 ～하기 위한 • I bought a new swimming suit. 주격보어 ～하는 것 • Her hobby is dancing.

8-1 분사의 종류

• 분사: 동사의 모양이 바뀐 분사는 명사를 수식하거나 주어나 목적어의 상태를 설명하는 형용사의 역할을 한다. 동사원형에 '-ing'를 붙이면 현재분사, '-ed'를 붙이면 과거분사가 된다.

◆ 현재분사와 과거분사

	현재분사	과거분사
역할	동사원형＋ing ～하고 있는 (진행) / ～하게 하는 (능동)	동사원형＋ed, 불규칙 과거분사 ～한 (완료) / ～된, ～해진 (수동)
쓰임	진행 • It was surprising to me. • She heard surprising news.	완료 • Mom cleaned the broken water jar. • A guitar string has broken.
	능동 • Jack read an interesting book. • A magician's job is interesting.	수동 • There are some boiled eggs. • The water is boiled.

Answer Keys p. 39

A 다음 괄호 안에서 알맞은 것을 고르시오.

1 They are (baking / to bake) some bread.

2 They found the vase (breaking / broken).

3 Minju has just (finished / finish) her homework.

4 They were (danced / dancing) in front of many people.

5 Rainy days makes us (depressed / depressing).

6 They saw the (rising / risen) sun.

7 People are (moved / moving) by the documentary.

Answer Keys p. 39

8   The glass is (filling / filled) with coke.

9   That movie was too (boring / bored).

10 Mom was (disappointed / disappointing) because I told a lie.

B   다음 주어진 단어를 알맞은 분사 형태로 바꾸어 문장을 완성하시오.

1   Mom moved the ___sleeping___ baby carefully. (sleep)

2   When I arrived there, she had already _____. (leave)

3   The teacher's first love story makes us _____.(excited)

4   This roller coaster is very _____, so I can't ride it. (frighten)

5   Those pictures were _____ by William. (hang)

6   He has _____ French for five years. (study)

7   Jane saw Tim _____ on the street. (walked)

8-2 명사를 꾸며주는 분사

• **명사를 꾸며주는 분사**: 형용사로 쓰여서 명사를 꾸며준다. 분사만 있을 경우 앞에서 명사를 꾸며주고, 분사 다음에 다른 말이 더 있을 경우 뒤에서 명사를 꾸며준다.

1. 명사 앞에서 수식: 분사가 단독으로 쓰일 경우

• The **singing** girl is my niece. [능동]
  (➡ girl 수식)

• Would you gather the **dried** fish? [수동]
  (➡ fish 수식)

2. 명사 뒤에서 수식

(1) 분사가 구를 이루어 수식하는 경우

• The man **standing over there** is a famous guitarist.
  (⬅ the man 수식)

• I watched the boxers **fighting in the ring** on TV.
  (⬅ boxers 수식)

(2) 의미상의 목적어, 보어가 있는 경우

• The girl **singing** the solo is Jack's girlfriend. [목적어]

• We looked at the portrait of a woman **called** Queen Elizabeth. [보어]

 **Check up!**

Answer Keys p. 39

A 다음 주어진 동사를 알맞은 형태로 바꾸어 빈칸에 쓰시오.

1 The woman ___making___ a speech is my mother. (make)

2 Her _____ wallet was found by the policeman. (steal)

3 The girl _____ a red skirt is my cousin. (wear)

4 The _____ boy was cured by Thomas. (wound)

5 I saw _____ leaves in my room. (fall)

6 He poured the _____ water into the jar. (boil)

7 Look at the cat _____ down the street. (run)

8 Jina started to raise money to help _____ animals. (abandon)

9 Do you know the girl _____ on the bench? (sit)

10 Youngnam looked at a picture _____ by Picasso. (draw)

11 The man _____ with Sara is not her boyfriend. (talk)

12 I don't buy a _____ car. (use)

8-3 보어로 쓰이는 분사

• 보어로 쓰이는 분사: 분사가 be동사나 감각동사 뒤에 나오면 주격보어로,
목적어 뒤에 나오면 목적격보어로 쓰인다.

1. 주격보어: 주어의 상태나 행동을 설명
- The scenery of the lake looks **calming**. (lake의 상태를 설명)
- Jane acted **embarrassed**. (Jane의 행동을 설명)

2. 목적격보어: 목적어의 상태나 행동을 설명
- Harry wanted his desk **cleaned** all the time. (desk의 상태를 설명)
- I fell in love with her **dancing** on the stage. (her의 행동을 설명)

Answer Keys p. 39

A 괄호 안의 동사를 알맞은 분사의 형태로 바꾸어 빈칸을 채우고 어떤 역할을 하
는지 쓰시오.

1 He looked ___*surprised*___. (surprise)   ___(주격보어)___

2 We saw the woman _____ on the street. (cry)   _____

3 She was _____ because of the movie. (fright)   _____

4 I heard my name _____. (call)   _____

5 They were _____ because of the training. (exhaust)

_____

6 That dog is _____. (scare)   _____

7 Mr. Kim kept his client _____ in the lobby. (wait)

_____

8 The dress was _____ in two. (tear)   _____

9 Tom saw the girl _____ in the park. (jog)   _____

10 Helen got her arm _____ due to the accident. (break)

_____

11 I saw the cat _____ tuna. (eat)   _____

12 He and I were _____ when we saw the play. (move)

_____

13 Jane caught the thief _____ away. (run)   _____

8-4 현재분사와 동명사

• 현재분사와 동명사: 둘 다 동사 뒤에 -ing를 붙여 사용하기 때문에 문장 안에서 쓰인 의미와 역할의 차이로 구분한다.

◈ 현재분사와 동명사

	현재분사	동명사
역할	형용사로서 명사를 수식하거나, 주어나 목적어를 설명하는 보어의 역할을 한다.	명사로서 주어나 보어로 쓰이며, 동사나 전치사의 목적어 역할을 한다.
형태	동사원형＋ing	동사원형＋ing
쓰임	〈상태, 동작〉 ~하는, ~하고 있는 • A sleeping baby is cute. 　(잠자고 있는 아기) • Sam watched a dancing robot. 　(춤추고 있는 로봇) 〈진행〉 ~하고 있는 중 • Dad is baking cookies. (Dad≠baking cookies)	〈목적, 용도〉 ~하기 위한 • I need a sleeping bag for camping. 　(침낭) • Anna bought new dancing shoes. 　(무용화) 〈주격보어〉 ~하는 것 • Dad's hobby is baking cookies. (Dad's hobby = baking cookies)

Check up!

Answer Keys p. 39

A 밑줄 친 부분의 역할이 같은 것을 보기 에서 고르시오.

> 보기
> **A** The boy is reading a book. (현재분사)
> **B** His hobby is reading. (동명사)

1 My father is having dinner. _____(A)_____

2 Her dream is traveling all over the world. _____

3 The girl playing the piano is our class president. _____

4 Tina was frightened by the barking dog. _____

5 John's job is taking a photo of a baby. _____

6 I need to buy a new swimming suit. _____

7 The woman making cookies is my aunt. _____

8 There are many delicious foods in the dining room. _____

9 Sara is jogging in the park. _____

10 His hobby is writing plays. _____

Practice More I

A 괄호 안에서 알맞은 것을 고르시오.

1 Helen is trying to find her (lost / losing) wallet.

2 I saw the boy (walking / walked) down the street.

3 My sister volunteered to care for some soldiers (wounding / wounded) in combat.

4 The bike (stolen / stealing) by Gitae was found in his garden.

5 On Jeju Island, we saw many horses (lying / laid) on the ground.

6 She was (wearing / worn) a red dress at the party.

7 Linda looks (tiring / tired) today.

8 The girl (standing / stood) in front of the building is my sister.

9 Our team must get our project (finished / finishing) by this Saturday afternoon.

10 The hunter found a deer (grazing / grazed) beside the river.

B 다음 괄호 안의 동사를 알맞은 형태로 바꿔 빈칸에 쓰시오.

1 Tim and John could not remember their ____given____ tasks. (give)

2 The officer said people should not _____ on the roadway. (walk)

3 Linda received a claim for _____ luggage from passengers. (miss)

4 I was praised for my _____ English skills by my teacher. (improve)

5 John doesn't like the recently _____ desk. (purchase)

6 Andrew was responsible for _____ items. (damage)

7 The manager _____ us is too careful. (interview)

8 We discussed the issue of _____ good habits. (have)

9 I refused to accept the project _____ by the community. (propose)

10 She is reading the article _____ in the magazine. (feature)

Note
- **volunteer** 자원하다
- **cure** 치료하다
- **in combat** 전투 중에
- **graze** 풀을 뜯다
- **roadway** 도로, 차도
- **propose** 제안하다
- **community** 지역사회,단체
- **feature** ~을 특집 기사로 다루다

C 다음 밑줄 친 부분의 쓰임이 같은 것을 보기 에서 골라 번호를 쓰시오.

보기
① Saving money is a good habit.   ② She is jogging in the park.

③ His job is making a book.   ④ I know the man talking to Lily.

⑤ She enters the waiting room.

1   Paul is making bulgogi for his mom.   ②

2   Using SNS has merits and faults.   _____

3   The woman writing the article is our chief editor.   _____

4   We need to buy a new answering machine.   _____

5   Their favorite activity is flying kites.   _____

D 다음 두 문장을 분사를 이용하여 알맞게 한 문장으로 완성하시오.

1   He bought a book. It was written by James Brown.
    ➡ _____He bought a book written by James Brown._____

2   We watched the news. That was shocking.
    ➡ _____

3   I saw the man. He was baking bread in the bakery.
    ➡ _____

4   There is a man in our company. He is called 'yes-man'.
    ➡ _____

5   The students were studying. They were sleepy.
    ➡ _____

6   The boys are exercising in the gym. They are Aron and Jim.
    ➡ _____

7   I saw the smoke. It came out of the window.
    ➡ _____

8   The roof is covered with leaves. It looks dirty.
    ➡ _____

9   They know a woman. She is cooking in the kitchen.
    ➡ _____

10 The soldiers were injured. They were taken to a hospital.
    ➡ _____

Answer Keys p. 39~40

E 우리말과 같은 뜻이 되도록 주어진 단어를 사용하여 문장을 바르게 배열하시오.

1 John이 새로 작곡한 노래는 훌륭했다.

(the, great, new, John, by, song, was, composed)

➡ _____ *The new song composed by John was great.*

2 이 케이크를 포장하자. (get, this, wrapped, let's, cake)

➡ _____

3 내 숙제는 프랑스어로 쓰인 시를 읽는 것이다.

(my, homework, French, reading, a, is, in, written, poem)

➡ _____

4 Jenny는 자기의 방이 깨끗하기를 원한다.

(cleaned, Jenny, her, wants, room)

➡ _____

5 너는 주어진 문장들을 외워야 한다.

(you, sentences, should, the, memorize, given)

➡ _____

6 인도에서 수입해온 이 그릇이 깨졌다.

(this, broken, imported, bowl, India, from, was)

➡ _____

7 나는 동물원에서 곡예를 하는 원숭이들을 보았다.

(monkeys, saw, at, I, zoo, juggling, the)

➡ _____

8 Tim은 그녀의 눈에 눈물이 가득 찬 것을 보았다.

(tears, Tim, her, saw, fill, eyes, with)

➡ _____

9 그 경찰관은 길에서 도망가는 강도를 쫓아갔다.

(the policeman, street, chased, down, away, the robber, the, running)

➡ _____

10 나는 정원에서 내 이름이 불리는 것을 들었다.

(I, garden, called, my, in, heard, the, name)

➡ _____

Point Check II

◆ **분사구문**: 접속사가 있는 부사절의 접속사와 주어를 생략하고 동사를 분사의 형태로 만들어 사용하는 문장을 말한다.

◆ **형용사로서의 분사**: 사물이 주어일 때 현재분사를 사용하며, 사람이 주어일 때는 과거분사를 사용한다.

1. 분사구문 만들기

As I don't sleep well, I am tired every day.	
• 접속사와 주어를 없앤다.	don't sleep well, I am tired every day.
• 부정형일 경우, 'not'을 문장 맨 앞으로 놓는다.	Not sleep well, I am tired every day.
• '동사+ing'의 형태를 만든다.	Not sleeping well, I am tired every day.
• **Not sleeping well, I am tired every day.**	

2. 분사구문의 시제

• 부사절과 주절의 주어가 다를 경우 <u>주어는 생략하지 않는다.</u>	• When <u>she</u> gave me a rose, <u>I</u> was so surprised. = She giving me a rose, I was so surprised.
• 부사절의 동사가 be동사일 경우 **'Be+ing'의 형태는 생략 가능**	• As she <u>was</u> excited, she laughed loudly. (Being) Excited, she laughed loudly. [→ excited – 과거분사의 형용사 역할]
• 부사절의 보어가 분사가 아닐 경우 **'being'은 생략 불가능**	• As he was <u>kind</u>, he gave me a lollipop. Being kind, he gave me a lollipop. [→ kind – 형용사]

3. with+명사+분사

• 명사와 분사의 관계가 <u>능동</u> ➡ 현재분사	• I was washing the dishes while Jerry was watching TV. ➡ I was washing the dishes, <u>with Jerry watching</u> TV. [Jerry : watching = 능동]
• 명사와 분사의 관계가 <u>수동</u> ➡ 과거분사	• She is posing for pictures, and a camera is fixed on the tripod. ➡ She is posing for pictures, with <u>a camera fixed</u> on the tripod. [a camera : fixed = 수동]

8-5 감정을 나타내는 분사

- 감정을 나타내는 현재분사와 과거분사는 사실상 형용사로 쓰인다.
- **현재분사 형용사**: 사물을 꾸미거나 사물인 주어의 상태를 나타낼 때 사용한다.
- **과거분사 형용사**: 사람을 꾸미거나 사람인 주어의 상태를 나타낼 때 사용한다.

현재분사 (-ing) ~한 감정을 느끼게 하는	과거분사 (-ed, 불규칙 과거분사) ~한 감정을 느끼는
• The math class is boring.	• I'm bored with the math class.
• What you mean is confusing.	• I'm confused about what you mean.
• That party was surprising.	• I was surprised by the party.
• Working for a long time is tiring.	• Working for a long time makes me tired.
• Rainy days are so depressing.	• Rainy days make depressed.
• The documentary movie was moving.	• I was moved by the documentary movie.
• The service at the hotel is satisfying.	• I'm satisfied with the service at the hotel.
• The magic show was amazing.	• I was amazed at the magic show.
• Meeting with him is very pleasing.	• I was pleased to meet with him.

★Check up!

Answer Keys p. 40

A 다음 주어진 단어를 문맥에 맞게 알맞은 형태로 바꾸어 문장을 완성하시오.

1 Studying all night makes me ___exhausted___. (exhaust)

2 The taste of this coffee is _____. (satisfy)

3 I was _____ with his absence. (confuse)

4 People were _____ by her performance. (move)

5 Today was _____ for me. (tire)

6 Ann was _____ because the event was canceled. (depress)

7 Her song was _____. (amaze)

8 They are _____ at his accident. (surprise)

9 The movie was too _____ for children to watch. (shock)

8-6 분사구문 (1)

> • 분사구문: 접속사가 있는 부사절의 접속사와 주어를 생략하고 분사를 사용한 형태를 말한다.

1. 분사구문 만들기

As I was left alone, I started to clean the house. [부사절이 있는 평서문]	
① 접속사 As를 없앤다.	A̶s̶ I was left alone, I started to clean the house.
② 부사절과 주절의 주어가 같을 경우, 부사절의 주어를 없앤다.	I̶ was left alone, I started to clean the house.
③ 부사절의 동사를 ing 형태로 바꾼다. (동사가 수동태일 경우 be동사＋ing)	w̶a̶s̶ left alone, I started to clean the house. was → being
➡ **Being left alone, I started to clean the house.** [분사구문]	

2. 분사구문의 의미상의 주어

(1) 의미상의 주어를 생략하는 경우

- As **she** arrived home, **she** washed her hands first.
  <u>(부사절)</u>　　　　<u>(주절)</u>
  ➡ 부사절과 주절의 주어가 같을 경우 부사절의 주어를 생략한다.
  Arriving home, **she** washed her hands first.

(2) 의미상의 주어를 쓰는 경우

- As **he** gave much homework, **I** couldn't play at all.
  <u>(부사절)</u>　　　　<u>(주절)</u>
  ➡ 부사절과 주절의 주어가 다를 경우 부사절과 주절의 주어를 모두 사용한다.
  He giving much homework, **I** couldn't play at all.

3. 분사구문의 시제

(1) 부사절과 주절의 동사의 시제가 일치하는 경우 '동사원형＋ing'를 사용한다.

(2) 부사절의 동사가 be동사인 경우 즉, 수동형 분사구문에서 'be＋ing (being)'은 생략이 가능하다

- As he was very tired, he was late for work.

  = **(Being) Tired**, he was late for work.

(3) 부사절이 2형식이고, 보어가 분사가 아닐 경우 being은 생략할 수 없다.

- As it was dark, he turned on the light.

  = **It being dark**, he turned on the light. (dark는 분사가 아닌 형용사이다.)

4. 분사구문의 부정: 분사 앞에 'not'을 붙인다.

- As I **didn't bring** any stationery, Mary lent me some.

  = **Not bringing** stationery, Mary lent me some.

Answer Keys p. 40

A 두 문장의 뜻이 같도록 분사구문을 이용하여 문장을 완성하시오.

1 While he is waiting for her, he reads the novel.

➡ ___*Waiting for her*___, he reads the novel.

2 After she cleaned my room, mom started cooking.

➡ _____ my room, mom started cooking.

3 Although she was tired, she went to the concert.

➡ _____, she went to the concert.

4 Because she woke up late today, she couldn't go on a picnic.

➡ _____ late today, she couldn't go on a picnic.

5 I lie down on my bed, and turn on the radio.

➡ I lie down on my bed, _____ the radio.

6 When she finished her homework, she could go outside.

➡ _____ her homework, she could go outside.

7 If you are interested in listening to K-pop, you may like her songs.

➡ _____ to K-pop, you may like her songs.

8 As I don't have enough time, I cannot take a nap.

➡ _____ enough time, I cannot take a nap.

9 Because she felt hungry, she began to cry.

➡ _____, she began to cry.

10 If I pass the exam, I felt entitled to a new coat.

➡ _____ the exam, I felt entitled to a new coat.

분사구문 (2)

• '접속사＋주어＋동사'와 같은 부사절의 경우 접속사와 주어를 생략한 후 분사구문으로 고칠 수 있다.

1. 시간: while, before, after, when

• **When** Anna goes to school, she takes the subway.

= **Going** to school, she takes the subway.

2. 원인, 이유: because, as, since

• **Because** he is too weak, he cannot hold heavy things.

= **Being** too weak, he cannot hold heavy things.

3. 조건: if, unless

• **If** you go straight one block, you'll see the post office.

= **Going** straight one block, you'll see the post office.

4. 양보: although, though, even if

• **Although** I wanted to talk with you, I had no courage.

= **Wanting** to talk with you, I had no courage.

5. 동시 동작: while, when, as

• **While** we walked in the park, we met Mr. Black.

= **Walking** in the park, we met Mr. Black.

6. 연속 동작: and

• Jerry lies on the bed, **and** he reads a book.

= Jerry lies on the bed, **reading** a book.

A 다음 우리말 해석에 맞게 괄호 안의 단어를 이용하여 분사구문을 완성하시오.

1 다음에 무엇을 할지 몰라서 나는 선생님을 기다렸다. (know)

➡ _____Not knowing_____ what to do next, I waited for the teacher.

2 나는 파리에 살고 있는데도 불구하고 에펠탑을 못 보았다.

➡ _____, I didn't see the Eiffel Tower. (live)

3 왼쪽으로 돌면 이탈리아 레스토랑이 하나 있을 것이다.

➡ _____, you will see an Italian restaurant. (turn)

4 그녀는 너무 어려서 학교에 갈 수 없었다. (be)

➡ _____, she couldn't go to school.

5 거리를 걸어 내려가는 동안에 나는 길을 잃은 아이를 보았다. (walk)

➡ _____ the street, I saw the lost child.

6 많은 돈이 없어서 그들은 유럽으로 여행을 가지 못했다. (have)

➡ _____ much money, they couldn't travel to Europe.

7 늦잠을 잤기 때문에 Sam은 아침을 먹지 못했다. (get up)

➡ _____, Sam couldn't eat breakfast.

8 내 남동생을 지나쳤을 때 나는 그가 방에서 자고 있던 것을 보았다. (pass)

➡ _____, I saw him sleeping.

9 너무 많은 옷이 있어서 나는 옷들을 조금 팔기로 결심했다. (have)

➡ _____, I decided to sell some of them.

10 그녀는 커피를 마시면서 그를 기다리고 있었다. (drink)

➡ She was waiting for him, _____.

8-8 with + 명사 + 분사

• 어떠한 상황에 덧붙여 따라오는 상황을 표현하며, '~한 채로, ~하는 동안'의 뜻으로 동시 동작을 나타낸다.

1. 현재분사: 명사와 분사의 관계가 능동일 경우

• I was having dinner <u>while my brother was taking a shower</u>.

= I was having dinner **with** my brother **taking** a shower. [with+명사+현재분사]
<u>(mybrother : taking = 능동)</u>

2. 과거분사: 명사와 분사의 관계가 수동일 경우

• James is painting a picture, <u>and his box of crayons is opend(open)</u>.

= James is painting a picture **with** <u>his box of crayons **opened**(open)</u>. [with+명사+과거분사]
<u>(his box of crayons : opened = 수동)</u>

Grammar Plus +

• 'with + 명사 + 분사' 구문에서 현재분사와 과거분사의 구분
명사와 분사의 관계를 '주어 + 동사'의 관계로 바꾸었을 때 능동이면 현재분사를, 수동이면 과거분사를 사용한다.
• Sam is singing a song <u>with Jenny playing the drums</u>. [능동_현재분사]
<u>(=while Jenny is playing the drums)</u>
• Paul played the drums <u>with his eyes closed</u>. [수동_과거분사]
<u>(=and his eyes were closed)</u>

※ 'open'은 동사의 뜻 외에 형용사의 뜻도 있기 때문에 '열린'이라는 의미로 사용이 가능하다. 이러한 것은 'with+명사+분사'에서 분사는 형용사의 역할을 하기 때문에 분사 대신 형용사가 올 수 있기 때문이다.

☆Check up!

Answer Keys p. 40

A 다음 괄호 안에 주어진 동사를 알맞은 형태로 바꾸어 빈칸에 쓰시오.

1 Jack couldn't see well with an eye _*bandaged*_. (bandage)

2 She was laughing at me with her finger _____ at my new hair style. (point)

3 I always fall asleep with the light _____ on. (turn)

4 Judy danced with her friends with the music _____. (play)

5 Lane went out of the room with his hand _____. (wave)

Answer Keys p. 40

B 다음 짝지어진 두 문장의 뜻이 같도록 'with + 명사 + 분사'를 이용하여 빈칸을 채우시오.

1 Mr. Lee was eating breakfast while his son was watching TV.
➡ Mr. Lee was eating breakfast ___*with his son watching TV*___ .

2 Linda was speaking and tears were falling down her cheeks.
➡ Linda was speaking _____ .

3 They went away and their hands were waved.
➡ They went away _____ .

4 His daughter was flying a kite while Mike was jogging.
➡ His daughter was flying a kite _____ .

5 He is having lunch and his cell phone was ringing.
➡ He is having lunch _____ .

6 Youngmin listened to music and his head was nodded.
➡ Youngmin listened to music _____ .

7 We enjoyed the festival and the woman was dancing in the street.
➡ We enjoyed the festival _____ .

8 Tom leaned on the door and his arms were crossed.
➡ Tom leaned on the door _____ .

9 She was cooking while her baby was sleeping.
➡ She was cooking _____ .

10 Lisa was driving her car and her hair was flying.
➡ Lisa was driving her car _____ .

Practice More II

Answer Keys p. 41

A 보기와 같이 주어진 단어를 이용하여 빈칸을 채우시오.

> 보기
>
> The news was <u>shocking</u>.
> We were <u>shocked</u> at the news. (shock)

1 The movie was _____. / I was _____ with the movie. (bore)

2 Staying up all night is _____. / I'm _____ by staying up all night. (exhaust)

3 That novel is _____. / I am _____ in that novel. (interest)

4 His answer is _____. / I'm _____ by his answer. (confuse)

5 Jackson's performance was _____. / I was _____ at Jackson's performance. (amaze)

6 Her speech is so _____. / I'm so _____ by her speech. (move)

7 The exam was _____. / We were _____ by the exam. (puzzle)

8 The service is _____. / We're _____ with the service. (satisfy)

B 다음 문장에서 어법상 어색한 것을 찾아 바르게 고치시오.

1 She being sick, she can't go to the concert.

<u>She being</u> ➡ <u>Being</u>

2 Listened to music, I prepared for the party.

_____ ➡ _____

3 Knowing not where to go, he was so confused.

_____ ➡ _____

4 I started to feel boring.   _____ ➡ _____

5 Study hard, he thought he could get an A on the test.

_____ ➡ _____

6 Mom baked chocolate cookies, sing a song.

_____ ➡ _____

7 John was sitting on the sofa with his arms crossing.

_____ ➡ _____

8 She arriving home, she began to cry.

_____ ➡ _____

9 Pushing a boy by mistake, I apologizing to him.

_____ ➡ _____

10 I was sleeping with my dog sat beside me.

_____ ➡ _____

C 주어진 접속사 중 알맞은 것을 골라 밑줄 친 부분을 부사절로 바꿔 쓰시오.

보기

| since | while | when | as | if | although |

1 Satisfying with our restaurant's service, please take part in our survey.

➡ *If you are satisfied with our restaurant's service*, please take part in our survey.

2 Entering the room, Linda found her room cleaned.

➡ _____, she found her room cleaned.

3 Calling Joe's name, his mom came to him.

➡ His mom came to Joe _____.

4 Being rich, he wanted to earn more money.

➡ _____, he wanted to earn more money.

5 Finishing my speech, I could take a nap.

➡ _____, I could take a nap.

6 Having dinner, they discussed today's issue.

➡ _____, they discussed today's issue.

D 다음 우리말과 같은 뜻이 되도록 주어진 단어를 이용하여 분사구문을 완성하시오.

1 Tom을 우연히 마주쳤을 때 그녀는 울기 시작했다. (come across)

➡ _____*Coming across Tom*_____, she began to cry.

2 그 코너에서 오른쪽으로 돌면 약국을 볼 수 있습니다. (corner, turn)

➡ _____, you can see the pharmacy.

3 시험 결과를 확인하고서 그녀는 아무 말도 할 수 없었다. (check, test results)

➡ _____, she couldn't say anything.

4 어떻게 자동차를 고쳐야 할지 몰라서 나는 정비사에게 전화했다. (know, fix)

➡ _____, I called the mechanic.

5 낮에 낮잠을 너무 많이 자서 John은 밤에 잠을 잘 수가 없었다. (sleep, daytime)

➡ _____, John couldn't sleep at night.

6 Jina는 불을 끄고 영화를 보았다. (watch the movie)

➡ Jina turned off the light,_____

E 우리말과 같은 뜻이 되도록 주어진 단어를 배열하여 문장을 쓰시오.

1 시험에 합격하면 네가 원하는 무엇이든 가질 수 있다. (passing, you, will, the exam, get, be able to, want, you, anything)

➡ *Passing the exam, you will be able to get anything you want.*

2 역으로 가는 방법을 몰랐기 때문에 나는 그에게 물어봐야만 했다. (knowing, station, how, ask, not, get, I, to, to, had to, him, the)

➡ _____

3 외국에서 학교를 다녔음에도 불구하고 그는 한국에 많은 친구들이 있다. (going, a foreign, has, to school, in, Korea, he, in, friends, many, country)

➡ _____

4 피곤하고 배가 고팠기 때문에 우리는 아무것도 할 수 없었다. (feeling, and, we, anything, tired, could, hungry, not, do)

➡ _____

5 나무에서 떨어져서 Cindy는 다리가 부러졌다. (broken, falling, the tree, Cindy, had, from, her leg)

➡ _____

6 돈이 매우 많이 있음에도 불구하고 그녀는 가난한 사람들을 돕는 것을 원하지 않는다. (having, she, a lot of, the poor, money, help, doesn't, to, want)

➡ _____

내신 최다 출제 유형

01 다음 밑줄 친 부분의 쓰임이 보기 와 같은 것을 고르시오. [출제 예상 90%]

> 보기
> Do you know the smiling man?

① This is a good sleeping bag.
② This washing machine works very well.
③ The girls are watching an interesting game.
④ Asking for help is necessary.
⑤ Her hobby is collecting stamps.

02 다음 중 어법상 어색한 것을 고르시오. [출제 예상 85%]

① The falling leaves make me depressed.
② They are exciting at the festival.
③ We went to the art show.
④ She was bored of doing the dishes.
⑤ He was interested in riding a bicycle.

03 다음 중 짝지어진 문장의 의미가 다른 것을 고르시오. [출제 예상 80%]

① Because he is busy, he cannot help me.
  → Being busy, he cannot help me.
② If you read this book, you'll be happy.
  → Reading this book, you'll be happy.
③ While I took a walk, I saw Mr. and Mrs. Smith.
  → Taking a walk, I saw Mr. and Mrs. Smith.
④ When we watched the movie, we were moved.
  → Watching the movie, we were moved.
⑤ Though the shirt is cheap, it is nice.
  → Cheap the shirt is nice.

04 다음 밑줄 친 부분의 의미로 알맞은 것을 고르시오. [출제 예상 80%]

> Living in the country, they can grow vegetables and fruits.

① They live in the country
② Because they live in the country
③ Because they living in the country
④ Because they are living in the country
⑤ Because live in the country

05 다음 밑줄 친 부분 중 쓰임이 나머지 넷과 다른 것을 고르시오. [출제 예상 85%]

① Mary finally finished writing the book report.
② It is exciting to play tennis with my sister.
③ The book you recommended is boring.
④ I saw her washing the dishes.
⑤ The boy wearing a blue jacket is my brother.

06 다음 빈칸에 들어갈 말이 바르게 짝지어진 것을 고르시오. [출제 예상 80%]

> • I am not afraid of the _____ dog.
> • Helping sick people is a _____ job for me.

① barked − satisfied
② barking − satisfied
③ barked − satisfying
④ barking − satisfying
⑤ bark − satisfy

[01~03] 다음 빈칸에 들어갈 알맞은 말을 고르시오.

01

> Jane had her wallet _____ on the bus.

① stolen　　② stole　　③ steal
④ to steal　　⑤ stealing

02

> When I watched the news, I was _____ .

① surprise　　② surprised　　③ to surprise
④ surprises　　⑤ surprising

03

> _____ in easy English, we can understand the book easily.

① Write　　② Wrote　　③ Written
④ To write　　⑤ Writing

[04~05] 다음 밑줄 친 부분이 어법상 어색한 것을 고르시오.

04 ① There lived a queen named Elizabeth.
② We like the article posting on her blog.
③ Who is the boy dancing on the ground?
④ The movie directed by Steven Spielberg is moving.
⑤ I saw some students studying in the library.

05 ① All the people were excited.
② This Bible is written in English.
③ The flowers in my garden are watered.
④ We will not buy a used car.
⑤ I think the movie was bored.

Note　a used car 중고차

[06~07] 다음 중 밑줄 친 부분이 어법상 옳은 것을 고르시오.

06 ① I was disappointing with his behavior.
② Stop using confused words.
③ Please tell me a moved story.
④ They are embarrassing to hear his lies.
⑤ She was surprised at the accident.

07 ① I'm looking forward to playing an interested computer game.
② They were shocking at the rumor.
③ I was boring with his studying.
④ Apple mangoes eaten by Koreans are imported.
⑤ The cloudy weather makes us depressing these days.

[08~10] 다음 빈칸에 들어갈 말이 순서대로 알맞게 연결된 것을 고르시오.

08

> A　_____ by the camp fire, I played the guitar.
> B　Your playing makes us _____ .

① Sit − smiles　　② Sit − smiled
③ Sitting − smile　　④ Sat − smiling
⑤ To sit − smile

09

- A _____ accident happens every day in the world.
- They were _____ with the water show.

① surprised – satisfying
② surprised – satisfied
③ surprising – satisfied
④ surprising – satisfying
⑤ surprise – satisfy

10

A Was the concert _____?
B No, it was so _____.

① excited – bore
② excited – bored
③ excited – boring
④ exciting – boring
⑤ exciting – bored

[11~13] 다음 밑줄 친 곳의 쓰임이 나머지와 다른 하나를 고르시오.

11
① These days many women enjoy driving cars.
② Walking in the park is good for our health.
③ The man picking up a bag is under the bridge.
④ I am good at speaking Chinese.
⑤ Jogging is better than any other exercise.

12
① Her hobby is cooking Japanese food.
② We're planning to go hiking this Saturday.
③ Many kids enjoyed going to Everland.
④ I don't like watching TV.
⑤ His dream is helping elderly people.

★★★
13
① They saw an exciting show last weekend.
② My sleeping kitten makes a funny sound.
③ We expected satisfying results on our final test.
④ I gave up memorizing some English words.
⑤ We are running with our puppy.

[14~15] 다음 밑줄 친 부분을 분사구문의 형태로 바르게 고친 것을 고르시오.

14

Because they felt tired and hot, they wanted to do nothing.

① Feeling tired and hot
② Feel tired and hot
③ Feeling they are tired and hot
④ They feel tired and hot
⑤ They feeling tired and hot

15

Since he was shocked by his grade, he decided to study harder.

① Shock by his grade
② Be shocking by his grade
③ Be shocked by his grade
④ Being shocking by his grade
⑤ Being shocked by his grade

[16~17] 다음 빈칸에 들어갈 말로 알맞은 표현을 고르시오.

★★★
16

A hurricane hit America, _____.

① being destroy all the houses
② destroys all the houses
③ being destroys all the houses
④ destroyed all the houses
⑤ destroying all the houses

★★★
17

_____, I worked at my father's company.

① Need some money to buy a cell phone
② Needing some money to buy a cell phone
③ Needed some money to buy a cell phone
④ To needing some money to buy a cell phone
⑤ Needs some money to buy a cell phone

[18~20] 다음 주어진 우리말을 영어로 바르게 옮긴 것을 고르시오.

★★★
18

Jessy는 TV를 보며 소파에 앉아 있었다.

① Jessy was sitting on the sofa watch TV.
② Jessy was sitting on the sofa to be watch TV.
③ Jessy sits on the sofa watching TV.
④ Jessy was sitting on the sofa watching TV.
⑤ Jessy sat on the sofa watched TV.

★★★
19

그는 무엇을 해야 할지 알고 싶어서 나에게 물어보았다.

① Want to know what to do, he asked me.
② Wanted to know what to do, he asked me.
③ Wanting to know what to do, he asked me.
④ Wanted knowing what to do, he asked me.
⑤ Want knowing what to do, he asked me.

★★★
20

뭔가를 속삭이고 있는 소녀는 Sophia이다.

① The girl whispering something is Sophia.
② The girl whispers something is Sophia.
③ The girl whispered something is Sophia.
④ The girl whispering is Sophia.
⑤ The girl whispered is Sophia.

[21~23] 다음 중 문장의 전환이 <u>잘못된</u> 것을 고르시오.

21
① If you leave right now, you can take the bus.
→ Leaving right now, you can take the bus.

② Although I was busy, I took part in the meeting.
→ Being busy, I took part in the meeting.

③ While Max read a book, he fell asleep.
→ Reading a book, Max fell asleep.

④ Because she had no money, she couldn't buy the car.
→ Having no money, she couldn't buy the car.

⑤ He sat in the chair and he was reading a book.
→ Sat in the chair, he was reading a book.

22
① When I didn't know what to say, I kept silent.
→ Not knowing what to say, I kept silent.

② As she arrived home, she noticed she had lost her wallet.
→ Arriving home, she noticed she had lost her wallet.

③ Although she did not finish her work, she went to the party.
→ Not finishing her work, she went to the party.

④ Because it was rainy, we just stayed at home.
→ Being rainy, we just stayed at home.

⑤ Because I was tired, I went to bed early.
→ Being tired, I went to bed early.

★★★
23
① After we sat on the grass, we started to eat lunch.
→ Sitting on the grass, we started to eat lunch.

② Some people waste water, while others have no water to drink.
→ Some people waste water, having no water to drink.

③ When you bite your nails, you are nervous.
→ Biting your nails, you are nervous.

④ When she saw the lion, she screamed.
→ Seeing the lion, she screamed.

⑤ He took a nap after he fixed his car.
→ He took a nap, fixing his car.

[24~25] 다음 빈칸에 알맞은 말을 고르시오.

24

> • When she doesn't understand, she asks her teacher.
> ➡ _____, she asks her teacher.

① Doesn't understanding
② Not understanding
③ No understanding
④ Understanding
⑤ Not to understanding

25

> • Maggie talked on the phone _____ a picture.

① paints
② painted
③ painting
④ to paint
⑤ paint

[26~27] 다음 중 어법상 <u>틀린</u> 것을 <u>모두</u> 고르시오.

26
① You can see the birds flying in the sky.
② He painted a mother looking at her kids.
③ I finally found a hiding truth.
④ This is the castle built five hundred years ago.
⑤ I couldn't read anything wrote on the paper.

27
① The opera was amazing.
② I was shocking to hear about the news.
③ They were disappointed at the changed rules.
④ Some children were frightening of the dog.
⑤ My sister and I were excited to watch the dolphin show.

★★★
28 다음 밑줄 친 부분의 쓰임이 [보기] 와 같은 것을 <u>모두</u> 고르시오.

> [보기]
> We saw something <u>burning</u> on the mountain.

① I smiled, <u>waving</u> both of my hands.
② <u>Taking</u> care of a baby is difficult.
③ They began <u>running</u> for the finish line.
④ They picked up a pair of <u>dancing</u> shoes.
⑤ They are <u>volunteering</u> at the orphanage.

(Note) orphanage 고아원

[29~30] 다음 글을 읽고 물음에 답하시오.

> I ① <u>like to</u> ② <u>go skiing</u> in winter. It makes me ③ <u>exciting</u>.
> But it is ④ <u>disappointing</u> that I can't go to a ski resort ⑤ <u>this winter</u>.

29 윗글의 밑줄 친 부분 중 어법상 <u>어색한</u> 것을 고르시오.

①   ②   ③   ④   ⑤

30 윗글의 밑줄 친 부분 중 어법상 <u>어색한</u> 부분을 바르게 고쳐 쓰시오.

_____ ➡ _____

★★★
31 다음 분사구문 문장 중 '양보'의 뜻을 가진 문장을 <u>고르시오.</u>

① Going to school, he takes a bus.
② Being too weak, I cannot hold these boxes.
③ Not having enough money, he helps the poor regularly.
④ Walking in the park, I met Annie.
⑤ Larry lies on the bed, listening to music.

32 다음의 밑줄 친 부분과 바꿔 쓸 수 있는 말이 바르게 짝지어진 것을 고르시오.

> • <u>Living</u> in Jeju Island, she became a woman diver.
> • <u>Living</u> by the sea, he cannot swim well.

① She lives — He lives
② As she lived — Although he lives
③ Because she's living — Although he lives
④ Because she is living — Though he is living
⑤ As she live — Although he live

[33~34] 다음 중 어법상 옳은 문장을 <u>모두</u> 고르시오.

33 ① I was embarrassing by the event.
② Computer games are interesting.
③ The news was very shocking.
④ We're tiring of too much work.
⑤ The music was so depressed.

34 ① Being tired by my work, I wanted to take a rest.
② Wanting not to buy it, I had to buy it.
③ Happy, I feel like I am flying in the sky.
④ Turning right at the corner, you'll find the building.
⑤ Danced on the street, he listened to music.

35 다음 밑줄 친 문장과 바꿔 쓸 수 있는 것을 고르시오.

> <u>Taking care of my brother</u>, I can't go outside to play.

① When I take care of my brother
② Because I take care of my brother
③ Although I take care of my brother
④ After I take care of my brother
⑤ As I taking care of my brother

◇◇◇◇◇◇◇◇◇ 서술형 평가 ◇◇◇◇◇◇◇◇◇

[36~40] 다음 괄호 안의 단어를 문맥에 맞게 바르게 변경하여 쓰시오.

36
> • There is a little boy (cry) on the bench.
> • Helena was (shock) by her grade.

➡ (cry) − ＿＿＿＿＿＿＿
　(shock) − ＿＿＿＿＿＿＿

37
> • Who are you (wait) for at the flower shop?
> • Many people are (move) by his songs.

➡ (wait) − ＿＿＿＿＿＿＿
　(move) − ＿＿＿＿＿＿＿

38

The (frighten) animals by the hunters ran into the deep forests.

➡ (frighten) − _____

39

When he failed the test, he couldn't hide his (disappoint) face.

➡ (disappoint) − _____

40

Our teacher was (satisfy) with our last music concert.

➡ (satisfy) − _____

[41~42] 다음 문장을 분사구문으로 전환할 때 빈칸에 알맞은 말을 쓰시오.

41

Because the report is written in English, there are some mistakes.

➡ _____,
  the report has some mistakes.

➡ _____

42

She was eating some fruit while her sister was reading comic books.

➡ She was eating some fruit with

  _____.

➡ _____

[43~44] 다음 괄호 안의 단어를 사용하여 밑줄 친 부분을 부사절로 고쳐 쓰시오.

43

Studying in class, you should turn off your cell phone. (while)

➡ _____,
  you should turn off your cell phone.

➡ _____

44

Jenny is drawing a picture with her crayon box opened. (and)

➡ Jenny is drawing a picture,

  _____.

➡ _____

[45~46] 다음 괄호 안의 단어를 우리말에 맞게 바르게 배열하여 문장을 완성하시오.

★★★

45

잠시 쉬고 나서 우리는 연습을 하기 시작했다.

(practicing / short / break / a / started / we / taking / after)

➡ _____

★★★

46

너는 솔직하지 못했기 때문에 친구를 사귈 수 없었다.

(not / honest / you / being / friends / make / couldn't / any)

➡ _____

Note

09
Chapter
형용사와 부사

Point Check I

◆ **형용사:** 사람이나 사물의 성질, 특징 등을 나타내는 말로, 명사 앞뒤에서 꾸며주기도 하고 동사 뒤에서 주어나 목적어의 상태를 설명해주기도 한다.

1. 형용사의 쓰임

한정적 용법	형용사 + 명사	• Those are heavy <u>boxes</u>. [heavy – boxes를 꾸며줌]
	명사 + 형용사	• They want to learn some <u>activities</u> that are helpful to others. [helpful – activities를 꾸며줌]
서술적 용법	주격보어	• <u>Her singing tone</u> is beautiful. [beautiful – Her singing tone을 설명]
	목적격보어	• He made <u>us</u> glad. [glad – us의 상태를 설명]

2. the + 형용사 : '~하는 사람들'

- **The young** should have huge ambition.
  [=Young people]
- **The old** are weak, so we should help them.
  [=Old people]

3. 고유 형용사 : 나라의 이름에서 파생된 형용사들을 말하며, 때로는 명사처럼 쓰이기도 한다.

국가명	형용사 (언어, 국적)	개인 (단수)	개인 (복수)	국민 (전체)
Korea	Korean	a Korean	Koreans	the Koreans
America	American	an American	Americans	the Americans
China	Chinese	a Chinese	Chinese	the Chinese

4. 형용사의 어순

서수	기수	성질	크기	신/구	색깔	국적	재료
first	one	good	middle	new	white	Korean	wooden

5. 감각동사 : be동사처럼 뒤에 보어 역할을 하는 형용사가 온다.

• look, seem	• feel	• smell
• sound	• taste	

Lesson 9-1 형용사

형용사의 역할과 쓰임

> • **형용사**: 형용사는 사람이나 사물의 생김새, 성질 등을 나타내는 말이다. 명사 앞에서 꾸며주거나, 동사 다음에 나와서 주어, 목적어가 어떤 상태인지 알려주는 보어 역할도 한다.

1. 한정적 용법: 명사의 앞이나 뒤에 위치해 명사의 모습이나 성질을 나타낸다.

(1) 형용사 + 명사

- Jane is a **positive** woman. (positive → woman 수식)
- Paul is a **charming** man. (charming → man 수식)

(2) 명사 + 형용사

① -thing, -one, -body로 끝나는 명사의 경우 형용사는 뒤에 위치한다.

- Phillip wants to do something **special**. (special → something 수식)

② 형용사 뒤에 다른 어구가 따라올 때 명사를 뒤에서 꾸며준다.

- Liah has some data **useful** for your research. (useful → data 수식)

◈ **한정적 용법으로만 쓰이는 형용사**

• only	• elder	• lonely	• live
• former	• major	• golden	• wooden

2. 서술적 용법: 주격보어나 목적격보어의 자리에서 주어나 목적어의 상태를 알려준다.

(1) 주격보어

- His playing was **wonderful**. (wonderful → his playing 설명)

(2) 목적격보어

- I thought her voice **husky**. (husky → her voice 설명)

◈ **서술적 용법으로만 쓰이는 형용사**

• afraid	• alone	• asleep	• alike
• alive	• awake	• glad	

A 괄호 안에서 알맞은 것을 고르시오.

1 James is (awake / wake).

2 The babies are (sleep / asleep) in the room.

3 Jane wants to eat (sweet something / something sweet).

4 I think (negative thinking / thinking negative) makes people depressed.

5 Inho and Inha look (alike / like).

6 Look at the (cheerful / glad) boy!

7 It was (an impressive movie / a movie impressive).

8 I'd like to meet (friendly anyone / anyone friendly).

9 I think their performance was (awesome / wonderfully).

10 Mika is ten years (older / elder) than Jessica.

B 주어진 단어를 알맞게 배열하여 문장을 다시 쓰시오.

1 Mr. Lee thinks _____ *all of the dogs are asleep* _____.
(asleep, all of the dogs, are)

2 They went to the stadium to _____.
(game, an exciting, watch, baseball)

3 She is looking for _____.
(smart, someone, for the job)

4 He couldn't buy _____.
(weekend, anything, last, expensive)

5 Minho said he had _____.
(nothing, tell, me, to)

6 I'd like to _____.
(have, chocolate, ice cream, a)

7 Lina has a lot of _____.
(books, read, interesting, to)

the + 형용사, 고유 형용사

- **the + 형용사**: 정관사 'the' 뒤에 형용사가 오면 '~ 한 사람들'이란 뜻을 가진다.
- **고유 형용사**: 나라의 이름에서 파생된 형용사들을 말한다.
  이 형용사들은 명사로 '언어'와 '국적'을 나타내기도 하고, 관사가 붙어 '국민 개인'이나 '국민 전체'를 나타내기도 한다.

1. the + 형용사: ~한 사람들(복수명사 취급)

the rich = rich people	the poor = poor people
the old = old people	the young = young people

- A famous doctor went to Africa to help **the sick**. [the sick = sick people]

- **The young** try to find their purpose in life. [The young = Young people]

2. 고유 형용사

국가명	형용사 (언어, 국적)	개인 (단수)	개인 (복수)	국민 (전체)
Korea	Korean	a Korean	Koreans	the Koreans
America	American	an American	Americans	the Americans
Australia	Australian	an Australian	Australians	the Australians
China	Chinese	a Chinese	Chinese	the Chinese
Denmark	Danish	a Dane	Danes	the Danish
England	English	an Englishman	Englishmen	the English
France	French	a Frenchman	Frenchmen	the French
Germany	German	a German	Germans	the Germans
Italy	Italian	an Italian	Italians	the Italians
Japan	Japanese	a Japanese	Japanese	the Japanese
Russia	Russian	a Russian	Russians	the Russians

- This is **Korean** food. [형용사: 한국의, 한국적인]

- **Korean** is interesting to learn. [명사: 한국어]

- I'm **a Korean**. They are **Koreans**, too. [명사: 한국인]

- **The Koreans** like to eat kimchi. [국민 전체 → 복수 취급]

Answer Keys p. 43

A 다음 괄호 안에서 알맞은 것을 고르시오.

1   This is my friend Jane. She is (Chinese / the Chinese).

2   The rich (has / have) their own know-how to earn money.

3   Is he an (English / Englishman)?

4   (A / The) young should respect old people.

5   (The Italy / The Italians) like to eat pasta and pizza.

6   Three (German / Germans) asked me the way to the station.

7   She is taking care of (the weak / a weak).

8   The Koreans (likes / like) to sing and dance.

9   I like (a Japanese / Japanese) food very much.

10 The blind (learn / learns) languages in a special way.

11 People think we should help the (poor / poors).

12 (English / The English) consists of vowels and consonants.

13 I want to be a doctor to heal (the sick / the sicks).

9-3 형용사의 어순

- 형용사의 어순: 한 문장에 2개 이상의 형용사가 있는 경우 쓰이는 순서를 말한다.

1. 형용사의 어순

서수	기수	성질	크기	신/구	색깔	국적	재료
first	one	nice	big	new	green	Korean	wooden
second	two	pretty	large	old	pink	American	rocky
third	three	smart	small	young	purple	English	metal
fourth	four	delicious	long	used	blue	French	plastic

- They have a **small young white** cat.
- Jane and Tommy are making a **pretty small pink wooden** dollhouse.

2. 형용사 앞에 다른 수식어가 올 때

all	both
double	half

정관사	the
지시 형용사	this that these those
소유격	my your his her its our their

- Harry likes **all his old blue** shirts.

☆Check up!

Answer Keys p. 43

A 주어진 단어를 바르게 배열하여 빈칸에 쓰시오.

1 _a small white_ bird (white, small, a)

2 _____ words (two, first, the)

3 _____ table (wooden, new, blue, all)

4 _____ girls (pretty, those, young)

5 _____ friend (new, my, kind, English)

6 _____ dress (pink, the, beautiful)

7 _____ bread loaves
(delicious, two, French, large)

8 _____ chair
(large, new, green, comfortable, plastic, a)

9 _____ dogs
(German, four, his, white, small)

10 _____ skirt (new, a, Korean, green)

불완전 자동사와 감각동사

- **불완전 자동사**: 동사만으로는 뜻을 나타내기 부족하기 때문에 주격보어가 필요한 동사를 말한다.
- **감각동사**: be동사와 비슷한 것으로 이 감각동사 뒤에는 주격보어로 형용사가 나와 주어가 어떠한 상태인지 알려준다.

1. '상태의 유지' 또는 '변화'를 나타내는 불완전 자동사: become, stay, get

- She **became** bankrupt.
- They **stay** healthy by exercising every day.
- I didn't sleep well last night, so I **got** tired.

2. 감각동사

• look, seem	• feel	• smell
• sound	• taste	

- They **looked** rushed.
- It's raining. And I **feel** chilly.
- It **smelled** so bad. It might be rotten.
- That **sounds** wonderful.
- This soup **tastes** awesome.

Grammar Plus +

- **look like, feel like** + 명사/동명사
  'like'는 '~와 같은, ~처럼'이란 뜻의 전치사로 쓰였기 때문에 이들 뒤에는 명사나 동명사가 와야 한다.

  ① look like ~처럼 보이다, ~할 것 같다
  - Julie **looks like** an old woman.
  - It **looks like** snowing/snow.

  ② feel like ~한 느낌이 들다, ~하고(갖고) 싶다
  - She doesn't **feel like** going there.
  - I **feel like** a bowl of warm soup.

A   다음 문장에서 어법상 <u>어색한</u> 것을 찾아 바르게 고치시오.

1   This cookie tastes sweety.   _sweety_ ➡ _sweet_

2   John looked palely.   _____ ➡ _____

3   His daughter looked happily.   _____ ➡ _____

4   He looks like magical.   _____ ➡ _____

5   I feel like to eat something spicy. _____ ➡ _____

6   Jane will stay wake.   _____ ➡ _____

7   The red dress looks familiarly.   _____ ➡ _____

8   This cake smells badly.   _____ ➡ _____

9   It sounds strangely.   _____ ➡ _____

10 He feels like leave now.   _____ ➡ _____

Practice More I

A 괄호 안에서 알맞은 것을 고르시오.

1 Amy would like to drink (something cold / cold something)

2 This documentary is so (moving / moved).

3 She can touch a (live / alive) snake.

4 Mr. Choi's acting was so (badly / bad) last night.

5 They looked really (sadly / sad).

6 You should be (quiet / quietly) here.

7 Englishmen (is / are) usually gentle.

8 He wanted to become a doctor to help (the sick / a sick people).

9 The Frenchmen (enjoy / enjoys) drinking wine.

10 Helen looked (pale / palely).

11 Daniel brought his (new car / newly car).

12 The baby was (asleep / sleep) in the room.

13 My sister loves (beautiful things / things beautiful).

14 To live a successful life is (major / important), but it's not my goal of life.

15 His chair was so (comfortable / comfortably).

B 다음 문장에서 어법상 어색한 것을 찾아 바르게 고치시오.

1 John looked happily. ___happily___ ➡ ___happy___

2 Put the book on that white small table.

   _____ ➡ _____

3 Gray knows the both handsome guys.

   _____ ➡ _____

4 The deaf goes to a special school.

   _____ ➡ _____

5 He is looking for cheerful someone for the job.

   _____ ➡ _____

6 He did a lot of great things for the poors.

   _____ ➡ _____

7 I'll find funny something. _____ ➡ _____

8　You look so nervously.　　＿＿＿＿＿＿＿＿ ➡ ＿＿＿＿＿＿＿＿

9　Father said the spider was live.

　　　　　　　　　　　　＿＿＿＿＿＿＿＿ ➡ ＿＿＿＿＿＿＿＿

C　보기 에서 알맞은 형용사를 골라 다음 문장의 빈칸을 채우시오.

> 보기
>
> homeless　　blind　　young　　disabled　　old
> Chinese　　rich　　poor　　positive

1　__The blind__　use braille when they read a book.

2　Some people think that ＿＿＿＿＿＿ should do society a favor
　by donating to charity.

3　Which brand is the most popular with ＿＿＿＿＿＿, especially
　in their early 20s?

4　Every year, ＿＿＿＿＿＿ visit Korea for sightseeing.

5　The government should prepare a bill to take care of ＿＿＿＿＿＿.

6　People should not sit on the seats for ＿＿＿＿＿＿.

7　Everyone's happiness depends on their ＿＿＿＿＿＿ thinking.

8　Jane went to Africa to help ＿＿＿＿＿＿ and the sick.

9　＿＿＿＿＿＿ are wiser than the young.

D　주어진 단어를 알맞게 배열하여 문장을 완성하시오.

1　Mr. Harrison ＿＿＿＿_was a great English teacher._＿＿＿＿
　(a, teacher, was, English, great)

2　＿＿＿＿＿＿＿＿＿＿＿＿＿＿＿＿＿＿＿＿ last night.
　(Americans, us, two, played, with)

3　＿＿＿＿＿＿＿＿＿＿＿＿＿＿＿＿＿＿＿＿＿＿
　(romantic, are, the, usually, French)

4　＿＿＿＿＿＿＿＿＿＿＿＿＿＿＿＿＿＿＿＿＿＿
　(movies, I, very, Korean, much, like)

5　If you study English hard, ＿＿＿＿＿＿＿＿＿＿＿＿＿＿
　(better, your, get, English, will)

6　＿＿＿＿＿＿＿＿＿＿＿＿＿＿＿＿＿＿＿ with their friends.
　(the, to, young, hang out, like)

Point Check Ⅱ

◆ **수량 형용사 :** 명사 앞에 쓰여 수나 양을 표시하는 것을 말한다.

1. 수량 형용사 (1)

	많은		조금의, 약간의		거의 없는
셀 수 있는 명사	many, a number of	a lot of, lots of, plenty of	a few	some, any	few
셀 수 없는 명사	much, a good deal of		a little		little

- many, some, any, a few, few + 셀 수 있는 명사의 <u>복수형</u>
- much, some, any, a little, little + 셀 수 없는 명사의 <u>단수형</u>
- some : 긍정문, 권유의 의문문에 사용
- any : 부정문, 의문문에 사용

2. 수량 형용사 (2)

each 각각의 every 모든	+ 단수명사 (항상 단수 취급)	not ~ any = no 아무 ~도 없는	+ 복수명사
both 둘의, 두 개의 several 몇몇의	+ 복수명사 (항상 복수 취급)	all 모든, 전부의 most 대부분의	+ 복수명사

3. 기수, 서수, 배수사

기수	일반적인 숫자	one, two, three, four, five, six
서수	순서를 나타내는 숫자	(the) first, second, third, fourth, fifth, sixth
배수사	'수의 배'를 나타내는 숫자	once, twice, three times, four times, five times

- '명사 + 기수' = '서수 + 명사' : lesson five = the fifth lesson
- 분수 읽기 : 분자에서 분모 순서로 읽고, 분자는 기수, 분모는 서수로 표현한다.

$\dfrac{1}{2}$ – a half, one half $\dfrac{3}{5}$ – three fifths

9-5 수량 형용사_many / much / a lot of

- **수량 형용사:** 명사 앞에 쓰여서 수나 양을 표시하는 것을 말한다.
- **many, much, a lot of :** '많은'이라는 뜻으로 'many'는 셀 수 있는 명사의 복수형, 'much'는
  셀 수 없는 명사의 복수형에 쓰이며, 'a lot of'는 셀 수 있는 명사와
  셀 수 없는 명사의 복수 모두에 사용할 수 있다.

◆ **many, much, a lot of**

many (= a number of)	+ 셀 수 있는 명사의 복수	• There are many <u>oranges</u> in the basket.
much (= a good deal of)	+ 셀 수 없는 명사의 복수	• There is much <u>water</u> in the bottle.
a lot of (= lots of, plenty of)	+ 셀 수 있는 명사 / 셀 수 없는 명사의 복수	• There are a lot of <u>books</u> on the shelf. • There is a lot of <u>honey</u> in the jar.

➡ 'much', 'a lot of'가 셀 수 없는 명사의 양을 표현할 때 동사는 단수 동사를 사용한다.

☆Check up!

Answer Keys p. 44

A 다음 빈칸에 many, much 중 알맞은 것을 바르게 넣으시오.

1 How __*many*__ apples did you eat yesterday?

2 This research will not be _____ help for your studies.

3 Too _____ exercise sometimes makes you sick.

4 Were there _____ people in the amusement park?

5 He earned _____ money through the business.

6 Ann made _____ mistakes last week.

7 Don't spend too _____ time complaining about your
    school.

8 There are _____ cars in the parking lot.

9 We had better not have too _____ hope to win the game.

10 There are _____ ways to enjoy summer.

수량 형용사_(a)few / (a)little

· **(a) few / (a) little** : (a) few는 셀 수 있는 명사, (a) little는 셀 수 없는 명사에 사용한다.

1. (a) few/(a) little

a few 약간의, 조금의	+ 셀 수 있는 명사 (복수형)	· There are a few chairs in the hall.
few 거의 없는		· There are few available tables in the cafe.
a little 약간의, 조금의	+ 셀 수 없는 명사	· There is a little sugar in this bread.
little 거의 없는		· There is little juice in the glass.

➡ '조금' 또는 '거의 없다'는 뜻으로 사용되는 'a few, few'는 아주 조금이라도 남아 있다는 뜻이므로 반드시 복수 동사를 써 주어야 한다.

2. quite a few/quite a little

· quite a few (= not a few) : 꽤 많은, 상당한 수의

I collected **quite a few** mini toy cars.

· quite a little (= not a little) : 꽤 많은, 상당한 양의

Phillip has drunk **quite a little** water a day.

3. little, a little : 종종 부사로 사용돼 형용사, 동사, 다른 부사를 꾸미기도 한다.

· The musical was **a little** boring.

· I studied **little** for the test.

☆Check up!

Answer Keys p. 44

A 다음 문장의 빈칸에 a few와 a little 중 알맞은 것을 쓰시오.

1 Peter eats ___*a little*___ coffee everyday.

2 Tim has _____ trouble in preparing food for the party.

3 Sam has _____ knowledge about fixing cars.

4   Linda came back to school _____ hours later.

5   Put _____ sugar in the bowl.

6   I bought this car _____ years ago.

7   It took _____ time to solve the problem.

8   Amy has _____ jazz albums.

9   She came home _____ days ago.

10   There is _____ ice in the cup.

11   I spread _____ jam on the bread.

12   Tina has been there _____ times.

13   They bought _____ bread because it was almost sold out.

14   _____ people were absent because of the disease.

15   I have _____ money. So, I have to stay home this weekend.

B   다음 문장에서 어법상 어색한 부분을 찾아 바르게 고치시오.

1   She uses a few salt when she cooks.

                  a few   ➡   _a little_

2   Why don't we plant a little trees?

                  _____ ➡ _____

3   Do you have few money?

                  _____ ➡ _____

4   I want to drink a few apple juice.

                  _____ ➡ _____

5   There are little people in the park.

                  _____ ➡ _____

6   There was few water in the pond.

                  _____ ➡ _____

7   Jane has a little friends to ask help.

                  _____ ➡ _____

9-7 수량 형용사 _ some / any

- **some, any** : '조금의, 약간의'의 뜻을 가지며, 주로 'some'은 긍정문과 권유문(제안문)에, 'any'는 부정문과 의문문에 사용한다.

◆ some, any

some	• Jack likes to give some <u>advice</u> to his friends. [긍정문]
	• Would you like to eat some <u>cookies</u>? [제안문]
any	• He doesn't have any ideas about it. [부정문]
	• Do you have any plans for the Halloween party? [의문문]

➡ 'some'과 'any'는 셀 수 있는 명사와 셀 수 없는 명사에 모두 사용할 수 있다.

✪Check up!

Answer Keys p. 44

A 괄호 안에서 알맞은 것을 고르시오.

1 She had ((some) / any) orange juice in the morning.

2 There are (some / any) buses that you can take.

3 Can I borrow (some / any) pens to write with?

4 Does she have (any / some) plans to go to a foreign country?

5 Do you have (some / any) problems? Just call me.

6 The news said (some / any) people evaded a huge amount of taxes.

7 Do you have (any / some) questions?

8 Why don't you have (some / any) tea?

B 다음 빈칸에 some, any 중 알맞은 것을 쓰시오.

1 Do you have _____any_____ books written by professor Han?

2 _____ people were injured by the accident.

3 Are there _____ good French restaurants?

4 I can speak _____ foreign languages.

5 I needed _____ advice, so I visited Diana.

6 Susan heard _____ strange sounds last night.

7 I don't have _____ time to study English.

Note

- **plan** 계획
- **foreign** 외국의
- **foreign country** 외국
- **evade** 피하다, 벗어나다
- **tax** 세금
- **advice** 충고, 조언
- **injure** 상처를 입히다, 다치게 하다

9-8 수량 형용사 _ all / each / both / no

- **all, each, both**: all은 셋 이상의 '모든 것의', each는 '각각의', both는 '둘 다의'라는 뜻을 가지고 있다.
- **no**: 'not ~ any'와 같이 '아닌, 없는'의 뜻을 가진다.

◈ all, each, both, no

each 각각의 every 모든	+ 단수 명사 (항상 단수 취급)	• Each animal has its own way of surviving. • Every person has their own lifestyle.
both 둘의, 두 개의 several 몇몇의	+ 복수 명사 (항상 복수 취급)	• Phillip likes both sports, basketball and soccer. • There are several people at the beach.
not ~ any = no 아무 ~도 없는	+ 복수 명사	• There weren't any cakes at the bakery. (= There were no cakes at the bakery.)
all 모든, 전부의 most 대부분의	+ 복수 명사	• All the people in Korea respect King Sejong. • Most students in the class have smartphones.

➡ 'every + 단수 명사'는 문법적으로는 단수 취급을 하지만 우리말로 옮길 때는 '복수'의 뜻으로 해석한다.

☆Check up!

Answer Keys p. 44

A 괄호 안에서 알맞은 것을 고르시오.

1 Helen knows (both / any) men.

2 All (student / students) must be quiet in the library.

3 They like (every / most) action movies.

4 There is (any / no) way to arrive there on time.

5 Everything (was / were) wonderful last week.

6 I have two best friends. Both (are / is) kind and thoughtful.

7 Linda saw the boy several (time / times) at the park.

8 Each (country / countries) has a different culture.

9 All (the boys / the boy) are running around the field.

10 I know every (person / person's) name in our soccer club.

기수와 서수를 사용한 숫자 표현

- **기수**: 일반적인 숫자로 '～개', '～명'을 나타내는 것을 만한다.

- **서수**: 숫자를 나타내는 '～번째'를 뜻하며, 서수 앞에는 정관사 'the'를 붙인다.
  숫자 뒤에는 '-th'를 붙여서 서수를 표현한다.

1. [명사+숫자]

- Lesson 7 – lesson seven, the seventh lesson

➡ '명사 + 기수' 또는 '서수 + 명사'로 읽을 수 있다.

2. 분수 읽기

- $\frac{2}{3}$ - two third**s**

- $\frac{1}{2}$ - a half, one half

- $\frac{3}{5}$ - three fifth**s**

➡ 분자에서 분모의 순서로 읽으며 분자는 기수, 분모는 서수로 읽고, 분자가 복수일 경우 분모는
복수형(-s)을 쓴다.

Answer Keys p. 44

A 숫자가 들어가는 표현을 영어로 읽을 때 다음 빈칸에 알맞은 수를 쓰시오.

1   World War Ⅱ ➡ World War _two_ ➡ _the Second_ World War

2   Part 7 ➡ part _____ ➡ _____ part

3   George Ⅲ ➡ George _____

4   Act 5 ➡ act _____ ➡ _____ act

5   $\frac{3}{4}$ ➡ _____

6   $2\frac{4}{6}$ ➡ _____

7   $\frac{9}{13}$ ➡ _____

8   $5\frac{8}{10}$ ➡ _____

9   Lesson 14 ➡ lesson _____ ➡ _____ lesson

10 $\frac{2}{15}$ ➡ _____

• **배수사**: 1배 (once), 2배 (twice)를 제외하고 3배부터는 '숫자 + times'로 나타낸다.

• My family has been to Switzerland **once**.

• Jeremy's room is **twice** <u>as big as</u> his sister's.
  (= Jeremy's room is **twice** <u>bigger than</u> his sister's.)

• They have **three times** as many toys as we have.

Grammar Plus +

• **원급 비교에서 배수사를 사용할 때**: 배수사 + as + 형용사/부사 + as (...배 더 ~하다)
                                    (= 배수사 + -er(more) than)
Min got **four times** <u>as many candies as</u> I got.
(= Min got **four times** <u>more candies than</u> me.)

Check up!

Answer Keys p. 44

A 우리말 해석과 같은 뜻이 되도록 빈칸에 알맞은 말을 쓰시오.

1 하루에 세 번 강연이 있습니다.
  ➡ We have lectures ___*three times*___ a day.

2 저는 한 달에 네 번 바다 사진을 찍습니다.
  ➡ I take a picture of the sea _____ a month.

3 그들은 오키나와에 두 번 가본 적이 있다.
  ➡ They have been to Okinawa _____.

4 나는 딱 한 번 그녀를 제주도에서 만난 적이 있다.
  ➡ I met her only _____ in Jeju Island.

5 이 컵은 저 컵보다 두 배 더 크다.
  ➡ This cup is _____ as large as that cup.

6 노란색 코트는 파란색 코트보다 세 배 더 짧다.
  ➡ The yellow coat is _____ shorter than the blue one.

7 John은 일주일에 다섯 번 수영을 가곤 했다.
  ➡ John used to go swimming _____ a week.

8 그녀는 1년에 열 번 산을 오른다.
  ➡ She climbs mountains _____ a year.

9 지난달에 스키 강습을 몇 번이나 걸렀니?
  ➡ How _____ did you skip ski lessons last month?

Practice More II

A 괄호 안에서 알맞은 것을 고르시오.

1 I need (many / ⟨much⟩) time to prepare for the party.

2 Nari has a (little / few) friends to talk with.

3 Don't put too (many / much) sugar in the bowl.

4 Could you give her (any / some) help?

5 There isn't (some / any) jam in the pot.

6 Every dog (has / have) his day.

7 Can you speak (some / any) foreign languages?

8 She didn't buy (any / some) juice last night.

9 I only know (a few / a little) words of German.

10 There are (little / few) differences among the girls.

B 다음 문장에서 어법상 어색한 것을 찾아 바르게 고치시오.

1 The act second was so boring. So, I walked out of the musical.

second ➡ _two_

2 Could you bring me any hot water?

_____ ➡ _____

3 All teacher at Joy's school prepared for the graduation party.

_____ ➡ _____

4 Most Japan restaurants serve fresh sushi.

_____ ➡ _____

5 All the child looked happy. _____ ➡ _____

6 Every student want to go to the picnic this weekend.

_____ ➡ _____

7 I think chapter fourth is too difficult to study.

_____ ➡ _____

8 Sam and Harry have a concert two a day.

_____ ➡ _____

9 All visitor must stay calm in this place.

_____ ➡ _____

10 My son has few interest in math. I'm so worried about that.

_____ ➡ _____

11 They don't have many food to eat.

_____ ➡ _____

12 He lost his shoes much times before.

_____ ➡ _____

C 다음 우리말에 맞게 빈칸에 알맞은 말을 쓰시오.

1 조금의 설탕과 함께 그것들을 섞으세요.
➡ Mix them with ___a little___ sugar.

2 마실 물이 거의 없다.
➡ There is _____ water to drink.

3 약간의 회원들만이 나의 의견에 동의했다.
➡ _____ members agreed with my opinion.

4 파이 위에 상당한 양의 크림이 있었다.
There were quite _____ cream on the pie.

5 8막
Act 8 = act _____ = _____ act

6 7분의 3
$$\frac{3}{7} = \underline{\hspace{3cm}}$$

7 오늘은 학생들이 아무도 없다.
There _____ students today.
= There are no students today.

8 따뜻한 핫초코를 조금 마시는 게 어때?
Why don't you have _____ hot chocolate?

9 그녀는 그녀의 일을 그만둘 어떤 이유도 없다.
She doesn't have _____ reason to quit her job.

10 바구니 안에는 아주 많은 계란들이 있다.
There are _____ eggs in the basket.

Practice More II

Answer Keys p. 45

D 다음 우리말 해석에 맞게 주어진 단어를 배열하시오.

1 그는 4막에서 하품을 세 번 했다.

(the, three, in, act, fourth, times)

➡ He yawned ___ ___ three times in the fourth act

2 나는 John이 더 이상 문제를 일으키지 않기를 바란다.

(John, any more, doesn't, any, trouble, make)

➡ I hope _____

3 너희 각각은 아름답고 특별하다.

(each, special, of, is, you, beautiful, and)

➡ _____

4 Mr. Lee는 2000년대에 캐나다를 세 번 방문했다.

(Mr. Lee, three, Canada, visited, times)

➡ _____ in 2000s.

5 살을 빼기 위해서는 junk food를 먹지 않는 것이 좋다.

(you, junk food, had better, any, not, eat)

➡ To lose weight, _____

6 모든 소년들은 축구 경기에서 이기기 위해 열심히 연습했다.

(every, the soccer game, hard, boy, win, to, practiced)

➡ _____

7 우리는 몇 분 후에 베이스캠프에 도착할 것이다.

(we, minutes, the base camp, in, arrive at, will, a few)

➡ _____

8 매일이 똑같아. 나는 해외로 나가고 싶다.

(every, to, the same, I, go, day, is, abroad, want)

➡ _____

9 트럭 안에는 약간의 과일이 있었다.

(there, truck, some, was, in, fruit, the)

➡ _____

10 내 생각에는 이 다리가 저 다리보다 다섯 배 더 긴 것 같아.

(this, five, longer, that, bridge, than, one, is, times)

➡ I think _____

Point Check Ⅲ

◆ **부사:** 다른 말을 도와서 자세한 정보를 주는 역할을 한다.

동사, 형용사, 다른 부사, 그리고 문장 전체를 꾸며준다.

1. 부사의 위치

동사 + 부사	• She can <u>run</u> fast.
부사 + 형용사	• He drinks very <u>cold</u> water.
부사 + 부사	• I play the piano very <u>well</u>.
부사 + 문장 전체	• Luckily, <u>they all entered the university</u>.

2. 형용사로 부사 만들기

규칙		단어	
-y로 끝나는 경우	y를 i로 바꾸고 -ly	happy – happily	heavy – heavily
-e로 끝나는 경우	e를 없애고 -ly	true – truly	
-le로 끝나는 경우	e를 없애고 -y	simple – simply	gentle – gently
-ic로 끝나는 경우	-ally를 붙임	basic – basically	scientific – scientifically

3. 빈도부사

always	**usually**	**often**	**sometimes**	**seldom**	**rarely**	**never**
항상	보통, 대개	종종, 자주	가끔, 때때로	드물게	거의 ~않는	결코 ~않는

100% ◄──────────────────────────────► 0%

➡ rarely = hardly 거의 ~않는 (부정의 의미)

4. 빈도부사의 위치

(1) **일반동사 앞:** [주어 + 빈도부사 + 일반동사]

• Elly usually <u>washes</u> the dishes after meals.

(2) **be동사와 조동사 뒤:** [주어 + be동사 + 빈도부사], [주어 + 조동사 + 빈도부사]

• They <u>were</u> **never** telling the truth.

• She <u>will</u> **sometimes** visit you.

부사

부사의 역할과 종류

• **부사**: 다른 말을 도와 더 자세한 정보를 준다. 문장 안에서 동사, 형용사, 다른 부사, 또는 문장 전체를 꾸며준다.

1. 부사의 역할: 부사는 주로 동사나 형용사를 꾸며주며, 문장 내의 다른 부사나 문장 전체를 꾸며준다.

(1) [동사 + 부사]

• The hummingbird <u>moves</u> its wings **quickly**. (quickly → moves 수식)

(2) [부사 + 형용사]

• We were **very** <u>impressed</u>. (very → impressed 수식)

(3) [부사 + 부사]

• The soccer team can play **very** <u>well</u>. (very → well 수식)

(4) [부사 + 문장 전체]

• **Fortunately**, <u>I could barely pass the exam</u>. (Fortunately → 문장 전체 수식)

2. 부사의 종류

1. 방법, 방식	quickly, softly, heavily
2. 장소	here, there, upstairs, downstairs, abroad, inside, outside
3. 시간	tomorrow, yesterday, now, then, already, recently
4. 빈도, 횟수	once, twice, sometimes, usually, rarely
5. 정도, 강조	completely, nearly, entirely, really, quite

☆Check up!

Answer Keys p. 45

A 다음 문장에서 부사를 찾아 모두 쓰시오

1 I get up early in the morning. _____*early*_____

2 Fortunately, they won the game. _____

3 She didn't know exactly what to do tomorrow.

_____

4   He solved the problem easily. I think he may be a genius.

_____

5   I'm so worried about him because he looked seriously ill.

_____

6   Helen cried endlessly because she failed to pass the exam.

_____

7   Unfortunately, the concert has already started.

_____

8   He could speak English fluently and quickly.

_____

9   My father built the farm well.   _____

10 Linda was ignored completely by the crowd.

_____

형용사로 부사 만들기

- 단어 자체가 부사인 경우도 있지만, '형용사 + ly'의 형태로 부사를 만들 수도 있다.

1. 규칙 변화: [형용사 + ly]

규칙		단어
-y로 끝나는 경우	y를 i로 바꾸고 -ly	happy – happily heavy – heavily easy – easily
-e로 끝나는 경우	e를 없애고 -ly	true – truly
-le로 끝나는 경우	e를 없애고 -y	simple – simply gentle – gently
-ic로 끝나는 경우	-ally를 붙임	basic – basically scientific – scientifically

2. 불규칙 변화: 형태는 같으나 뜻이 다른 부사

단어	뜻	예문
late	형 늦은	• Jack was late for the meeting.
	부 늦게	• She has to study late at night.
hard	형 열심인, 어려운	• Lily is a hard ballerina.
	부 열심히	• We decided to study and play hard as we can.
early	형 이른	• The special delivery arrived in the early morning.
	부 일찍	• I got to the appointment 30 minutes early.
fast	형 빠른	• The KTX is a very fast train in Korea.
	부 빠르게	• Because of the rising water, the river flows very fast.
high	형 빠른, 높은	• I can surf the Internet at a high speed.
	부 높이, 높게	• An eagle flies high into the sky.
long	형 긴	• Barbie has long blond hair.
	부 오래, 길게	• He was waiting for her too long.
enough	형 충분한	• We prepared enough food for everyone.
	부 충분히	• Your sister is old enough to go to school.

Answer Keys p. 45

Grammar Plus +

• lively, lonely, lovely, friendly, manly, yearly, monthly 등은 원래의 형태가 '-ly'로 끝나는 형용사이며, 따로 부사 형태는 없다.

☆Check up!

A 다음 형용사의 부사형을 쓰시오.

1	happy	➡ *happily*	2	real	➡ _____
3	quick	➡ _____	4	whole	➡ _____
5	true	➡ _____	6	final	➡ _____
7	gentle	➡ _____	8	easy	➡ _____
9	polite	➡ _____	10	full	➡ _____
11	mad	➡ _____	12	pretty	➡ _____
13	sad	➡ _____	14	lucky	➡ _____
15	careful	➡ _____	16	terrible	➡ _____
17	successful	➡ _____	18	brave	➡ _____
19	basic	➡ _____	20	simple	➡ _____
21	hard	➡ _____	22	different	➡ _____
23	visible	➡ _____	24	serious	➡ _____
25	wide	➡ _____	26	busy	➡ _____
27	comfortable	➡ _____	28	dull	➡ _____
29	angry	➡ _____	30	anxious	➡ _____
31	clear	➡ _____	32	full	➡ _____
33	loud	➡ _____	34	sudden	➡ _____
35	reasonable	➡ _____	36	slight	➡ _____
37	slow	➡ _____	38	nice	➡ _____
39	safe	➡ _____	40	foolish	➡ _____

9-13 뜻이 다른 두 가지 형태의 부사

• 부사에 '-ly'가 있으나 뜻이 완전히 다른 부사들도 있다.

◆ 뜻이 다른 부사

단어	뜻	예문
late	늦게	• He worked late all this week.
lately	최근에	• The weather has been so sunny lately. (= recently)
hard	열심히	• They worked hard all day.
hardly (=rarely)	거의 ~않다	• She could hardly rest last week.
high	높이	• I threw the ball high over the wall.
highly	매우, 높이 평가하여	• Audrey Hepburn was highly respected as not only an actress but also a humanitarian.
near	가까이에	• The orchestra hall is near City Hall.
nearly (=almost)	거의	• That picture is nearly 500 years old.

Check up!

Answer Keys p. 46

A 괄호 안에서 알맞은 것을 고르시오.

1 I was (late / lately) for the appointment.

2 They studied (hard / hardly) to pass the graduation exam.

3 Tim is so busy (lately / late) because of the project.

4 Tim and Sam lived (nearly / near) Central Park.

5 Director Park is one of the (highly / high) respected directors in Korea.

6 The box is (near / nearly) three hundred kilogram.

7 He jumped (high / highly) to reach the shelf.

8 Have you ever seen John (late / lately)?

9 Mijin could (hardly / hard) understand the lecture.

10 The kite was flying (high / highly).

11 Jackson woke up (lately / late) this morning.

Note

• humanitarian
인도주의자

빈도부사

• 빈도부사: 어떤 일이 얼마나 빈번하게 일어나는지에 대하여 알려주는 부사를 말한다.

1. 빈도부사의 종류

always	usually	often	sometimes	seldom	rarely	never
항상	보통, 대개	종종, 자주	가끔, 때때로	드물게	거의 ~않는	결코 ~않는

100% ◀━━━━━━━━━━━━━━━━━━━━━▶ 0%

➡ rarely ＝ hardly 거의 ~않는 (부정의 의미)

2. 빈도부사의 위치

(1) **일반동사 앞**: [주어 + 빈도부사 + 일반동사]

• Elly **often** goes to the library to read books.

• Luke **rarely** goes to the opera theater.

(2) **be동사와 조동사 뒤**: [주어 + be동사 + 빈도부사], [주어 + 조동사 + 빈도부사]

• You were **sometimes** taking a nap when I visited you.

• Timmy will **seldom** ask **you** for some help.

• I can **never** swim without a life jacket.

➡ 'never'는 자체에 부정의 의미가 있으므로 'not'과 함께 쓰일 수 없다.

☆Check up!

Answer Keys p. 46

A 다음 문장에서 어법상 어색한 것을 찾아 바르게 고치시오

1 He comes always on time.

comes always ➡ *always comes*

2 I sometimes can dance without music.

＿＿＿＿＿＿ ➡ ＿＿＿＿＿＿

3 James never think he is smart.

＿＿＿＿＿＿ ➡ ＿＿＿＿＿＿

4 Amy always is happy.

＿＿＿＿＿＿ ➡ ＿＿＿＿＿＿

5 Kate eats never vegetables.

＿＿＿＿＿＿ ➡ ＿＿＿＿＿＿

6 Suzy is late seldom for class.

＿＿＿＿＿＿ ➡ ＿＿＿＿＿＿

7 They always are ready to go on a trip.

＿＿＿＿＿＿ ➡ ＿＿＿＿＿＿

Practice More Ⅲ

A   다음 형용사의 부사형을 쓰시오.

1   happy   ➡   *happily*

2   basic   ➡   _____

3   comfortable ➡   _____

4   fast   ➡   _____

5   realistic   ➡   _____

6   honest   ➡   _____

7   quick   ➡   _____

8   terrible   ➡   _____

9   whole   ➡   _____

10 polite   ➡   _____

B   다음 빈칸에 들어갈 단어를 보기 에서 골라 쓰시오.

> 보기
>
> late   long   hard   fast   high   enough

1   It's ___hard___, but I won't give up. I'll do my best.

2   Her hair is _____. Jane is proud of it.

3   I want to have _____ time to think about my future.

4   _____ time no see, Daniel.

5   I can run as _____ as Jane.

6   A plane is flying _____ up in the sky.

7   Max always worked _____ to succeed, so he could live a successful life.

8   He is not old _____ to go to school.

9   You can surf the Internet at a _____ speed in Korea.

10 I was _____ for the English class.

C   다음 괄호 안에서 알맞은 것을 고르시오.

1   She (hard /(hardly)) watches horror movies.

2   She (often goes / goes often) to the gym to exercise.

3   I haven't read any books (late / lately).

4   They think Jane danced (beautifully / beautiful).

5   The kite was flying (high / highly).

6   My birthday is (near / nearly).

7   I can't remember his name (exact / exactly).

8   Jane could (hardly / hard) hear anything after she had an accident.

9   Please, listen (careful / carefully).

D   다음 주어진 부사를 알맞은 곳에 넣어 문장을 다시 쓰시오.

1   Tim comes on time. (usually)

➡ _____ *Tim usually comes on time.* _____

2   My son likes to wear his red coat in winter. (often)

➡ _____

3   I see Helen these days. (rarely)

➡ _____

4   I think they will catch up with me. (never)

➡ _____

5   When she is alone, she calls me. (usually)

➡ _____

6   Because he exercised too much, he could walk. (hardly)

➡ Because he exercised too much, _____

7   He closes the window. (always)

➡ _____

8   James and his mom go to the movies together. (sometimes)

➡ _____

9   I buy luxurious things such as jewelry. (rarely)

➡ _____

10   What do you do on holidays? (usually)

➡ _____

Point CheckIV

◆ **이어 동사:** '타동사+부사'의 형태에서 목적어가 명사인지 대명사인지에 따라 타동사와 부사 사이, 또는 타동사와 부사 뒤에 오는 위치가 달라진다.

1. 여러 가지 부사

already	– 긍정문과 의문문에 사용된다. • Did you already finish your homework?
yet	– 의문문과 부정문에 사용되며, 주로 문장의 끝에 위치한다. • We haven't eaten it yet.
still	– 긍정문과 의문문에 사용된다. • They still like to take trips.
too	– 긍정문에 사용된다. • You are pretty. You sister is pretty, too.
either	– 부정문에 사용된다. • He didn't like bananas. I didn't like bananas, either.
very	– 형용사와 부사의 원급을 수식한다. • This is very cold.
much	– 형용사와 부사의 비교급을 수식한다. • Lions are much stronger than deer.
else	– 수식하고자 하는 말 뒤에 위치한다. • Have you had anything else?
even	– 수식하고자 하는 말 앞에 위치한다. • He didn't even say sorry to her.
ago	– 시간을 나타내는 말과 함께 쓰이고, 과거 시제와 함께 사용된다. • They went back to England two years ago.
before	– 과거의 시점을 기준으로 그 이전에 일어난 일을 나타낼 때 쓰며, 과거완료 시제와 함께 사용된다. • We've cured for the disease a few years before.

2. So do I. / Neither do I.

- **So do I:** 긍정문에 동의할 때 [So + (조)동사 + 주어]
- **Neither do I:** 부정문에 동의할 때 [Neither + (조)동사 + 주어]

3. 이어 동사

- [타동사 + 부사 + 명사 목적어] = [타동사 + 명사 목적어 + 부사]

  Try on this new dress. = **Try** this new dress **on**.

- [타동사 + 목적어(대명사) + 부사]

  Don't **put** it **off**.

already / yet / still

- **already / yet**: 모두 '이미, 벌써'의 뜻을 가진다. 'already'는 긍정문이나 의문문에서 사용되며, 'yet'은 부정문과 의문문에서 사용된다.
- **still**: 주로 긍정문, 의문문에 쓰이며 계속되는 행위를 말할 때 사용한다.

already 이미, 벌써	– 긍정문과 의외나 놀라움을 나타내는 의문문에서 사용된다. • Did you already write a letter? [의외] • The tailor already made two suits. [긍정문]
yet 이제, 아직 (이미, 벌써)	– 의문문과 부정문에 사용되며, 주로 문장의 끝에 위치한다. • Have they left yet? [의문문] • We haven't finished it yet. [부정문]
still 여전히, 아직도	– 긍정문과 의문문에 쓰이며, 계속되는 행위를 강조할 때는 부정문에 쓰이기도 한다. • He still likes to tell funny stories. [긍정문] • Do they still enjoy playing badminton after dinner? [의문문] • I still can't stop going shopping on weekends. [부정문]

➡ 이 부사들은 일반동사 앞, be동사 뒤에 온다.
　하지만 'still'의 경우, 부정문을 강조하려고 쓰일 때 부정어 앞에 위치한다.

Grammar Plus +

- **'still'과 'yet'의 비교급 강조**: 비교급 문장에 쓰일 때는 '훨씬, 더욱'이라는 뜻을 가진다.
  - This dress is still shinier than that one.
  - To make a yet more interesting tale, I combined at least two more stories.

- **부정문에서 'still'과 'yet'의 위치**
  부정문: 'still not' / 'not yet'의 형태로 쓰이며 '아직'이라는 뜻으로 쓰인다.

☆Check up!

Answer Keys p. 46

A　보기와 같이 빈칸에 already, yet, still 중 알맞은 것을 쓰시오.

보기

① I <u>already</u> finished my homework.
② I'm <u>still</u> doing my homework.
③ I haven't finished my homework <u>yet</u>.

1 ① They ___already___ talked to Helen.

   ② They are ___still___ talking to Helen.

   ③ They haven't talked to Helen ___yet___.

2 ① Are you _____ reading the book?

   ② Have you read the book _____?

   ③ Did you _____ read the book?

3 ① Mijin is _____ sending an email.

   ② Mijin _____ sent an email.

   ③ Mijin hasn't sent an email _____.

4 ① Linda is _____ cleaning her house.

   ② Linda hasn't cleaned her house _____.

   ③ Linda _____ cleaned her house.

5 ① Sally _____ prepared for her daughter's birthday party.

   ② Sally is _____ preparing for her daughter's birthday party.

   ③ Sally hasn't prepared for her daughter's birthday party _____.

B 빈칸에 알맞은 것을 쓰시오.

1 Does she ___still___ work on that project?

2 I _____ had my breakfast.

3 Have you written the letter _____?

4 John has _____ left.

5 I haven't decided where to go _____.

6 Max _____ loves her.

7 Does he _____ know the answer?

8 They haven't completed the course _____.

9 I _____ have his picture.

10 Mrs. Brown _____ made the dress.

too / either

> • too와 either : 둘 다 문장 끝에 쓰여 '~도 또한'이라는 뜻을 가진다. 앞의 내용에 동의하는 부사로 'too'는 긍정문에, 'either'는 부정문에 쓰인다.

◆ too와 either

too ~도 또한, 역시	– 긍정문에 사용된다. • Ally is a fashion model. You are a fashion model, too. • **A** I want to eat a lobster. **B** Me, too. (=I want to eat a lobster, too)
either ~도 또한, 역시	– 부정문에 사용된다. • I don't enjoy playing chess. She doesn't enjoy it, either. • **A** I didn't bring anything to the party. **B** I didn't bring anything, either.

Grammar Plus +

• **not either = neither** : '~도 또한'의 뜻으로 부정문에 사용된다.

  A I don't want to mix more vegetables into the soup, **either**.

  B Me, **neither**.

☆Check up!

Answer Keys p. 46

A 빈칸에 알맞은 것을 써 넣으시오.

1 I like baseball, and my brother likes baseball, ___too___.

2 Max doesn't listen to the radio. Max doesn't read books, _____.

3 He is smart. He is gentle, _____.

4 I can't read French. Helen can't read it, _____.

5 John comes from LA. Amy comes from LA, _____.

6 He doesn't like to eat pasta. His wife doesn't like to, _____.

7 **A** I don't want to go to Europe this summer.
  B Me, _____.

8 I didn't finish the project, and James didn't finish, _____.

9 She is not a teacher. She is not a nurse, _____.

10 **A** I can't remember his name. **B** Me, _____.

So do I / Neither do I

- 'So do I'와 'Neither do I'는 모두 '나도 그래'라는 뜻을 가지지만, 'So do I'는 긍정문에, 'Neither do I'는 부정문에 쓰인다.

◈ So do I / Neither do I

	긍정문에 동의할 때 [So + (조)동사 + 주어]	부정문에 동의할 때 [Neither + (조)동사 + 주어]
be동사	• A I am so glad. B So <u>am</u> I.	• A He wasn't angry at Tommy. B Neither <u>was</u> I.
일반동사	• A Larry likes to talk. B So <u>does</u> Julie.	• A I didn't get an email from professor Joe. B Neither <u>did</u> I.
조동사	• A They can dance very well. B So <u>can</u> we.	• A She can't pole-jump. B Neither <u>can</u> I.

☆Check up!

Answer Keys p. 47

A 다음 대화의 빈칸에 so, neither를 알맞게 쓰시오.

1 A I'm so moved.

　　B _So am_ I.

2 A Kate thought Tom's answer was right.

　　B _____ I.

3 A I didn't know what day tomorrow was.

　　B _____ I.

4 A She was not happy with the present.

　　B _____ my daughter.

5 A Eunhye likes to talk.

　　B _____ Mina.

6 A I didn't realize it was too late.

　　B _____ I.

7 A Joe didn't read the book.

　　B _____ Jungmin.

8 A I can't swim in the sea.

　　B _____ I.

very / much / else / even

- **very / much**: 형용사나 부사를 수식하여 의미의 정도를 나타낸다.
- **else / even**: 수식하는 말 앞이나 뒤에 위치한다.

◈ very와 much

	very 너무, 매우	**much** 훨씬, 더욱
형용사 수식	원급을 수식한다. • This math quiz is very <u>difficult</u>.	비교급을 수식한다. • Max is much <u>smarter</u> than Jimmy.
부사 수식	원급을 수식한다. • Akiko speaks English very <u>well</u>.	비교급을 수식한다. • Lily studies science much <u>better</u> than Jenna. (부사: better)

◈ else와 even

else 그 밖에	**even** ~조차
• 수식하고자 하는 **말 뒤에 위치한다.** • Have you worked anywhere else? • What else should we bring? ➡ 'else'가 의문대명사나 부정대명사 뒤에 올 때는 형용사의 역할을 한다.	• 수식하고자 하는 **말 앞에 위치한다.** • I didn't even know it was a holiday. • Even children can do better than that. • Even when you go to bathroom, you should tell your teacher.

☆Check up!

Answer Keys p. 47

A 다음 괄호 안에서 알맞은 것을 고르시오.

1 The car was ((very)/ much) expensive.

2 Sam arrived at the concert (very / much) early.

3 After the snow, the weather became (very / much) warmer.

4 I didn't realize that the car was (much / very) cheaper than my car.

5 The information that he gave was (very / much) useful.

6 She can make cakes (much / very) better than she could last year.

7 My baby likes James more than anyone (else / even).

8 We work hard (else / even) on holidays!

9 Where (even / else) can I get the photos taken by him?

ago / before

- **ago** : 현재를 기준으로 과거의 어느 시점에 일어난 일을 나타낼 때 사용한다.

- **before** : 과거의 어느 한 시점을 기준으로 그 이전에 일어난 일을 나타낼 때 사용한다.

◈ **ago / before** : ～전에

ago	before
'ago'는 홀로 사용될 수 없어 항상 시간을 나타내는 말과 함께 쓰이며, **과거 시제와 함께 사용된다.** • There were a lot of trees and flowers in this garden a long time ago. • Jessy moved to Seoul from Gwangju five years ago.	'before'는 과거의 한 시점을 기준으로 그 이전에 일어난 일을 나타낼 때 쓰이며, 과거완료시제와 함께 사용된다. • Miyu has been to Europe twice before. • We heard that you had traveled in Germany a few months before.

Grammar Plus +

- **before**

  'before'는 시간을 나타내는 말 없이도 홀로 쓰일 수 있다. 이때는 현재완료, 과거, 과거완료 시제와 함께 사용될 수 있다.

  We've never **seen** fireworks **before**.

  It was cold because it **had rained before** the party.

☆Check up!

Answer Keys p. 47

A 다음 괄호 안에서 알맞은 것을 찾으시오.

1 Mary and Linda have been to Korea three times (before / ago).

2 Tommy moved to Busan from Seoul six years (ago / before).

3 Tomorrow morning, I have to arrive at the station (before / ago) ten o'clock.

4 They came here ten minutes (before / ago).

5 My teacher told us the schedule seven days (before / ago).

6 She has to leave here (before / ago) 2 o'clock.

7 I have seen John (ago / before).

8 Jina finished the project two hours (before / ago).

9 My nephew moved to another country three days (ago / before).

10 You should make a reservation one day (before / ago) you want to go to the restaurant.

Lesson 9-20

이어 동사 _ 타동사 + 부사(+ 목적어)

- **이어 동사**: 목적어가 명사인지 대명사인지에 따라 그 위치가 달라진다.

  목적어가 명사이면 동사와 부사 사이 또는 부사 뒤에 위치하고,

  목적어가 대명사이면 동사와 부사 사이에 위치한다.

1. [타동사 + 부사 + 명사 목적어] = [타동사 + 명사 목적어 + 부사]

- **Put on** the new shoes. = **Put** the new shoes **on**.

2. [타동사 + 목적어(대명사) + 부사]

- **Throw** it **away** over there. (**O**)

- Throw away it over there. (**X**)

3. [타동사 + 부사]로 쓰이는 동사

• turn on/off	(TV, 스위치 등을) 켜다/끄다	• turn down	(소리, 온도 등을) 줄이다
• take off	(옷, 모자 등을) 벗다	• give up	포기하다
• put on	(옷, 모자 등을) 입다	• pick up	집어 들다, 차로 데리러 가다
• try on	시험 삼아 해보다, 옷을 입어보다	• put off	연기하다, 미루다
• see off	배웅하다	• throw away	내버리다, 던지다

Grammar Plus +

- **[자동사 + 전치사]**: '자동사 + 전치사' 는 두 개가 합쳐져 하나의 타동사로 쓰인다.

  두 단어는 분리될 수 없으며, 목적어가 명사인지 대명사인지 상관없이 무조건 전치사 뒤에 위치한다.

◈ **[자동사+전치사]로 쓰이는 동사**

look for	look at	listen to	talk about	depend on	agree with

We are waiting for her. (**O**) / We are waiting her for. (**X**)

A 괄호 안에 알맞은 말을 <u>모두</u> 찾으시오.

1 Could you (turn it off / turn off it)?

2 She is (looking for a dictionary / looking a dictionary for).

3 (Look at the picture / Look the picture at)! I love it.

4 Don't (give it up / give up it)! You should do your best.

5 Alex will (pick you up / pick up you) at seven.

6 Well, (wake him up / wake up him) right now.

7 He is (waiting for her / waiting her for) outside.

8 When you are inside, (take off your shoes / take your shoes off).

9 I don't (agree you with / agree with you).

10 Many people tend to (depend on their parents / depend their parents on).

11 Inho (put the hat on / put on the hat) before he went out with her.

12 People should not (throw garbage away / throw away garbage) here.

13 Will you (check them out / check out them) for me?

14 I (listened to the radio / listened the radio to) yesterday.

15 My son is (sitting on the chair / sitting the chair on).

Practice More IV

Answer Keys p. 47~48

A 괄호 안에서 알맞은 것을 고르시오.

1 I don't know how to play chess. I don't know how to play
   Baduk, (either / neither).

2 Jane (hasn't still / still hasn't) start her homework.

3 A I'm so pleased to see you again.   B So (do / am) I.

4 Tim is (very / much) slimmer than Alex. Alex should start
   exercising to lose weight.

5 Have you lived (anywhere else / else anywhere)?

6 Ann (yet / already) knows the fact.

7 They didn't (realize even / even realize) that she was Sally.

8 A Hey, I didn't remember that today is Kim's birthday.

   B (Neither / Either) did I.

9 Mary started to make the yellow dress two hours (ago /
   before).

10 A I can't swim in the sea.   B Neither (can / can't) I.

B 다음 빈칸에 알맞은 말을 넣어 문장을 완성하시오.

1 A I've had dinner.

   B I've had dinner, ____too____.
      Me, ____too____. / So ____have____ I.

2 A I can't remember Jack's phone number.

   B I can't remember Jack's phone number, _____.
      Me, _____. / _____ can I.

3 A I went to see a baseball game last week.

   B I went to see a baseball game last week, _____.
      Me, _____. / So _____ I.

4 A I didn't hear the news.

   B I didn't hear the news, _____.
      Me, _____. / _____ did I.

5 A I like to watch horror movies.

   B I like to watch horror movies, _____.
      Me, _____. / So _____ I.

Practice More IV

6 **A** I didn't realize it was Sunday.

    B I didn't realize it was Sunday, _____.
Me, _____. / _____ did I.

7 **A** I think Amy should lose weight for her health.

    B I think Amy should lose weight for her health, _____.
Me, _____. / So _____ I.

8 **A** She likes dancing in front of an audience.

    B Lina likes dancing in front of an audience, _____.
Lina, _____. / So _____ Lina.

9 **A** I will go to LA over summer vacation.

    B I want to go there, _____.
Me, _____. / So _____ I.

C 밑줄 친 명사를 괄호 안의 대명사로 바꾸어 문장을 다시 쓰시오.

1 You have to turn in the paper by tomorrow morning. (it)

➡ _____ *You have to turn it in by tomorrow morning.* _____

2 Jack will pick up his friends at the airport. (them)

➡ _____

3 You should take off your hat when you enter a room. (it)

➡ _____

4 Don't turn off the TV. I need to watch Amy's talk show tonight. (it)

➡ _____

D 다음 문장에서 어법상 어색한 것을 찾아 바르게 고치시오.

1 Jane is looking a map for to find the station.

___ *a map for* ___ ➡ ___ *for a map* ___

2 Listen carefully and write down it.

_____ ➡ _____

3 I know him. I have met him ago.

_____ ➡ _____

4 Are you already reading the book?

_____ ➡ _____

5 John is yet cleaning her room.

        _____ ➡ _____

6 His research was much impressive.

        _____ ➡ _____

7 What can else I do for them?

        _____ ➡ _____

8 Sam would like to try on them.

        _____ ➡ _____

9 I think this winter is very colder than last year.

        _____ ➡ _____

10 Would you mind turning off it?

        _____ ➡ _____

E 다음 우리말 해석에 맞게 주어진 단어를 바르게 배열하여 문장을 완성하시오.

1 그가 그들을 공항에 데리러 갈 예정이다.

    (he, at the airport, pick, is, to, them, going, up)

    ➡   *He is going to pick them up at the airport.*

2 창 밖으로 쓰레기를 버리면 안 된다.

    (don't, the window, garbage, throw, out)

    ➡ _____

3 Minji는 방에서 그것을 입었다. (Minji, the, it, in, put, room, on)

    ➡ _____

4 포기하지 마. 끝까지 최선을 다하자!

    (don't, up, do, best, give, your)

    ➡ _____

5 불 좀 꺼줄래? 나는 지금 자야 해.

    (the, would, off, you, light, turn)

    ➡ _____? I have to sleep now.

6 너는 그것을 미루면 안 돼. 마감 기한은 금요일이야.

    (you, Friday, shouldn't, it, the due date, put, is, off)

    ➡ _____

내신 최다 출제 유형

01 다음 빈칸에 들어갈 말이 바르게 짝지어진 것을 고르시오. [출제 예상 80%]

> • Jenny gave me _____ information about the test.
> • I have _____ money.

① some – a few　② any – few
③ some – a little　④ any – a little
⑤ some – few

02 다음 중 어법상 옳은 것을 고르시오. [출제 예상 90%]

① I want warm something to eat.
② Did you find interesting something?
③ She has a youngest sister.
④ We helped a lot of poor people.
⑤ He is very funny man.

03 다음 빈칸에 들어갈 말로 알맞지 않는 것을 고르시오. [출제 예상 85%]

> Very early in the morning, Melisa _____.

① woke him up
② woke up him
③ woke her sister up
④ woke up her sister
⑤ woke up my friend

04 다음 중 어법상 어색한 것을 고르시오. [출제 예상 85%]

① You should take some medicine.
② Would you like some water?
③ We're in the third grade.
④ That sounds interesting.
⑤ Exciting something will happen to them.

05 다음 밑줄 친 부분의 쓰임이 어색한 것을 모두 고르시오. [출제 예상 85%]

① Would you like any coffee?
② I bought some apples at the market.
③ She didn't have some friends.
④ I put some food in my bag.
⑤ Do they have any special plans for the party?

06 다음 날짜 중 영어로 바르게 표현한 것을 모두 고르시오. [출제 예상 80%]

① 5월 15일 – the fifteen of May
② 1958년 – nineteen five-eight
③ 12월 28일 – December the twenty-eighth
④ 2009년 – two thousand nine
⑤ 11월 1일 – the one of November

07 다음 중 밑줄 친 부분의 쓰임이 맞는 것을 고르시오. [출제 예상 85%]

① We need a large strong box.
② Her big blue eyes are beautiful.
③ Jane has an old big car.
④ Jacky has a white small cat.
⑤ My all friends study hard.

[01~02] 다음 중 두 단어의 관계가 나머지 넷과 <u>다른</u> 것을 고르시오.

01
① slow − slowly
② kind − kindly
③ nice − nicely
④ short − shortly
⑤ love − lovely

02
① heavy − light
② pretty − ugly
③ angry − mad
④ long − short
⑤ big − small

[03~05] 다음 빈칸에 들어갈 말로 알맞은 것을 고르시오. (답이 여러 개일 경우 <u>모두</u> 고르시오.)

03

_____ minutes later, she came to me and asked me the way to City Hall.

① Little
② A little
③ A few
④ Any
⑤ Much

04

A Why are you so _____?
B My mom got angry with me.

① happily
② gladly
③ pleasing
④ upset
⑤ sad

05

There are _____ people in the concert hall.

① lots of
② much
③ a little
④ little
⑤ any

[06~09] 다음 중 어법상 옳은 문장을 고르시오.

★★★
06
① He them took out and looked at them.
② He took out them and looked at them.
③ He took them out and looked at them.
④ He took out them and looked them at
⑤ He took them out and looked them at.

★★★
07
① She wore a pink long skirt with a cute green ribbon.
② She wore a long pink skirt with a cute green ribbon.
③ She wore a long pink skirt with a ribbon cute green.
④ She wore a long pink skirt with a green cute ribbon.
⑤ She wore a pink long skirt with a green cute ribbon.

08
① He bought many butter to make some cookies.
② The seven-years-old boy is my son.
③ She doesn't look happily.
④ I want to eat something hot.
⑤ We saw a photo interesting yesterday.

09
① They haven't finished it already.
② It's more important than anything else.
③ He is very more famous than her.
④ She didn't visit me, too.
⑤ Please make him stopping crying.

[10~13] 다음 중 어법상 <u>어색한</u> 문장을 고르시오.

10
① Sara went on a picnic with her family.
② There once lived a prince in the country.
③ Clean up your room by seven.
④ She made some money last vacation.
⑤ Do good something for your parents.

11
① Jessica usually is kind.
② We never drink coffee.
③ Teddy is often late for school.
④ They usually go to church on Sundays.
⑤ I sometimes go swimming.

★★★
12
① I got a good grade, too.
② Eating regularly is well for your health.
③ Helen is much better than you.
④ Harry sometimes goes to the park.
⑤ I always meet my friends on Friday night.

★★★
13
① My baby nephew is asleep.
② He was very afraid of snakes.
③ Jena is alone all the time.
④ My sister and I look like.
⑤ Some flowers are alive.

[14~15] 다음 우리말을 영어로 바르게 옮긴 것을 고르시오.

14

이 동물원에는 많은 원숭이들이 있다.

① There is a number of monkeys in this zoo.
② There are number of monkeys in this zoo.
③ There are a number of monkeys in this zoo.
④ There is numbers of monkeys in this zoo.
⑤ There aren't a number of monkeys in this zoo.

15

Jack 또한 형제가 없었다.

① Jack didn't have any brothers, either.
② Jack didn't have any brother, neither.
③ Jack didn't have any brothers, too.
④ Jack didn't have any brothers, also.
⑤ Jack didn't have any brothers, neither.

★★★
16 다음 짝지어진 두 문장의 뜻이 같은 것을 고르시오.

① I have lots of toys.
= I have a few toys.
② They have some money.
= They have a few money.
③ I got some presents.
= I got a few presents.
④ We have a lot of homework.
= We have some homework.
⑤ Flowers need a little water.
= Flowers need little water.

Answer Keys p. 48~49

17 다음 대화의 밑줄 친 문장 중 어법상 어색한 것을 고르시오.

> A ① This Thursday is my birthday.
> B We know. ② What do you want to do?
> A Well, ③ I just want to do interesting something.
> B That sounds good. But ④ we'll think about it more.
> A Okay. Anyway, ⑤ my party will be very fun.

18 다음 중 빈칸에 들어갈 말로 알맞지 않은 것을 고르시오.

> Seon and Sally are _____ classmates.

① friendly   ② nice
③ kind   ④ carefully
⑤ polite

★★★
19 주어진 분수를 영어로 바르게 표현한 것을 고르시오.

> $$\frac{2}{7}$$

① two seven   ② second sevens
③ two seventh   ④ second sevenths
⑤ two sevenths

20 다음 괄호 안의 단어를 순서대로 배열했을 때 다섯 번째에 오는 단어를 고르시오.

> (we / such / a / graceful / woman / have / never / seen)

① seen   ② a   ③ never
④ such   ⑤ graceful

[21~23] 다음 대화의 빈칸에 들어갈 알맞은 표현을 고르시오.

21
> A Have you ever read, "The Great Gatsby"?
> B No, I haven't read it _____.

① yet   ② either   ③ neither
④ already   ⑤ too

22
> A I'd love to go camping, but I can't.
> B _____?

① Good   ② Okay   ③ Why not
④ Of course   ⑤ I'm sorry

23
> A _____ does Timmy go to band practice?
> B He goes to the band twice a week.

① How long   ② How many
③ How much   ④ Haw far
⑤ How often

24 다음 문장의 밑줄 친 much와 의미가 다른 것을 고르시오.

> Beth is much nicer than Elie.

① She is much taller than me.
② We enjoyed singing very much.
③ I feel much better today.
④ Tommy can jump much higher than Jim.
⑤ He is much fatter than before.

★★★
25 다음 밑줄 친 부분이 어색한 것을 모두 고르시오.

① I carried it very carefully.
② Why does she walk so fastly?
③ We look different.
④ Have you listened to music late?
⑤ He catches the ball quickly.

[26~27] 다음 글의 밑줄 친 부분이 어색한 것을 고르시오.

26

> ① Many people think it is ② more important to be ③ health ④ than to have ⑤ a lot of money.

27

> Jenny ① must be very ② hungry. Because she ③ only drank ④ a glass of milk and had ⑤ else nothing today.

[28~29] 다음 괄호 안의 주어진 단어를 바르게 배열한 것을 고르시오.

28

> Jack (sometimes / will / late / be) for work.

① will sometimes be late
② sometimes will be late
③ will be sometimes late
④ be will sometimes late
⑤ will late be sometimes

29

> If there's (anything / you / with / wrong), I'll help you anytime.

① wrong anything with you
② anything with you wrong
③ anything wrong with you
④ wrong with anything you
⑤ you wrong anything with

30 다음 밑줄 친 부분의 뜻으로 알맞지 않은 것을 모두 고르시오.

① Stella has little water to drink.
　　(거의 ~ 없는)
② Clare didn't have much money to buy it with.
　　(많은)
③ We bought a few oranges.
　　(거의 ~ 없는)
④ Plenty of people were cheering.
　　(약간)
⑤ There are many students in the gym.
　　(많은)

★★★
31 다음 중 어법상 올바른 것을 <u>모두</u> 고르시오.

① We want professional someone for this work.
② Can you find something fun to do on this island?
③ I wrapped up them myself.
④ He took out it from her bag.
⑤ Joan doesn't have anything interesting.

32 다음 밑줄 친 부분과 바꿔 쓸 수 있는 단어를 고르시오.

> I have bought <u>some</u> pretty postcards for my friends.

① any ② a little ③ few
④ a few ⑤ little

33 다음 질문에 대한 대답으로 옳은 것을 고르시오.

> **A** How far is the subway station from here?
> **B** _____.

① It's thirty minutes.
② I can't go there.
③ Not at all.
④ I'll pick you up.
⑤ It's about two blocks from here.

34

> **A** Have you ever been to Africa?
> **B** No, I haven't. Have you?
> **A** _____.

① Me, too. ② Me, neither.
③ Yes, I am. ④ No, I don't.
⑤ Me, also.

◇◇◇◇◇◇◇◇◇ 서술형 평가 ◇◇◇◇◇◇◇◇◇

35 다음 주어진 문장에서 틀린 곳을 찾아 바르게 고치시오.

> Annie finished the audition successful last Saturday.

_____ ➡ _____

36 빈칸에 알맞은 단어를 넣어 대화를 완성하시오.

> **A** I decided to learn Chinese.
> **B** I don't want to learn.
> **C** I don't want to learn, _____.

➡ _____

37 다음 우리말에 알맞은 영어 표현을 쓰시오.

> **A** I'm not good at speaking foreign languages.
> **B** <u>나도 그래.</u>

➡ _____

38 다음 우리말과 같은 뜻이 되도록 빈칸에 알맞은 단어를 쓰시오.

> 나는 Woody가 가진 것보다 네 배 많은 장난감을 가지고 있다.
> = I have _____ _____ as many toys as Woody has.

➡ _____ _____

★★★
39 다음의 분수를 영어로 바르게 쓰시오.

(1) $\frac{2}{5}$ – _____

(2) $\frac{6}{3}$ – _____

(3) $3\frac{5}{6}$ – _____

40 다음 글에서 어색한 부분을 찾아 고쳐 쓰시오.

> It was not hard to find the post office. We could easy find it.

_____ ➡ _____

41 다음 빈칸에 공통으로 들어갈 알맞은 말을 쓰시오.

> (A) I want to drink _____ water.
> (B) There is _____ money left.

➡ _____

[42~44] 다음 괄호 안의 단어를 바르게 배열하여 문장을 완성하시오.

★★★
42
> (Emily / looking / is / exciting / something / for)

➡ _____

★★★
43
> (unhappy / are / the / always / poor / not)

➡ _____

44
> (how / you / Art Gallery / to / get / did / the)

➡ _____

[45~46] 다음 질문에 대한 알맞은 대답을 쓰시오.
(세 단어로 표현 하시오.)

45
> A Larry likes to play badminton.
> B Judy도 그래.

➡ _____

46
> A Tory can't sing well.
> B 나도 그래.

➡ _____

10

Chapter
비교구문

Point Check I

◆ **비교구문**: 형용사와 부사의 형태를 변화시켜서 두 개 이상의 것을 비교하는 것을 말한다.
비교구문은 '원급, 비교급, 최상급'으로 나눌 수 있다.

1. 비교급과 최상급 형태

	비교급 [~보다 ~한]	최상급 [가장 ~한]
대개의 경우	• 형용사/부사-er + than	• the 형용사/부사-est
2음절 이상의 형용사	• more 형용사/부사 + than	• the most 형용사/부사

2. 원급 / 비교급 비교하기

원급과 비교급	예문
as 원급 as	• [as + 형용사/부사 + as + A] A만큼 ~한(하게) Beth is **as smart as** her sister.
	• [not as(so) + 형용사/부사 + as + A] A만큼 ~하지 않은(않게) I am **not as tall as** you.
비교급 than	• [형용사/부사 비교급 + than ...] ...보다 더 ~한 Victoria is **more popular than** he is. [= 목적어 him]
	• [not + 형용사/부사 비교급 + than ...] ...보다 더 ~하지 않은 Richard is **not kinder than** you are. [= 목적어 you]

3. 비교급의 여러 가지 표현

(1) [There is nothing~ 비교급 + than ...] ...보다 더 ~한 것은 없다

　　• **There is nothing** Jenny **likes better** than cooking.

(2) [비교급 and 비교급]: 점점 더 ~한(하게)

　　• Sammy was getting **thinner and thinner**.

(3) [the + 비교급 + 주어 + 동사, the + 비교급 + 주어 + 동사]: ~하면 할수록 더 ...한(하게)

　　• **The harder** I study, **the better** I will do.

10-1 비교급과 최상급 만들기 _ 규칙변화

- **비교급과 최상급**: 형용사와 부사의 형태를 변화시켜 만든다.
- **비교급**: [형용사(부사)-er / -r + than] ~보다 더 ...한
- **최상급**: [the+형용사(부사)-est / -st] 가장 ~한

* 2음절 이상의 단어들은 '-er / -r' 대신에 'more'를, '-est / -st' 대신에 'most'를 단어 앞에 붙여준다.

◆ 비교급과 최상급의 규칙변화 (1)

대개의 경우	원급 + -er/-est	cold – colder – coldest low – lower – lowest	hard – harder – hardest long – longer – longest
'-e'로 끝나는 경우	원급 + -r/-st	close – closer – closest nice – nicer – nicest	large – larger -largest wise – wiser – wisest
자음 + y	y를 'i'로 바꾸고 + -er/-est	dirty – dirtier – dirtiest busy – busier – busiest	lazy – lazier – laziest easy – easier – easiest
단모음 + 단자음	마지막 자음을 한 번 더 쓰고 + -er/-est	big – bigger – biggest fat – fatter – fattest	hot – hotter – hottest thin – thinner – thinnest

◆ 비교급과 최상급의 규칙변화 (2)

2음절 이상의 형용사		famous – more famous – the most famous helpful – more helpful – the most helpful
분사 형태의 형용사	more / the most + 원급	exciting – more exciting – the most exciting boring – more boring – the most boring
형용사+ly		exactly – more exactly – the most exactly careful – more careful – the most careful

A 다음 단어의 비교급과 최상급을 쓰시오.

1   hard   ➡ _____harder_____ ➡ _____hardest_____

2   hot   ➡ _____ ➡ _____

3   cold   ➡ _____ ➡ _____

4   fast   ➡ _____ ➡ _____

5   easy   ➡ _____ ➡ _____

6   happy ➡ _____ ➡ _____

7   large ➡ _____ ➡ _____

8   long   ➡ _____ ➡ _____

9   high   ➡ _____ ➡ _____

10 low   ➡ _____ ➡ _____

11 close ➡ _____ ➡ _____

12 early ➡ _____ ➡ _____

13 heavy ➡ _____ ➡ _____

14 pretty ➡ _____ ➡ _____

15 dirty ➡ _____ ➡ _____

16 fresh ➡ _____ ➡ _____

17 thin   ➡ _____ ➡ _____

18 thick ➡ _____ ➡ _____

19 deep   ➡ _____ ➡ _____

20 big   ➡ _____ ➡ _____

21 exactly ➡ _____ ➡ _____

22 mild   ➡ _____ ➡ _____

23 poor   ➡ _____ ➡ _____

24 cold   ➡ _____ ➡ _____

25 useful ➡ _____ ➡ _____

26 fluent ➡ _____ ➡ _____

27 tired ➡ _____ ➡ _____

28 fat   ➡ _____ ➡ _____

29 kind   ➡ _____ ➡ _____

비교급과 최상급 만들기 _ 불규칙변화

• 비교급과 최상급을 만들 때 일부 형용사나 부사는 의미에 따라 형태가 불규칙적으로 변화한다.

◈ 비교급과 최상급의 불규칙변화

불규칙변화의 단어		예문
good – better – best	좋은	• This car is better than that one.
well – better – best	건강한, 잘	• Timmy sings better than Jason.
bad – worse – worst	나쁜	• His personality is worse than we think.
ill – worse – worst	병든	• Her grandfather is worse than last week.
old – older – oldest	나이 든, 늙은	• Her sister is older than my sister.
old – elder – eldest	연장의, 손위의	• Luna is my elder sister.
late – later – latest	(시간) 늦은	• We were later to the party than they thought.
late – latter – last	(순서) 늦은	• The latter part of this book is very exciting.
far – farther – farthest	(거리) 먼	• We went farther than we planned.
far – further – furthest	(정도) 먼	• We'll talk about this problem further next time.
many – more – most	(수) 많은	• She has more troubles than we knew.
much – more – most	(양) 많은	• I begged him to give me more time.
few – fewer – fewest	(수) 적은	• There are fewer pencils on the left side than the right side.
little – less – least	(양) 적은	• There is less juice now than 30 minutes ago.

A 다음 단어들의 비교급과 최상급을 쓰시오.

1 bad   ➡ _worse_ ➡ _worst_

2 late (시간) ➡ _____ ➡ _____

3 much   ➡ _____ ➡ _____

4 little   ➡ _____ ➡ _____

5 ill   ➡ _____ ➡ _____

6 well   ➡ _____ ➡ _____

7 old (연장의) ➡ _____ ➡ _____

8 few   ➡ _____ ➡ _____

9 far (거리) ➡ _____ ➡ _____

10 far (정도) ➡ _____ ➡ _____

B 괄호 안에서 알맞은 것을 고르시오

1 This cake is (more / most) delicious than that one.

2 She sings (well / better) than her sister.

3 Mike is (older / elder) than Jack.

4 The (later / latter) part of this movie was very moving.

5 James is (worse / worst) than last week.

6 Please, give me (many / more) time.

7 Nick and I couldn't go (farther / further) because of the storm.

as 원급 as

• **as 원급 as** : 'as~as...' 사이에는 형용사 또는 부사의 원형이 들어간다.

비교하는 두 대상이 비슷하거나 같을 때 사용하며, '...만큼(처럼) ~한'이라고 해석한다.

* 원급은 형용사와 부사의 원래 형태를 말한다.

1. [as + 형용사/부사 + as + A]: A만큼 ~한(하게)

• Betty is **as tall as** her father.

• Jeremy plays soccer **as well as** professional players.

2. [not as(so) + 형용사/부사 + as + A]: A만큼 ~하지 않은(않게)
(= less + 형용사/부사 + than A)

• I am **not as fat as** you.

= I am **less fat than** you.

• She does **not** study **as hard as** me.

= She studies **less** hard **than** me.

3. [as + 형용사/부사 + as + 주어 + can(could)]: ~가 할 수 있는 한 ...하게
(= possible)

• He will do that **as quickly as** he **can**.

= He will do that **as quickly as possible**.

• They had to come back home **as soon as they could**.

= They had to come back home **as soon as possible**.

Grammar Plus +

• **as ~ as...**

① 비교할 대상은 서로 같은 종류, 같은 성질의 것이어야 한다.

• My sister is **as pretty as** that model.

• This ruler is **as long as** that belt.

② 'as ~ as' 사이에 들어가는 것이 형용사인지 부사인지를 판단할 때는 앞의 'as'를 빼고 다음 'as' 직전까지의 문장을 보고 판단한다.

➡ 대개의 경우 동사가 일반동사일 경우엔 부사를, be동사일 경우엔 형용사를 넣는다.

• Miranda <u>plays</u> the piano as **well** as her mom.

• Her playing is as **good** as yours.

A 우리말 뜻과 같도록 괄호 안에서 알맞은 단어를 고르시오.

1   나는 가능한 한 빨리 집에 돌아가야 한다.
➡ I have to go back home as soon as (possible / could).

2   Sue는 Jina보다 키가 작다.
➡ Sue is not as tall (as / than) Jina.

3   나는 Jack만큼 많은 공을 가지고 있다.
➡ I have as (many / much) balls as Jack.

4   그의 차는 내 차만큼 새 것이다.
➡ His car is as (new / newer) as mine.

5   내 바지는 그의 바지보다 길지 않다.
➡ My pants are not as (long / longer) as his pants.

6   바나나가 빵보다 더 무겁지 않다.
➡ The banana is not as heavy (as / than) the bread.

7   John은 그가 할 수 있는 한 세게 창을 던졌다.
➡ John threw the spear as hard as he (could / can).

8   나는 너만큼 일찍 일어나지 않는다.
➡ I don't get up as (early / earlier) as you.

9   우리 강아지는 너의 강아지만큼 귀엽다.
➡ My dog is as cute as (your / yours).

10   Jack은 가능한 한 빨리 뛰어야 했다.
➡ Jack had to run as (quickly / quick) as he could.

비교급의 비교

> • 비교급의 비교: 둘을 비교할 때 사용하는 비교급은 형용사나 부사 뒤에 '-er' 또는 'more'를 붙여 'than'과 함께 사용한다. 우리말로는 '더 ~한'이라는 뜻으로 쓰인다.

1. [형용사/부사 비교급＋than...] : ...보다 더 ~한

- Veronica is **prettier than** you are. [you are : 주어＋동사]

  = Veronica is **prettier than** you. [you : 목적격]

  ➡ 'than' 뒤에는 비교하고자 하는 대상(주어)과 동사가 온다. 하지만, '주어＋동사'를 목적격으로 바꿔 사용할 수 있다.

- He can run **faster than** I can.

  = He can run **faster than** me.

- I am not **more diligent than** my sister.

2. [There is nothing~ 비교급＋than...] : ...보다 더 ~한 것은 없다

- **There is nothing** I like **better than** singing.

  (= I like singing the best.)

Grammar Plus +

- 비교 대상이 주어와 같은 종류일 경우 소유대명사로 나타낼 수 있다.
  My hat is nicer than **yours**.

 **Check up!**

Answer Keys p. 50

A 주어진 단어를 비교급의 형태로 바꾸어 빈칸에 쓰시오.

1 He woke up ____earlier____ than yesterday because he will go to the hospital today. (early)

2 Which is _____, this bag or that one? (good)

3 They are too tired to walk any _____. (far)

4 Weather conditions are _____ than last week. (bad)

5 My shirt is _____ than yours. (big)

6 She was _____ than she expected. (nervous)

7 He arrived at the meeting _____ than us. (late)

8 Minji earned _____ money than her husband did. (many)

9 This suit is _____ than that one. (neat)

비교급 and 비교급

- 비교급 and 비교급: '점점 더 ~한(하게)'의 뜻으로 사용한다.
- the + 비교급, the + 비교급: '~하면 할수록 더 ...한(하게)'의 뜻으로 사용한다.

1. 비교급 and 비교급: 전전 더 ~한(하게)
   - Sultan Kosen is getting **taller and taller**.
   - The eagle flies **higher and higher**.

2. **the + 비교급 + 주어 + 동사, the + 비교급 + 주어 + 동사**: ~하면 할수록 더 ...한(하게)
   - **The more** you practice, **the better** you will do.
   - **The more positive** you think, **the happier** you will be.

☆Check up!

Answer Keys p. 50

A 다음 우리말에 맞게 빈칸에 알맞은 말을 쓰시오.

1 네가 더 많이 공부할수록 너는 더 똑똑해진다.
   ➡ ___The more___ you study, ___the smarter___ you will be.

2 풍선이 점점 더 하늘 높이 날아갔다.
   ➡ The balloon flew _____.

3 Tom의 얼굴이 점점 더 창백해지고 있다.
   ➡ Tom's face turned _____.

4 너는 더 많은 사람들을 만날수록 시야를 더 넓힐 수 있다.
   ➡ _____ you meet people, _____ your insight.

5 John은 화가 날수록 잠을 더 많이 잔다.
   ➡ _____ John gets, _____ he sleeps.

6 기온이 점점 더 내려가고 있다.
   ➡ The temperature is getting _____.

7 사람들이 많이 모일수록 그녀는 점점 더 부끄러워졌다.
   ➡ _____ people gathered, _____ she was.

8 Jim은 더 많이 베풀수록 점점 더 행복을 느낀다.
   ➡ _____ Jim gives, _____ he feels.

9 그 나무는 점점 더 크게 자란다.
   ➡ The tree grows _____.

Practice More Ⅰ

Answer Keys p. 50

A 다음 단어의 비교급과 최상급을 쓰시오.

1 far (정도) ➡ _____further_____ ➡ _____furthest_____

2 much ➡ _____ ➡ _____

3 few ➡ _____ ➡ _____

4 cheap ➡ _____ ➡ _____

5 small ➡ _____ ➡ _____

6 late (순서) ➡ _____ ➡ _____

7 bad ➡ _____ ➡ _____

8 young ➡ _____ ➡ _____

9 little ➡ _____ ➡ _____

10 useless ➡ _____ ➡ _____

11 happy ➡ _____ ➡ _____

12 convenient ➡ _____ ➡ _____

13 great ➡ _____ ➡ _____

14 easily ➡ _____ ➡ _____

15 lonely ➡ _____ ➡ _____

B 괄호 안에서 알맞은 것을 고르시오.

1 John's car is (older / elder) than mine.

2 They have to go (farther / further) to find the hat store.

3 Sally finished her homework (later / latter) than she expected.

4 Her hair is not so (darker / dark) as mine.

5 The ears of a rabbit are longer than (those of a dog / this of a dog).

6 My test results are not (such / so) good as his results.

7 Tim studied as (hardly / hard) as Sean did.

Practice More Ⅰ

C 주어진 문장과 같은 뜻이 되도록 빈칸을 완성하시오.

1 I bought this car forty-five years ago.

   Harry also bought his car forty-five years ago.

   ➡ My car is _____as old as_____ Harry's.

2 He ran to me as fast as possible.

   ➡ He ran to me _____.

3 I have ten dollars. Linda has ten dollars, too.

   ➡ I have _____ money _____ Linda.

4 She has to turn in the paper soon. She will do her best.

   ➡ She has to turn in the paper _____ possible.

5 Andrew goes to bed at 11:00 p.m. Joy goes to bed at 12:00 p.m.

   ➡ Joy doesn't go to bed _____ Andrew.

D 다음 우리말에 맞게 빈칸에 알맞은 단어를 쓰시오.

1 비행기가 점점 높이 올라가자 점점 마을이 작게 보였다.

   ➡ _The higher_ the airplane flew, _the smaller_ the village looked.

2 날이 따뜻해질수록 더 많은 꽃이 피었다.

   ➡ _____ it gets, _____ flowers blossom.

3 Helen은 점점 배가 고파왔다.

   ➡ Helen grew _____.

4 우리가 산에 높이 올라갈수록 공기가 점점 더 상쾌해졌다.

   ➡ _____ we climbed the mountain, _____
   the air was.

5 네가 점점 피곤할수록 집중할 수 없다.

   ➡ _____ you are, _____ you can't concentrate.

6 가로등이 밝을수록 더 많은 하루살이들이 모여들었다.

   ➡ _____ the lamp was, _____ mayflies gathered.

7 날이 더울수록 사람들이 화를 더 많이 낸다.

   ➡ _____ it becomes, _____ people get.

Answer Keys p. 50

E 다음 주어진 단어를 바르게 배열하여 문장을 완성하시오.

1 He tried to _____ *listen as carefully as possible.* _____
   (as, possible, carefully, listen, as)

2 Jane _____
   (as, helped, much, possible, the injured, as, soldiers)

3 Please let her know _____
   (as, his, possible, soon, name, as)

4 He _____
   (taller, brother, is, his, than)

5 She found the way _____
   (could, as, she, fast, as)

6 Stanley _____
   (he, has to, early, as, can, arrive, as)

7 Let's study _____
   (can, as, we, hard, as)

8 Josh _____
   (possible, mountains, as, climbs, as, often)

Point Check Ⅱ

◆ 원급과 비교급의 앞에 위치하는 부사어는 '매우, 훨씬'이라는 뜻으로 원급과 비교급을 강조하는 역할을 한다.

◆ 최상급은 셋 이상을 비교할 때 쓰이며 반드시 정관사 'the'가 앞에 온다.

1. 원급과 비교급 강조

원급 강조 (매우)	비교급 강조 (훨씬)
very, so, pretty	even, far, much, still, a lot
• Jeremy is pretty <u>happy</u>.	• Peggy became much <u>more beautiful</u> than before.

2. 최상급의 표현

the + 최상급	• I think the light bulb is the best invention.
in + 장소	• Eric is the most handsome boy in this club.
of + 복수명사 / 집단	• Sherry is the kindest of her friends.
one of the + 최상급 + 복수명사	• *Myeongnyang* is one of the best movies in Korea.
관계대명사절	• Mr. Pitt is the nicest teacher that I've seen.

3. 최상급의 다른 표현

the + 최상급 : 가장~한	• The brothers are the best writers of fairy tales.
= No (other) ~ as(so) + 원급 + as + A A만큼 ~한(다른) 것은 없다	• No (other) writers of fairy tales are as good as the brothers.
= No (other) ~비교급 + than A A보다 ~한(다른) 것은 없다	• No (other) writers of fairy tales are better than the brothers.
= A~비교급 + than any other + 단수명사 A는 다른 어떤 (단수명사) 보다 ~하다	• The brothers are better than any other writer.
= A~비교급 + than all the other + 복수명사 A는 다른 어떤 (복수명사) 보다 ~하다	• The brothers are better than all the other writers.

10-6 원급 / 비교급의 강조

> • 원급 / 비교급 강조하는 부사어: 원급과 비교급의 앞에 위치하여 '매우, 훨씬'이라는 뜻으로 형용사와 부사를 더욱 강조한다.

1. **원급 강조**: very, so, pretty 등은 형용사 또는 부사 원형 앞에서 '매우'라는 뜻으로 사용된다.

   • Jerry looks **so** <u>happy</u>.

   • The police officer runs **very** <u>fast</u>.

2. **비교급 강조**: even, far, much, still, a lot 등은 비교급 앞에서 '훨씬'이라는 뜻으로 사용된다.

   • Penny is **much** <u>fatter</u> now than before.

   • She is **still** <u>more famous</u> than him.

   • He bought **far** <u>more</u> fish than her.

☆Check up!

Answer Keys p. 51

A 다음 문장에서 밑줄 친 부분의 쓰임이 옳으면 O, 옳지 않으면 X를 하시오.

1 He is <u>so taller</u> than his father.   _____X_____

2 John looks <u>very happy</u> to see her again.   _____

3 This book is <u>much cheaper</u> than that one.   _____

4 She could run <u>even fast</u> than Minsu.   _____

5 Your computer is <u>still newer</u> than mine.   _____

6 Today is <u>very colder</u> than yesterday.   _____

7 We are <u>pretty interested</u> in making movies.   _____

8 John's grade is <u>even great</u> than Helen's.   _____

9 They can run <u>very faster</u> than us.   _____

10 Goeun drives <u>far more</u> badly than Daniel.   _____

최상급의 비교

- **최상급**: 셋 이상을 비교할 때 쓰이며 '가장~한'이라는 뜻을 가진다.
  형용사나 부사 뒤에 '-est / -st' 또는 'most'를 붙여서 최상급 형태를 만들며, 정관사
  'the'와 함께 쓰인다.

1. 최상급의 표현

(1) the + 최상급

- This is **the cheapest** dish in this restaurant.

(2) in + 장소

- Who is **the most beautiful in the class**?

(3) of + 복수명사/집단

- Wendy is **the smartest of her friends**.

(4) 관계대명사절

- This is **the most interesting** play (**that**) I've done.

2. [one of the + 최상급 + 복수명사]: 가장 ~한 …중의 하나

- *Spiderman* is **one of the most famous characters** in movies.
- Michelangelo is **one of the greatest painters**.

 Answer Keys p. 51

A   괄호 안의 단어를 최상급의 형태로 바꾸어 빈칸에 쓰시오.

1   Jane is ____the smartest____ student in our community. (smart)

2   She is one of _____ women in the world. (beautiful)

3   You are _____ man that I have ever met.
(handsome)

4   This is _____ book I've read. (interest)

5   Yesterday was _____ day of my life. (good)

6   That is _____ movie I've ever seen. (fun)

7   One of _____ ways to lose weight is to exercise
regularly. (easy)

8   You are _____ professor in our university. (old)

9   It was _____ thing that Tom has done. (foolish)

Lesson 10-8 최상급의 다른 표현

- 'the + 최상급' 외에도 원급과 비교급을 이용해서 최상급의 의미를 나타낼 수 있다.

◆ 최상급의 다른 표현

the + 최상급 : 가장 ~한	• Brooke is the prettiest woman in her town.
= **No (other) ~ as(so) + 원급 + as + A** A만큼 ~한(다른) 것은 없다	• No (other) woman in her town is as pretty as Brooke.
= **No (other) ~비교급 + than A** A보다 ~한(다른) 것은 없다	• No (other) woman in her town is prettier than Brooke.
= **A ~ 비교급 + than any other + 단수명사** A는 다른 어떤 (단수명사)보다 ~하다	• Brooke is prettier than any other woman in her town.
= **A ~ 비교급 + than all the other + 복수명사** A는 다른 어떤 (복수명사)보다 ~하다	• Brooke is prettier than all the other women in her town.

Grammar Plus +

- [No (other) + 비교급 + than] / [No (other) + as + 원급 + as]

  No (other) **student** is lazier than Mike.

  = No (other) **student** is as lazy as Mike.

Answer Keys p. 51~52

A 다음 주어진 문장들이 같은 뜻이 되도록 빈칸에 알맞은 말을 쓰시오.

1 This is the tallest tree in our village.

➡ ___No other___ tree in our village is ___as tall as___ this.

➡ ___No other___ tree in our village is ___taller than___ this one.

➡ This tree is ___taller than any other___ tree in our village.

➡ This tree is ___taller than all the other___ trees in our village.

2 This is the funniest novel in our library.

➡ _____ novel in our library is _____ this novel.

➡ _____ novel in our library is _____ this one.

➡ This is _____ novel in our library.

➡ This is _____ novels in our library.

3   He is the heaviest person on the team.

➔ _____ person on the team is _____ him.

➔ _____ person on the team is _____ him.

➔ He is _____ man on the team.

➔ He is _____ men on the team.

4   Van Gogh is the most famous artist in history.

➔ _____ artist is _____ Van Gogh in history.

➔ _____ artist is _____ Van Gogh in history.

➔ Van Gogh is _____ artist in history.

➔ Van Gogh is _____ artists in history.

5   She is the smartest girl in our class.

➔ _____ girl in our class is _____ her.

➔ _____ girl in our class is _____ her.

➔ She is _____ girl in our class.

➔ She is _____ girls in our class.

6   Harry is the shortest boy in our class.

➔ _____ boy in his class is _____ him.

➔ _____ boy in his class is _____ him.

➔ He is _____ boy in his class.

➔ He is _____ boys in his class.

7   A computer is the most useful thing.

➔ _____ thing is _____ a computer.

➔ _____ thing is _____ a computer.

➔ A computer is _____ thing.

➔ A computer is _____ things.

8   Elizabeth is the most graceful woman in the country.

➔ _____ woman in the country is _____ Elizabeth.

➔ _____ woman in the country is _____ Elizabeth.

➔ Elizabeth is _____ woman in the country.

➔ Elizabeth is _____ women in the country.

Practice More II

Answer Keys p. 52

A 괄호 안에서 알맞은 것을 고르시오.

1   Harry is the (more / (most)) popular singer in England.

2   The girl is more beautiful than (any other / all the other)
    girls in the school.

3   The ring is (very / much) more expensive than the necklace.

4   I'm one of the smartest (student / students) in our class.

5   There is nothing (more / most) exciting than bungee jumping.

6   Cindy is the tallest (in / of) her family.

7   (No other / No others) cookie in our store is as delicious as
    this one.

8   The later we slept, the (more tired / tired) we were.

9   This book is (most / the most) expensive in my room.

10 One of (the fastest / the faster) ways to lose weight is
    changing menu.

B 다음 문장에서 어법상 어색한 것을 찾아 바르게 고치시오.

1   In the summer, the days get long and long.

                    long and long ➡ _longer and longer_

2   He is the smarter person in the community.

                    _____ ➡ _____

3   I am the shortest girl of the gym.

                    _____ ➡ _____

4   This desk is very much wider than that one.

                    _____ ➡ _____

5   You are one of the most handsome boy in the class.

                    _____ ➡ _____

6   The pants are still expensive than I expected.

                    _____ ➡ _____

7   The giraffe has the very longest neck of all animals.

   _____ ➡ _____

8   Jane is most richest person in our village.

   _____ ➡ _____

9   Nick is the funniest students of his friends.

   _____ ➡ _____

10   He is more braver than I.

   _____ ➡ _____

C 다음 우리말 해석과 일치하도록 주어진 단어를 이용하여 최상급 문장을 완성하시오.

1   치타는 세상에서 가장 빠른 동물이다. (fast, animal)
   ➡ Cheetahs are _____the fastest animal_____ in the world.

2   내일이 나의 인생에서 가장 중요한 날이다. (important)
   ➡ Tomorrow is _____ of my life.

3   그것은 Helen에게 가장 어려운 문제다. (difficult, question)
   ➡ It is _____ for Helen.

4   여름은 그에게 가장 힘든 시간이다. (hard)
   ➡ Summer is _____ for him.

5   그 책은 Jane이 쓴 가장 재미있는 책이다. (interest)
   ➡ The book is _____ Jane has ever written.

6   그 영화는 내가 본 영화 중 가장 무서운 영화이다. (scare)
   ➡ The movie is _____ I've ever seen.

7   오늘은 올해 들어 가장 더운 날이다. (hot)
   ➡ Today is _____ this year.

8   우리 가게에는 이것보다 더 화려한 드레스가 없다. (fancy)
   ➡ No other dress in our store is _____ this one.

9   역사상 그만큼 위대한 장군은 없었다. (great)
   ➡ He is _____ than _____ general in history.

10 이것은 John이 지금까지 진행한 것 중 최고의 프로젝트였다. (good, project)
   ➡ This was _____ that John has ever managed.

내신 최다 출제유형

01 다음 중 어법상 잘못된 문장을 고르시오. [출제 예상 90%]

① She is one of the smartest student in her class.
② An unhappy peace is even worse than war.
③ Scientists will be able to find a cure for cancer.
④ Mars is colder than the earth.
⑤ No student is as diligent as Mary.

02 다음 중 어법상 올바른 것을 고르시오. [출제 예상 85%]

① History is more interesting math.
② We feel best than yesterday.
③ Are Benny's running shoes cheaper than Jack's?
④ Mike is the heavier in his class.
⑤ She has more books of them all.

03 다음 주어진 문장과 같은 뜻의 문장을 고르시오. [출제 예상 80%]

> Alice is not as slim as Laura.

① Alice is slimmer than Laura.
② Alice is less slim than Laura.
③ Alice is so slim as Laura.
④ Laura is not as slim as Alice.
⑤ Laura is not slimmer than Alice.

04 다음의 두 문장을 한 문장으로 쓸 때 빈칸에 알맞은 말을 고르시오. [출제 예상 80%]

> • I got three flowers.
>   You got nine flowers.
> = You got _____ flowers as me.

① twice as fewer
② three times as many
③ three as many
④ three times as much
⑤ trice as more

05 다음 표의 내용과 일치하지 않는 것을 고르시오. [출제 예상 85%]

	Mary	Jane	Kelly	Christine
Grade	B	A+	A	B

① Jane is the smartest girl of them.
② Mary is not smarter than Kelly.
③ Mary is as smart as Christine.
④ Christine is smarter than Kelly.
⑤ Kelly is not as smart as Jane.

06 다음 빈칸에 알맞지 않은 것을 고르시오. [출제 예상 85%]

> If you put a little pepper into the food, it will be _____ better than before.

① very   ② much   ③ a lot
④ far   ⑤ even

[01~03] 다음 중 '원급-비교급-최상급'이 잘못 짝지어진 것을 고르시오.

01
① slim − slimer − slimest
② large − larger − largest
③ small − smaller − smallest
④ thin − thinner − thinnest
⑤ fast − faster − fastest

02
① easy − easier − easiest
② little − less − least
③ good − better − best
④ much − many − more
⑤ great − greater − greatest

03
① expensive − more expensive − most expensive
② hard − harder − hardest
③ good − gooder − goodest
④ pretty − prettier − prettiest
⑤ famous − more famous − most famous

[04~05] 다음 중 빈칸에 들어갈 알맞은 말을 고르시오.

04
What is the _____ popular food in Korea?

① better   ② more   ③ well
④ good   ⑤ most

05
Benny is _____ diligent than Paul.

① most   ② well   ③ more
④ some   ⑤ better

[06~07] 다음 중 빈칸에 들어갈 수 없는 단어를 고르시오.

06
Perry's new car is _____ better than mine.

① much   ② very   ③ a lot
④ even   ⑤ far

07
Melissa is _____ smarter than before.

① a lot   ② still   ③ pretty
④ far   ⑤ even

[08~09] 다음 중 어법상 어색한 것을 고르시오.
★★★
08
① The bigger animals are, the longer they live.
② The sharks are swimming faster and faster.
③ The more you save, the more you can spend later.
④ Benjamin looks as old as an old man.
⑤ Turtles live the very longest life.

09 ① This was a much wonderful opera.

② Alex is the tallest boy in his class.

③ Billy gets up earlier than his mom.

④ Minsu is the laziest boy.

⑤ Daeun is as pretty as Chaerin.

[10~11] 다음 주어진 문장과 의미가 같은 문장을
고르시오.

10

> This is the mightiest animal of all.

① This is mightier than all the other animal.

② This is mightier than all the other animals.

③ This is mightier than any other animals.

④ This is mightier than the other animals.

⑤ This is the mightiest all the other animals.

(Note) **mighty** 거대한, 대단히 큰

11

> Leo likes drawing the best.

① There is nothing Leo likes most than
drawing.

② There is nothing Leo likes best drawing.

③ There is nothing Leo likes better than
drawing.

④ There is nothing Leo likes drawing better.

⑤ There is nothing Leo likes drawing best.

[12~13] 다음 주어진 우리말과 같은 뜻이 되도록 빈칸에
알맞은 말을 고르시오.

12

> 이것은 내가 읽어본 책 중 가장 지루한 책이다.
> = This is _____ book I've
> ever read.

① the best boring   ② the borest

③ the boringest   ④ the most

⑤ the most boring

13

> Mary는 누구보다 멀리 달렸다.
> = Mary ran _____ than anyone
> else.

① longer   ② farther   ③ farthest

④ faster   ⑤ further

★★★
14 다음 짝지어진 문장 중 어법상 <u>어색한</u> 것을 고르시오.

① Cheetahs are faster than horses.

   = Horses are slower than cheetahs.

② Jenny's sister is prettier than her.

   = Jenny is uglier than her sister.

③ Kelly is thinner than Jerry.

   = Jerry is fatter than Kelly.

④ The airplane is more expensive
   than the train.

   = The train is cheaper than the airplane.

⑤ Giraffes are taller than deer.

   = Deer are more shorter than giraffes.

★★★
15 다음 짝지어진 두 문장의 뜻이 서로 <u>다른</u> 것을 고르시오.

① Both tennis and badminton are exciting.
   = Tennis is as exciting as badminton.
② That is the cheapest thing in this shop.
   = No other thing in this shop is cheaper than that.
③ Jinny is less tall than her sister.
   = Jinny's sister is not as tall as Jinny.
④ I studied as hard as I could.
   = I studied as hard as possible.
⑤ The actor and I are the same age.
   = The actor is as old as I am.

16 다음 문장 중 의미하는 바가 나머지 넷과 <u>다른</u> 것을 고르시오.

① Nothing is bigger than Shanghai in China.
② Shanghai is bigger than any other city in China.
③ No other city in China is as big as Shanghai.
④ Shanghai is the biggest city in China.
⑤ Shanghai is the biggest of all the other cities in China.

★★★
17 다음 우리말을 영어로 옮긴 것 중 바르지 <u>못한</u> 것을 고르시오.

① 이 인형이 저 인형보다 훨씬 싸다.
   → This doll is vcry cheaper than that doll.
② 더 많이 가질수록 우리는 더 많이 원한다.
   → The more we have, the more we want.
③ 우리는 지각하지 않기 위해 가능한 한 빨리 달렸다.
   → We ran as fast as possible not to be late.
④ 날씨가 점점 더 서늘해지고 있다.
   → The weather is getting cooler and cooler.
⑤ 나는 그보다 똑똑하지 않다.
   → I am not as smart as him.

[18~19] 다음 빈칸에 들어갈 알맞은 말로 짝지어진 것을 고르시오.

18
> • I am _____ than my sister.
> • Japanese food is not _____ than Korean food.

① fat − hotter
② fatter − hotter
③ fatter − hoter
④ fater − hoter
⑤ fat − hot

19
> • Soccer is _____ than baseball.
> • Jogging is a _____ exercise to lose your weight.

① excitinger − better
② exciting −the best
③ more exciting − better
④ more exciting − gooder
⑤ exciting − good

[20~21] 다음 두 문장이 같은 뜻이 되도록 빈칸에 알맞은 말로 짝지어진 것을 고르시오.

20

> • Mt. Halla is the highest mountain in Korea.
> = _____ mountain in Korea is as high _____ Mt. Halla.

① No − more
② No − than
③ As − as
④ No any − as
⑤ No other − as

21

> • We like reading books the best.
> = There is _____ we like _____ than reading books.

① nothing − good
② no thing − best
③ nothing − better
④ none − best
⑤ nothing − best

[22~23] 다음 중 밑줄 친 부분이 어법상 옳은 것을 고르시오.

★★★
22 ① I don't make <u>more money as</u> him.
② She is not <u>shorter than</u> me.
③ An ant is <u>smaller as</u> a ladybug.
④ We are as <u>good than</u> you.
⑤ He is <u>more older</u> than her.

23 ① Summer is <u>hotter as</u> winter.
② I am <u>the happyest</u> person.
③ Your English is <u>good than</u> me.
④ This building is <u>as taller as</u> that one.
⑤ Yoga is <u>more interesting than</u> running.

[24~25] 다음 주어진 우리말을 영어로 바르게 옮긴 것을 고르시오.

24

> 과학은 영어보다 더 어렵다.

① English is harder than science.
② Science is not harder than English.
③ Science is as hard as English.
④ Science is harder than English.
⑤ Science is not as hard as English.

★★★
25

> 하와이의 날씨는 캘리포니아만큼 맑다.

① The weather of Hawaii is not sunnier than that of California.
② The weather of Hawaii is less sunny than that of California.
③ The weather of Hawaii is as sunny as that of California.
④ The weather of California is sunnier than that of Hawaii.
⑤ The weather of California is not as sunny as that of Hawaii.

[26~27] 다음 표를 보고 물음에 답하시오.

	grade	Final test score
Sam	5th grade	A+
John	4th grade	C
Molly	6th grade	B

26 다음 표의 내용을 설명한 문장 중 올바른 것을 고르시오.

① Sam is not smarter than Molly.

② Sam's grade is higher than Molly.

③ Molly is the oldest of them.

④ John is as smart as Sam.

⑤ Molly is as smart as Sam.

27 위의 표를 참고하여 다음 빈칸에 들어갈 알맞은 말을 고르시오.

> No other students are _____
> Sam.

① the smartest   ② as smart as

③ smartest   ④ smarter than

⑤ as smarter than

★★★
28 다음 우리말을 영작한 것 중 잘못된 것을 고르시오.

① 농구는 가장 인기 있는 운동 중 하나다.
→ Basketball is one of the most popular sports.

② 네 성적이 점점 나빠지고 있다.
→ Your grades are getting worse and worse.

③ 열심히 놀수록 시험은 더욱 어려워질 것이다.
→ The more you play, the harder the exam won't be.

④ 나는 너보다 꽃을 두 배 더 많이 샀다.
→ I bought twice more flowers than you.

⑤ 그는 우리나라에서 가장 잘생긴 배우이다.
→ He is the most handsome actor in Korea.

29 다음 중 어법상 올바른 것을 고르시오.

① That sounds a lot of fun.

② James is the smaller than Harry.

③ We just want three cartons of milk.

④ Harrison is tallest boy of all the classmates.

⑤ This is hottest item in the store.

30 다음 중 어법상 어색한 것을 고르시오.

① My mom is the kindest person in the world.

② Jay is much nicer than other students.

③ This is the seriousest problem in my life.

④ The weather is getting colder and colder.

⑤ She is the most thinnest in my class.

◇◇◇◇◇◇◇◇◇ 서술형 평가 ◇◇◇◇◇◇◇◇◇

31 다음 대화에서 <u>틀린</u> 곳을 찾아 고쳐 쓰시오.

> **A** California is one of the most famous city in the world.
> **B** You're right. I'm going there this summer.

_____ ➡ _____

32 다음 밑줄 친 단어의 형태를 바르게 고쳐 쓰시오.

> • Writing is often <u>difficult</u> than reading.
> • The question was the <u>easy</u> of all.

➡ • difficult − _____

   • easy − _____

33 다음 보기 를 참고하여 빈칸에 들어갈 알맞은 말을 쓰시오.

> 보기
> Jinsu 178cm, Minho 174cm,
> Gangho 175cm

➡ (A) Jinsu is _____ _____
    short _____ Minho.

 (B) Gangho is _____ _____
    Minho.

 (C) Jinsu is _____ _____ of
    them.

[34~35] 다음 글을 읽고 물음에 답하시오.

> I visited Chinchilla, Australia with my family last winter. There was a watermelon festival at that time. Luckily, we could attend the festival. There were some funny events, such as throwing watermelons, beating watermelons, watermelon bungee jumping, watermelon skiing, and so on. Those things were ⓐ (fun) than computer games. I especially enjoyed watermelon skiing. ⓑ <u>The watermelon skiing is the funniest game than I've ever played.</u>

34 윗글 ⓐ의 괄호 안의 단어를 알맞은 형태로 바꿔 쓰시오.

➡ _____

★★★
35 윗글의 밑줄 친 ⓑ문장과 뜻이 같도록 빈칸에 알맞은 말을 쓰시오.

➡ (1) No other games I've ever done is as
   _____ _____ watermelon
   skiing.

 (2) Watermelon skiing is _____
   _____ _____ _____
   _____ game I've ever played.

[36~38] 다음 그림을 보고 물음에 답하시오.

$10 $200 $150 $35

36 What is the most expensive thing?
➡ _____

37 What is the cheapest thing?
➡ _____

★★★
38 Compare an umbrella and sneakers.
(Use the word 'expensive')
➡ _____

[39~42] 다음 우리말에 맞게 괄호 안의 단어를 바르게
배열하여 문장을 완성하시오.

39
> 상황은 점점 나아지고 있다.
> (the / getting / condition / better / is /
> better / and)

➡ _____

40
> 나일 강은 세계에서 가장 긴 강이다.
> (the Nile / is / river / the / longest / the
> / world / in)

➡ _____

41
> 루브르 박물관은 세계에서 가장 인기 있는
> 박물관 중 하나이다.
> (Louvre / one / of / popular / most / is
> / the / the / in / world / museums)

➡ _____
_____

42
> 테니스를 하는 것보다 흥미로운 것은 없다.
> (there / nothing / is / playing / than /
> tennis / exciting / more)

➡ _____
_____

11

Chapter
가정법

Point Check I

◆ **가정법 :** 어떤 일이 일어날 가능성이 거의 없을 때 그 사실에 대해 반대의 의미를 가정해 나타낼 때 사용한다.

◆ 가정법의 종류

가정법 과거 현재 사실과 반대	• [If + 주어 + 과거..., 주어 + would / could 동사원형] 만약 ...한다면 ~할 텐데
가정법 과거완료 과거의 사실과 반대	• [If + 주어 + had + 과거분사..., 주어 + would / could... + have + 과거분사 ~] 만약...했다면 ~이었을 텐데
I wish + 가정법 과거 현재나 미래에 이룰 수 없는 소망	• [I wish + 주어 + 과거동사] ~라면 좋을 텐데
I wish + 가정법 과거완료 과거사실과 반대되는 일을 소망	• [I wish + 주어 + had + 과거분사] ~했더라면 좋을 텐데
현재 + as if + 가정법 과거 현재의 사실과 반대되는 것을 그러한 것처럼 표현	• [주어 + 현재 동사 + as if + 주어 + 과거동사...] 마치 ...처럼 ~하다
현재 + as if + 가정법 과거완료 과거의 사실과 반대되는 것을 그랬던 것처럼 표현	• [주어 + 현재 동사 + as if + 주어 + had + 과거분사...] 마치 ...이었던 것처럼 ~하다

조건의 부사절
어느 정도 실제로 가능할 경우 사용
	• [만약 ...라면 ~일 텐데]
	  ➡ 현재는 현재형을, 미래는 미래형을 사용한다.
	     단, if절에서는 미래를 현재형으로 표현한다.

11-1 가정법의 종류

- **가정법**: 가정법은 어떤 일이 일어날 가능성이 거의 없을 때, 그 사실에 대해 반대의 의미를 가정해서 나타낼 때 사용한다.

◈ **가정법의 종류**

가정법 과거 현재 사실과 반대	[If + 주어 + 과거..., 주어 + would / could / should + 동사원형~] 만약 ...한다면 ~할 텐데 • If she <u>worked</u> hard, she <u>would make</u> more money.
가정법 과거완료 과거의 사실과 반대	[If + 주어 + had + 과거분사..., 주어 + would / could / should + have + 과거분사~] 만약 ...했었다면 ~이었을 텐데 • If she <u>had worked</u> hard, she <u>would have made</u> more money.
I wish + 가정법 과거 현재나 미래에 이룰 수 없는 소망	[I wish + 주어 + 과거동사] ~라면 좋을 텐데 • I wish he <u>practiced</u> more.
I wish + 가정법 과거완료 과거사실과 반대되는 일을 소망	[I wish + 주어 + had + 과거분사] ~했더라면 좋을 텐데 • I wish he <u>had practiced</u> more.
현재 + as if + 가정법 과거 현재의 사실과 반대되는 것을 그러한 것처럼 표현	[주어 + 현재 동사 + as if + 주어 + 과거동사...] 마치 ...처럼 ~하다 • Whitney talks <u>as if</u> she <u>watched</u> the concert.
현재 + as if + 가정법 과거완료 과거의 사실과 반대되는 것을 그랬던 것처럼 표현	[주어 + 현재 동사 + as if + 주어 + had + 과거분사...] 마치 ...이었던 것처럼 ~하다 • Whitney talks <u>as if</u> she <u>had watched</u> the concert.
조건의 부사절 어느 정도 실제로 가능할 경우 사용	[만약 ...라면 ~일 텐데] ➡ 현재는 현재형을, 미래는 미래형을 사용한다. 　단, if절에서는 미래를 현재형으로 표현한다. 　• If you <u>do</u> your best, you <u>will get</u> a good grade. 　• If it <u>is</u> sunny tomorrow, we <u>will go</u> on a picnic.

A 다음 우리말 해석에 맞게 문장을 완성하시오.

1 그가 공부를 열심히 한다면 졸업 시험을 통과할 텐데.
➡ If ___he studied___ hard, he ___could pass___ the graduation exam.

2 그는 마치 부자인 것처럼 말한다.
➡ He talks as if _____ rich.

3 James가 책을 많이 읽었더라면, 더 똑똑해졌을 텐데.
➡ If _____ many books, he _____ smarter.

4 그녀가 피아노 연주를 잘 한다면 좋을 텐데.
➡ _____ she _____ well.

5 그녀는 마치 여배우였던 것처럼 행동한다.
➡ She acts _____ an actress.

6 내일 Sam이 온다면 우리는 소풍을 갈 거예요.
➡ If Sam _____ tomorrow, we _____
on a picnic.

7 그들이 축구 연습을 열심히 한다면, 그들은 결승에 진출할 것이다.
➡ If they _____ soccer hard, they _____ to the finals.

8 너는 마치 그 책이 재미있는 것처럼 말한다.
➡ You talk _____ the book _____.

9 내게 시간이 충분히 있다면, 너의 숙제를 도와줄 텐데.
➡ If I _____, I _____ you do the homework.

10 우리 가족이 서울에 살았다면 좋을 텐데.
➡ _____ our family _____ in Seoul.

11 내가 아기라면 하루 종일 잘 수 있을 텐데.
➡ If _____ a baby, I _____ all day.

12 우리가 Helen을 이해해줬으면 좋을 텐데.
➡ _____ we _____ Helen.

13 그는 모든 것을 알고 있었던 것처럼 말한다.
➡ He talks _____ everything.

14 내가 키가 작지 않다면, 야구선수가 될 수 있을 텐데.
➡ If _____, I _____ a baseball player.

15 그녀가 현명했더라면, 그렇게 행동하진 않았을 텐데.
➡ If she _____, she _____ like that.

가정법 과거

- **가정법 과거**: 현재의 사실과 반대되는 일이나 현재에 일어날 것 같지 않은 일을 가정해서 말할 때 사용한다.

※ 우리말 해석과는 달리 영어에서는 현재의 일을 가정하면서 과거형 동사를 사용하기 때문에 '가정법 과거'라고 한다.

1. 가정법 과거: 현재의 사실과 반대되는 가정을 말한다.

의미	만약 ...한다면(...라면) ~일 텐데
형태	[If + 주어 + 과거 동사, 주어 + would (could/should/might) + 동사원형~]
예문	• If <u>we</u> had enough money, <u>we</u> could buy that car. = We don't have enough money, so we can't buy that car. = As we don't have enough money, we can't buy that car.

2. 직설법 문장을 가정법 문장으로 전환

- **As** you **are** young, you **can't get** the job.

= **If** you **weren't** young, you **could get** the job.

➡ <u>직설법의 긍정은 가정법에서 부정으로 나타내고</u>, <u>직설법의 부정은 가정법에서 긍정으로 나타낸다</u>.

3. 가정법 과거의 be동사: If절의 be동사는 인칭에 상관없이 'were'를 사용한다.

- **If** she **were** diligent, she **would not be** late.

= She **is not** diligent, so she **will be** late.

➡ 구어체 (회화)에서는 인칭에 따라 'was'를 사용하기도 한다. (하지만 문어체에서는 쓰지 않는다.)

- **If** I **was** a bird, I would fly to you.

A 다음 문장을 If로 시작하는 가정법 문장으로 바꿔 쓰시오.

1 My father is short, so I am short.

➡ *If my father were not short, I would not be short.*

2 As she has a telescope, she can see the star.

➡

3 John works hard, so he earns a lot of money.

➡

4 My test result isn't good, so I am disappointed.

➡

5 The MP3 player is not mine, so I can't lend it to her.

➡

6 She doesn't know the answer, so she can't solve the problem.

➡

7 Sam practices the piano hard, so he can win the competition.

➡

8 Steve has enough money, so he can buy a new car.

➡

9 The weather is fine, so we can go on a picnic with our family.

➡

10 My brother isn't old enough, so he can't understand the lecture.

➡

B 다음 문장을 주어진 접속사를 넣어 직설법 문장으로 바꿔 쓰시오.

1 If she knew the fact, she could tell it to me. (as)

➡ *As she doesn't know the fact, she can't tell it to me.*

2 If it snowed a lot, we could not go to the festival. (so)

➡

3 If she liked him, she might write a letter to him. (as)

➡

4 If I didn't do my best, I could not get an A on the final test. (so)

➡

5 If he had enough time, he could meet her again. (so)

➡

11-3 가정법 과거완료

> • **가정법 과거완료**: 과거의 사실과 반대되는 일이나 일어날 것 같지 않은 과거의 일을 가정해서 말할 때 사용한다.

1. 가정법 과거완료: 과거 사실과 반대되는 가정을 말한다.

의미	만약 ...했었다면(...이었다면) ~했었을(이었을) 텐데
형태	[If + 주어 + <u>had</u> + 과거분사, ...주어 + would (could/should/might) + <u>have</u> + 과거분사~] ➡ if절에서 과거보다 더 앞선 과거인 대과거 시제를 사용한다.
예문	• If I had had more time, I could have been with them. = I didn't have more time, so I couldn't be with them. = As I didn't have more time, I couldn't be with them.

2. 직설법 문장을 가정법 문장으로 전환

• **As** he **practiced** hard, he **became** a famous musician.

= **If** he **had not practiced** hard, he **could not have become** a famous musician.

➡ 직설법의 긍정은 가정법에서 부정으로 나타내고, 직설법의 부정은 가정법에서 긍정으로 나타낸다.

Grammar Plus +

• **should have** + 과거분사: ~했어야 했다 [과거에 하지 못한 일을 후회]
   Jerry **should have told** us the truth.
• **should not have** + 과거분사: ~하지 말았어야 했다 [과거에 한 일을 후회]
   We **should not have fought** with them.

 Check up!

Answer Keys p. 54

A 다음 괄호 안의 동사를 알맞은 형태로 바꾸어 빈칸을 채우시오.

1 If she ____*had read*____ the book, she would have written the report. (read)

2 If you had not been ill, you _____ with us. (travel)

3 If I _____ enough time, I could have finished the project on time. (have)

4   If he had studied hard, he _____ the exam. (pass)

5   If it had been warm, they _____ the fireworks. (enjoy)

6   If I _____, I could have bought the house. (rich)

7   If John had known you were coming, he _____ at home. (stay)

8   If I _____ her, I would have participated in the competition. (be)

9   If she had been more thoughtful, she _____ like that. (say)

10 If you had read many books, you _____ all these questions. (answer)

B   다음 주어진 문장을 If를 이용한 가정법 문장으로 바꿔 쓰시오.

1   Linda was very busy, so she couldn't visit her grandparents.
    ➡ *If Linda had not been busy, she could have visited her grandparents.*

2   As I didn't have a car, I couldn't pick up Jane at the airport.
    ➡ _____

3   He was so busy, so he forgot about Sally's party.
    ➡ _____

4   She didn't keep her promise, so they were disappointed.
    ➡ _____

5   I didn't clean my room, so my mom was really angry.
    ➡ _____

11-4 조건절 if

• **조건절:** '조건의 if'는 '~한다면, ~라면'의 뜻으로 현재나 미래에 실제로 일어날 수 있는 상황에 대한 가능성을 이야기할 때 사용한다.

1. 조건의 부사절: 어느 정도 실현 가능하고, 반대 상황에 대한 가정이 아닐 경우 사용한다.

의미	만약 ...라면, ~일 텐데
형태	[If + 주어 + 동사, ...주어 + 동사~]
예문	• If you leave now, you can take the bus. [➡ 가능성이 있음] • If you look after him, he will be better soon. [➡ 실제와 반대 상황이 아님]

Grammar Plus +

• **if와 when**

① **if:** 어떤 일에 대해 확실하지 않을 경우 사용

If I draw him, I will draw you, too.

② **when:** 어떤 일에 대해 확실할 경우 사용

When I draw him, I will draw you, too.

☆Check up!

Answer Keys p. 55

A 다음 문장에서 어법상 <u>어색한</u> 것을 찾아 바르게 고치시오.

1 If you will meet him, please call me.

<u> will meet </u> ➡ <u> meet </u>

2 If you took a taxi, you will arrive on time.

<u>   </u> ➡ <u>   </u>

3 If he like Cindy, he will write a letter to her.

<u>   </u> ➡ <u>   </u>

4 If I finish homework, I go to the party.

<u>   </u> ➡ <u>   </u>

5 If he was rich, he will donate much money.

<u>   </u> ➡ <u>   </u>

6 If she has a map, she could find the way.

<u>   </u> ➡ <u>   </u>

7 If he practices hard, he win the game.

<u>   </u> ➡ <u>   </u>

8 If she will read the book, she can complete the report.

<u>   </u> ➡ <u>   </u>

9 If I know the answer, I help her solve the problem.

<u>   </u> ➡ <u>   </u>

11-5 I wish 가정법

- **I wish 가정법**: 현재 또는 과거의 사실과 반대되는 소망을 말할 때 사용하는 표현이다.

1. I wish + 가정법 과거: 현재나 미래에 이룰 수 없는 일을 소망할 때 사용

의미	~라면 좋을 텐데 (➡ 하지만 아니다)
형태	I wish + 주어 + 과거 동사

예문	• I wish I passed the exam.
	  = I didn't study, but I want to pass the exam.
	• I wish Jane and David would make up.
	  = Jane and David will not make up, but I want them to make up.

(Note)

• **make up** 화해하다

2. I wish + 가정법 과거완료: 과거 사실과 반대되는 일을 소망할 때 사용

의미	~였더라면 (했더라면) 좋을 텐데 (➡ 그런데 아니었다)
형태	I wish + 주어 + had + 과거분사

예문	• I wish I had had lunch.
	  = I didn't have lunch, so I was hungry.
	• I wish they had not come to the party.
	  = They came to the party, but I didn't like it.

☆Check up!

Answer Keys p. 55

A 다음 두 문장의 의미가 같도록 빈칸을 채우시오.

1 I'm sorry he is wrong.
  ➡ I wish he _____weren't_____ wrong.

2 I wish I had passed the exam.
  ➡ I'm sorry I _____ the exam.

3 I'm sorry it's cold today.
  ➡ I wish it _____ cold today.

4 I'm sorry Jane didn't remember our promise.
  ➡ I wish Jane _____ our promise.

5 I wish I were diligent.

➡ I'm sorry I _____ diligent.

6 I'm sorry Tina didn't study hard.

➡ I wish Tina _____ hard.

7 I wish there were flowers on the table.

➡ I'm sorry there _____ flowers on the table.

8 I'm sorry I'm not good at speaking English.

➡ I wish I _____ good at speaking English.

9 I'm sorry I didn't attend the meeting.

➡ I wish I _____ the meeting.

10 I'm sorry we didn't visit her in the hospital.

➡ I wish we _____ her in the hospital.

B 다음 우리말 해석에 유의하여 괄호 안의 말을 이용하여 문장을 완성하시오.

1 내가 그때 그녀와 통화를 했었다면 좋을 텐데. (talk)

➡ I wish I ___*had talked*___ on the phone with her then.

2 내가 그를 위해 무엇인가를 사면 좋을 텐데. (buy)

➡ I wish I _____ something for him.

3 그녀가 영어를 잘하면 좋을 텐데. (speak)

➡ I wish she _____ English well.

4 그들이 바쁘지 않았다면 좋을 텐데. (be)

➡ I wish they _____ busy.

5 내가 Jessy의 이메일 주소를 알면 좋을 텐데. (know)

➡ I wish I _____ Jessy's email address.

6 그 상점의 모든 것들이 싸면 좋을 텐데. (be)

➡ I wish everything _____ very cheap in the store.

7 그가 어제 그렇게 놀지 않았다면 좋을 텐데. (play)

➡ I wish he _____ so much yesterday.

as if 가정법

• **as if 가정법**: 현재의 사실과 반대되는 일이나 일어날 것 같지 않은 현재의 일을 가정해서 말할 때 사용한다.

1. 현재시제 주절＋as if＋가정법 과거: 현재의 사실과 반대되는 것을 그러한 것처럼 표현

의미	마치 ...처럼 ～하다
형태	[주어＋동사의 현재형＋as if＋주어＋과거 동사...]
예문	• James talks as if he taught all students. [➡ In fact, he doesn't teach all students.] • Emily acts as if she were a little kid. [➡ In fact, she isn't a little kid.]

2. 현재시제의 주절＋as if＋가정법 과거완료: 과거의 사실과 반대되는 것을 그랬던 것처럼 표현

의미	마치 ...이었던 것처럼 ～하다
형태	[주어＋동사의 현재형＋as if＋주어＋had＋과거분사...]
예문	• Sara talks as if she had been the May Queen of her university. [➡ In fact, she was not the May Queen of her university.] • It sounds as if he had studied a lot last night. [➡ In fact, he didn't study a lot last night.]

Grammar Plus +

• **as if＋직설법**
사실과 반대가 아니라 그러할 가능성이 있을 경우, 가정법이 아닌 직설법 문장을 사용한다.
Mary looks **as if** she **has** a lot of friends. [➡ 사실 친구가 많을 수도 있다.]

☆Check up!

Answer Keys p. 55

A 다음 주어진 문장을 참고하여 as if를 사용한 가정법 문장을 완성하시오.

1 In fact, he doesn't like eating chocolate cake.

➡ He eats _____*as if he liked eating chocolate cake.*_____

2 In fact, Jane was not a singer.

➡ Jane pretends _____

3 In fact, Tim slept well last night.

➡ Tim looks _____

4 In fact, Jessica sings very well.

➡ Jessica talks _____

5 In fact, she couldn't play the piano.

➡ She acts _____

6 In fact, my parents didn't like to go fishing.

➡ My parents pretends _____

7 In fact, she doesn't have a cold.

➡ She acts _____

8 In fact, it wasn't her idea.

➡ She talks _____

9 In fact, I didn't hide anything from him.

➡ I pretend _____

10 In fact, John was not good at dancing.

➡ John speaks _____

B 다음 우리말과 같은 뜻이 되도록 주어진 단어를 이용하여 문장을 완성하시오.

1 그는 전에 나를 만난 적이 있었던 것처럼 대했다. (meet)

➡ He treated me ___as if___ he ___had met___ me before.

2 그 여자는 마치 모델인 것처럼 걷는다. (be)

➡ The woman walks _____ she _____ a model.

3 그 남자는 마치 오랫동안 씻지 않았던 것처럼 보인다. (wash)

➡ The man looks _____ he _____ for a long time.

4 그들은 마치 진실을 알고 있는 것처럼 행동한다. (know)

➡ They act _____ they _____ the truth.

5 너는 마치 부자인 것처럼 돈을 쓴다. (be)

➡ You spend money _____ you _____ a rich.

6 Nami는 마치 런던에 다녀온 적이 있었던 것처럼 말한다. (be)

➡ Nami talks _____ she _____ to London.

Practice More Ⅰ

A 다음 괄호 안에 주어진 동사를 알맞은 형태로 고쳐 빈칸에 쓰시오.

1 If it is cold tomorrow, I _____*will go*_____ to central park to ice skate. (go)

2 If you had come to the party, you could _____ delicious food. (enjoy)

3 I wish I _____ a good memory then. (have)

4 If I had had a robot, I could _____ with them. (play)

5 He looks as if he _____ spicy food. (eat)

6 If she _____ a driver's license, she could _____ me up. (have / pick)

7 I wish she _____ our offer that day. (accept)

8 He talks as if he _____ everything. In fact, he can't fix anything. (fix)

9 As I _____ work today, I can't go to the concert. (have to)

10 If you eat healthy food, you _____ healthier. (be)

B 다음 주어진 문장과 같은 의미가 되도록 빈칸에 알맞은 말을 넣으시오.

1 If I were a bird, I could fly everywhere.
   ➡ As I ___*am not a bird*___, I ____*can't fly*____ everywhere.

2 Jack was not careful, so he made a big mistake.
   ➡ If Jack _____ careful, he _____ a big mistake.

3 In fact, John is in trouble.
   ➡ John acts as if he _____.

4 I'm sorry Daniel agreed with her.
   ➡ I wish Daniel _____ her.

5 She doesn't have enough time, so she can't go on a picnic with us.
   ➡ If she _____, she _____ go on a picnic with us.

6 I wish she trusted Mr. Park.
   ➡ I'm sorry she _____ Mr. Park.

7 If I were you, I could solve the problem.

  ➡ As _____ you, I _____ the problem.

8 If you had not had an appointment, you could have come to the party.

  ➡ As you _____, you _____ to the party.

9 As you didn't talk about it, Lina made a big mistake.

  ➡ If you _____ about it, Lina _____ a big mistake.

10 He was tired, so he couldn't attend the meeting.

  ➡ If he _____ tired, he _____ the meeting.

11 I wish he weren't busy today.

  ➡ I'm sorry he _____ today.

12 If I had been good at singing, I could have become a singer.

  ➡ As I _____ singing, I _____ a singer.

13 She talks as if she were popular among her friends.

  ➡ In fact, she _____ among her friends.

C 다음 문장을 우리말로 해석하시오.

1 He acts as if he didn't have a job.

  ➡ _____ 그는 직업이 없는 것처럼 행동한다. _____

2 If I were you, I would do my best to pass the exam.

  ➡ _____

3 If he had believed her, she could have won the tennis game.

  ➡ _____

4 I wish my son had not wasted time.

  ➡ _____

5 If he got up early, he could climb the mountain.

  ➡ _____

6 He talks as if he saw her again.

  ➡ _____

7 She acts as if she were fat.

  ➡ _____

Practice More Ⅰ

Answer Keys p. 55~56

D 다음 가정법 문장을 직설법 문장으로 바꿔 쓰시오.

1 If I had visited the festival, I could have eaten many delicious foods. (so)

➡ _I didn't visit the festival, so I couldn't eat many delicious foods._

2 He talks as if he had been poor in his youth. (in fact)

➡ _____

3 If you had not littered, you would have not paid a fine. (as)

➡ _____

4 If Mr. Kim didn't exercise regularly, he would become fat. (so)

➡ _____

5 I wish she had won the contest. (I'm sorry)

➡ _____

6 If she didn't have much work, she could sleep more. (as)

➡ _____

7 If you didn't live in Seoul, you could not see the night view. (so)

➡ _____

8 If they had learned how to make cookies, they could have helped Sean. (as)

➡ _____

E 다음 괄호 안의 단어를 알맞게 배열하여 우리말을 영어로 옮기시오.

1 그가 좀 더 책을 많이 읽었더라면 좋을 텐데.
(I, books, he, wish, many, read, had)

➡ _I wish he had read many books._

2 그는 그녀를 전에 만나본 적이 없는 것처럼 얘기한다.
(he, if, met, before, as, never, talks, had, he, her)

➡ _____

3 John이 노래를 잘했더라면 그 밴드의 리드보컬이 되었을 텐데.
(John, of, have been, could, well, the lead singer, the band, if, sung, he, had)

➡ _____

Answer Keys p. 56

내신 최다 출제 유형

01 다음 빈칸에 들어갈 말이 바르게 짝지어진 것을 고르시오 [출제 예상 80%]

> (A) If she _____ a liar, she would not tell the truth.
> (B) If you _____ every morning, you would be healthy.

① was – jogs
② were – jogged
③ were – had jogged
④ had been – jogged
⑤ had been – had jogged

02 다음 주어진 문장과 의미가 같은 것을 고르시오. [출제 예상 90%]

> I didn't know the whole story.

① I wish I hadn't known the whole story.
② I wish I had known the whole story.
③ I wish I known the whole story.
④ I wish I didn't know the whole story.
⑤ I wish I knew the whole story.

03 다음 중 어법상 올바른 문장을 모두 고르시오. [출제 예상 90%]

① If you will come with her, you will enjoy the party.
② It sounds as if she were good at speaking English.
③ He wished he became more popular.
④ If she followed his advice, she could made a better decision.
⑤ In fact, she not see the accident.

04 다음 중 밑줄 친 부분이 어법상 어색한 것을 고르시오. [출제 예상 90%]

① We wish the big hurricane didn't hit the city.
② They acted as if they had known the result.
③ If there were a book store near here, I could buy some books.
④ If I had taken piano lessons, I would have become a pianist.
⑤ I wish we have more holidays in summer.

05 다음 빈칸에 알맞은 말을 고르시오. [출제 예상 80%]

> If we _____ a camping car, we would have traveled around the country.

① had   ② have   ③ will have
④ have had   ⑤ had had

[01~02] 다음 빈칸에 들어갈 알맞은 말을 고르시오.

01

> If you _____ early, you won't be late.

① get up   ② got up
③ wakes up   ④ will get up
⑤ woke up

02

> Jenny would not have met me if they _____ late.

① had have   ② had been
③ have be   ④ have been
⑤ had had

[03~05] 다음 중 어법상 어색한 것을 고르시오.

★★★
03 ① If you study hard, you'll get a good grade.
② If you lose weight, you'll be able to wear this skirt.
③ If he passes the test, his parents will be happy.
④ If it will be sunny tomorrow, we'll go on a picnic.
⑤ If they come to my party, we'll have a good time.

★★★
04 ① We wish you could spend Christmas with us.
② I hope that I can meet him again.
③ If you didn't tell the truth, I couldn't have helped you.
④ I wish there were no pollution in the world.
⑤ I'm sorry I didn't visit him yesterday.

★★★
05 ① I wish you could come to my party.
② If you don't get it, I will not try it again.
③ He talks as if he were my uncle.
④ If I were you, I wouldn't marry her.
⑤ She wishes him was here with her.

[06~07] 다음 주어진 문장을 가정법으로 바르게 바꾼 것을 고르시오.

★★★
06

> As you are busy, you can't go to the concert with them.

① If you are busy, you can go to the concert with them.
② If you weren't busy, you could go to the concert with them.
③ If you aren't busy, you could go to the concert with them.
④ If you were busy, you can't go to the concert with them.
⑤ If you were busy, you could go to the concert with them.

★★★
07

In fact, I didn't graduate from Oxford.

① I pretend as if I had not graduated from Oxford.
② I look as if I had not graduated from Oxford.
③ I sound as if I would graduate from Oxford.
④ I act as if I didn't graduate from Oxford.
⑤ I act as if I had graduated from Oxford.

[08~09] 다음 주어진 문장과 의미가 같은 문장을 고르시오.

08

If she had enough money, she could buy all the books.

① Although she doesn't have enough money, she can buy all the books.
② As she has enough money, she can buy all the books.
③ Because she doesn't have enough money, she can't buy all the books.
④ Because she didn't have enough money, she couldn't buy all the books.
⑤ Though she has enough money, she can't buy all the books.

09

If I studied much harder, I could get first prize.

① Though I studied much harder, I could get first prize.
② I don't study much harder, so I can't get first prize.
③ As I study much harder, I can get first prize.
④ Unless I studied much harder, I could get first prize.
⑤ Because I don't study much harder, I couldn't get first prize.

10
다음 중 의미상 자연스러운 것을 모두 고르시오.

① If you get up late, you may catch the first bus.
② If she eats too many candies, she'll have good teeth.
③ If you want to go camping, be nice to your parents.
④ If she studies hard, she may fail the test.
⑤ If you turn the radio on, you can listen to the news.

11
다음 중 앞뒤 문장의 연결이 어색한 것을 고르시오.

① I can't sleep well at night. I wish I could sleep well at night.
② I don't know Japanese. I wish I didn't know Japanese.
③ She can't swim in the sea. She wishes she could swim in the sea.
④ I don't have much free time. I wish I had more free time.
⑤ He isn't good at cooking. He wishes he were good at cooking.

[12~13] 다음 글에서 어법상 어색한 것을 고르시오.

12

- If I ① were an American, I ② would speak English well.
- If I ③ had lived in France, I ④ would ⑤ had visited Paris.

13

① If you ② went there ③ by bus, you ④ won't ⑤ arrive on time.

★★★
14 다음 중 어법상 바르지 않은 것을 모두 고르시오.

① If we had had the key, we could have entered there.

② If I had lived there, I would had visited them often.

③ If she wasn't sick, she could take a trip with me.

④ If he had not been at work, he could have come to the party.

⑤ If I had made them, I could have given them to the children.

[15~16] 다음 빈칸에 들어갈 말들이 알맞게 짝지어진 것을 고르시오.

15

As Rachel has many good friends, she is happy.

= If Rachel _____ many good friends, she _____ happy.

① has − will be

② had not have − would not be

③ didn't have − were not

④ didn't have − would not be

⑤ had − was

16

Practice it again and again, and she can play the piano very well.

= If she _____ again and again, she _____ the piano very well.

① practice − can play

② practices − can play

③ practiced − can play

④ had practiced − could have played

⑤ had not practice − could not have played

17 다음 두 문장의 뜻이 같아지도록 빈칸에 들어갈 알맞은 말을 고르시오.

If you don't listen carefully, you won't get it.

= Listen carefully, _____ you won't get it.

① and   ② but   ③ or

④ therefore   ⑤ so

18 다음 중 어법상 바르게 쓰인 것을 고르시오.

① If she will grow up, she will understand me.

② If it rains a lot, the field trip will be canceled.

③ When you will arrive, I will go to you.

④ If he drives too fast, he might have had an accident.

⑤ If they go to bed early, they would not be tired.

[19~20] 다음 주어진 우리말을 영어로 바르게 옮긴 것을 고르시오.

★★★
19

네가 어리지 않다면 그것을 함께 탈 수 있을 텐데.

① As you are young, you couldn't ride it together.

② As you aren't young, you can ride it together.

③ If you aren't young, you can't ride it together.

④ If you weren't young, you can ride it together.

⑤ If you weren't young, you could ride it together.

★★★
20

그녀가 좀 더 현명했다면 좋을 텐데.

① I wish she is wiser.

② I wish she had been more wise.

③ I wish she is wise.

④ I wish she was wise.

⑤ I wish she had wise.

★★★
21 다음 밑줄 친 부분 중 어법상 올바른 것을 모두 고르시오.

① If she were your friend, she <u>could help</u> you.

② If he had eaten a lot of ice cream, he <u>would have</u> a stomachache.

③ If I were you, I <u>bought</u> the car.

④ What would you do if you <u>picked up</u> the wallet?

⑤ If I were not sick, I <u>could have played</u> with friends.

★★★
22 다음 밑줄 친 부분 중 어법상 틀린 것을 모두 고르시오.

① If you <u>hadn't enjoy</u> reading books, you would have wasted your time.

② Tommy could have finished it if we <u>helped</u> them.

③ We would have had a good time if we <u>had not worked</u>.

④ If they <u>had saved</u> money, they would have bought their house.

⑤ If you <u>had clever</u>, you would have decided not to do it.

★★★
23 다음 중 짝지어진 문장의 뜻이 같은 것을 고르시오.

① I wish my parents had not been angry with me.
= I am sorry my parents are angry with me.

② I wish I was slim.
= I am sorry I wasn't slim.

③ I wish I could speak Spanish well.
= I am sorry I spoke Spanish well.

④ I wish I were a famous dancer.
= I am sorry I was not a famous dancer.

⑤ I wish I weren't busy these days.
= I am sorry I am busy these days.

[24~25] 다음 두 문장들의 내용이 같지 <u>않은</u> 것을 고르시오.

24 ① If his bike were repaired, he could ride it with me.
= As his bike is not repaired, he can't ride it with me.

② Judy used my cell phone, so I couldn't call my mom.
= If Judy didn't use my cell phone, I could have called my mom.

③ If I had had enough money, I could have helped the poor.
= As I didn't have enough money, I couldn't help the poor.

④ If you had a dream, you would study hard.
= You don't have a dream, so you don't study hard.

⑤ If he hadn't broken his arm, he could have played hockey.
= As he broke his arm, he couldn't play hockey.

25 ① Martin had his ticket, so he could enter the concert.
= If Martin hadn't had his ticket, he couldn't have entered the concert.

② As I don't have a good skill, I can't make a kite.
= If I had a good skill, I could make a kite.

③ If Lina had been alone, she would have got lost.
= Lina was alone, so she got lost.

④ They are smart, so they can win a prize.
= If they weren't smart, they couldn't win a prize.

⑤ If you hadn't helped me, I couldn't have finished it.
= As you helped me, I could finish it.

26 다음 문장의 빈칸에 이어질 표현으로 알맞은 것을 고르시오.

> If we had enough money, _____ _____.

① we bough a new camera

② we can buy a new camera

③ we would buy a new camera

④ we would have bought a new camera

⑤ we wouldn't have bought a new camera

★★★
27 다음 주어진 문장과 의미가 같은 것을 고르시오.

> As this is a horror movie, I am so
> nervous.

① If this movie wasn't a horror movie, I
would be so nervous.
② If this movie wasn't a horror movie, I
wouldn't be so nervous.
③ If this weren't a horror movie, I wouldn't
be so nervous.
④ If this movie weren't a horror movie, I
would be so nervous.
⑤ If this wasn't a horror movie, I wouldn't
be so nervous.

[28~30] 다음 괄호 안의 알맞은 동사의 형태가 바르게
짝지어진 것을 고르시오.

28

> • I wish I (join) the music club last
> month.
> • If she (buy) a new bike, she would
> ride it.

① join − bought
② had joined − bought
③ joined − bought
④ have joined − had bought
⑤ had joined − buy

29

> • She talks as if she (be) an actress.
> • They talk as if they (win) the game
> last year.

① was − won
② were − won
③ had been − had won
④ were − had won
⑤ had been − won

30

> • If I had been more diligent, I (finish)
> cleaning the house.
> • I wish I (write) a story in English.

① could have finished − wrote
② could finished − could written
③ finished − wrote
④ couldn't finished − can't write
⑤ could have finish − can write

◇◇◇◇◇◇◇◇◇ 서술형 평가 ◇◇◇◇◇◇◇◇◇

[31~33] 다음 주어진 우리말과 같은 뜻이 되도록 주어진
동사를 활용하여 빈칸에 알맞은 말을 쓰시오.

31

> 나의 조부모님들께서 여기에 계셨더라면 좋
> 을 텐데.
> = I wish my grandparents _____
> _____ here. (be)

➡ _____

中간 기말고사 **예상문제**

32

우리가 지난달에 유럽 여행을 했더라면 좋을 텐데.

= We wish we _____ _____ to Europe last month. (travel)

➡ _____

33

그녀가 조금만 더 일찍 일어났다면 그녀는 산에 오를 수 있었을 텐데.

= If she _____ _____ a little earlier, she would _____ _____ the mountain. (get up, climb)

➡ _____

[34~36] 다음 두 문장의 뜻이 같아지도록 빈칸에 알맞은 말을 쓰시오.

34

There is no Italian restaurant in this town.

= I wish there _____ _____ _____ _____ in this town.

➡ _____

35

Go to bed early, and you will not get up late.

= _____ you go to bed early, you _____ get up late.

➡ _____

36

In fact, they are not rich.

= They act _____ _____ they were rich.

➡ _____

[37~38] 다음 괄호 안의 말을 이용하여 문장을 완성하시오.

37

If he _____ harder, he could have succeeded. (work)

➡ _____

38

If she _____ so busy, she would visit Tom's house together. (be not)

➡ _____

[39~40] 다음 주어진 문장을 다시 쓸 때 괄호 안의 동사를 이용하여 빈칸에 알맞은 말을 쓰시오.

39

As you aren't honest, you don't have many friends.

➡ If you were honest, _____ many friends. (have)

40

He feels as if today were Sunday.

➡ In fact, ＿＿＿＿＿＿＿＿ Sunday. (be)

[41~43] 다음 주어진 문장을 가정법 문장으로 바꿔 쓰시오.

★★★
41

In fact, William isn't very silly.

➡ ＿＿＿＿＿＿＿＿＿＿＿＿＿＿

★★★
42

As I don't prepare a tent, I will come back home tonight.

➡ ＿＿＿＿＿＿＿＿＿＿＿＿

43

Unless he minds it, we can go to the festival together.

➡ ＿＿＿＿＿＿＿＿＿＿＿＿

[44~45] 다음 주어진 그림과 내용이 일치하도록 괄호 안의 단어를 이용하여 가정법 문장을 쓰시오.

44

(more money / buy / the new bike)

➡ If he ＿＿＿＿＿＿＿＿＿＿＿＿＿,

＿＿＿＿＿＿＿＿＿＿＿＿＿ now.

45

(practice / hard / win the game)

➡ If they ＿＿＿＿＿＿＿＿＿＿＿＿,

＿＿＿＿＿＿＿＿＿＿＿＿ last year.

Note

12

Chapter
관계사

Point Check I

◆ **관계대명사**: 두 개 문장의 공통된 부분을 하나로 연결하는 역할을 하는 것을 말한다.
선행사에 따라 쓸 수 있는 관계대명사가 다르다.

◆ **선행사**: 관계대명사가 이끄는 절이 설명하는 대상을 선행사라고 한다.

1. 관계대명사의 종류

선행사 \ 격	주격	목적격	소유격
사람	who	who(m)	whose
사물, 동물	which	which	of which / whose
사람, 사물(동물)	that	that	–
선행사 없음	what (~하는 것)	what (~하는 것)	–

2. 관계대명사를 사용한 문장 만들기

(1) 선행사와 선행사를 꾸밀 문장 선택	• Jane has a good friend. He is always kind to others. 　　　　　[선행사]　　　　　　　　　　　[선행사를 수식할 문장]
(2) 수식할 문장에서 선행사와 같은 대명사 삭제	• Jane has a good friend. He is always kind to others. 　　[a good friend = he]
(3) 두 문장을 관계대명사로 연결	• Jane has a good friend who(that) is always kind to others.

3. 목적격 관계대명사 생략하기

목적격 관계대명사	예문
who(m)	• He was **a teacher**. My mom met **him** yesterday. ➡ He was a teacher (whom) my mom met yesterday.
which	• I ate **dim sum**. Ching-ching recommended **it** to me. ➡ I ate some dim sum (which) Ching-ching recommended to me.
that	• Neil finished **the work**. His boss gave **it** to him. ➡ Neil finished the work (that) his boss gave him.

4. 주격 관계대명사 + be동사 + 분사

• The actor **(who is) playing** Hamlet on the stage is my boyfriend.
['주격관계대명사+be동사' 생략]

12-1 관계대명사의 역할과 종류

> • **관계대명사**: 두 문장을 하나로 연결하는 접속사이면서 앞에 나온 명사를 대신하는 대명사의 역할을 한다. 관계대명사에는 'who, what, which, that'이 있으며, 선행사에 따라 사용하는 것이 달라진다.

1. 관계대명사의 역할: 관계대명사절은 앞에 있는 명사를 꾸며주는 형용사절이며, 꾸밈을 받는 명사를 선행사라고 한다.

형 태	[접속사 + 대명사 = 관계대명사]
예 문	• I know **a girl**. + She dances very well. [a girl = she] ➡ I know **a girl** and she dances very well. [a girl = she] ➡ I know <u>**a girl**</u> who dances very well. [a girl = who dances very well] [선행사] [관계대명사 이하의 문장은 'a girl'을 꾸미는 형용사절]

2. 관계대명사의 종류: 선행사에 따라 관계대명사가 결정되며, 관계대명사가 이끄는 절에서 주격, 소유격, 목적격이 결정된다.

선행사＼격	주격	목적격	소유격
사람	who	who(m)	whose
사물, 동물	which	which	of which / whose
사람, 사물(동물)	that	that	–
선행사 없음	what (~하는 것)	what (~하는 것)	–

➡ 관계대명사 'that'은 선행사가 사람, 사물, 동물에 상관없이 모두 쓰일 수 있다.

3. 관계대명사를 사용하여 문장 만들기

(1) 선행사와 선행사를 꾸밀 문장 선택	• I have a friend. He speaks English well. 　　　[선행사]　　　　　[선행사를 수식할 문장]
(2) 수식할 문장에서 선행사와 같은 대명사 삭제	• I have a friend. speaks English well. 　　　[a friend = he]
(3) 두 문장을 관계대명사로 연결 ➡ • 선행사가 사람 　• 지워진 'he'가 주어 　⇒ 주격 관계대명사 사용	• I have a friend who(that) speaks English well.

A 문장 안의 선행사에 밑줄을 긋고 알맞은 관계대명사를 고르시오.
(선행사가 없는 경우도 있음)

1 I want to read <u>the book</u> ((which) / who) was written by James.

2 Sam wants to buy the bag (whose / whom) color is black.

3 This is (what / that) I want to say.

4 The baby (which / who) is wearing the yellow hat is my son.

5 You can see the house (who / whose) roof is green.

6 Jane met a boy (who / whom) speaks English fluently.

7 I have a friend (whom / whose) hobby is playing soccer.

8 John bought me some tea (which / of which) was good for relieving stress.

9 They believe (what / that) you told them.

10 That is the table (which / whose) I want to buy.

B 주어진 문장에서 동그라미 친 선행사를 꾸미는 관계대명사절을 찾아 밑줄을 치시오.

1 The song which my father composed was really great.

2 I'll lend you my car whose color is red.

3 The girl whom I met last week is my best friend, Helen.

4 The island that we visited last winter is Jeju Island.

5 I like movies that have super heroes who save the world.

6 Jina couldn't pass the exam which she took yesterday.

7 This is the house which I lived in for seventeen years.

8 John started to write the book whose topic was how to live a successful life.

9 I have a boyfriend who lives in Busan.

10 Choose the title that attracts many people to our performance.

12-2 관계대명사 who

• 관계대명사 who : 관계대명사가 설명해 주는 선행사가 '사람'일 경우 사용한다.

◈ 관계대명사 who

격	의미 및 예문
who (주격)	관계대명사가 이끄는 절 안에서 주어 역할을 한다. • Jenny is my sister. She is pretty and smart. = Jenny is my sister who is pretty and smart.
whose (소유격)	관계대명사가 이끄는 절 안에서 관계대명사 바로 뒤에 나오는 명사를 꾸며주는 역할을 한다. • I met a man. His hair style is weird. = I met a man whose hair style is weird.
whom (목적격)	관계대명사가 이끄는 절 안에서 목적어 역할을 한다. (회화체에서는 'whom' 대신 'who'를 쓰기도 한다.) • They are soccer players. Mr. Park trained them. = They are soccer players who(m) Mr. Park trained.

Answer Keys p. 58

A 다음에 주어진 두 문장을 관계대명사를 이용하여 한 문장으로 쓰시오.

1 I know the girl. She jogs every morning.

➡ *I know the girl who jogs every morning.*

2 Tim and Jane are singers. I love them.

➡ _____

3 Do you remember Jane? She was our class president.

➡ _____

4 I have a sister. She has a long blond hair.

➡ _____

5 There is a man. I want to talk with him.

➡ _____

6 She met a boy. His brother is a dentist.

➡ _____

7 I saw a man and a bird. They were sitting on the bench.

➡ _____

8 Mary is a student. She got the first prize in English speaking contest.

➡ _____

9 He remembered Jane. She was sitting next to Linda.

➡ _____

10 They respect James. He has a lot of wisdom.

➡ _____

B 우리말 해석과 일치하도록 주어진 단어와 관계대명사를 이용하여 문장을 완성하시오.

1 나는 Sam 옆에 앉아 있던 소년을 좋아한다. (who, sit)
➡ I liked the boy ____*who was sitting next to Sam.*____

2 나는 거리를 뛰어 내려가는 소년을 안다. (who, run)
➡ I know the boy _____

3 그는 모든 어려운 문제에 대답 할 수 있는 학생이다. (who, answer)
➡ He is a student _____

4 Andrew는 내가 만나고 싶었던 영화감독이다. (whom, meet)
➡ Andrew is a movie director _____

5 초록색 코트의 여성 분이 우리 할머니이시다. (whose, coat)
➡ The lady _____

6 나는 거리를 청소하곤 했던 여인을 만났다. (who, used to)
➡ I met a lady _____

7 Harry는 개를 찾고 있는 소년을 보았다. (who, look for)
➡ Harry saw the boy _____

8 호텔에서 일하는 사람들은 매우 친절하다. (who, work)
➡ The people _____ are very kind.

9 그 금발머리 소녀의 이름은 무엇이니? (whose, blond)
➡ What is the name of the girl _____?

10 나의 생일 파티에 초대한 나의 친구들 몇몇은 오지 않았다. (whom, invite)
➡ Some of friends _____ didn't come.

12-3 관계대명사 which

- **관계대명사 which**: 선행사가 사물 또는 동물로 주어 역할을 할 때는 주격으로, 목적어 역할을 할 때는 목적격으로 'which'를 사용한다.

◈ 관계대명사 which

격	의미 및 예문
which (주격)	주어 역할을 한다. • Look at my sports car. It is new. = Look at my sports car which is new.
whose (소유격)	관계대명사 바로 뒤에 나오는 명사를 꾸며주는 역할을 한다. • Cathy has a cat. Its fur is so fluffy. = Cathy has a cat whose fur is so fluffy.
which (목적격)	목적어 역할을 한다. • Johnny drew some pictures. I liked them. = Johnny drew some pictures which I liked.

Check up!

Answer Keys p. 58

A 괄호 안에 주어진 단어 중 알맞은 것을 고르시오.

1 Mom made the dress ((which) / of which) I would wear to the party.

2 I want to buy the chair (which / whose) legs don't break easily.

3 The books which (is / are) on the sofa are Tim's.

4 Kate entered the room (whose / which) window was opened.

5 There is a house (whose / which) is going to be repainted.

6 My hobby is making cookies (which / what) takes many hours.

7 Tell me about the accident (which / whose) you saw last night.

8 He wants to have a pet (who / which) can talk.

9 I like the castle (which / whose) has many windows.

10 Ostriches are birds (which / who) cannot fly.

Answer Keys p. 58

B   which, whose를 이용하여 두 문장을 한 문장으로 연결하시오.

1   This is a desk. Father made it for me.

➡ *This is a desk which father made for me.*

2   I have a cat. It has black and white fur.

➡ _____

3   This is the car. I fixed it by myself.

➡ _____

4   Jane likes to read the book. Its cover is black.

➡ _____

5   The song is good. Harry made it for his wife.

➡ _____

6   Edward made some food. I liked them.

➡ _____

7   This is my daughter's room. Its walls are green.

➡ _____

8   This letter was so moving. Jim wrote it to me.

➡ _____

9   Tim should clean his car. It is too dirty.

➡ _____

10   I want to buy the camera. Many people like it.

➡ _____

12-4 관계대명사 that

- 관계대명사 that: 'who(m)'이나 'which' 대신 사용할 수 있으며, 선행사가 사람, 사물, 동물인 경우 모두 쓸 수 있다. 주격과 목적격의 형태가 같으며 소유격은 쓰이지 않는다.

1. 관계대명사 that

격	의미 및 예문
that (주격)	주어 역할을 한다. • I like the boy. He is smiling at me over there. = I like the boy that(who) is smiling at me over there.
that (목적격)	목적어 역할을 한다. • I have some coins. You gave me them. = I have some coins that(which) you gave me.

2. 다음과 같은 경우 주로 'that'을 쓴다.

(1) 최상급, 서수, the only, the very, the same, all 등이 선행사를 수식하는 경우

- It's the same question **that** you asked me.

(2) '-thing'으로 끝나는 대명사 또는 '사람 + 사물(동물)'이 선행사인 경우

- They didn't buy anything **that** their kids wanted.

- He likes to play with James and his dog **that** are the best friends to him.

Answer Keys p. 59

A 괄호 안에 주어진 관계대명사 중 알맞은 것을 모두 고르시오.

1 The man (that / whom) I met last night was very handsome.

2 He saved the driver and the car (whose / that) fell into the river.

3 She is the most beautiful girl (which / that) I've ever seen.

4 There will be many dishes (that / which) you can eat.

5 Mike didn't say anything (that / which) related to the accident.

6 Mom didn't like those clothes (which / that) I bought yesterday.

7 Mary is the first girl (that / whom) finished the project.

8 There is much information (that / whose) I can get.

9 Let me introduce John (who / that) is a great scientist.

10 That's the only mistake (that / which) you made.

12-5 관계대명사 what

- 관계대명사 what : 'what'은 자체적으로 선행사를 갖고 있는 유일한 관계대명사이다.
  what이 이끄는 관계대명사는 '~하는 것'의 뜻을 가지며, 명사 역할을 하면서
  주어, 목적어, 보어로 쓰인다.

1. 관계대명사 what

명사 역할	예문
주어	• What they want is to travel all over the world. = The thing that(which) they want is to travel all over the world.
목적어	• The students don't understand what the principal means. = The students don't understand the thing that(which) the principal means.
보어	• That is what I want to buy. = That is the thing that(which) I want to buy.

➡ 관계대명사 'what'은 'the thing that(which)'으로 바꿔 쓸 수 있다.

Grammar Plus +

- 의문사와 관계대명사의 차이

	의문사	관계대명사
역할	'누구, 어떤(어느) 것, 무엇'의 뜻을 갖는다.	선행사를 수식하는 '접속사 + 대명사'의 역할을 한다.
who	• Who is that man? [누구]	• Everyone knows the boy who is the most hadsome in this school. [the boy = who]
which	• Which do you like better, a sweater or a jacket? [어느 것]	• I want to have a CD which has his autograph on. [a CD = which]
what	• What is the matter? [무엇]	• What I want to say is just a funny joke. [what ~하는 것]

A　괄호 안에서 알맞은 것을 고르시오.

1　(What / That) I want is to go to the amusement park.

2　I can't understand (what / that) Tom said.

3　Today's class was (what / which) I expected.

4　Horror movies are (what / that) I really like to watch.

5　(That / What) is not (what / that) he meant.

6　Think about (what / which) you started first.

7　(That / What) Jane wants to do now is to eat lunch.

8　That is the thing (that / what) my mother wants to buy.

9　That is not (what / that) I want to do the most.

10　This is (what / which) I'd like to discuss with you.

B　다음 주어진 문장을 관계대명사 what을 이용해 고쳐 쓰시오.

1　I don't believe the thing that you said to Tim.
　➡　*I don't believe what you said to Tim.*

2　Mother bought the thing that I wanted for my graduation present.
　➡ _____

3　The thing that you prepared for your son's birthday party will make him happy.
　➡ _____

4　That movie is not the thing that I want to watch.
　➡ _____

5　I think Jane has to do the thing that is best for her.
　➡ _____

6　The thing that Lisa needed was paper and pencils for her study.
　➡ _____

7　They wanted to know the thing which Helen wanted to have for New Year's Day.
　➡ _____

관계대명사의 생략

· 관계대명사의 생략 : 문장 안에서 관계대명사가 목적격으로 쓰일 경우 생략할 수 있다.

1. 목적격 관계대명사의 생략

목적격 관계대명사	예문
who(m)	· He is **a doctor**. I met **him** last Sunday. ➡ He is a doctor (whom) I met last Sunday.
which	· We traveled to **Rome**. Amy recommended **it** to us. ➡ We traveled to Rome (which) Amy recommended to us.
that	· Does she practice **the song**? Ms. Apple chose **it** for her. ➡ Does she practice the song (that) Ms. Apple chose for her?

2. 주격 관계대명사＋be동사＋분사 : '주격 관계대명사＋be동사' 생략가능

· The woman **(who is) playing** the violin on the stage is my aunt Alison.

· Paul gave me a necklace **(which was)** made of silver.

Grammar Plus +

· 전치사가 관계대명사 앞에 쓰인 경우는 관계대명사를 생략 할 수 없고, 'that'은 쓸 수 없다.
Chicago was a city **(which)** I have lived **in**.
➡ Chicago was a city **in which** I have lived. (in which 생략 불가능)
➡ Chicago was a city in that I have lived. (X)

Check up!

Answer Keys p. 59

A 다음 문장에서 생략해도 되는 부분이 있다면 그 단어에 괄호를 표시하시오.
(없을 경우 X 하시오.)

1 Try this pasta (which) I've made now.

2 My friend who loves watching movies was Jane.

3 This is the wallet that I lost last night.

4 I recommended the musical that Nick was cast as the leading role.

5 The book which was written by James recorded one billion in sales.

6 Everything that she wrote is false.

7 This is the building which my father built.

Practice More I

Answer Keys p. 59

A 괄호 안에서 알맞은 것을 고르시오.

1 The boy (who / which) was singing on the stage was my nephew.

2 He is the inventor (who / whom) I met yesterday in the conference.

3 This is the car (whose / which) I am going to buy.

4 Find the store (which / whose) door is green.

5 These are glasses (which / whose) my friend bought for me.

6 I visited my grandmother's home (that / who) was in London.

7 They need a hint (that / whose) helps them solve the problem.

8 This is the writer (whose / who) book was a best seller.

9 I like the writer (who / whom) Lisa took a picture of.

10 I like the band (whose / which) performance was great last night.

B 다음 문장에서 어법상 <u>어색한</u> 것을 찾아 바르게 고치시오.

1 They have a dog whose bites people.

_____whose_____ ➡ ___which (that)___

2 I want to meet more people which can teach me.

_____ ➡ _____

3 They are restaurants which menus are different.

_____ ➡ _____

4 I can fix my car whose was broken yesterday.

_____ ➡ _____

5 I know the person whose you helped.

_____ ➡ _____

6 That's that I want to say.

_____ ➡ _____

7 I'm the first person which wore the coat.

_____ ➡ _____

8 I called my sister whom lives in Germany.

_____ ➡ _____

Practice More I

9 Jane remembered the man what she met before.

      _____ ➡ _____

10 He was a scientist whose is most respected.

      _____ ➡ _____

C 다음 문장에서 생략할 수 있는 부분에 동그라미 치시오.

1 This is the house which is made by his father.

2 The girls who are playing chess are my students.

3 The movie which was directed by Tom was great.

4 The book which is written in English is so difficult to read.

5 I like to eat fish which are caught in the river.

6 They bought the car that he wants to buy.

7 There are many people whom we met during the rock festival.

8 I love the woman who is playing violin on the stage.

D 다음에 주어진 두 문장을 관계대명사를 이용하여 한 문장으로 연결하시오.

1 This is a school. My daughter will attend the school next year.

  ➡ *This is a school which my daughter will attend next year.*

2 The boy is a famous dancer. He has lived in this city for five years.

  ➡ _____

3 She was going to the tower. Its night view was awesome.

  ➡ _____

4 The woman is wearing a red raincoat. She is running down the street.

  ➡ _____

5 I have a friend. I can depend on him.

  ➡ _____

6 This is the last thing. He had it in his pocket.

  ➡ _____

7 There is a restaurant. It opens early in the morning.

  ➡ _____

8 The man is our math teacher. He said we should study hard for the final exam.

  ➡ _____

> **Note**
> - **play chess**
>   체스를 두다
> - **direct** 감독하다
> - **the rock festival**
>   록 축제
> - **design** 설계하다
> - **attend school**
>   학교에 통학하다(다니다)
> - **night view** 야경
> - **awesome**
>   굉장한, 훌륭한

◆ **관계부사**: 선행사를 수식하는 절을 이끌면서 '접속사＋부사'의 역할을 하는 것을 말하며,
'전치사＋관계대명사'로 바꿔 쓸 수 있다.

1. 관계부사의 종류 및 쓰임

when (시간)	• I remember the day when I first had a job interview. [관계부사 (＝전치사＋관계대명사 on which)]
where (장소)	• Paris is a romantic city where I visited. [관계부사 (＝전치사＋관계대명사 in which)]
why (이유)	• We didn't know the reason why our teacher was angry. [관계부사 (＝전치사＋관계대명사 for which)]
how (방법)	• He'll tell you how to make a kite. ＝ He'll tell you the way to make a kite. [관계부사 (＝전치사＋관계대명사 in which)]

2. 관계부사의 생략 : 선행사가 있을 경우 생략이 가능하다.

관계사	선행사	관계사	선행사
where	the place, the house, the town, the city	**when**	the time, the day, the month, the year
why	the reason	**how**	(the way)

3. 선행사의 생략 : 관계부사의 대표적인 선행사의 경우 생략이 가능하다.

관계사	선행사	예문
when	the time, the day	• Jessy doesn't remember when Mike left. [선행사: the day 또는 the time 생략]
where	the place	• They'll visit where Jenny moved to. [선행사: the place 생략]
why	the reason	• He couldn't say why he cried yesterday. [선행사: the reason 생략]

4. 관계사의 계속적 용법과 한정적 용법

계속적 용법	• 관계사 앞에 '콤마(,)'가 있으며, 순서대로 해석한다. Tina has two baskets of apples, which are so fresh.
한정적 용법	• 콤마 없이 문장과 문장 사이에 관계사가 존재하며, 관계부사절을 먼저 해석한다. Laura had to know why Jimmy was angry with her.

• 관계부사: 문장 안에서 앞 문장의 선행사를 꾸며 주면서 시간, 장소, 이유, 방법 등을 나타내며, '전치사+관계대명사'의 부사구를 대신한다.

◆ 관계부사의 종류

	선행사	관계부사	전치사 + 관계대명사
장소	the place, the house, the town, the city	where	at/in/to which
시간	the time, the day, the month, the year	when	at/in/to which
이유	the reason	why	for which
방법	(the way)	how	in which

• This is the place **where** I got married.
  = This is the place **in which** I got married. [in + 장소]

• July 16th is the day **when** Sherry met her husband.
  = July 16th is the day **on which** Sherry met her husband. [on + 날짜]

• That's the reason **why** we got angry.
  = That's the reason **for which** we got angry.

• That's **how** I learned English. (= That's **the way** I learned English.)
  = That's the way **in which** I learned English.

➡ 방법을 표현할 때 'how'와 'the way'는 함께 사용할 수 없으므로 둘 중 하나만 써야 한다.

☆Check up!

Answer Keys p. 60

A 다음 문장의 빈칸에 알맞은 관계 부사를 쓰시오.

1 Paris is the city ___where___ I have lived for fifteen years.

2 March 13th is the day _____ my sister was born.

3 I could learn _____ to fix the watch by myself.

4 2002 was the year _____ all the people were enthusiastic about the World Cup.

5 Mr. Jung taught us _____ we read French exactly.

6 This is the place _____ I found my dog.

7 Kate told us the reason _____ she broke up.

8 I want to buy the new house _____ my family can live.

9 I can't remember the day _____ we first met.

12-8 관계부사 when, where

- **when**: 선행사가 '시간, 때'를 나타낸다.
- **where**: 선행사가 '장소'를 나타낸다.

1. **관계부사 when**: 시간을 선행사로 한다. 관계대명사 'on/at/in which'로 바꾸어 쓸 수 있다.

- I can't forget the day. + We first watched the musical on the day.

  = I can't forget the day **and** we first watched the musical on that day.
  (접속사)   (시간의 부사구)
  = I can't forget the day **when** we first watched the musical.
  관계부사 (= 전치사 + 관계대명사 on which)
  = I can't forget the day **on which** we first watched the musical.

2. **관계부사 where**: 장소를 선행사로 한다. 관계대명사 'in/at/to which'로 바꾸어 쓸 수 있다.

- Hong Kong is a big city. + I live there.

  = Hong Kong is a big city **and** I live there.
  (접속사)   (장소의 부사구)
  = Hong Kong is a big city **where** I live.
  관계부사 (= 전치사 + 관계대명사 in which)
  = Hong Kong a big city **in which** I live.

☆Check up!

Answer Keys p. 60

A 다음 보기 에서 알맞은 단어를 골라 빈칸에 쓰시오.

> where   the day   when   the place

1 Does she know a restaurant ___where___ we can have a nice dinner?

2 I didn't know the time _____ Chris came back home.

3 The theater _____ we watched the musical was not big.

4 October 23rd is _____ when my father celebrates his birthday.

5 This is _____ where I was born.

Answer Keys p. 60

B   다음 두 문장을 관계부사를 이용하여 한 문장으로 바꿔 쓰시오.

1   I remember the day. My son gained his feet for the first time on the day.

➡ *I remember the day when my son gained his feet for the first time.*

2   Tokyo is the city. I want to go there.

➡ _____

3   She went to America. She was an elementary school student at that time.

➡ _____

4   This is the place. I lost my bike here.

➡ _____

5   He doesn't forget the day. He bought his first car on the day.

➡ _____

6   Busan is a big city. My best friend lives there.

➡ _____

7   Sam still remembers the day. He first met his girlfriend on the day.

➡ _____

8   April first is the day. People can be forgiven for their lies that day.

➡ _____

9   This is the building. They have built this for five years.

➡ _____

10   Kate told me the day. She left for China that day.

➡ _____

11   Nick waited for her in the park. They usually exercise there.

➡ _____

12   We will go hiking this Saturday. Our parents celebrate their wedding anniversary on that day.

➡ _____

_____

12-9 관계부사 why, how

- **why**: 선행사가 '이유'를 나타낸다.
- **how**: 선행사가 '방법'을 나타낸다.

1. **관계부사 why**: 이유를 선행사로 한다. 관계대명사 'for which'로 바꾸어 쓸 수 있다.

- She didn't know the reason. + Tom broke his promise for that reason.

= She didn't know the reason **and** Tom broke his promise for that reason.
(접속사) (이유의 부사구)
= She didn't know the reason **why** Tom broke his promise.
관계부사 (= 전치사 + 관계대명사 for which)
= She didn't know the reason **for which** Tom broke his promise.

2. **관계부사 how**: 방법을 선행사로 한다. 'the way'와 'how'를 같이 사용하지 않는다.
관계대명사 'in which'로 바꾸어 쓸 수 있다.

- I'll tell you the way. + You write a letter in English in the way.

= I'll tell you the way **and** you write a letter in English in the way.
(접속사) (방법의 부사구)
= I'll tell you **how** you write a letter in English.

= I'll tell you **the way** you write a letter in English.
(= 전치사 + 관계대명사 in which)
= I'll tell you the way **in which** you write a letter in English.

 Answer Keys p. 60

A 다음 두 문장을 관계부사를 이용하여 한 문장으로 바꿔 쓰시오.

1 Tim didn't know the reason. His mom was angry for the reason.

➡ *Tim didn't know the reason why his mom was angry.*

2 I can't understand the reason. She cries for the reason.

➡ _____

3 I'll teach you the way. You can write a good novel this way.

➡ _____

➡ _____

4 They didn't know the reason. She left suddenly for that reason.

➡ _____

5   She'll tell me the way. I can fix my oven by myself in this way.

➡ _____

➡ _____

6   Tell me the reason. She gave up the competition for the reason.

➡ _____

7   Can you tell me? The way you solved all the problems.

➡ _____

➡ _____

8   I didn't know the reason. He didn't come to the party last night for the reason.

➡ _____

9   John learned the way. The chef made the pasta in that way.

➡ _____

➡ _____

10 Does he tell the reason? He has to get up early tomorrow because of it.

➡ _____

B   다음 우리말과 같은 뜻이 되도록 괄호 안의 말을 이용하여 알맞은 말을 쓰시오.

1   네가 그 종이학을 접는 법을 가르쳐 줄래? (folded, the paper crane)

➡ Could you teach me _how (the way) you folded the paper crane_ ?

2   내가 그림을 잘 그리는 법을 말해 줄게. (draw pictures)

➡ I'll tell you _____ .

3   우리의 지구가 위험에 처한 이유를 알고 있니? (reason)

➡ Do you know _____ why the earth is in danger?

4   그녀가 어떻게 일등을 했는지 이해가 안 가. (got)

➡ I don't understand _____ .

5   내가 그 일을 해야 하는 이유를 말해줘요. (should, do)

➡ Please tell me the reason _____ the work.

Lesson

12-10 관계부사의 생략

- 관계부사의 생략: 방법을 나타내는 'how'는 원래 선행사와 함께 쓰일 수 없지만, 다른 관계부사들은 선행사가 나올 경우 생략할 수 있다.

1. 관계부사의 생략: 선행사가 있을 경우 생략이 가능하다.

관계부사	선행사
when (시간)	the day, the time, the year...
where (장소)	the place, the city, the house, the country...
why (이유)	the reason
how (방법)	the way

- This is the restaurant. I eat tomato spaghetti at this restaurant.
  = This is **the restaurant** (**where**) I eat tomato spaghetti.
  [선행사: the restaurant, 관계부사 생략: where]

- I want to know the reason. Emily and Jack are fighting for that reason.
  = I want to know **the reason** (**why**) Emily and Jack are fighting.
  [선행사: the reason, 관계부사 생략: why]

2. 선행사의 생략: 각 관계부사의 대표적인 선행사의 경우 생략이 가능하다.

관계부사	선행사	예문
when (시간)	the time the day	• He didn't remember when we came here. [선행사: the day 또는 the time 생략]
where (장소)	the place	• Henry and I are traveling where Jenny lives now. [선행사: the place 생략]
why (이유)	the reason	• We couldn't know why Helen told a lie to us. [선행사: the reason 생략] • He couldn't tell why he cried yesterday. [선행사: the reason 생략]

Answer Keys p. 60~61

A   다음 두 문장을 [보기]와 같이 한 문장으로 바꾸어 쓰시오.

> [보기]
>
> I know the place. My family has lived there for ten years.
> ➡ I know the place where my family has lived for ten years.
> ➡ I know where my family has lived for ten years.

1   I can remember the day. We first met that day.

➡ _____

➡ _____

2   Tell me the reason. They were late for the reason.

➡ _____

➡ _____

3   We remember the city. My son was born in the place.

➡ _____

➡ _____

4   Do they know the time? Our performance will begin at the time.

➡ _____

➡ _____

5   I can't remember the way. Koreans make kimchi in that way.

➡ _____

➡ _____

6   We are going to the place. We got married in that place.

➡ _____

➡ _____

7   Helen got up at that time. The alarm went off at that time.

➡ _____

➡ _____

8   I know the reason. She resigned from her position for that reason.

➡ _____

➡ _____

9   We want to know the day. She will graduate that day.

➡ _____

➡ _____

12-11 관계사의 계속적 용법

> • **계속적 용법**: 선행사에 대해 부가적인 설명을 덧붙일 때는 관계사 앞에 ', (콤마)'를 쓰며, 문장 순서대로 해석한다.

1. 관계사의 계속적 용법과 한정적 용법

계속적 용법	• 관계사 앞에 '콤마(,)'가 있으며, 순서대로 해석한다. Neil has two brothers, who are lawyers. ➡ 순서대로 해석한다.
한정적 용법	• 콤마 없이 문장과 문장 사이에 관계사가 존재한다. Harry went to the restaurant where is known as Naengmyeon. [where가 선행사 the restaurant을 수식하며, 관계부사절을 먼저 해석한다.]

2. 관계대명사의 계속적 용법

• I made **a new friend. She** is from India. [a new friend = she]

= I made a new friend, **and she** is from India.

= I made a new friend, **who** is from India.

• Jason wrote **a book. It** became a bestseller. [a book = it]

= Jason wrote a book, **and it** became a bestseller.

= Jason wrote a book, **which** became a bestseller.

3. 관계부사의 계속적 용법

• We went to **the department store. It** was on sale. [the department store = it]

= We went to the department store, **and it** was on sale.

= We went to the department store, **where it** was on sale.

4. 관계사절이 문장 가운데 있을 경우

: 계속적 용법의 관계사절이 문장 중간에 위치할 경우 앞뒤에 '콤마(,)'를 붙여준다.

• Peter got the role of Romeo. He auditioned last month.

= Peter, **who got the role of Romeo**, auditioned last month.

A 다음 문장을 관계대명사나 관계부사의 계속적 용법으로 바꿔 쓰시오.

1 John made a new movie and it was really exciting.

➡ *John made a new movie, which was really exciting.*

2 This is my friend and she majored in English education.

➡ _____

3 Mr. Park was my professor and he recieved an honor last week.

➡ _____

4 We went to the store and there were many beautiful flowers.

➡ _____

5 I have three sons and they are actors.

➡ _____

6 Amy took me to the seminar and we could taste a variety of food.

➡ _____

7 I want to introduce my husband, Jack and he likes to play soccer.

➡ _____

8 My mother got a new job last month. and she was really happy.

➡ _____

9 He read about the person. The person invented the washing machine.

➡ _____

10 I watched the drama and it was really boring.

➡ _____

Practice More II

Answer Keys p. 61~62

A 다음에 주어진 두 문장을 한 문장으로 연결할 때 빈칸에 알맞은 관계사를 넣으시오. (빈칸에 관계사를 넣을 수 없는 것도 있음)

1 This is the house. My family lived there for twenty years.
   ➡ This is the house _____*that*(*which*)_____ my family lived in for twenty years.

2 Tell me the way. She made the cake in that way.
   ➡ Tell me the way _____ she made the cake.

3 This is the movie theater. He and I visited the theater last week.
   ➡ This is the movie theater _____ he and I visited last week.

4 November 22nd is the day. We participated in the soccer competition that day.
   ➡ November 22nd is the day _____ we participated in the soccer competition.

5 Does he know the way? I can go to the shopping center in that way.
   ➡ Does he know the way _____ I can go to the shopping center?

6 John teaches the thing. The thing is useful to me.
   ➡ John teaches _____ is useful to me.

7 We are going to the city. I met him.
   ➡ We are going to the city _____ I met.

8 Tell me the reason. She was crying for that reason.
   ➡ Tell me the reason _____ she was crying.

B 다음 문장에서 밑줄 친 곳을 바르게 고치시오.

1 Eric made the pasta, <u>that</u> was really delicious.
   _____*which*_____

2 This is the shelf <u>in that</u> I found my wallet.
   _____

3 The test result is <u>that</u> we expected.
   _____

4 Do you know <u>the way how</u> to go to the bus stop?
   _____

Practice More II

5 <u>This is</u> important thing is to finish the project on time.

_____

6 I want to go to the city <u>which</u> my mom was born.

_____

7 This is the house <u>how</u> I designed last month.

_____

8 I read the book <u>what</u> was written by James.

_____

C 다음에 주어진 두 문장을 관계부사 또는 관계대명사를 이용하여 각각 한 문장으로 바꿔 쓰시오.

1 Do you know the place? Jade and Amy will get married in that place.

➡ _Do you know (the place) where Jade and Amy will get married?_ (관계부사)

2 This is the cafe. Jane sometimes drinks juice there.

➡ _____ (관계부사)

➡ _____ (전치사+관계대명사)

3 My uncle is working in China for a month. He is a businessman.

➡ _____ (관계사 계속적용법)

4 Can you remember the place? We lived in the place for fifty years.

➡ _____ (관계부사)

➡ _____ (전치사+관계대명사)

5 My mother scolded us in a certain way. We liked the way.

➡ _____ (how)

➡ _____ (the way)

6 I often go to Namsan Tower. I can see squirrels there.

➡ _____ (관계사 계속적용법)

7 Do you know the reason? She didn't come to the party for the reason.

➡ _____ (the reason+관계부사)

8 He watched the TV talk show. I watched the same show at Linda's house.

➡ _____ (관계사 계속적용법)

D 다음 주어진 단어를 알맞게 배열하여 우리말 해석에 맞게 문장을 완성하시오.

1 선생님이 우리에게 원하는 것은 항상 최선을 다하는 것이다.
(what, is, teacher, our, the, do, wants, best, to, us)

➡ _____ *What the teacher wants us is to do our best.* _____

2 나는 그들이 살았던 집에서 낡은 라디오를 발견했다.
(I, lived, the, in, where, found, an old radio, house, they)

➡ _____

3 우리는 당신이 우리와 처음 만났던 날을 기억한다.
(remember, first, you, met, the, day, we, when, us)

➡ _____

4 그 어린 소년은 13살인데, 영어로 유창하게 말할 줄 안다.
(the, old, young, fluently, boy, can, who, is, speak, English, years, thirteen)

➡ _____

5 아이들이 놀고 있는 놀이공원을 보아라. (are, look at, where, the amusement park, playing, the, children)

➡ _____

6 그는 시험이 끝나는 다음 주에 고향으로 돌아간다. (he, the, test, goes, back, next week, home, when, ends)

➡ _____

7 나는 미국에서 새로운 친구를 만났는데, 그는 뮤지컬 배우였다.
(I, actor, musical, a, new, in America, was, friend, a, who, made)

➡ _____

8 Mr. Park은 나의 오랜 영어 선생님이었는데, 그는 영문학을 공부하기 위해 미국으로 갔다. (Mr. Park, to, literature, English, who, study, to, America, old, my, English teacher, went, was)

➡ _____

9 나는 부모님의 50주년 결혼기념일을 기억하지 못했다.
(I, parents', 50th, of, my, the day, wedding anniversary, didn't, remember)

➡ _____

10 나는 그가 하는 말을 이해할 수가 없다.
(I, understand, he, means, don't, what)

➡ _____

내신 최다 출제 유형

01 다음 빈칸에 들어갈 말이 나머지 넷과 <u>다른</u> 것을 고르시오. [출제 예상 95%]

① We want to buy the camera _____ color is pink.

② I'm the only friend _____ she has.

③ She wants the same toy _____ I bought last week.

④ Look at the cat and the woman _____ are playing.

⑤ There is something _____ I can do for them.

02 다음 밑줄 친 부분 중 생략할 수 <u>없는</u> 것을 고르시오. [출제 예상 90%]

① Have you heard green music <u>that</u> plants like?

② The buildings <u>that were</u> destroyed by the typhoon have been rebuilt.

③ They can see the rabbits <u>which</u> are hopping on the grass.

④ I don't understand the reason <u>why</u> he doesn't like me.

⑤ We remember the day <u>when</u> we met them.

03 다음 중 어법상 <u>어색한</u> 것을 고르시오. [출제 예상 90%]

① Do you believe what she told us?

② Tell me the way how you finished the homework.

③ Winter is the season when we go skiing.

④ He'll give me what I like best.

⑤ What I don't know is the last sentence.

04 다음 빈칸에 that을 쓸 수 <u>없는</u> 것을 고르시오. [출제 예상 85%]

① The tree _____ grows in the garden is a persimmon tree.

② Look at the huge statue _____ is a sculpture of Buddha.

③ She is the most talented girl _____ I have ever seen.

④ I met a man _____ shirt is so colorful.

⑤ Jennifer bought a house _____ is located downtown.

05 다음 두 문장이 같은 뜻이 되도록 빈칸에 알맞은 것을 고르시오. [출제 예상 85%]

This is the thing that Eric bought in Hong Kong for my mom.
= This is _____ Eric bought in Hong Kong for my mom.

① which   ② who   ③ what
④ what   ⑤ whose

06 다음 빈칸에 공통으로 들어갈 알맞은 말을 고르시오. [출제 예상 80%]

• Jenny, _____ you ate was chicken soup, not mushroom soup.
• Most of people believe _____ they see.

① who   ② what   ③ which
④ that   ⑤ whom

[01~03] 다음 빈칸에 들어갈 말이 바르게 짝지어진 것을 고르시오.

01

- I need a helper _____ can cook Chinese food.
- The statue _____ stands in front of the fountain is wonderful.

① who − who
② who − which
③ which − who
④ what − what
⑤ what − which

02

- The quiz show _____ plays on Channel 10 is exciting.
- The model _____ stands beside the flower shop is my aunt.

① that − who
② what − which
③ who − that
④ what − which
⑤ what − what

03

- Nancy painted a girl _____ was playing with a ball.
- Teddy has an electronic dictionary _____ is broken.

① who − that
② that − whom
③ whom − who
④ which − that
⑤ whose − that

[04~05] 다음 글에서 어법상 어색한 부분을 고르시오.

04

She ① is ② the woman ③ whom ④ can ⑤ speak Spanish very well.

05

Can you ① tell ② me ③ the reason ④ why ⑤ is she angry?

[06~08] 다음 중 빈칸에 들어갈 알맞은 말을 고르시오.

06

There lived a prince _____ had a beautiful wife.

① whom
② which
③ but
④ who
⑤ whose

07

The building _____ windows are big was built in the 1800s.

① which
② whose
③ who
④ that
⑤ what

08

We arrived at the place _____ Jack and Jill's old house was.

① when
② which
③ what
④ where
⑤ that

[09~10] 다음 중 밑줄 친 부분의 쓰임이 나머지 넷과 다른 하나를 고르시오.

09 ① I don't know who is shorter, Jenny or me.
② She knew the girl who drew this picture.
③ Can you tell us who you are.
④ I just guessed who your brother is.
⑤ Who makes you so happy?

10 ① What you do will be nice.
② This is what I want to have.
③ I don't know what day it is today.
④ This is better than what I bought.
⑤ The music is what makes me depressed.

[11~13] 다음 밑줄 친 부분과 바꿔 쓸 수 있는 것을 고르시오.

11
> A train which runs every hour goes to Chuncheon.

① that ② who ③ what
④ whose ⑤ when

12
> The cook tells us the way to make these chocolate cookies.

① why ② what ③ how
④ which ⑤ when

13
> Owen has some dried leaves that his mother gave him.

① what ② whose ③ which
④ who ⑤ when

[14~15] 다음 주어진 문장의 밑줄 친 부분과 쓰임이 같은 것을 모두 고르시오.

14
> Badminton is what he likes most.

① What did she do last week?
② What you said to me was awesome.
③ That is what I've found.
④ They will tell you what to buy.
⑤ I didn't know what to say.

15
> Harrison is the teacher who taught us English.

① She is the police officer who helped me.
② Tell us who she is playing with.
③ Who borrowed your dictionary?
④ There are children who can focus well in the class.
⑤ Do you know who that man is?

[16~17] 다음 주어진 두 문장을 한 문장으로 바르게 바꾸어 쓴 것을 고르시오.

16

> He baked some bread with blueberries.
> He grew the blueberries.

① He baked some bread with the blueberries he grew.
② He baked some bread with the blueberries and he grew.
③ He baked some bread with the blueberries, and he grew the blueberries.
④ He baked some bread with he grew the blueberries.
⑤ He baked some blueberries bread with he grew.

17

> Jenny drew many pictures of fables.
> They influenced my paintings.

① Jenny drew many pictures of fables they influenced my paintings.
② Jenny drew many pictures of fables which influenced my paintings.
③ Jenny drew many pictures which influenced my paintings of fables.
④ They influenced my paintings that Jenny drew many pictures of fables.
⑤ They influenced my paintings Jenny drew pictures of fables.

[18~19] 다음 밑줄 친 부분 중 생략할 수 <u>없는</u> 것을 고르시오.

18
① I have a cap <u>that</u> Tom gave me.
② I met a girl <u>who has</u> long blond hair.
③ Look at the boy <u>who is</u> playing baseball.
④ This is the car <u>which</u> I bought last month.
⑤ This is the apartment <u>which</u> she lives in.

19
① This is the prize <u>that</u> my brother got.
② This is the novel <u>which</u> my mother wrote.
③ A little girl likes the story <u>that</u> her grandfather told.
④ The man <u>who</u> is walking along the river is my teacher.
⑤ I like the glasses <u>that</u> my dad is wearing.

[20~21] 다음 밑줄 친 관계대명사 중 쓰임이 나머지 넷과 <u>다른</u> 것을 고르시오.

20
① Here are some drinks <u>which</u> you drink.
② This is the picture <u>which</u> my father drew.
③ I have a wooden table <u>that</u> Johnny made.
④ She likes the skirt <u>that</u> I am wearing.
⑤ This is the boy <u>that</u> uses magic.

21 ① I showed that those students are honest.
② Harry knew that the boy was a genius.
③ How did she know that I was crying?
④ She thinks that she must be very tired.
⑤ Everything that I told her was a white lie.

22 다음 글에서 'who were'가 생략된 부분을 고르시오.

All ① the people ② living in the town ③ helped ④ each other ⑤.

[23~24] 다음 중 어법상 어색한 것을 모두 고르시오.

23 ① Madonna is the first one that arrived here.
② My elder sister bought me shoes which color was pink.
③ She is the only person which helped me.
④ What you need is just cold water.
⑤ We saw someone who works at the park.

24 ① I have a pen pal that lives in Canada.
② A bat is the animal which lives in a cave.
③ The old man who was sitting on the bench was my neighbor.
④ A planet is a large round object what moves around the sun.
⑤ This is the restaurant who I heard about.

25 다음 문장의 빈칸에 'who'를 쓸 수 없는 것을 고르시오.

① This is the kid _____ broke the window.
② I gave her something _____ was important.
③ There are many doctors _____ take care of sick people.
④ She is the woman _____ Sam likes.
⑤ It rescues people _____ are in danger.

26 다음의 빈칸에 공통으로 들어갈 알맞은 말을 고르시오.

• Suzie is interested in music _____ makes people happy.
• The woman _____ is wearing short pants and boots is Jessie.

① who   ② that   ③ whose
④ how   ⑤ which

27 다음 주어진 문장의 밑줄 친 that과 쓰임이 같은 것을 고르시오.

I think that Jenny will be my best friend.

① We like the drama that we saw last night.
② Can you return me the book that I gave you before?
③ Don't throw away anything that can be reused.
④ We think that she's so diligent.
⑤ The lid that is on the table is useless.

★★★
28 다음 주어진 두 문장이 어법상 어색한 것을 고르시오.

① Sally is my student. She is from Kenya.
= Sally is my student who is from Kenya.

② Mr. White is a painter. He drew a lot of pictures.
= Mr. White is a painter whom drew a lot of pictures.

③ This is the tablet. I bought it last week.
= This is the tablet which I bought last week.

④ This is the ring. I'm looking for it.
= This is the ring that I'm looking for.

⑤ I have a girl friend. She is a cook.
= I have a girl friend who is a cook.

29 다음 중 어법상 올바른 것을 모두 고르시오.

① There is someone at the corner who wants to see you.

② In this hot weather, what we want is to just stay at home.

③ She is the only person whose can help me.

④ I bought some pictures whom title I couldn't remember.

⑤ Jack is the last student arrived here.

30 다음 빈칸에 들어갈 알맞은 말을 고르시오.

| A What's the reason _____ you can't buy that car? |
| B Because we don't have enough money to buy it. |

① when   ② why   ③ how
④ what   ⑤ which

[31~32] 다음 문장에서 생략할 수 있는 것을 고르시오.

31
| The MP3 player which is on my desk did not work. |

① which   ② is   ③ on
④ did not   ⑤ which is

32
| They are good ski jumpers who all Koreans are proud of. |

① good ski jumpers   ② who
③ who all Koreans   ④ Koreans
⑤ of

[33~34] 다음 빈칸에 들어갈 말이 다른 하나를 고르시오.

33 ① People _____ work with me are very nice.

② There are some adults _____ act like children.

③ The little girl _____ uniform is neat looks nice.

④ This is the boy _____ dances very well.

⑤ The woman _____ informed me was so unkind.

34 ① I have a friend _____ has a twin brother.

② Pass me the pepper _____ is on the left side of the table.

③ Do you have any special stamps _____ you collected so far?

④ This is the ball _____ you and your brother played with.

⑤ This is the office in _____ I worked.

35 다음 밑줄 친 부분이 바르게 쓰인 것을 고르시오.

① Sunday is the day <u>which</u> we aren't excited about the next day.

② This city has many little parks. That's <u>what</u> we live here.

③ We'll visit Paris <u>which</u> is loved by many people.

④ This is the way <u>how</u> my sister makes me happy.

⑤ Tell him the reason <u>how</u> you broke the radio.

◇◇◇◇◇◇◇◇◇ **서술형 평가** ◇◇◇◇◇◇◇◇◇◇

[36~38] 다음 빈칸에 알맞은 말을 쓰시오.

36

He can't remember the month _____ Thomas came back.

➡ _____

37

She couldn't believe _____ he said at that time.

➡ _____

38

Look at the little girls and dog _____ are playing together.

➡ _____

39 다음 주어진 문장에서 생략 가능한 두 단어와 이유를 쓰시오.

Look at the balloons which are stuck in the trees.

➡ 단어 : _____

➡ 이유 : _____

_____

[40~42] 다음 우리말과 같은 뜻이 되도록 괄호 안의 단어를 바르게 배열하여 문장을 완성하시오.

40

> 토요일은 내가 테니스를 치는 날이다.
> (Saturday / when / is / I / the day / tennis / play)

➡ _____

41

> 우리는 다른 사람들의 생각하는 방식을 존중해야 한다.
> (we / think / should / the way / others / respect)

➡ _____

42

> 이 마을에 살고 있는 다른 사람들을 찾아보자.
> (Let's / town / in / this / find / other / people / who / live)

➡ _____

[43~45] 다음 주어진 두 문장을 관계대명사 또는 관계부사를 이용하여 한 문장으로 완성하시오.

43

> We know the boy. Everyone loves him so much.

➡ _____
_____

44

> These are the CDs of English grammar. My brother bought them for me.

➡ _____
_____

45

> This is the biggest bookstore I shop at. I usually buy books here.

➡ _____
_____

Note

13

Chapter
접속사

Point Check I

◆ **접속사**: 단어와 단어, 표현과 표현을 연결하는 말이다.

◆ **접속사의 종류**: 등위접속사, 상관접속사, 종속접속사, 그리고 접속부사가 있다.

◆ 접속사의 종류 및 의미

		주격	의미
등위접속사		and	～와, 그리고, ～하고 나서
		but	하지만, 그러나
		or	또는, 아니면
		so	그래서, 그러므로
		for	왜냐하면, ～하기 때문에
상관접속사		both A and B	A와 B 둘 다 ～이다
		either A or B	A와 B 둘 중 하나는 ～이다
		neither A nor B	A와 B 둘 다 ～아니다
		not only A but (also) B (=B as well as A)	A뿐만 아니라 B도 ～이다
종속 접속사	명사절을 이끄는 접속사	that	주어 (～하는 것은) 목적어 (～하는 것을) 보어 (～하는 것이다)
		whether	～인지 아닌지
		if	～인지 아닌지
	시간의 부사절을 이끄는 접속사	when	～할 때
		while	～하는 동안, ～하면서
		before	～하기 전에
		after	～한 후에
		until	～할 때까지
		as	～할 때, ～하자마자, ～하면서
		since	～이래로, ～이후로
		as soon as	～하자마자
		every time	～할 때마다 (매번)
		each time	
		whenever	

등위접속사

• 등위접속사: 문법적 역할이 서로 대등한 말을 연결하는 역할을 한다.

◈ 등위접속사

의미	소유격
and ~와, 그리고, ~하고 나서	앞뒤의 말이 서로 대등하거나 비슷한 것, 이어지는 행위일 때 사용
but 하지만, 그러나	앞뒤의 말이 서로 반대, 대조될 때 사용
or 또는, 아니면	여러 가지 가능성이나 선택 사항 중 하나를 고를 때 사용
so 그래서, 그러므로	앞뒤의 문장이 원인과 결과일 때 사용
for 왜냐하면, ~하기 때문에	앞뒤의 문장이 결과와 이유일 때 사용

• Sally bought a pink hat **and** a white hat.

• Dexter wanted to buy comic books **but** couldn't buy them.

• Do they want to travel to Greece **or** Italy?

• There was a traffic accident, **so** the police came.

• He was absent yesterday, **for** he was very sick.

Grammar Plus +

• 등위접속사의 앞뒤 내용은 서로 대등하여야 한다.
   This dress is pretty **and** cheap. [단어＋단어]
   Do you like playing soccer **or** watching game? [구＋구]
• 접속사 앞뒤 절의 주어가 같을 때는 접속사 뒤에 나오는 주어를 생략 할 수 있다.
   She was very tired **but** (she) had to finish it.
• 'so' 뒤에는 결과가 나온다.
• 'for' 뒤에는 이유가 나온다.

A 괄호 안에서 알맞은 것을 고르시오.

1 Kate is smart, (so / or) everyone asks her to solve difficult questions.

2 Mina doesn't like playing chess (but / and) she likes playing tennis.

3 Which one do you prefer, spicy food (or / and) sweet food?

4 I was really sleepy (but / so) I had to finish my homework.

5 Do you want to go hiking (or / and) go swimming?

6 Sean was tired, (so / and) he took a nap.

7 Mike wants to go to Linda's concert, (so / for) he likes her songs.

8 Will they arrive on Monday (or / so) on Friday?

9 We went to the theater (but / so) we couldn't see the movie.

10 These pants are too long (and / for) these shirts are too short.

13-2 명령문과 and / or

- **명령문과 and / or** : 'and'와 'or'이 명령문 뒤에 나와서 평서문과 연결해 주는 역할을 한다.
- **명령문, and~** : 'and'는 '그러면'이라는 뜻으로 앞의 명령문을 행했을 때의 결과를 나타내며, 주로 긍정의 의미를 갖는다.
- **명령문, or~** : 'or'는 '그렇지 않으면'이라는 뜻으로 앞의 명령문을 행하지 않았을 때의 결과를 나타내며, 주로 부정의 의미를 갖는다.

1. 명령문, and~ (= If you..., you will~) : ~해라, 그러면 …일 것이다. – 긍정
   - Read many kinds of books, **and** you'll be a wise person.
     = **If you** read many kinds of books, **you will** be a wise person.

2. 명령문, or~ (= If you don't..., you will~)
   : ~하지마라(~해라), 그렇지 않으면 …일 것이다. – 부정
   - Be nice to your friends, **or** they will leave you.
     = **If you are not** nice to your friends, they will leave you.
     (= Unless you are)

Check up!

Answer Keys p. 64

A 두 문장이 같은 뜻이 되도록 빈칸에 and, or 중 알맞은 것을 쓰시오.

1. If you study hard, you will pass the exam.
   ➡ Study hard, ___*and*___ you will pass the exam.

2. If you don't arrive on time, you will miss the train.
   ➡ Arrive on time, _____ you will miss the train.

3. If you exercise regularly, you'll succeed in losing weight.
   ➡ Exercise regularly, _____ you will succeed in losing weight.

4. If he doesn't go there, he can't get some useful information.
   ➡ He should go there, _____ he can't get some useful information.

5. If you clean the room, mom will make you a chocolate shake.
   ➡ Clean the room, _____ mom will make delicious chocolate shake.

Note
- **on time** 제시간에, 정각에
- **succeed in −ing** ~하는 데 성공하다
- **useful** 유용한

13-3 상관접속사

- **상관접속사**: 두 개 이상의 단어가 짝을 이뤄 함께 쓰이는 접속사로서, 강조나 첨가의 의미를 갖는다.

◈ 상관접속사

상관접속사		동사의 사용
both A and B	A와 B 둘 다 ~이다	복수 동사 사용
either A or B	A와 B 중 하나는 ~이다	'B'의 인칭에 동사 일치
neither A nor B	A와 B 둘 다 ~아니다	
not only A but (also) B (=B as well as A)	A뿐만 아니라 B도 ~이다	

- I like **both** Chinese food **and** Japanese food.

- **Either** Jenny **or** Mary will be captain of the team.

- **Neither** I **nor** my sister likes pizza and hamburgers. [➡ 'my sister'에 동사의 수를 맞춤]

- Jinsu can speak **not only** Spanish **but (also)** English.

= Jinsu can speak English **as well as** Spanish.

Grammar Plus +

- 'both A and B'가 주어일 때는 복수 취급을 한다.
  Both Larry **and** Peter are very smart brothers.
- 'not only A but (also) B'와 'B as well as A'는 같은 뜻이지만, 'A와 B'의 위치가 바뀐다.
  이들이 주어로 쓰일 때 동사는 'B'에 해당하는 인칭에 일치시켜 사용한다.
  Not only Lucy **but (also)** you don't like playing tennis. (B: you)
  = You **as well as** Lucy don't like playing tennis. (B: you)

☆Check up!

Answer Keys p. 64

A 다음 빈칸에 알맞은 접속사를 쓰시오.

1 I like to play ___both___ soccer and baseball.

2 Either John _____ Eunhyuk will be late for the meeting.

3 I'll buy _____ the pants nor the coat.

4 Mijin can cook _____ pasta but also a beef stew.

5 My height as _____ as your height is 180 centimeters.

6 John is neither a nurse _____ a dentist.

7 He should not only get up early _____ exercise.

B 다음 문장에서 어법상 <u>어색한</u> 것을 찾아 바르게 고치시오.

1 Both Jane and Jina has gone to America.

_____*has*_____ ➡ _____*have*_____

2 Peter should decide to go to either China nor Japan.

_____ ➡ _____

3 I play either basketball nor soccer after school.

_____ ➡ _____

4 David will meet either Tommy and Paul.

_____ ➡ _____

5 Neither Harry nor Tim don't like to eat spicy food.

_____ ➡ _____

6 Andrew as well as his sons go hiking every weekend.

_____ ➡ _____

7 Both Helen and my wife is having dinner together.

_____ ➡ _____

8 My brother as well as I like coffee and tea.

_____ ➡ _____

9 Not only this cup but also that table are mine.

_____ ➡ _____

10 Either Helen or John buy those flowers.

_____ ➡ _____

13-4 종속접속사 _ that

• 종속접속사: 접속사가 이끄는 문장(종속절)을 접속사가 없는 주된 문장(주절)과 연결하는 것을 말한다.

1. 명사절을 이끄는 that

'that + 주어 + 동사'의 형태로 주어, 목적어, 보어로 쓰인다.

주어	'~라는 것은'의 뜻을 가지며, 주로 가주어 it을 쓰고, 진주어 that절은 뒤로 보낸다.
	• That my sister likes puppies is true. [주어] = It is true that my sister likes puppies. 　　(가주어)　　　　　(진주어)
목적어	'~라는 것을'의 뜻을 가지며, 동사의 목적어로 쓰인다. 이때 'that'은 생략이 가능하다. • 함께 쓰이는 동사: believe, say, know, think 등
	• We believe (that) we can visit another planet someday. [목적어]
보어	보어 역할을 하며, '~라는 것이다'의 뜻을 가진다. • 함께 쓰이는 동사: be동사, seem 등
	• The problem is that Mike didn't finish his work yet. [보어] • It seems that Mary and Anna are alike. [보어] 　= Mary and Anna seem to be alike.

2. 명사와 동격인 절을 이끄는 that

접속사 that은 앞에 나온 명사를 설명하는 동격절을 이끌기도 한다. 이때 that은 생략할 수 없다.

• I didn't know **the news that** he was hurt in a plane crash.

(the news = he was hurt in a plane crash)

☆Check up!

Answer Keys p. 64

A 다음 문장에서 that의 역할을 적으시오.

1 The problem is that I don't have enough time to go.　　(보어)

2 I believe that they can win the competition.　　_____

3 The fact is that she didn't steal anything.　　_____

4 That Max died is a rumor.　　_____

5   John thought that she made a big mistake.   _____

6   It is true that Sam will come back to Korea next week.

_____

7   The reason is that we don't have enough money.   _____

8   Jane knew that you couldn't arrive on time.   _____

9   It was wrong that drinking much water harms your health.

_____

B   다음 문장에서 that이 명사절과 동격절 중 어떤 것을 이끄는지 쓰시오.

1   I know that tomorrow is Jane and Tim's wedding anniversary.

_____ (명사절)

2   The fact is that the costs of college get higher every year.

_____

3   My point was that he doesn't like her.

_____

4   Mom knows that I lied to her last night.

_____

5   I agreed with the idea that teenagers must not.

_____

6   I remember the proverb that you told me.

_____

7   He said that we didn't throw the garbage away there.

_____

13-5 종속접속사 _ whether / if

- **whether/if** : '~인지 아닌지'의 뜻을 가진다.
  문장 앞에 쓰여 의문의 뜻을 가지며, 문장 전체가 명사로 되어 문장 안에서 주어,
  보어, 목적어의 역할을 한다.

◈ whether / if

주어	• Whether they come here (or not) doesn't matter.
목적어	• I asked her whether she can cook Asian food (or not). = I asked her whether (or not) she can cook Asian food. = I asked her if she can cook Asian food. ➡ 'whether or not'을 붙여서 쓸 때는 'if'와 바꿔 쓸 수 없다. ➡ 접속사 'if'는 목적어 역할로만 쓰인다.
보어	• The important thing is whether we can watch the game (or not).

Answer Keys p. 64

A 괄호 안에서 알맞은 것을 고르시오.

1 (Whether / If) I am tired or not doesn't matter.

2 I asked mom (whether / if) or not she will make a chocolate cake.

3 People are wondering (that / if) Sally will answer the question.

4 He is not sure (that / whether) this statement is true or not.

5 I don't know (if / that) she studied hard or not.

6 Her question is (whether / that) John will attend the meeting or not.

7 The important thing is (that / whether) we pass the graduation exam or not.

8 I asked him (if / that) he could prepare decorations for my daughter's birthday party.

9 The question is (that / whether) he wants to help us or not.

10 They are wondering (if / that) it will snow tomorrow.

11 (If / Whether) you can lend us your car is really important.

12 My concern is (that / whether) Mr. Park can teach us or not.

13-6 종속접속사 _ 시간이나 때를 나타내는 접속사

• **시간을 나타내는 접속사**: 시간이나 때를 나타내는 접속사가 문장 앞에 올 경우 문장 전체가 시간이나 때를 표현하는 문장으로 된 부사절이 된다.

◈ 시간을 나타내는 접속사

접속사		예문
when	~할 때	• When I arrived at the theater, the opera started.
while	~하는 동안 ~하면서	• Mary was reading a book while she was listening to music.
before	~하기 전에	• Wash your hands before you eat a meal.
after	~한 후에	• Nancy had to write a report after she came back from the museum
until	~할 때까지	• The copy machine didn't work until it was fixed.
as	~할 때 ~하자마자 ~하면서	• We watched Mr. and Mrs. White cross the street as we drank tea at the cafe.
since	~이래로 ~이후로	• Jamie has played the drums since she was 15 years old.
as soon as	~하자마자	• As soon as we heard the news, we surfed the Internet.
every time	~할 때마다 (매번)	• Miranda draws a picture every time she sees a good subject. = Miranda draws a picture each time she sees a good subject. = Miranda draws a picture whenever she sees a good subject.
each time		
whenever		

Grammar Plus +

• 부사절이 주절의 앞에 놓일 경우 '콤마(,)'를 써서 두 문장을 구분해 준다.
  After he comes back, just call me.
• 시간을 나타내는 접속사가 이끄는 부사절에서는 현재형이 미래형을 대신한다.
  When you finish the work, please let me know.
• 'since'는 주로 과거형의 부사절을 이끌며, 주절에는 현재완료형이 온다.
  I have studied Chinese **since** I was very young.

A 괄호 안에서 알맞은 것을 고르시오.

1 (Since / (After)) he finished his homework, he is taking a nap.

2 Tim has lived in Busan (since / when) he graduated from middle school.

3 (Every time / As for as) you need anything, please call me.

4 (When / Before) you meet Peter, tell him to bring my bag.

5 Linda likes to listen to the radio (while / since) she studies English.

6 We have studied judo (since / while) we were very young.

7 The girl was crying (before / until) her brother returned her doll.

8 Write in your diary every night (before / as) you go to sleep.

9 I stayed at Susan's house (since / until) mom called me.

10 The cat was lying on the sofa (since / when) Jane came home.

11 We have practiced hard (each time / since) we lost a game.

12 Hana has been a teacher (when / since) her daughter was five.

13 When you (will read / read) this letter, I will not be in Korea.

14 (Until / When) I am with old friends, I'm happy.

15 I have worked for this company (since / when) 2015.

16 (As / Until) I realized my mistake, I apologized to her.

17 She is reading a book (when / while) she is waiting for him.

Practice More I

Answer Keys p. 65

A 보기 에서 알맞은 등위접속사를 골라 빈칸에 쓰시오.

보기

and but or so for

1 I want to become a professor _____or_____ an architect.

2 This table is small _____ comfortable.

3 I stayed up all night, _____ I didn't get up early in the morning.

4 He stopped eating junk food _____ started exercising.

5 It took a long time, _____ there many people waiting for the show.

6 It's rainy today, _____ we should cancel our hiking plan.

7 She read the detective novel _____ the romantic novel.

8 We didn't study enough last night _____ passed the exam fortunately.

9 Maybe she is doing homework _____ writing in her diary now.

10 We wanted to eat ice cream, _____ today was hot.

11 Keep notes, _____ you can't achieve your goal.

12 Take notes, _____ you will not forget anything important.

B 다음 문장에서 밑줄 친 부분을 바르게 고치시오.

1 He went to the hospital, so he had a cold.

_____for_____

2 He likes eating snacks and to read books.

_____

3 Either he nor Minji should become a team leader.

_____

4 She asked me that I can donate money to her charity.

_____

5 Not only Mr. Kim but also his son are tall.

_____

Practice More I

6 Both Jane and Kate <u>goes</u> to the gym everyday.

_____

7 I'm not sure <u>if</u> or not she is American.

_____

8 You can leave <u>either</u> on Saturday nor on Sunday.

_____

9 They can't remember what they did or what <u>saying</u>.

_____

10 My point is <u>whether</u> Inho should take care of my dog.

_____

C 빈칸에 that, whether, if 중 알맞은 접속사를 모두 쓰시오.

1 Did you hear the rumor _____*that*_____ she will retire next month?

2 I don't care _____ you love her.

3 _____ he will move to Seoul is wrong.

4 Tony is wondering _____ or not she arrived on time.

5 I can't believe _____ he married Helen.

6 I'll ask them _____ they can teach us how to play soccer.

7 It is true _____ he doesn't like me anymore.

8 The question is _____ we can trust Sam.

9 The problem is _____ we don't know how to get there.

10 She asked me _____ or not Sandra could come to the party.

11 Did you know the reason _____ Max quit his job?

12 They are not sure _____ they can go hiking next week.

13 She's wondering _____ or not she made the same mistake.

Grammar Master Level 2

D 우리말 해석에 맞게 주어진 단어를 알맞게 배열하여 문장을 완성하시오.

1 Helen과 그녀의 아버지는 모두 매일 밤 9시 뉴스를 본다.
(Helen, every night, both, the nine o'clock news, her father, and, watch)

➡ *Both Helen and her father watch the nine o'clock news every night.*

2 수미나 유미 둘 중 하나는 우리 반 반장을 맡아야 한다. (Yumi, Sumi, the class president, should, or, as, serve, either)

➡ _____

3 Tom은 컴퓨터를 하는 것뿐만 아니라 퍼즐을 하는 것도 싫어한다.
(doesn't, like, a puzzle, computer games, not, also, but, playing, only, doing, Tom)

➡ _____

4 나는 그가 지금 떠나는 것인지 아닌지 궁금하다. (I, now, or not, he, wonder, leave, will, whether)

➡ _____

5 나는 지금 파스타도 피자도 먹고 싶지 않다.(I, now, pizza, eat, to, neither, want, pasta, nor)

➡ _____

6 그녀는 독서를 하면서 음악 듣는 것을 좋아한다.
(she, to, books, likes, while, music, she, reads, listen to)

➡ _____

7 내 남동생은 축구를 할 때마다 다리를 다친다.
(my brother, every time, hurts, plays, his leg, soccer, he)

➡ _____

Point Check II

◆ **종속접속사:** 명사절을 이끄는 that, 시간을 나타내는 접속사 외에, '조건, 이유, 목적, 결과, 양보'를 나타내는 부사절을 이끄는 접속사가 있다.

◆ **접속부사:** 부사이면서 접속사처럼 문장과 문장을 연결하는 역할을 한다.

◈ 종속접속사와 접속부사

종속접속사	조건	if	만약 ~라면
		unless	만약 ~가 아니라면
	이유나 원인	because	~때문에, 왜냐하면
		as	
		since	
	목적	so that	~하기 위해서, ~하려고
		in order that	
	결과	so ~ that...	너무 ~해서 ...하다
	양보	though	~에도 불구하고, 비록 ~할지라도
		although	
		even though (= even if)	
접속부사	대조	however	그러나
	결과	therefore	그러므로
	첨가	in addition (= moreover, besides)	게다가
	예시	for example	예를 들면

13-7 if / unless / because

- **if / unless**: 조건의 부사절을 이끄는 종속접속사이다.
- **because (= as, since)**: 이유나 원인의 부사절을 이끄는 종속접속사이다.

1. if / unless

if 만약 ~라면	• If you like this cap, I will buy it for you. • She will be kind if you are polite to her.
unless (= if ~ not) 만약 ~아니라면	• Unless it is rainy tomorrow, we'll take a train trip. = If it isn't rainy tomorrow, we'll take a train trip.

2. because (= as, since)

because + 문장 **(= as, since)** ~때문에, 왜냐하면	• Because it is getting dark, we have to go back home. • You must wear a life vest since you will swim in the river. • We are so tired as we practiced basketball a lot.
because of + 명사(구) ~때문에	• We couldn't take a trip because of a hurricane.

Grammar Plus +

- **That is because + 원인**
  We like Jim. **That is because** he is smart and kind.

- **That is why + 결과**
  Sammy is tall and fast. **That is why** he became a basketball player.

★ Check up!

Answer Keys p. 65

A 빈칸에 unless와 if 중 알맞은 것을 쓰시오.

1 ___*If*___ it snows tomorrow, we will go skiing.

2 _____ you turn it off, you can't concentrate on your homework.

3 _____ you need a car, I will lend mine to you.

4 _____ she wears her raincoat, she will have a cold.

5 Let's go out tomorrow _____ you are busy.

6 _____ Jane asks for his help, he will help her.

7 We can ride a bike _____ it rains tomorrow.

13-8 so that / so ~ that...

- **so that (= in order that)**: '~하기 위해서'의 뜻을 가지며, 문장 전체가 목적을 나타내는 부사가 된다.
- **so ~ that...**: '너무 ~해서 ...하다'의 뜻을 가지며, 문장 전체가 결과를 나타내는 부사가 된다.

◈ so that / so ~ that...

so that (= in order that) ~하기 위해서	• I take an English class so that I can speak English well. • I practiced singing a lot in order that I can sing at the concert.
so ~ that ... 너무 ~해서 ...하다	• The sun is so strong that we have to wear sunscreen to protect our skin. • It was so cold that she didn't go outside to play.

Grammar Plus +

- 'so that'과 'in order that'은 목적을 나타내기 때문에 가능을 뜻하는 조동사 can(could)이 온다.
- in order that+절(문장) / in order to+동사원형
- so ~ that...에서 so와 that 사이에는 형용사 또는 부사가 온다.
- 등위접속사 so(그래서) 뒤에는 결과를 나타내는 내용이 온다.

☆Check up!

Answer Keys p. 65

A 다음 두 문장을 so that을 이용하여 한 문장으로 바꿔 쓰시오.

1 I am saving money. I want to study abroad next year.
   ➡ *I am saving money so that I can study abroad next year.*

2 They practiced hard. They wanted to get the gold medal.
   ➡ _____

3 Please turn off the light. My baby should sleep now.
   ➡ _____

4 I registered for the baking class. I wanted to learn how to bake bread.
   ➡ _____

5 He took photos of her. He wanted to keep memories of her.

➡ _____

6 Mina quit her job. She wanted to start her own company.

➡ _____

7 He called me. He wanted to make an appointment.

➡ _____

B 다음 우리말 해석에 맞게 빈칸을 채우시오.

1 그 코트는 너무 길어서 내가 입을 수 없었다.

➡ The coat was ___*so long that*___ I ___*couldn't*___ wear it.

2 그 케이크는 너무 달아서 아빠는 드시지 않는다.

➡ The cake is _____ father _____ eat it.

3 Helen은 너무 긴장해서 한 마디도 하지 않았다.

➡ Helen was _____ she _____ say anything.

4 그녀는 너무 똑똑해서 모든 어려운 수학 문제를 풀 수 있다.

➡ She is _____ she _____ solve all difficult
   math problems.

5 나는 너무 바빠서 Jake의 생일을 기억하지 못했다.

➡ I was _____ I _____ remember Jake's
   birthday.

6 우리는 너무 피곤해서 일찍 일어나지 못했다.

➡ We were _____ we _____ get up early.

7 벽이 너무 단단해서 우리는 부술 수 없었다.

➡ The wall was _____ we _____ break it.

13-9 though / although / even though

· though/although/even though : '~에도 불구하고' 또는 '비록 ~일지라도'의 뜻을 가졌으며, 문장에서 양보의 역할을 한다.

◈ though/although/even though : 비록 ~일지라도, ~에도 불구하고

though	· Though it was raining, we enjoyed swimming in the sea.
although	· Although the mood of the restaurant was good, the food was not delicious.
even though (= even if)	· Even though (if) he didn't pass the exam, he will be able to take next year's classes.

 Check up!

Answer Keys p. 65

A 문맥에 맞게 보기 에서 알맞은 문장을 찾아 빈칸을 채우시오.

> 보기
> · Although he is Korean   · Even though she seemed sad
> · though I got first place in the English speaking contest
> · Although he didn't get the best actor award
> · although his goal was to lose weight
> · although there was only a small chance of being a member of the national soccer team
> · Though she is five   · although he doesn't come back home
> · though I want to go to bed   · Even though she was sick

1   _Although he is Korean_ , he doesn't know Korean history well.

2   Mom didn't praise me _____

3   _____, she attended the meeting.

4   _____, John is truly a good actor.

5   I have to study for the math exam _____

6   _____, she didn't cry.

7   He didn't start exercising _____

8   I practiced hard _____

9   They won't care _____

10   _____, she can stay alone at home.

13-10 접속부사

• 접속부사: 원래는 부사이지만 접속사처럼 문장과 문장을 연결할 수 있는 말을 접속부사라고 한다. 접속부사는 앞뒤에 '콤마(,)'를 찍어서 문장의 다른 단어와 구분되도록 한다.

◆ 접속부사

대조	however 그러나 (= but)	Tommy is the smartest boy in his town. However, he is very rude.
결과	therefore 그러므로	I read 'Little Women.' I have to hand in a book report on it by tomorrow. Therefore, I have to start it right now.
	finally 결국	Neil was interested in music a lot. Finally, he became a musician.
첨가	in addition 게다가 (= besides, moreover)	The actress is pretty and famous. In addition, she is very kind.
예시	for example 예를 들면	There are several special holidays in the world. For example, Christmas, Thanks Giving Day and New Year's Day.

☆Check up!

Answer Keys p. 66

A 우리말 해석에 맞게 빈칸에 알맞은 접속부사를 쓰시오.

1 나는 너와 함께 가고 싶다. 그러나 나는 이곳에서 해야 할 일이 있어.
➡ I want to go with you. _____However_____, I have work to do here.

2 이번 주에 태풍이 올 예정이다. 그러므로 우리는 계획을 변경해야 한다.
➡ A Typhoon will come this week. _____, we should change our plans.

3 그녀는 그 배우가 연기를 잘해서 좋아한다. 게다가 그는 친절하고 정중하다.
➡ She likes the actor because he acts well. _____, he is kind and gentle.

4 우리나라에는 많은 문화유산이 있다. 예를 들면, 경복궁과 다보탑 등이 있다.
➡ There are many cultural heritage sites in our country. _____, Gyeongbok palace and Dabotop.

5 Tim은 춤을 잘 춘다. 그러나 그는 노래는 잘하지 못한다.
➡ Tim dances well. _____, he doesn't sing well.

6 그녀는 2시간 동안 그를 기다렸다. 마침내, 그가 방으로 들어왔다.
➡ She waited for him for two hours. _____, he entered the room.

Practice More II

A 다음 밑줄 친 부분을 어법에 맞게 고치시오.

1 I couldn't concentrate on studying <u>if</u> the TV volume was too loud.
   <u>since (because / as)</u>

2 Please ask her <u>though</u> she can't understand this lecture.
   _____

3 Don't call me <u>since</u> you apologize to me.
   _____

4 He was so <u>that surprised</u> he couldn't remember anything.
   _____

5 She took an English class <u>that</u> she could speak English well.
   _____

6 He couldn't complete the report <u>if</u> the laptop was broken.
   _____

7 Her headache is so bad <u>it</u> she can't sleep well.
   _____

8 Linda was happy <u>though</u> her daughter got first place.
   _____

9 <u>If</u> it rains tomorrow, I won't change my travel plans.
   _____

10 I like him <u>because</u> his personality.
    _____

B 알맞은 접속사를 보기 에서 골라 빈칸에 쓰시오.

> 보기
> | while | since | after | so ~ that | whenever |
> | until | although | before | as soon as | so that |

1 He usually drinks coffee ___whenever___ he is tired.

2 _____ having dinner, we went to the park for a walk.

3 Sam studied _____ the sun rose.

4 I was _____ nervous _____ I couldn't speak well in the meeting.

5 She couldn't get a job _____ she did her best.

6 They have lived here _____ they were middle school students.

7 He went to Japan _____ he could learn how to make sushi.

8 _____ he was sleeping, the thief came into his house.

9 She came in _____ I called her.

10 We took a picture _____ we left for the station.

C 주어진 표현을 이용하여 다음 두 문장을 한 문장으로 연결하시오.

1 I must sleep now. I go to the mountain in the morning. (so that)
➡ _I must sleep now so that I can go to the mountain in the morning._

2 I was scared. I couldn't enjoy the horror movie. (so ~ that)
➡ _____

3 The service was very bad. The food was delicious. (although)
➡ _____

4 The zoo is small. We can see it in a day. (so ~ that)
➡ _____

5 The traffic was very heavy. We could arrive on time. (though)
➡ _____

6 We should save money. We will go to America next year. (in order to)
➡ _____

7 Today was hot. I had to reapply sunscreen all day. (so ~ that)
➡ _____

8 I worked hard. I got a promotion faster than any other employee. (so ~ that)
➡ _____

9 He turned down the light. His baby slept well. (so that)
➡ _____

10 The pizza was large. All of our family could eat it. (so ~ that)
➡ _____

13. 접속사 **453**

Practice More II

Answer Keys p. 66

D 주어진 문장 다음에 이어질 문장을 보기 에서 골라 기호를 쓰시오.

보기

A However, some people hate it now.

B Therefore, she came back home early.

C Therefore, I changed the location.

D For example, I love watching "The Silence of the Lambs."

E However, she couldn't take a rest.

F Moreover, she is good at math.

G For example, there are roses and lilies.

H Therefore, you should write the date.

I However, I'm still waiting for him.

J Therefore, I didn't want to eat anything.

1   He didn't want to go to the zoo.   (C)

2   In the past, people ate raw meat.   _____

3   Linda has a lot of housework to do.   _____

4   There are many flowers in her garden.   _____

5   This appointment is very important.   _____

6   I enjoy watching horror movies.   _____

7   He told us he would never come back.   _____

8   I was sad all day long.   _____

9   Helen was sick.   _____

10 My mother is an English teacher.   _____

내신 최다 출제 유형

01 다음 밑줄 친 부분 중 어법상 틀린 것을 고르시오.

[출제 예상 85%]

① Which do you like better, listening to Psy or listen to Big Bang?
② She thinks that I am handsome.
③ Every time I listen to Wonder Girls' music, I feel very happy.
④ My favorite hobby is reading books.
⑤ Loud music may not be good for studying.

02 다음 밑줄 친 부분의 쓰임이 나머지 넷과 다른 것을 고르시오.

[출제 예상 90%]

① It is certain that I will keep my promise.
② It is true that Jessica is the prettiest girl in class.
③ Her wish is that she will be able to write a letter in English.
④ This is the only present that I got from my friends.
⑤ I think that keeping pets teaches me many things.

03 다음 중 어법상 어색한 것을 고르시오. [출제 예상 90%]

① I saw flowers bloom.
② She listened to him play the guitar.
③ Before Jane slept, she read a book.
④ She had to finish the work by 8 o'clock.
⑤ After I get up I made the bed.

04 다음 우리말을 바르게 영작한 것을 고르시오.

[출제 예상 85%]

> 강당이 너무 더워서 Tim은 재킷을 벗었다.

① It was hot, so Tim took off his jacket.
② It was very hot in the hall, so Tim took off his jacket.
③ It was too hot in the hall that Tim took off his jacket.
④ It is very hot in the hall, so Tim takes off his jacket.
⑤ It is very hot in the hall, so Tim took off his jacket.

05 다음 글의 밑줄 친 부분과 바꾸어 쓸 수 있는 것을 고르시오. [출제 예상 80%]

> If you do not build a strong fence, some wild animals will destroy it.

① Unless   ② Whether   ③ As
④ Or   ⑤ But

06 다음 중 어법상 올바른 것을 모두 고르시오.

[출제 예상 90%]

① His mom will get angry with him and he fails the exam.
② We'll leave for Seoul which Jack arrives.
③ When he saw me, I was swimming in the river with my friends.
④ I'll tell you the truth if we will meet again.
⑤ If I remember correctly, you are an engineer.

[01~05] 다음 빈칸에 들어갈 알맞은 말을 고르시오.

01

_____ you stay here, you'll feel better.

① So   ② That   ③ Then
④ If   ⑤ Besides

02

She was disappointed _____ she didn't get any Valentine's Day cards.

① because   ② because of ③ so
④ but   ⑤ if

03

_____ they were riding a roller coaster, we took some pictures.

① And   ② So   ③ But
④ Finally   ⑤ While

04

She thinks _____ many Americans act in free.

① who   ② that   ③ which
④ if   ⑤ when

05

_____ you open your mind, you will not make any friends.

① If   ② So   ③ Unless
④ Because   ⑤ But

06 다음 중 밑줄 친 that의 쓰임이 나머지 넷과 다른 하나를 고르시오.

① I feel that I am very lucky.
② She was so glad at that time.
③ One bad point is that the class is so noisy.
④ She knows that fast food is not good.
⑤ Are you sure that she wants to go with us?

07 다음 글의 빈칸에 들어갈 말로 알맞은 것을 고르시오.

Jane, Minsu and I were talking about the new rule in our class. Jane and I said it was very easy to follow it. _____, Minsu didn't agree with us. He said one more rule might make us too regimented.

① And   ② Or
③ However   ④ For example
⑤ Anyway

08 다음 밑줄 친 when의 쓰임이 나머지 넷과 다른 하나를 고르시오.

① When is your birthday?
② When I was young, I couldn't ride a bike.
③ Where did you stay when you visited Tokyo?
④ Bring your picnic blanket when you go camping.
⑤ When he saw me, I just smiled at him.

09 다음 문장에서 that이 들어갈 알맞은 곳을 고르시오.

An interesting ① fact ② about eating ③ is ④ some people use the right hand ⑤ when they eat.

10 다음 문장의 밑줄 친 부분과 같은 의미로 쓰인 것을 고르시오.

<u>As</u> he was passing by my house, he saw my sister.

① <u>As</u> she missed the bus, she couldn't be there on time.
② <u>As</u> I was playing soccer, someone called.
③ Jenny got smarter <u>as</u> she grew older.
④ Tony is as handsome <u>as</u> Phillip.
⑤ They were used <u>as</u> money at that time.

[11~13] 다음 빈칸에 공통으로 들어갈 알맞은 말을 고르시오.

11

• We met both Jane _____ Mary.
• Both my mom _____ dad are doctors.

① either   ② that   ③ and
④ but   ⑤ also

12

• She'll tell me the truth _____ I see her.
• _____ you swim in a river, you should wear a life vest.

① where   ② when   ③ what
④ why   ⑤ who

13

• I enjoy playing computer games. _____, my parents don't like me to play them.
• Some people think pandas are cute. _____, other people don't like them.

① Therefore   ② And   ③ So
④ At first   ⑤ However

[14~16] 다음 문장의 빈칸에 들어갈 말로 바르게 짝지어진 것을 고르시오.

14

• _____ you cross the street, you should be careful.
• I spend a lot of time playing _____ my pet dog.

① When – to   ② When – with
③ That – to   ④ That – for
⑤ Where – in

15

- This restaurant is popular _____ the food is delicious and cheap.
- _____ you want to fail the test, you must study harder.

① so – So
② because of – Although
③ so – Because
④ that – That
⑤ because – Unless

16

Everyone likes her _____ she always smiles at her friends.
= Everyone likes her _____ her smile.

① because – because
② because of – because
③ because – because of
④ that – because
⑤ because of – because

17 다음 밑줄 친 부분과 바꿔 쓸 수 있는 것을 고르시오.

Martin didn't give up and kept practicing for three hours. <u>In the end</u>, he won first place in the music contest.

① At most   ② At least   ③ However
④ Finally   ⑤ Sometimes

18 다음 주어진 문장의 밑줄 친 부분과 쓰임이 같은 것을 고르시오.

I go to music cafe <u>when</u> I feel sad.

① <u>When</u> Judy came back home, she had to clean the house.
② <u>When</u> does the show begin?
③ <u>When</u> is your wedding anniversary?
④ <u>When</u> will they meet each other?
⑤ <u>When</u> is the biggest holiday in Korea?

19 다음 두 문장을 한 문장으로 만들 때 빈칸에 들어갈 단어가 바르게 짝지어진 것을 고르시오.

Taesu can't speak Japanese. Sumi can't speak Japanese, either.
= _____ Taesu _____ Sumi can speak Japanese.

① Either – or   ② Both – and
③ Either – nor   ④ Neither – nor
⑤ Neither – or

★★★
20 다음 두 문장을 한 문장으로 바르게 바꾼 것을 고르시오.

We're hungry. We can eat pizza within ten minutes.

① We're so hungry that we can't eat pizza within ten minutes.
② We're hungry when we can eat pizza within ten minutes.
③ We're too hungry that we can eat pizza within ten minutes.
④ We're hungry which we can eat pizza within ten minutes.
⑤ We're so hungry that we can eat pizza within ten minutes.

[21~23] 다음에 이어질 표현으로 올바른 것을 고르시오.

21
> Science is so difficult _____.

① I can't understand it
② that I can't understand it
③ that I could understand it
④ that I couldn't understand it
⑤ that I understand it

22
> Exercise regularly, _____.

① and you'll lose weight
② or you'll lose weight
③ and you'll be weak
④ or you'll be weak
⑤ and you'll be ugly

23
> Take this medicine, _____.

① and you'll be sick
② and you won't get better
③ or you won't have a cold.
④ or you'll be better
⑤ or you won't get better.

24 다음 빈칸에 들어갈 알맞은 말을 고르시오.
> Miranda has a lot of caps, _____ _____. She herself designs and makes them.

① and she doesn't spend much money on caps
② but she didn't spend much money on caps
③ but she doesn't spend much money on caps
④ but she don't spend much money on caps
⑤ and she spends much money on caps

25 다음 주어진 문장의 밑줄 친 as와 같은 의미로 쓰인 것을 고르시오.
> We talked about Leonardo da Vinci as we walked home together.

① As he isn't honest, everyone doesn't like him.
② My brother knocked as he came into my room.
③ On Halloween, American children dress up as ghosts.
④ I started working as a manager in the restaurant.
⑤ As she got up late, she didn't have breakfast.

[26~28] 다음 밑줄 친 부분에 들어갈 알맞은 것을 고르시오.

26

He asked me _____ I can cook well.

① if not　　　　② whether not
③ whether　　　④ unless
⑤ which

27

Jin is listening to music _____ she is drinking coffee.

① while　　② what　　③ if
④ but　　　⑤ before

28

I enjoy taking pictures _____ I am free.

① all time　　② as soon as　③ each
④ every　　　⑤ every time

[29~30] 다음 우리말에 맞게 영어로 바르게 옮긴 것을 고르시오.

★★★
29

비가 오기 시작했기 때문에 우리는 뛰어야 했다.

① Because we had to run, it started raining.
② Because it started raining, we had to run.
③ It started raining, because we had to run.
④ We had to run it started raining because.
⑤ Because it started raining, we ran.

★★★
30

그녀는 예쁘다. 그러나 똑똑하지는 않다.

① She is pretty and she is not smart.
② She is pretty. Therefore, she is not smart.
③ She is pretty. In addition, she is not smart.
④ She is pretty. However, she is not smart.
⑤ She is pretty. Finally, she is not smart.

[31~35] 다음 빈칸에 들어갈 알맞은 말을 고르시오.

31

_____ most teenagers like fast food, I like Korean food more.

① Unless　　② if　　　③ Although
④ Whether　⑤ Because

32

Peter wants to make a movie himself, _____ he'll join the movie club.

① so　　　② but　　③ whether
④ that　　⑤ however

33

We used to live in a small town _____ we were young.

① and　　② what　　③ when
④ while　⑤ which

34

Saving energy, we should not use electricity when we don't need it. _____, turn off the light when you go out.

① Even though　② For example
③ Unless　④ Moreover
⑤ At last

35

It grew dark, _____ we went home in a hurry.

① and　② but　③ if
④ although　⑤ so

[36~38] 다음 밑줄 친 부분과 바꿔 쓸 수 있는 것을 고르시오.

36

Jeremy is kind. <u>However</u>, he is not smart.

① Therefore　② Though
③ Even though　④ And
⑤ But

37

Maria is good at singing. <u>In addition</u>, she dances very well, too.

① Since　② Even though
③ Beacause　④ Moreover
⑤ For example

38

<u>If</u> you <u>don't</u> want to go there, I won't go there, either.

① Whether　② Whether or not
③ Unless　④ Unless ~ don't
⑤ Why

★★★
39 다음 중 어법상 어색한 것을 모두 고르시오.

① If you read many books, you'll be wiser.
② Unless there is water, all plants will die.
③ Although he couldn't drive, he wanted to buy a car.
④ People left the restaurant because the fire.
⑤ We'll show this video when they will come back.

★★★
40 다음 밑줄 친 부분이 어법상 올바른 것을 모두 고르시오.

① My sister is not studying but <u>reading</u> comic books.
② When it rains, my mom either stays at home or <u>watches</u> a video.
③ Jane is not only a good singer but also <u>dances well</u>.
④ Both loving and <u>be loved</u> make people happy.
⑤ She fell in love with Harrison as well as <u>I</u>.

◇◇◇◇◇◇◇◇◇ 서술형 평가 ◇◇◇◇◇◇◇◇◇

[41~45] 다음 보기 에서 알맞은 단어를 찾아 쓰시오.

보기
| in addition | for example | but |
| so that | though |

41

Jacky studied very hard _____ he could pass the final exam.

➡ _____

42

Mary is so nice and kind. _____, she is so pretty.

➡ _____

43

We want to buy something for Jane, _____ we don't know what she likes.

➡ _____

44

_____ it's very cold, we enjoyed playing in the snow.

➡ _____

45

Jenny is a lovely girl. She has many good qualities. _____, she likes to help other people and she is polite.

➡ _____

[46~49] 다음 두 문장을 하나로 만들 때 빈칸에 알맞은 말을 써 넣으시오.

46

My parents read the newspaper. And then they started having breakfast.
= _____ my parents read the newspaper, they started having breakfast.

➡ _____

47

At the age of eight, I learned Chinese letters.
= _____ I was eight, I learned Chinese letters.

➡ _____

48

If you study hard, you'll get a good grade.
= Study hard, _____ you'll get a good grade.

➡ _____

49

나의 가족은 런던과 뉴욕 두 곳 모두에서 살았었다.
= My family has lived in _____ London _____ New York.

➡ _____

14

Chapter
전치사

Point Check I

◆ 전치사: 명사나 대명사 앞에 위치하여 시간, 장소, 위치, 방향, 수단 등을 나타낸다.

1. 시간, 때를 나타내는 전치사

전치사	예시			
at	at 3 o'clock	at night	at that time	at the end of this year
on	on Saturday	on my birthday	on this weekend	on Monday night
in	in 2012	in (the) spring	in the morning	in the future

during	~동안	특정 기간	before	~전에	구체적인 시간이나 특정 시점이와 시간의 전후 관계를 표현
for		시간의 길이를 나타내는 숫자로 표현	after	~후에	
by	~까지	특정 시간까지 어떤 일이 완료됨을 표현	from	~부터	시작된 시점을 표현
until		특정 시간까지 어떤 상태가 계속됨을 표현	since	~이후	과거의 일이 지금까지 계속 되는 것을 표현, 완료형과 쓰임

2. 장소를 나타내는 전치사

전치사	예시			
at	at the cafe	at a party	at school	at the station
on	on the road	on the wall	on an airplane	on the first floor
in	in a train	in space	in the bucket	in America

3. 위치를 나타내는 전치사

under	~아래에	under the chair	next to		next to the school
over	~위로	over the wall	beside	~옆에	beside the store
below	~아래에	below the bridge	by		by the vase
above	~위에	above the rainbow	near	~가까이에	near the house
in front of	~앞에	in front of the tree	between	~사이에 (둘)	between jam and cream
behind	~뒤에	behind the door	among	~사이에 (셋 이상)	among three dogs

14-1 전치사의 역할

• **전치사**: 명사나 대명사 앞에 위치하여 시간, 장소, 위치, 방향, 수단 등을 나타낸다.

1. 전치사의 역할: '전치사＋명사'의 형태로 형용사, 부사, 명사 역할을 한다.

형용사 역할	바로 앞의 명사를 수식하거나 서술	• The building on the left side is old. [한정적] • This English book is of great use to me. [서술적]
부사 역할	바로 앞의 동사를 수식	• We run along the river.
명사 역할	의미상으로 형용사, 동사의 목적어 역할	• I'm sorry for being late. [형용사의 목적어] • We couldn't rely on his word. [동사의 목적어]

2. 전치사의 목적어: 전치사의 목적어로는 '명사(절)'만 올 수 있으며, 전치사 뒤에 위치한다. 명사처럼 쓰이는 to부정사는 전치사의 목적어로 올 수 없다.

• We're playing volleyball **at** the beach. [명사]

• Peter cooks French food **for** her. [대명사]
  ➡ 전치사 뒤에 대명사가 올 때는 목적격 대명사가 온다.

• Jenny and Peggy are fond **of** making snowmen in winter. [동명사]

• They were surprised **at** what their baby said first. [명사절]

Answer Keys p. 68

A 전치사에 동그라미를 하고 다음에 오는 명사(구)에 밑줄을 치시오.

1 The French restaurant is next ⓣⓞ the hotel.

2 There is a book on the table.

3 We're sorry about the accident.

4 We walked along the street.

5 She was surprised at the news.

6 John wanted to study about the star.

7 I'm so tired of preparing for the party all day long.

8 Many people are sitting on the grass.

9 He has practiced playing the piano since last month.

10 My father bought the ring for my mother.

14-2 시간, 때를 나타내는 전치사 (1)

• 시간을 나타내는 전치사는 시간이나 때를 뜻하는 명사와 함께 쓰여 몇 시, 무슨 요일, 어떤 계절인지 등의 정확한 때를 표현해 준다.

◈ 시간, 때를 나타내는 전치사

전치사	쓰임	예시	
at	구체적인 시간	• at 3 o'clock	• at 5 : 45 p.m.
	특정한 시점	• at noon • at midnight • at that time • at the beginning of May	• at lunchtime • at night • at the end of this year
on	날짜 / 요일	• on July 14th	• on Saturday
	특정한 날	• on my birthday	• on Easter
	특정한 날의 아침, 점심, 저녁	• on Monday night • on Christmas afternoon	
in	아침, 점심, 저녁	• in the morning • in the evening	• in the afternoon
	월	• in February	• in October
	계절	• in (the) summer • in (the) spring	• in (the) winter • in (the) fall
	연도 / 세기	• in 2012	• in the 21st century
	과거, 현재, 미래	• in the past	• in the future

☆Check up!

Answer Keys p. 68

A 다음 각 문장의 빈칸에 at, on, in 중 알맞은 전치사를 쓰시오.

1 They will go to the concert _____*on*_____ Sunday.

2 Mr. Kim had a party _____ the end of this week.

3 My younger sister went to America _____ July 14th.

4 We will take the English exam _____ June.

5 _____ that time, I was very sick.

6 My family goes to church _____ Sundays.

7 I will go to China _____ Sunday.

8 It was raining _____ the last day of the year.

9 I usually get up early _____ the morning.

10 They will get married _____ August.

14-3 시간, 때를 나타내는 전치사 (2)

• 시간을 나타내는 전치사는 시간이나 때를 뜻하는 명사와 함께 쓰여 정확한 때를 표현해 준다.

◆ 시간, 때를 나타내는 전치사

전치사		쓰임	예시
before	~ 전에	구체적인 시간이나 특정 시점이 와서 시간의 전후 관계를 나타낸다.	• before noon • before 11 o'clock
after	~ 후에		• after dinner • after 2 o'clock
during	~ 동안	특정 기간이 온다.	• during summer vacation • during the holidays
for		시간의 길이를 나타내는 숫자 표현이 온다.	• for two hours • for five months
by	~ 까지	특정 시간에 어떤 일이 완료됨을 나타낸다.	• I have to finish it by 8:00.
until		특정 시간까지 어떤 상태가 계속됨을 나타낸다.	• We drew pictures until the bell rang.
from	~ 부터	시작된 시점을 나타낸다.	• I worked from last week to this week.
since	~ 이후	과거에 시작된 일이 지금까지 계속되는 것을 나타내며, 완료형과 함께 쓰인다.	• Mr. Jang has lived here since 2010.

Check up!

Answer Keys p. 68

A 다음 괄호 안에서 알맞은 것을 고르시오.

1   I took art lessons (since / (for)) two months.

2   We have dinner (after / during) seven o'clock.

3   She should pay attention (during / for) science class.

4   John and Jake stayed here (from / during) the morning.

5   They have been working in this company (since / from) 1995.

6   I raised a dog (until / from) last week.

7   Billy waited for her (until / by) five o'clock.

8   I wanted to take a nap (after / by) having lunch.

9   Joe will go to China (during / for) winter vacation.

10   I have lived in the house (since / during) 2010.

> **Note**
>
> • **from A to B**
> A에서 B까지
> (시간, 장소 모두 쓰임)

14-4 장소를 나타내는 전치사

• 장소를 나타내는 전치사: 명사나 대명사 앞에서 사람이나 물건이 있는 장소를 정확하게 말해준다.

◈ 장소를 나타내는 전치사

전치사	쓰임	예시	
at	지점을 나타낼 때	• at home • at the door	• at the bus stop
	건물의 용도를 나타낼 때	• at school	• at work
	행사나 모임을 말할 때	• at a party	• at a meeting
on	표면에 맞닿은 것을 말할 때	• on the wall • on the third floor	• on the playground
	길을 말할 때	• on the road	• on Main street
	교통수단을 말할 때	• on a bus • on a train	• on a bike
	통신수단을 말할 때	• on TV	• on the Internet
in	마을, 도시, 국가와 같은 넓은 장소일 때	• in a town • in Beijing	• in Korea • in the world
	건물, 운송수단, 용기 등의 내부를 말할 때	• in a car • in a bowl	• in the closet
	우주, 하늘을 말할 때	• in space	• in the sky

☆Check up!

Answer Keys p. 68

A 다음 각 문장의 빈칸에 at, on, in 중 알맞은 전치사를 쓰시오.

1 We played basketball _____*in*_____ the gym.

2 My dog is lying _____ the sofa.

3 We first met _____ the Christmas party.

4 There are lots of people _____ the park.

5 They ordered five dishes _____ the restaurant.

6 There are so many interesting things to do _____ Korea.

7 Put this bike _____ the front yard.

8 _____ school, students can improve communication skills.

9 They should discuss the issue _____ today's meeting.

10 There are three hundred cherry blossom trees _____ the town.

14-5 위치를 나타내는 전치사

• 위치를 나타내는 전치사: 명사나 대명사 앞에서 사람이나 물건이 있는 위치를 정확하게 말해준다.

◆ 위치를 나타내는 전치사

전치사		예시
under	~아래에	• under the table • under the tree → A key is under the sofa.
over	~위로	• over the rainbow • over the wall → A lot of birds are flying over the clouds.
below	~아래에	• below the bridge • below the surface → A little stream flows below the bridge.
above	~위에	• above the horizon → We saw the sun rising above the horizon.
in front of	~앞에	• in front of the shopping mall → There is a post office in front of the bank.
behind	~뒤에	• behind the computer → A little boy hides behind the tree.
next to	~옆에	• next to the door
beside		• beside the church → My kitten is playing next to me.
by		• by the school
near	~가까이에	• near the flower shop → There was a lake near the town.
between	~사이에 (둘)	• between two doors • between ham and cheese → There is a church between the school and the bookstore.
among	~사이에 (셋 이상)	• among ten flowers → There is a green rose among some white lilies.

 **Check up!**

Answer Keys p. 68

A 다음 약도를 보고 빈칸에 알맞은 전치사를 쓰시오.

| barber shop | Seoul middle school | bookstore |
| flower shop | | library |

| Moon street |

| restaurant | perfume store | gym |

1 The barber shop is _____*behind*_____ the flower shop.

2 The perfume store is _____ Seoul middle school.

3 The bookstore is _____ Seoul middle school.

4 The library is _____ the bookstore.

5 The gym is _____ the perfume store.

6 The Seoul middle school is _____ the barber shop _____ the bookstore.

7 The restaurant is _____ the flower shop.

8 There is nothing _____ the flower shop _____ the library.

9 The bookstore is _____ the library.

10 The flower shop is _____ the barber shop.

> **Note**
> • **across from**
>   ～맞은편에, 건너편에
> • **in front of**
>   ～앞에
> • **between A and B**
>   A와 B사이에

Practice More I

Answer Keys p. 68~69

A 괄호 안에서 알맞은 전치사를 고르시오.

1 There is a big tree ((among) / between) the buildings.

2 The cat is sleeping (next to / over) Tina.

3 The book you were looking for is (under / among) the table.

4 It rained (for / until) a while.

5 The birds are flying (over / in) the bridge.

6 There is a nice car (behind / in) her.

7 I met Yujin (at / to) the party yesterday.

8 There is a store (between / among) the museum and the school.

9 You can find me easily (among / under) the people.

10 There were many beautiful pictures (in / on) the gallery.

B 다음 빈칸에 알맞은 전치사를 보기 에서 골라 쓰시오.

보기
| before | by | during | for |
| from | at | after |

1 He will have lunch ____at____ noon.

2 I have to turn in the paper _____ six.

3 _____ starting the meeting, let me introduce our leader, Tim.

4 Tim waited for her _____ yesterday to today.

5 Can you play tennis _____ school?

6 I can stay here _____ three days.

7 Andy has worked at this company _____ five months.

8 Father said I should come back home _____ next morning.

9 _____ now on, you should start exercising regularly.

10 I planned to learn how to swim _____ summer vacation.

Practice More Ⅰ

C 다음 보기 에서 문장의 빈칸에 들어갈 알맞은 전치사구를 골라 쓰시오.

> 보기
>
> on the street   down the stairs   the Internet
>
> in the box   in Minhyuk's car   under the tree
>
> throughout the forest   in front of many people
>
> at the meeting   in university

1   There was a terrible car accident ___*on the street*___ yesterday.

2   We went to the beach _____.

3   A man is going _____.

4   There are some log cabins _____.

5   I taught English class _____.

6   There are some flowers _____.

7   They're not used to dancing _____.

8   You can use my laptop. Searching _____ is useful and quick.

9   They will have some tea _____.

10   I was sleeping _____.

D 다음 우리말과 같은 뜻이 되도록 주어진 단어를 알맞게 배열하여 영작하시오.

1   그는 다섯 마리의 강아지들과 산에서 살았다.
    (he, mountain, with, on, lived, dogs, five, the)
    ➡ _____*He lived with five dogs on the mountain.*_____

2   나는 일요일에 할머니를 찾아뵐 예정이다.
    (am, on, I, visit, Sunday, grandmother, going, to)
    ➡ _____

3   백화점은 향수 가게 앞에 있다.
    (the department store, the perfume store, front, is, of, in)
    ➡ _____

> **Note**
> - **terrible** 끔찍한
> - **car accident** 교통사고
> - **log** 통나무
> - **cabin** 오두막
> - **useful** 유용한
> - **laptop** 노트북
> - **perfume** 향수
> - **department store** 백화점

4   너는 지하철에서 소매치기를 조심하는 것이 좋다.

(you, watch, on the subway, had better, for, out, pickpockets)

➡ _____

5   Helen은 10월 3일까지 이 편지를 그녀의 아버지께 보내야 한다.

(Helen, by, should, to, this letter, October 3rd, send, her father)

➡ _____

6   많은 아름다운 그림들이 벽에 걸려 있다.

(many, on, the, beautiful, are, pictures, wall, hung)

➡ _____

7   Jane은 일요일에 미국으로 떠난다.

(Jane, on, leaving, for, is, Sunday, America)

➡ _____

8   내 여동생은 밤에는 물조차 마시지 않는다.

(my sister, at, drink, water, doesn't, even, night)

➡ _____

9   광장에는 많은 사람들이 몰려 있다.

(a, there, plaza, crowd, is, in, big, the)

➡ _____

10 우리는 Mr. Park와 내일 오후에 점심을 먹을 예정이다.

(we, tomorrow, are going to, Mr. Park, afternoon, have, with, lunch)

➡ _____

Note

• **had better**
  ~하는 게 좋겠다, 낫겠다

• **watch out**
  ~을 조심하다

• **pickpocket**
  명 소매치기
  통 소매치기하다

• **on the wall** 벽에

• **crow** 군중

• **plaza** 광장

Point Check II

◆ **전치사 :** 명사나 대명사 앞에 위치하여 시간, 장소, 위치, 방향, 수단 등을 나타낸다.

1. 방향을 나타내는 전치사

to	~로	out of	~밖으로	across	~을 가로질러
from	~로부터	up	~위로	along	~을 따라
into	~안으로	down	~아래로	through	~을 통하여

2. 도구, 수단을 나타내는 전치사

with ~을 가지고	• Sally always draws pictures with colored pencils.
by ~을 타고	• I often go to the park by bike.

3. 형용사와 함께 쓰는 전치사

be absent from	~에 결석하다	be tired of	~에 싫증나다
be different from	~와 다르다	be interested in	~에 관심이 있다
be afraid of	~을 두려워하다	be curious about	~에 호기심이 있다
be proud of	~을 자랑스러워하다	be good at	~을 잘하다
be full of	~으로 가득 차다	be sorry for (about)	~을 미안해하다
be famous for	~으로 유명하다	be ready for	~을 위한 준비가 되다
be late for	~에 지각하다	be responsible for	~에 책임이 있다

4. 동사와 함께 쓰는 전치사

listen to	~을 듣다	wait for	~을 기다리다	take care of	~을 돌보다
look at	~을 보다	put up with	~을 참다	depend on	~에게 의지하다

5. 기타 전치사

with	~와 함께	for	~을 위해	like	~처럼, ~같이
by	~에 의해	as	~로서	without	~없이
of	~의	to	~에게	about	~에 관하여

방향을 나타내는 전치사

• 방향을 나타내는 전치사: 명사나 대명사 앞에서 사람이나 물건이 있는 방향을 정확하게 말해준다.

◈ 방향을 나타내는 전치사

전치사		예시
to	~로	• We go to church.
from	~로부터	• She came back from the theater.
into	~안으로	• They were walking into the hall.
out of	~밖으로	• They were walking out of the classroom.
up	~위로	• Jack climbs up a tree.
down	~아래로	• I went down the mountain.
across	~을 가로질러	• The red ball rolls across the road.
along	~을 따라	• He walks along the river.
through	~을 통하여	• The ball flew through the window.
around	~주위에	• There are some people around the painter.

Check up!

Answer Keys p. 69

A 다음 빈칸에 알맞은 전치사를 쓰시오.

1 Linda walked ___through___ the forest.

2 The girl stood _____ and began to run.

3 The dog was running _____ the street.

4 I will travel all _____ the world.

5 She ran _____ the building because of the storm.

6 Because there was a fire, people ran _____ the hotel.

7 The bus passes _____ the tunnel once a day.

8 There is a beautiful bird _____ a tree.

9 The man is riding a bike _____ the river.

10 They are going to go _____ beach.

11 Put some sugar _____ the bowl.

12 There are many people _____ the corner.

도구 / 수단을 나타내는 전치사

• **도구, 수단을 나타내는 전치사**: 'with'는 도구와 함께 쓰여 '~을 가지고'의 뜻을 가지며, 'by'는 교통 수단과 함께 쓰여 '~을 타고'의 뜻을 가진다.

◈ 도구 / 수단을 나타내는 전치사

with [~을 가지고]	• I usually write a letter with pen and ink. • They are playing with toy robots.
by [~을 타고, ~로써]	• Jerry sometimes goes to work by taxi. • He always pays by cash.

◈ 전치사에 따라 달라지는 교통수단의 의미

in + 교통수단	교통수단의 내부에 초점을 맞추어 사용한다. 또는 작은 차, 개인용 비행기, 보트에 관해 말할 때 사용한다. • They came in a car.
on + 교통수단	공공 교통수단을 이용한 이동 과정을 나타내며, 타고 있는 상태를 말한다 (관사 a(an)와 함께 쓰인다.) • She must be on a train now. • We are taking on a bus.
by + 교통수단	'~로', '~을 이용해서'의 의미로 수단에 초점을 맞출 때 사용하며, 관사는 사용하지 않는다. • He goes to market by bicycle.

★Check up!

Answer Keys p. 69

A 다음 빈칸에 with와 by 중 알맞은 전치사를 쓰시오.

1 She took a picture _____*with*_____ a new camera.

2 I usually pay _____ credit card.

3 My son likes to play _____ a robot.

4 We planned to travel to Busan _____ bus.

5 Jane put some salt in a bowl _____ a spoon.

6 I always go to school _____ subway.

7 My dog likes to play _____ the doll.

8 Mom made some cookies _____ her new oven.

9 We heard her news _____ an email.

14-8 형용사와 함께 쓰는 전치사

- 형용사와 함께 쓰이는 전치사: 'be동사＋형용사＋전치사'의 형태를 가지고 있으며, 일상생활에서 자주 쓰인다.

◈ 형용사와 함께 쓰는 전치사

전치사		예시
be absent from	~에 결석하다	• I was absent from work yesterday.
be different from	~와 다르다	• This table is different from another one.
be afraid of	~을 두려워하다	• We are afraid of the horror story.
be proud of	~을 자랑스러워하다	• Her parents are proud of her graduation.
be full of	~으로 가득 차다	• This bucket is full of maple syrup.
be tired of	~에 싫증나다	• I was really tired of taking care of dogs.
be interested in	~에 관심이 있다	• Martin is interested in dancing at a club.
be curious about	~에 호기심이 있다	• She is always curious about everything that she experiences.
be good at	~을 잘하다	• We are good at reciting poems in English.
be sorry for (about)	~을 미안해하다	• He is sorry for the mistakes.
be famous for	~으로 유명하다	• Korea is famous for kimchi and bulgogi in the world.
be late for	~에 지각하다	• She is sometimes late for school.
be ready for	~을 위한 준비가 되다	• They were ready for the exam.
be responsible for	~에 책임이 있다	• I am responsible for this problem.

A 다음 문장의 빈칸에 알맞은 전치사를 써 넣으시오.

1 I was really afraid _____*of*_____ being in car accident.

2 Because she was sick, she was absent _____ English class.

3 Tim is ready _____ the piano competition.

4 She was responsible _____ the crash.

5 My baby is curious _____ everything all around her.

6 Mina is good _____ speaking Chinese.

7 They are interested _____ making movies.

8 You should remember that you are different _____ others. You are unique.

9 This restaurant is famous _____ its spicy pasta.

10 This cup is full _____ black coffee.

11 I'm sorry _____ the noise.

12 You should not be late _____ the appointment.

13 He was so tired _____ making food for the party.

14 Are you ready _____ the show?

15 I'm so proud _____ John. He was great in this movie.

14-9 동사와 함께 쓰는 전치사

• 동사와 함께 쓰이는 전치사: '자동사＋전치사'의 형태로 타동사가 되어서 그 다음에 목적어를 취한다.

◈ 동사와 함께 쓰는 전치사

전치사		예시
listen to	～을 듣다	• I was listening to classical music.
look at	～을 보다	• Teddy looked at a beautiful woman.
look for	～을 찾다	• We are looking for Jenny's new pencil case.
thank A for B	A에게 B에 대해 감사하다	• I thank her for helping me.
wait for	～을 기다리다	• You waited for him two hours, didn't you?
put up with	～을 참다	• I couldn't put up with my noisy neighbors.
take care of	～을 돌보다	• Maria takes care of her little sister.
depend on	～에게 의지하다	• She depends on her mother for everything.

Check up!

Answer Keys p. 69

A 다음 문장의 빈칸에 알맞은 전치사를 쓰시오.

1 Helen is looking _____for_____ some new movies to watch.

2 Look _____ the boy! He resembles his father.

3 I thanked her _____ inviting me to the party.

4 My mother couldn't put up _____ my dirty room.

5 He didn't care _____ my mistake.

6 The man was waiting _____ his wife.

7 He depended _____ me everything.

8 I take care _____ my old grandmother.

9 They thanked Mr. Park _____ writing the letter.

10 Kate was listening _____ the newest pop song.

Note

• care about
～에 마음 쓰다,
관심을 가지다

◈ 기타 전치사

전치사		예시
with	～와 함께	• Timmy will go camping with us.
by	～에 의해	• The magic show was directed by a famous magician.
of	～의	• The cloth of this jacket is made of something special.
for	～을 위해	• These raspberries are all for you.
as	～로서	• Jack leads the team as a captain.
to	～에게	• Our professor sent an email to us.
like	～처럼, ～같이	• I want to be a nice person like my parents.
without	～없이	• She can't see anything without her glasses.
about	～에 관하여	• We learn about old Korean literature.

☆Check up!

Answer Keys p. 69

A   보기 에서 알맞은 전치사를 골라 빈칸에 쓰시오.

보기

| to | like | without | for | about | as | of | by | with |

1   Let's go _____to_____ the concert this Saturday.

2   This movie is _____ World War Ⅱ.

3   He likes rock bands _____ many other boys.

4   The window was broken _____ Tim.

5   I can't live _____ you.

6   The title _____ this book was so impressive.

7   My son said he wanted to be a brave man _____ me.

8   You did your best _____ our team leader.

9   I donated some money _____ the charity.

10   Mike wrote a sad song _____ her.

11   These days, I started learning _____ Korean history.

12   Daniel is one _____ my best friends.

13   They will go hiking _____ their family.

14   This can will be used _____ a musical instrument.

15   She refused to talk _____ the rumor.

Practice More Ⅱ

Answer Keys p. 69~70

A 괄호 안에서 알맞은 것을 고르시오.

1 I made the green skirt (for / of) my daughter.

2 He must behave politely (as / to) a class president.

3 She was saddened (by / for) the news.

4 This mail was sent (to / for) you.

5 (As / By) a guide, I'm responsible for your tour.

6 All the players should know the rule (of / by) this game.

7 She looks (like / about) a butterfly.

8 Go out (with / to) your raincoat. It's raining today.

9 Tim went (to / by) the hospital for checkup.

10 It is exciting to travel (by / for) train.

> **Note**
>
> • **sadden**
> (수동태로) 슬프게 하다
> : **be saddened by~**
> ~에 의해 슬픔을 느끼다

B 다음 빈칸에 알맞은 전치사를 보기 에서 골라 쓰시오.

> 보기
>
> | around | to | up | along | into | out of |
> | --- | --- | --- | --- | --- | --- |
> | across | for | from | through | | |

1 I walked _____for_____ a while with Jane.

2 His hobby is climbing _____ mountains.

3 John dived _____ the pool.

4 We were running _____ the river.

5 The car passed _____ the forest.

6 People ran _____ the building because of a fire.

7 _____ now on, you should remember what you did.

8 There is a bridge _____ the river.

9 There is a French restaurant _____ the corner.

10 Some apples fell _____ the ground.

Practice More II

C   다음 문장의 빈칸에 알맞은 표현을 [보기] 에서 골라 고쳐 쓰시오.

[보기]

look for	buy ~ for	different from
thank ~ for	absent from	interested in
be famous for	be ready for	be good at listen to

1   She was ___looking for___ the key.

2   Why don't you _____ this doll _____ your son? I think he will really like it.

3   Was she _____ school yesterday?

4   _____ you _____ inviting me to your birthday party. It was really fun.

5   I was _____ composing songs. I have many songs that I made.

6   Although they are twins, they are _____ each other.

7   Sarah _____ everything related to physical activities such as basketball and swimming.

8   They _____ the hike.

9   Mother liked to _____ the radio while she was cooking.

10   This store _____ its very delicious cookies.

D   다음 우리말 뜻에 맞게 괄호에 주어진 단어를 활용하여 영작하시오.

1   그녀는 배를 타고 여행을 갈 것이다. (travel)
  ➡ _____ _She will travel by ship._ _____

2   그는 새 차로 그녀를 태웠다. (pick up)
  ➡ _____

3   John은 그의 펜 없이는 편지를 쓰지 않는다. (write, his pen)
  ➡ _____

Answer Keys p. 69~70

4 나는 새로운 피아노를 가지고 피아노 연습을 했다. (practice)

➡ _____

5 그녀는 자신의 고양이를 찾고 있었다. (look for)

➡ _____

6 Harry는 천둥을 두려워했다. (thunder)

➡ _____

7 Jim과 Sora는 그들의 할머니에 의해 양육되었다. (raise)

➡ _____

8 우리는 Tim의 컴퓨터로 숙제를 했다. (do homework)

➡ _____

9 엄마는 늘 택시를 타고 쇼핑을 간다. (go shopping)

➡ _____

10 나는 서울에서 오는 비행기를 기다리고 있는 중이다. (wait for)

➡ _____

중간 기말고사 예상문제

내신 최다 출제 유형

01 다음 빈칸에 들어갈 말이 바르게 짝지어진 것을 고르시오. [출제 예상 90%]

> • This sofa is different _____ the other one.
> • Writing stories _____ English is not easy.

① of – on   ② in – by
③ by – in   ④ from – in
⑤ from – by

02 다음을 우리말과 같도록 할 때 빈칸에 들어갈 알맞은 말을 고르시오. [출제 예상 85%]

> 아기들은 항상 새로운 무엇인가에 호기심을 가진다.
> = Babies are always curious _____ new things.

① in   ② with   ③ about
④ by   ⑤ for

03 다음 밑줄 친 부분이 어법상 어색한 것을 고르시오. [출제 예상 90%]

① Amelia is tired <u>at</u> taking piano lesson.
② I want to be a model <u>like</u> that woman.
③ We decided to send some cookies <u>to</u> her.
④ My little puppy depends <u>on</u> me for everything.
⑤ I really thank you <u>for</u> finding my wallet.

04 다음 그림과 어울리지 <u>않는</u> 문장을 고르시오. [출제 예상 85%]

① There is a girl between a table and a bed.
② There is a girl next to the table.
③ There is a girl by the bed.
④ There is a girl beside the table.
⑤ There is a girl on the bed.

05 다음 중 어법상 올바른 문장을 고르시오. [출제 예상 85%]

① Miranda leads the team by a leader.
② James asked a question about old American literature.
③ I was waiting of Johnny and Mina for two hours.
④ They are all ready at the field trip.
⑤ Mark is interested at a dance club.

06 다음 괄호 안의 단어를 우리말과 같도록 바르게 배열하시오. [출제 예상 90%]

> 그는 장갑 없이는 설거지를 하지 않는다.
> (he / wash / doesn't / gloves / dishes / without / the)

➡ _____

[01~05] 다음 빈칸에 들어갈 알맞은 말을 고르시오.

01

Nelson was born in Toronto _____ September 15, 1989.

① to   ② on   ③ in
④ at   ⑤ of

02

Write your address and stick a stamp _____ the envelope.

① in   ② at   ③ over
④ on   ⑤of

03

I like books. My room is full _____ old books.

① at   ② in   ③ of
④ to   ⑤ for

04

My mother prefers juice _____ coffee.

① than   ② on   ③ to
④ by   ⑤ in

05

When I come back home, my father is _____ the kitchen.

① on   ② in   ③ of
④ to   ⑤ by

06 다음 중 어법상 올바른 것을 고르시오.

① She likes this restaurant because its delicious food.
② My uncle's family lives at America.
③ She enjoyed to dance with me.
④ Why don't we take a picture next that tree?
⑤ Let's make it at 5:30 next to a city hall.

[07~09] 다음 우리말과 같은 뜻이 되도록 빈칸에 들어갈 알맞은 말을 고르시오.

07

나는 항상 토요일마다 오후까지 잔다.
I always sleep _____ noon on Saturdays.

① on   ② at   ③ until
④ of   ⑤ for

★★★
08

그는 꽃을 사기 위해 지갑에서 돈을 꺼낸다.
He takes the money _____ his wallet to buy some flowers.

① into   ② out of   ③ out
④ outside   ⑤ off

09

그는 고개를 가로젓음으로써 아니라고 말했다.
He said no _____ shaking his head.

① to   ② by   ③ on
④ of   ⑤ for

10 다음의 밑줄 친 부분과 쓰임이 같은 것을 고르시오.

> In the picture, my niece was smiling <u>in</u> a white wedding dress.

① There are some chocolate muffins <u>in</u> the basket.
② He doesn't get up early <u>in</u> the morning.
③ <u>In</u> fall, I gather the falling leaves.
④ Is there a bookshelf <u>in</u> your bedroom?
⑤ He looks young <u>in</u> his yellow shirt.

[11~14] 다음의 빈칸에 공통으로 들어가는 알맞은 것을 고르시오.

11

> • Pour some juice _____ the glass.
> • I will move _____ a new house next week.

① of　　② about　　③ into
④ on　　⑤ out of

12

> • The telephone was invented _____ Graham Bell.
> • The light bulb was invented _____ Thomas Edison.

① in　　② on　　③ with
④ by　　⑤ of

13

> • The old woman _____ curly silver hair is my grandmother.
> • I walked to the park _____ my friend, Jina.

① into　　② of　　③ and
④ with　　⑤ by

★★★
14

> • From now _____, I'm going to jog every day.
> • Harry and Helena went out for dinner _____ Friday evening.

① on　　② in　　③ of
④ at　　⑤ for

15 다음 밑줄 친 부분의 쓰임이 <u>어색한</u> 것을 고르시오.

① The contest was held <u>on</u> April fifteenth.
② I speak English <u>in</u> a second language.
③ We're going to travel <u>around</u> the country.
④ He is looking <u>for</u> a used car.
⑤ We should protect wild animals <u>like</u> bears.

[16~19] 다음 빈칸에 들어갈 말이 바르게 짝지어진 것을 고르시오.

16

> • She's good _____ singing songs.
> • The picture didn't fit _____ the frame.

① on － at　　② at － on　　③ of － in
④ in － at　　⑤ at － in

Answer Keys p. 70~71

17

- He breathed _____ the sweet smell of his salad.
- What is she playing _____?

① on − of   ② in − in
③ in − with   ④ by − with
⑤ out − of

18

- I think there is something wrong _____ the article.
- This movie looks interesting. Do you know what this movie is _____?

① with − with   ② by − with
③ at − about   ④ in − about
⑤ with − about

★★★
19

- Tony hurt his arm _____ he was playing baseball.
- I told my friends what I did _____ the winter vacation.

① while − for   ② while − during
③ during − during   ④ during − for
⑤ for − while

20 다음 중 밑줄 친 부분의 쓰임이 올바른 것을 <u>모두</u> 고르시오.

① Why don't we take a taxi instead <u>for</u> a bus?
② My friends and I like to go to the beach <u>in</u> summer.
③ You should take off your shoes in the house <u>in</u> Korea.
④ He didn't see her name <u>in</u> the list.
⑤ I talked to him <u>of</u> the phone.

21 다음 빈칸에 들어갈 말로 알맞은 것을 고르시오.

Lucy and I were bored. So we watched several movies _____ six hours.

① by   ② during   ③ for
④ until   ⑤ since

22 우리말과 같은 뜻이 되도록 빈칸에 들어갈 알맞은 말을 고르시오.

그는 에디슨처럼 훌륭한 과학자가 되고 싶었다.
= He wanted to be a scientist _____ Edison.

① alike   ② like   ③ become
④ liked   ⑤ with

★★★
23 다음 중 어법상 올바른 것을 고르시오.

① Jinny and Takuya went to Japan of a boat.
② My room is in the fifth floor.
③ There are a few buildings at the street.
④ Julie climbed in the ladder to reach the shelf.
⑤ I took a kitten out of the box.

★★★
24 다음 중 어법상 <u>어색한</u> 것을 고르시오.

① The bridge is on the river.
② Some birds are flying above the people.
③ We can see some ants under the tree.
④ When I was young, I liked to climb trees.
⑤ They walked down the mountain.

25 다음 빈칸에 공통으로 들어갈 알맞은 말을 고르시오.

> • Do you have these shoes _____ size 6?
> • Cut the apple _____ half.

① in   ② on   ③ at
④ by   ⑤ of

★★★
26 다음 빈칸에 들어갈 말이 바르게 짝지어진 것을 고르시오.

> I _____ $100 _____ these earrings.

① pay − of   ② paid − of
③ paid − for   ④ pay − on
⑤ paid − about

27 다음 빈칸에 들어갈 말이 바르게 짝지어진 것을 고르시오.

> • Where will you be _____ October?
> • His baby sister was born _____ June 27th.

① on − on   ② in − on   ③ in − in
④ on − in   ⑤ to − to

28 우리말과 같은 뜻이 되도록 빈칸에 들어갈 알맞은 말을 고르시오.

> 만약 네가 네 자신을 믿는다면, 너는 어려움을 극복할 수 있을 것이다.
> = If you believe _____ yourself, you'll be able to overcome difficulties.

① on   ② of   ③ by
④ at   ⑤ in

★★★
29 다음 문장 중 어법상 올바른 것을 모두 고르시오.

① They will live in Paris from April.
② I have played the piano for 2007.
③ Because of a big storm, I had to stay at home while three days.
④ The first modern Olympics was held in 1896.
⑤ Jim's family visits his grandparents every Saturdays.

30 다음 문장 중 어법상 어색한 것을 모두 고르시오.

① I don't drink coke at night.
② I am not in the home before 5 o'clock.
③ She did her homework after clean her room.
④ What did Jane get for her birthday?
⑤ Why don't we go to the theater on Friday night?

◇◇◇◇◇◇◇◇◇ **서술형 평가** ◇◇◇◇◇◇◇◇◇

[31~35] 다음 각각의 빈칸에 들어갈 알맞은 말을 쓰시오.

31
- I'll let you know _____ an email.
- Jessy and Mark have gone _____ Canada.

➡ _____

32
- Harry gave a bunch of roses _____ her.
- We are going to leave Seoul _____ Jeju Island.

➡ _____

33
- They stayed at my home _____ a month.
- She helped me write in my diary _____ English.

➡ _____

34
- Larry puts his books _____ the table.
- I am really tired _____ studying science and math.

➡ _____

35
- Judy and Nancy usually go to the park _____ school.
- Is anything wrong _____ your computer?

➡ _____

[36~38] 다음 우리말을 참고하여 괄호 안에서 알맞은 말을 고르시오.

36
나와 내 개는 언덕 아래로 달려가고 있는 중이다.

➡ I and my dog are running (up / down) the hill.

37
Brown 부부는 강을 따라 걷는 중이다.

➡ Mr. and Mrs. Brown are walking (along / alone) the river.

38
그 파랑새는 창문을 통과해 날아갔다.

➡ The blue bird flew (though / through) the window.

[39~42] 다음 우리말에 맞게 괄호 안의 단어를 이용하여 영작하시오.

★★★
39

일요일마다 나와 내 가족은 10시에 일어난다.
(every Sunday / get up)

➡ _____

40

나는 벽 위의 그림들을 바라보았다. (look at / wall / pictures)

➡ _____

41

우리는 그를 두시간 동안 기다리고 있는 중이다.
(wait for / two / hours)

➡ _____

★★★
42

많은 소년들이 Jessie 주위에 있고, 그들은 웃고 있다.
(boys / many / laugh / and)

➡ _____

[43~45] 다음 빈칸에 공통으로 들어갈 알맞은 전치사를 쓰시오.

43

• My grandmother can't see _____ her glasses.
• I cannot enjoy playing tennis _____ my friend, John.

➡ _____

44

• Bill wanted to be a great boxer _____ Muhammad Ali.
• Lina looks _____ her mother a lot.

➡ _____

45

• Jamie had to _____ _____ with his anger at the news.
• They didn't _____ _____ with each other.

➡ _____

15

Chapter
화법과 속담

Point Check I

◆ **화법 :** 다른 사람의 말을 전달하는 방법을 말한다.

◆ **직접화법 :** 누군가의 말을 따옴표(" ")를 사용해 직접적으로 전달하는 방법을 말한다.

◆ **간접화법 :** 누군가의 말을 전달하는 사람의 입장으로 바꿔 간접적으로 전달하는 방법을 말한다.

1. 평서문의 화법 전환

[직접화법] Mia said, "I have to do my homework now."

[간접화법] Mia said that she had to do her homework then.

① say → say, say to → tell ② 콤마(,)와 따옴표 (" ") 대신 'that' 사용

③ that절의 인칭대명사는 전달하는 사람의 입장으로 바꾼다. (that 생략 가능)

④ that절의 시제는 전달 동사의 시제와 일치 ⑤ 지시대명사나 부사(구)는 전달하는 사람의 입장으로 바꾼다.

2. 의문문의 화법 전환

의문사가 없는 의문문	[직접화법] He said, "Are you okay?" [간접화법] He asked if (whether) I was okay. ① say, say to → ask ② 콤마(,), 따옴표(" "), 물음표(?)를 없애고 'if' 또는 'whether'를 사용 ③ 인칭대명사와 시제를 바꾸고, 어순을 '주어＋동사'로 변경 ④ 지시대명사나 부사(구)는 전달하는 사람의 입장으로 바꾼다.
의문사가 있는 의문문	[직접화법] Harry said to me, "What do you want to do?" [간접화법] Harry asked me what I wanted to do. ① say, say to → ask ② 콤마(,), 따옴표(" "), 물음표(?)를 없애고 의문사로 두 문장을 연결 ③ 인칭대명사와 시제를 바꾸고, 어순을 '주어＋동사'로 변경 　단, 의문사가 주어인 경우 '의문사＋동사'의 어순을 그대로 유지

3. 명령문의 화법 전환

[직접화법] The teacher said to me, "Get in the line."

[간접화법] The teacher ordered me to get in the line.

① 전달 동사는 말투에 구분해서 사용 [명령: tell, order, command], [충고: advise], [부탁: ask, beg]

② • 명령문의 동사원형을 'to부정사'로 바꾼다.

　• 부정문일 경우 'not to부정사'로 바꾼다.

Lesson 15-1 평서문의 화법 전환

- **화법**: 다른 사람의 말을 전달하는 방법을 말한다.
- **직접화법**: 누군가의 말을 따옴표(" ")를 사용해 직접적으로 전달하는 방법이다.
- **간접화법**: 누군가의 말을 전달하는 사람의 입장으로 바꿔서 간접적으로 전달하는 방법이다.

1. 직접화법에서 간접화법으로 전환하기

[직접화법] She said, "I want to take a trip alone."

[간접화법] She said that she wanted to take a trip alone.

Peterson said, "I can make it well myself now." [직접화법] Peterson은 "이제 나 혼자서 그것을 잘할 수 있어"라고 말했다.	
① 직접화법의 동사 변환 say → say say to → tell	Peterson said
② 콤마(,)와 따옴표(" ") 대신 'that' 사용	Peterson said that
③ that절의 인칭대명사는 전달하는 사람의 입장으로 바꾼다. (that 생략 가능)	Peterson said that he
④ that절의 시제는 전달 동사의 시제와 일치시킨다.	Peterson said that he could make
⑤ 지시대명사나 부사(구)는 전달하는 사람의 입장으로 바꾼다.	Peterson said that he could make it well himself then.

➡ Peterson said (that) he could make it well himself then. [간접화법]
Peterson은 그때 그 스스로 잘할 수 있다고 말했다.

2. 간접화법으로 전환할 때의 지시대명사 또는 부사구

직접화법		간접화법	직접화법		간접화법
this/these	➡	that/those	here	➡	there
ago	➡	before	now	➡	then
yesterday	➡	the previous day (the day before)	today	➡	that day
tomorrow	➡	the next day (the following day)	last night	➡	the previous night (the night before)

- Jerry said, "**I'll** go to Gangwondo **tomorrow**."
  = Jerry said that he **would** go to Gangwondo **the next day**.

- Angela said to us, "I **want** to sing in the band."
  = Angela told us that she **wanted** to sing in the band.

Answer Keys p. 72

A 보기 와 같이 주어진 문장을 간접화법으로 바꿀 때 빈칸에 알맞은 단어를 쓰시오.

> 보기
>
> She said to me, "I'm very happy to see you again."
> ➡ She told me that she was very happy to see me again.

---

1 Minji said to him, "I know how to play the game."

   ➡ _____

2 My mother said to me, "You should be polite to everybody."

   ➡ _____

3 Jane said to us, "It's rainy today. so we should change the plans."

   ➡ _____

4 Mom said to my brother, "You should study hard."

   ➡ _____

5 Tom said, "I will be back next month."

   ➡ _____

6 He said, "I can't believe the rumor now."

   ➡ _____

7 Father said to me, "I'm going to go to Japan tomorrow."

   ➡ _____

8 Jim said to her, "I will love you forever."

   ➡ _____

9 Jane said to us, "I will attend the meeting in Busan."

   ➡ _____

10 Tim said to me, "I bought a new car last week."

   ➡ _____

B　보기와 같이 간접화법은 직접화법으로, 직접화법은 간접화법으로 바꾸시오.

> 보기
>
> He said, "I will go out with Jane."
>
> ➡　　　He said that he would go out with Jane.
>
> The English teacher told me that he played soccer on Saturday.
>
> ➡ The English teacher said to me, "I play soccer on Saturday."

1　My little sister said that she had broken Tim's window.

　　➡ _____

2　My friend said to me, "I'm going to quit my job."

　　➡ _____

3　The girl said, "I don't want to go hiking."

　　➡ _____

4　Jenny told her friends that she invited them to her birthday party.

　　➡ _____

5　Tim told his son that he had to save money.

　　➡ _____

6　Jina said to him, "I will make some food for the picnic."

　　➡ _____

7　Mike said that he would go to Jeju Island the following week.

　　➡ _____

15-2 의문문의 화법 전환

- **의문문의 화법 전환**: 직접화법에서의 전달 동사 'say (to)'를 'ask'로 바꿔준다.

1. 의문사가 없는 의문문의 화법 전환

<table>
<tr><td colspan="2">He said, "Are you going fishing now?" [직접화법]
그는 "너는 지금 낚시를 가는 중이니?"라고 말했다.</td></tr>
<tr><td>① say, say to → ask</td><td>He asked</td></tr>
<tr><td>② 콤마(,), 따옴표(" "), 물음표(?)를 없애고 'if' 또는 'whether'를 사용한다.</td><td>He asked if (whether)</td></tr>
<tr><td>③ 인칭대명사와 시제를 바꾸고, 어순을 '주어 + 동사'로 변경한다.</td><td>He asked if (whether) I was</td></tr>
<tr><td>④ 지시대명사나 부사(구)는 전달하는 사람의 입장으로 바꾼다.</td><td>He asked if (whether) I was going fishing then.</td></tr>
</table>

➡ He asked if (whether) I was going fishing then. [간접화법]
그는 그때 내가 낚시를 가고 있는 중인지 물었다.

2. 의문사가 있는 의문문의 화법 전환

<table>
<tr><td colspan="2">Sandra said to him, "What is your favorite subject?" [직접화법]
Sandra는 그에게 "너는 무슨 과목을 제일 좋아하니?"라고 말했다.</td></tr>
<tr><td>① say, say to → ask</td><td>Sandra asked him</td></tr>
<tr><td>② 콤마(,), 따옴표(" "), 물음표(?)를 없애고 의문사로 두 문장을 연결한다.</td><td>Sandra asked him what</td></tr>
<tr><td>③ 인칭대명사와 시제를 바르게 바꾸고, 어순을 '주어 + 동사'로 변경한다. 의문사가 주어인 경우 '의문사 + 동사'의 어순을 그대로 유지한다.</td><td>Sandra asked him what his favorite subject is.</td></tr>
</table>

➡ Sandra asked him what his favorite subject is. [간접화법]
Sandra는 그가 가장 좋아하는 과목이 무엇인지 물었다.

Answer Keys p. 72

A 보기와 같이 주어진 문장을 간접화법으로 바꾸시오.

> 보기
>
> He said to me, "How often do you exercise?"
> ➡ _____ He asked me how often I exercise. _____
>
> The woman said to him, "Do you like eating spicy food?"
> ➡ The woman asked him if he liked eating spicy food.

1 Kate said to me, "Can I borrow your car?"

➡ *Kate asked me if she could borrow my car.*

2 Father said, "Where is my key?"

➡ _____

3 Amy said to her, "Who's calling?"

➡ _____

4 The lady said to me, "Do you enjoy the party?"

➡ _____

5 The man said to her, "Can you say that again?"

➡ _____

6 She said, "Are you for or against my opinion?"

➡ _____

7 Andy said to me, "Are you looking for the book?"

➡ _____

8 He said to her, "What makes you cry?"

➡ _____

9 I said to Jack, "Where can I get the ticket?"

➡ _____

10 The gentleman said to her, "Where is the conference center?"

➡ _____

> **Note**
> · be + 주어 + for or against~?
> ~에 대해 찬성이니 반대이니?

15-3 명령문의 화법 전환

- **명령문의 화법전환**: 간접화법으로 전환할 때 두 문장을 연결해 주는 역할로 'to'를 사용한다.

1. 명령문의 화법 전환

Mr. Black said to us, "Listen carefully." [직접화법] Mr. Black은 우리에게 "잘 들어라."라고 말했다.	
① 명령문의 전달 동사는 말투에 따라 몇 가지 동사를 구분해서 사용한다.	Mr. Black told us
② · 명령문의 동사원형을 'to부정사'로 바꾼다. · 부정문일 경우 'do not, never'을 없애고 'not to부정사'로 바꾼다.	Mr. Black told us to listen carefully.

➡ Mr. Black told us to listen carefully. [간접화법]
Mr. Black은 우리에게 잘 들으라고 말했다.

2. 간접화법으로 전환할 때의 전달 동사

명령	tell, order, command
충고	advise
부탁 (주로 **please**가 있는 문장)	ask, beg

- My mother said to me, "**Don't go** to bed late."
  = My mother told me **not to go** to bed late.

☆Check up!

Answer Keys p. 72

A 〔보기〕와 같이 주어진 문장을 괄호 안의 단어를 이용하여 간접화법으로 바꾸시오.

〔보기〕

He said to me, "Concentrate on your studies." (advise)
➡ He advised me to concentrate on my studies.

The mother said to her son, "Watch out when you ride a bike." (tell)
➡ The mother told her son to watch out when he rode a bike.

1 She said to me, "Tell me why you cry." (tell)
 ➡ _____

2 The teacher said to her, "Study hard to pass the exam." (advise)

➡ _____

3 Mom said to my brother, "Get up early in the morning." (tell)

➡ _____

4 Jim said to her, "Exercise regularly." (tell)

➡ _____

5 Mom said to me, "Quit playing right now." (advise)

➡ _____

6 Mr. Kim said to us, "Don't be late tomorrow." (order)

➡ _____

7 She said to her son, "Pass me the salt." (tell)

➡ _____

8 John said to her, "Turn in your paper by five." (order)

➡ _____

9 Mrs. Anderson said to me, "Stop copying novels." (advise)

➡ _____

10 Tina said to me, "Don't play the piano at night." (tell)

➡ _____

15-4 속담 표현 익히기

◆ 속담

	영문	한글
1	A bad workman blames his tools.	서툰 목수가 연장 탓한다.
2	A friend in need is a friend indeed.	어려울 때 돕는 친구가 진정한 친구다.
3	A little is better than none.	조금이라도 있는 것이 없는 것보다 낫다.
4	A rolling stone gathers no moss.	구르는 돌에는 이끼가 끼지 않는다.
5	A soft answer turns away wrath.	부드러운 대답이 분노를 보내버린다. (말 한마디에 천 냥 빚도 갚는다.)
6	A picture is worth a thousand words.	백문이 불여일견이다.
7	A watched pot never boils.	지켜보는 냄비는 끓지 않는다.
8	Actions speak louder than words.	말보다 행동이다.
9	After a storm comes the calm.	폭풍 후에 평온함이 온다.
10	All that glitters is not gold.	반짝인다고 다 금은 아니다.
11	Better late than never.	늦는 것이 안 하는 것보다 낫다.
12	Blood is thicker than water.	피는 물보다 진하다.
13	Every dog has his day.	쥐구멍에도 볕 들 날이 있다.
14	Haste makes waste.	서두름이 낭비를 만든다.
15	He who laughs best laughs last.	최후에 웃는 사람이 승자다.
16	Heaven helps those who help themselves.	하늘은 스스로 돕는 자를 돕는다.
17	Iron not used soon rusts.	쇠는 쓰지 않으면 곧 녹이 슨다.
18	Knowledge is power.	아는 것이 힘이다.
19	Like father, like son.	그 아버지에 그 아들.
20	Luck comes to those who look after it.	행운은 찾는 사람에게 온다.
21	Many hands make light work.	많은 손이 가벼운 일을 만든다. (백지장도 맞들면 낫다.)
22	Necessity is the mother of invention.	필요는 발명의 어머니이다.
23	Out of the frying pan into the fire.	튀김 팬에서 불속으로. (갈수록 태산이다.)
24	Practice makes perfect.	연습이 완벽을 만든다.
25	Reading makes a full man.	독서가 완전한 인간을 만든다.
26	Rome was not built in a day.	로마는 하루아침에 세워지지 않았다.
27	One goes a long way step by step.	한 걸음 한 걸음 멀리 간다. (천 리 길도 한 걸음부터.)

28	Strike while the iron is hot.	쇠뿔도 단김에 빼라.
29	Teaching is learning.	가르치는 것이 배우는 것이다.
30	The foot of the candle is dark.	등잔 밑이 어둡다.
31	The pen is mightier than the sword.	펜은 칼보다 강하다.
32	Time flies like an arrow.	시간은 쏜살같이 지나간다.
33	Time is money.	시간이 돈이다.
34	When god closes one door, he opens another.	하늘이 무너져도 솟아날 구멍은 있다.
35	Where there is a will, there is a way.	뜻이 있는 곳에 길이 있다.

 **Check up!**

Answer Keys p. 72~73

A 다음 우리말 해석에 맞는 속담을 보기에서 골라 번호를 쓰시오.

> 보기
>
> ① Time flies like an arrow.
>
> ② Every cloud has a silver lining.
>
> ③ Better late than never.
>
> ④ The pen is mightier than the sword.
>
> ⑤ Where there is a will, there is a way.
>
> ⑥ Haste makes waste.
>
> ⑦ A watched pot never boils.
>
> ⑧ A little is better than none.
>
> ⑨ The foot of the candle is dark.
>
> ⑩ One goes a long way step by step.
>
> ⑪ A friend in need is a friend indeed.
>
> ⑫ Out of sight, out of mind.
>
> ⑬ Heaven helps those who help themselves.

1 괴로움 뒤에는 기쁨이 있다.   ②

2 급히 서두르면 일을 망친다.   _____

3 늦는 것이 안 하는 것보다 낫다.   _____

4 펜이 칼보다 강하다.   _____

5 뜻이 있는 곳에 길이 있다. _____

6 눈에서 멀어지면 마음에서 멀어진다. _____

7 천 리 길도 한 걸음부터. _____

8 하늘은 스스로 돕는 자를 돕는다. _____

9 어려울 때 친구가 진짜 친구다. _____

10 지켜보는 냄비는 끓지 않는다. _____

11 등잔 밑이 어둡다. _____

12 시간은 쏜살같이 지나간다. _____

13 조금이라도 있는 것이 없는 것보다 낫다. _____

B 다음 우리말에 맞게 빈칸에 알맞은 말을 쓰시오.

1 백지장도 맞들면 낫다.
➡ Many hands _____ *make light work.* _____

2 피는 물보다 진하다.
➡ Blood is _____

3 뜻이 있는 곳에 길이 있다.
➡ _____, there is a way.

4 지켜보는 냄비는 끓지 않는다.
➡ _____ never boils.

5 필요는 발명의 어머니다.
➡ _____ is the mother of _____.

6 가르치는 것이 배우는 것이다.
➡ _____ is _____.

7 구르는 돌에는 이끼가 끼지 않는다.
➡ A rolling stone gathers _____.

8 조금이라도 있는 것이 없는 것보다 낫다.
➡ _____ is better than _____.

9 최후에 웃는 사람이 승자다.
➡ He who laughs best _____.

10 김칫국부터 마시지 마라. (알을 까기도 전에 병아리 수를 세지 마라.)
➡ Don't count your chickens _____.

Practice More I

Answer Keys p. 73

A 다음 문장을 간접화법으로 고치시오.

1 Daniel said to me, "I don't forget your birthday."

➡ Daniel _____ *told me that he didn't forget my birthday.* _____

2 My brother said to me, "Can you go to the concert with me tonight?"

➡ My brother asked _____

3 Her boss said to her, "Send these letters today."

➡ Her boss ordered _____

4 Jane said to him, "I can't understand what you are saying."

➡ Jane told _____

5 The director said to John, "What are you looking for now?"

➡ The director asked _____

6 She said to James, "Can I borrow your car?"

➡ She asked _____

7 Sam said to her, "Don't throw garbage away here."

➡ Sam ordered _____

8 My father said to me, "Put on your raincoat because it's rainy today."

➡ My father told _____

9 Helen said to him, "I can't remember your name."

➡ Helen told _____

10 He said to his son, "Be careful when you drive a car."

➡ He told _____

B 다음 밑줄 친 부분을 바르게 고치시오.

1 He said that Helen <u>goes</u> to the park for exercise.

_____ *went* _____

2 Daniel <u>asked</u> that he was not a genius.

_____

3   She asked him what time was it then.

_____

4   The professor advised me to not watch the documentary.

_____

5   He asked me was who calling.

_____

6   Jane told her sister that she could buy the hat tomorrow.

_____

7   Mike asked me how old was she.

_____

8   She told me not speaking loudly in the library.

_____

9   John asked her that she had been to LA.

_____

10 Our leader ordered us wait a minute.

_____

C   다음 우리말 해석에 맞게 주어진 단어들을 알맞게 배열하시오.

1   최후에 웃는 사람이 승자다. (he, last, best, laughs, who, laughs)
    ➡ _____ He who laughs best laughs last. _____

2   필요는 발명의 어머니이다. (of, the mother, necessity, invention, is)
    ➡ _____

3   지켜보는 냄비는 끓지 않는다. (a watched, boils, pot, never)
    ➡ _____

4   어려울 때 친구가 진정한 친구다.
    (a friend, indeed, is, in, a friend, need)
    ➡ _____

5   폭풍 후에 평온함이 온다. (after, the calm, comes, a storm)
    ➡ _____

6 뜻이 있는 곳에 길이 있다.
(a way, there, a will, there, is, where, is)

➡ _____

7 로마는 하루아침에 세워지지 않았다.
(a day, Rome, built, was, in, not)

➡ _____

8 쇠뿔도 단김에 빼라. (hot, strike, the iron, while, is)

➡ _____

9 갈수록 태산이다. (fire, out of, into, the frying pan, the)

➡ _____

10 구르는 돌에는 이끼가 끼지 않는다.
(a rolling, gathers, no, stone, moss)

➡ _____

내신 최다 출제 유형

01 다음 빈칸에 들어갈 알맞지 <u>않은</u> 것을 고르시오.

[출제 예상 85%]

> Johnny said that _____.

① he would have dinner with Jane
② you would go fishing
③ he will go to France
④ he didn't like math
⑤ he changed his shirts.

02 다음의 문장을 간접화법으로 바르게 바꾼 것을 고르시오.

[출제 예상 90%]

> Hongdo said, "Are you full?"

① Hongdo asked that I was full.
② Hongdo asked if I was full.
③ Hongdo asked if I am full.
④ Hongdo asks if I am full.
⑤ Hongdo asks whether I was full.

03 다음 두 문장의 뜻이 같게 할 때 빈칸에 알맞은 것을 고르시오.

[출제 예상 85%]

> Mr. White said to us, "Be quiet."
> = Mr. White told us _____ quiet.

① to be   ② that be   ③ if be
④ whether be ⑤ should be

04 다음 문장의 빈칸에 알맞은 말을 쓰시오.

[출제 예상 85%]

> Mark said to me, "Don't be silly."
> = M a r k _____ m e _____ silly.

➡ _____

05 다음 문장들 중 간접화법으로 바르게 바꾼 것을 <u>모두</u> 고르시오.

[출제 예상 85%]

① He said to me, "Who are you?"
   = He asked me who was I.
② Mr. Lee said to us, "Pay attention."
   = Mr. Lee told us that pay attention.
③ I said to Annie, "I'll move to Jejudo next month."
   = I told Annie that I will move to Jejudo next month.
④ She said to him, "Do you like me?"
   = She asked him if he liked her.
⑤ Judy said to us, "Where are we going now?"
   = Judy asked us where we were going then.

01 다음 밑줄 친 부분이 잘못된 것을 고르시오.

> He said, "I don't have to write in my diary today."
> = He ① said ② that he ③ doesn't ④ have to write in his diary ⑤ that day.

[02~04] 다음 문장의 화법을 전환할 때 빈칸에 들어갈 알맞은 말을 고르시오.

02

> Peterson said to me, "What is this movie about?"
> = Peterson _____ me _____ that movie was about.

① asks — what   ② asking — what

③ asked — what   ④ ask to — what

⑤ asked to — what

03

> She says, "I will study hard for the first time in my life."
> = She said _____ she _____ hard for the first time in her life.

① if — would study

② that — would study

③ that — will study

④ that — studied

⑤ if — studied

04

> Mr. Han, my English teacher said to us, "Who wrote *Romeo and Juliet*?"
> = Mr. Han, my English teacher asked us _____ *Romeo and Juliet*.

① who writes   ② who write

③ who was writing   ④ who is writing

⑤ who had written

05 다음 문장의 화법 전환이 올바르게 된 것을 고르시오.

> Mia said, "I will keep his words in mind."

① Mia said that she keeps his words in mind.

② Mia said that she kept his words in mind.

③ Mia said that she will keep his words in mind.

④ Mia said that she would keep his words in mind.

⑤ Mia said that she would kept his words in mind.

[06~07] 다음 우리말과 같은 뜻이 되도록 빈칸에 알맞은 단어를 고르시오.

06

> 말 한마디에 천 냥 빚도 갚는다.
> = A soft answer _____ wrath.

① turns down   ② turns away

③ turns up   ④ turns off

⑤ turns on

07

선생님은 우리에게 복도에서 뛰지 말라고 명령하셨다.

= The teacher ordered us _____ in the hallway.

① to not run ② no run ③ not run

④ not to run ⑤ don't run

[08~09] 다음 괄호 안에 주어진 동사의 알맞은 형태를 고르시오.

08

Our teacher told us that the earth (go) around the sun.

① goes ② went ③ go

④ have gone ⑤ had gone

09

Mr. Smith told us (no, run) in the hallway and classroom.

① no run ② not to run

③ not running ④ don't run

⑤ run

[10~11] 다음 우리말을 바르게 영작한 것을 고르시오.

★★★
10

나는 그에게 그의 사무실이 어디에 있는지를 물었다.

① I ask him where his office was.

② I ask him where his office is.

③ I asked him where his office is.

④ I asked him where his office was.

⑤ I asked him where was his office.

★★★
11

그녀는 딸에게 "어디 아프니?"라고 말했다.

① She said her daughter, "Are you sick?"

② She says to her daughter, "Are you sick?"

③ She said to her daughter, "Were you sick?"

④ She said her daughter, "Are you sick?"

⑤ She said to her daughter, "Are you sick?"

[12~13] 다음 글과 어울리는 속담을 고르시오.

12

When Eric first came to our school, I didn't think much of him. He was small and very quiet. Because he didn't say much in class, I assumed he didn't know much. But as the semester went on, I realized how wrong I had been. That first semester at our school, he got the highest grade in all our classes.

① He who laughs best laughs last.

② Haste makes waste.

③ Knowledge is power.

④ Don't judge a book by its cover.

⑤ Many hands make light work.

13

M Thank you so much for your help, Julie.

W It's no problem. I am happy to help you.

M It is really kind of you to bring this homework home for me each day. Mr. Jackson says it's important I keep up with my schoolwork. I need another week off my leg, to make sure it heals properly.

W Well, don't worry. I'm happy to bring your schoolwork to you for the next week.

M Thanks again, Julie.

① A picture is worth a thousand words.

② A friend in need is a friend indeed.

③ A little is better than none.

④ After a storm comes a calm.

⑤ Every dog has his day.

[14~15] 다음 밑줄 친 부분 중 어법상 어색한 곳을 고르시오.

14

A What did Sally ① say to you?

B She ② told me ③ if she ④ would have a date ⑤ with James.

15

A Where are you ① going?

B The airport. Uncle Jack is coming, ② so I ③ told him ④ that I ⑤ will pick him up at the airport.

[16~17] 다음 주어진 문장을 간접화법으로 바르게 전환한 것을 고르시오.

16

★★★

She said, "Can I drink some water?"

① She asked that she could drink some water.

② She asks if she could drink some water.

③ She asked if she could drink some water.

④ She asks whether she could drink some water.

⑤ She asked whether she can drink some water.

17

★★★

Jane said to her father, "I want a bicycle."

① Jane told to her father that she wanted a bicycle.

② Jane told her father she want a bicycle.

③ Jane told her father that she wanted a bicycle.

④ Jane told her father that she a bicycle.

⑤ Jane told her father that she had a bicycle.

18 다음 빈칸에 들어갈 알맞은 말을 고르시오.

> Mom said to me, "I'm making invitations for your birthday."
> =Mom told me that she _____ invitations for my birthday.

① making　　② was making
③ makes　　④ made
⑤ to make

[19~20] 다음 우리말 속담을 영어로 바르게 표현한 것을 고르시오.

19

> 아는 것이 힘이다.

① Knowledge is power.
② The power is knowledge.
③ Having power is knowledge.
④ Studying hard is power.
⑤ Get knowledge, get power.

20

> 하늘은 스스로 돕는 자를 돕는다.

① Heaven helps people who help each other.
② The heaven helps the people.
③ Heaven help them who help themselves.
④ Heaven helps those who help themselves.
⑤ Heaven helped those who helped themselves.

21 다음의 문장을 직접화법으로 바르게 전환한 것을 고르시오

> Tony asked us what our plans were for Christmas.

① Tony said us, "What are your plans for Christmas?"
② Tony said, "What are your plans for Christmas?"
③ Tony said to us, "What were your plans for Christmas?"
④ Tony said to us, "What are your plans for Christmas?"
⑤ Tony said to us, "What is your plans for Christmas?"

◇◇◇◇◇◇◇◇◇ **서술형 평가** ◇◇◇◇◇◇◇◇◇

[22~23] 다음 주어진 간접화법 문장을 직접화법 문장으로 전환하여 다시 쓰시오.

★★★
22

> Phillip told me that he was pleased with the magic show.

➡ _____

23

> Ian said that his mom made aprons well.

➡ _____

[24~26] 다음 주어진 직접화법 문장을 간접화법으로
전환하여 다시 쓰시오.

24

Kelly said to us, "I am so happy now."

➡ _____

★★★
25

Nicole said to a woman, "Is the post office near here?"

➡ _____

_____

26

Robin said to Jennifer, "What are you doing?"

➡ _____

[27~28] 다음 괄호 안의 말을 이용하여 빈칸에 알맞은
형태로 쓰시오.

27

Mary thought that Sam _____ do anything just for her. (can)

➡ _____

28

I know that Lian _____ the subway to work every day. (take)

➡ _____

[29~31] 다음 괄호 안의 단어를 바르게 배열하여 문장
을 완성하시오.

★★★
29

(spaghetti / that / she / said / like / cream / didn't / with / sauce)

➡ Jinny _____.

★★★
30

(asked / movie / had watched / me / if / that / I)

➡ Brown _____.

★★★
31

(he / why / I / liked / asked / old music / me)

➡ _____

Grammar Master Level 2

펴낸이	임 병 업
펴낸곳	(주)월드컴 에듀
디자인	임예슬 · 김지현
저자	신은진
편집	김채원
감수	Amy Smith
주소	서울특별시 강남구 도곡동 411-2
	차우빌딩, 5층
전화	02)3273-4300 (대표)
팩스	02)3273-4303
홈페이지	www.wcbooks.co.kr
이메일	wc4300@wcbooks.co.kr

GRAMMAR MASTER 2

정답 및 해설

WorldCom Edu

Chapter 01 문장의 기본

Lesson 1-1 Yes/No 의문문

p. 012

A
1 Aren't the girls in the classroom?
2 Will Jane pass the exam?
3 Is the giraffe's neck long?
4 Do students have to follow the rules?
5 Can John speak Chinese?
6 Does Sally ride a bike?
7 Was he angry with Jessica?
8 Can't your father make cookies?

B
1 you can
2 he didn't
3 it was
4 he did
5 I have not(haven't)
6 she can
7 they weren't
8 it can

Lesson 1-2 부가의문문과 선택의문문

p. 014

A
1 didn't you
2 is it
3 couldn't he
4 have they
5 don't they
6 shall we
7 will you
8 doesn't it
9 hasn't she
10 isn't it

B
1 or
2 or
3 Jack or Harry
4 or
5 or not
6 Which
7 Which
8 can she
9 won't you

Lesson 1-3 간접의문문

p. 016

A
1 is Tommy → Tommy is
2 cookies bought → bought cookies
3 is his name → his name is
4 the window broke → broke the window
5 did she → she did
6 didn't she → she didn't

B
1 I wonder if Max is a businessman.
2 Let's ask Jim how he found it.
3 Please tell us how we can get to the station.
4 How do you think she can solve the problem?
5 Where do you believe Sean got it?
6 I wonder if (whether) you love John.
7 Please tell me if (whether) she passed the exam.

Practice More Ⅰ

p. 017~019

A
1 is the woman → the woman is
2 Whose → Which
3 can't you → will you
4 does he → he is
5 What → Which
6 that → if
7 Are → Do
8 won't → will
9 what → if/whether
10 was she → she was
11 Do you think where → Where do you think
12 Thinking → Think
13 leaves he → he leaves
14 isn't it → shouldn't it
15 does Inho's car → Inho's car is

B
1 I can't remember who James is
2 Please tell me why Linda left home.
3 Who do you believe will gain the final victory?
4 Let's ask him how we can get to the station.

5 Peter wanted to know if(whether) the book was sold out.

6 I don't know if(whether) Amy became a nurse.

7 When do you guess they will come back?

8 Can you tell me what that means?

9 I wonder if(whether) he broke the window.

10 Do you know who helped the old man last night?

11 I can't believe what he said.

C
1	didn't	**2**	aren't I
3	Whose	**4**	help
5	don't	**6**	doesn't
7	will	**8**	isn't
9	aren't	**10**	didn't

D
1 When do you guess he will

2 when Max's birthday is

3 Where did you find the key?

4 Don't be late again, will you?

5 Which food do you want to eat

6 What did you do last night?

7 what I want to be

8 Please draw my dog

9 Do you know what day today is?

10 Go to bed early, or you will be late for school.

Lesson 1-4 주어

Check up!   p. 022

A
1	I	**2**	Exercising
3	is	**4**	It
5	don't	**6**	There are
7	It	**8**	is
9	It	**10**	To keep a diary

B
1	This → It	**2**	was → were
3	Go → Going(To go)	**4**	That's → It's
5	wears → wear	**6**	Her → She
7	are → is	**8**	It → That
9	My → I	**10**	is → are

Lesson 1-5 동사

Check up!   p. 023~024

A
1	wears	**2**	wants
3	rises	**4**	study
5	them	**6**	swim
7	leave	**8**	went
9	empty	**10**	him

B
1 lose → lost

2 send → sent

3 become → becomes (became)

4 went → will go (are going)

5 said → say

6 making → made

7 is → was

8 have → had

9 your → you

10 the leader Sally → Sally the leader

Lesson 1-6 보어

Check up!   p. 025

A
1	comfortable	**2**	clean
3	dancing / dance	**4**	nice
5	sad	**6**	lovely
7	exciting	**8**	playing
9	surprising	**10**	boring
11	confused	**12**	happy

Lesson 1-7 목적어

Check up!   p. 026

A
1	me	**2**	him
3	her	**4**	to find
5	them	**6**	cooking
7	himself	**8**	her
9	yelling	**10**	to go

Lesson 1-8 부사어

Check up!
p. 027

A 1 well 2 peacefully
3 Strangely 4 in the morning
5 carefully 6 hastily
7 Unluckily 8 fast
9 specially 10 late / later

Practice More II
p. 028~029

A 1 pollute → polluting
2 to John → John
3 meeting → to meet
4 easy → easily
5 are → is
6 Watch → Watching
7 allowed → allow
8 being → to be

B 1 are 2 carefully
3 suddenly 4 Writing(To write)
5 study 6 late
7 arrived 8 well
9 disappointed 10 quickly
11 riding(ride) 12 laugh
13 climb 14 exciting
15 stolen

C 1 receive her salary this month
2 is writing novels and poems
3 He was impolite at the meeting.
4 James class president
5 to remember how to get there
6 This coffee doesn't taste bad.
7 Memorizing is what I am good at.
8 The news shocked us.
9 was diagnosed with lung cancer
10 My dog is running fast.
11 doesn't love her anymore
12 always exercise every morning

Lesson 1-9 1형식 동사_완전자동사

Check up!
p. 031

A 1 begins 2 happened
3 lived 4 come
5 left

Lesson 1-10 2형식 동사_불완전자동사

Check up!
p. 032

A 1 tired 2 spicy
3 writing 4 talking
5 became 6 proved
7 useful 8 true
9 come 10 chocolate, sweet

Lesson 1-11 3형식 동사_완전타동사

Check up!
p. 033

A 1 resemble like → resemble
2 doing → to do
3 to turn → turning
4 discussed about → discussed
5 wakes → wake
6 entered into → entered
7 traveling → to travel

Lesson 1-12 4형식 동사_수여동사

Check up!
p. 034~035

A 1 Mr. Kim will make a delicious cake for her.
2 The cook teaches baking cookies to me.
3 He bought a bunch of flowers for Jennifer.
4 My teacher told the story of his first love to us.
5 She gave difficult homework to me.
6 Eric got some chocolate for us.
7 I cooked a pasta salad for my father.
8 They showed their new house to us.

9 Sandra requires some information about the test of him.

10 Liam brought a cup of coffee to Angela.

B **1** I will lend Inho my car next week.

2 Jiho asked me a favor.

3 The policeman found Linda her lost daughter.

4 She offered her employees some new data.

5 I bought my son a robot.

6 The detective asked her many questions.

Lesson 1-13 5형식 동사_불완전타동사

Check up!

p. 037

A **1** to go   **2** fantastic

3 clean   **4** to solve

5 important   **6** angry

7 president   **8** Billy

9 to exist   **10** an angel

11 destroyed   **12** quiet

13 to jaywalk   **14** interesting

Practice More Ⅲ

p. 038~040

A **1** cowardly → coward

2 agreed → agreed with

3 was lead → led

4 happily → happy

5 truly → true

6 was happened → happened

7 for → to

8 quick → quickly

9 excite → exciting

10 sending → to send

11 to know → know

12 cut → to cut

13 easy → easily

14 peeling → peel

15 fool → a fool(foolish)

B **1** to stand   **2** broken

3 walk   **4** to solve

5 devastated   **6** important

7 (to) finish   **8** exhausted

9 cooperate   **10** eating

11 turn   **12** making

13 to loan   **14** closing

15 to buy

C **1** made the gloves for her son.

2 Would you mind opening the window?

3 asked a difficult question of me.

4 resembles her mother very much.

5 enjoys skating in winter.

6 lent his bicycle to Mary yesterday.

7 A cat is chasing after the dog

8 gave some cookies to his sister.

9 the movie would be a box-office failure.

10 Working late makes you tired.

11 always tell me to do my best.

중간 기말고사 예상문제

내신 최다 출제 유형

p. 041

01 ⑤   02 ①   03 ①,⑤   04 ②   05 ②

06 ②,⑤

해설

01 ① hasn't she – doesn't she, ② aren't we – shall we
③ doesn't he – does he, ④ don't they – haven't they

02 ② to cross – cross, ③ driving – drive, ④ cleaned – clean, ⑤ going to – to go

03 ① bought ~ for, ⑤ teaches ~ to

04 〈보기, ②〉 4형식 문장, ①,③,④ 3형식 문장, ⑤ 5형식 문장

05 ① What – How, ③ fooled – to fool (be sure+to부정사 ~이 확실하다), ④ nicely – nice, ⑤ How – What

06 ② will you – shall we, ⑤ did she – didn't she

p. 042~048

01 ①	02 ④	03 ②	04 ③	05 ②
06 ①	07 ②	08 ②	09 ①	10 ②
11 ⑤	12 ④	13 ③	14 ②	15 ③
16 ②	17 ④	18 ⑤	19 ②,③	20 ①,⑤
21 ③	22 ②	23 ④	24 ①	25 ⑤
26 ②	27 ③	28 ③	29 ⑤	30 ④
31 (1) ③, (2) ④, (3) ①, (4) ②		32 ②,④	33 ①,③	
34 ⑤	35 ②	36 ③,⑤	37 ②,④	

〈서술형 평가〉

38 exercise → to exercise

39 sadly → sad

40 No, I won't.

41 (1) aren't they (2) hasn't she (3) shall we

42 I wonder if she told her secret to everyone.

43 How does he think we can translate it into Korean?

44 joining

45 having

46 respect her as the best actress.

47 Can you tell me if there are flower shops

해설

01 ① 형용사 원급-비교급, ②,③,④,⑤ 동사-명사

02 ④ 동사-형용사, ①,②,③,⑤ 동사-명사

03 ② 동사-형용사, ①,③,④,⑤ 형용사-명사

04 ③ 동사-도구를 나타내는 명사, ①,②,④,⑤ 동사-사람을 나타내는 명사

05 told는 목적격보어로 to부정사를, 사역동사 let은 동사원형을 갖는다.

06 interest – interesting

07 'Which'의 선택의문문이다. 선택의문문에 대한 대답은 문제에 제시된 것 중 하나를 선택하여 대답하여야 한다.

08 부정의문문에 대답은 일반 의문문과 같다. 다만, 우리말 해석에 따라 다른 의미가 될 수 있다.
A: Isn't Sally a model? Sally는 모델이 아니야?
B: Yes, she is. 아니, 맞아. / No, she isn't. 응, 그렇지 않아.

09 take a class 수업을 듣다, take (a) prize 상을 받다

10 kind of~ ~종류, kind 친절한

11 직접의문문에서 의문사가 주어의 역할을 할 때 간접의문문에서의 문장 어순은 변하지 않는다.

12 생각이나 추측을 나타내는 'believe' 같은 동사가 주절에 있을 경우, 의문사는 문장의 맨 앞에 위치한다.

13 질문에 대한 대답으로 'with my brother'이라고 사람이 목적어로 왔으므로 누구와 함께 갔는지에 대한 질문이다 따라서 'who'가 정답이다.

14 주절은 긍정, 동사는 과거형이므로 부가의문에는 '과거형의 부정'을 나타내는 부가의문문이 온다.

15 'Why don't you ~?' ~하지 않을래? – 권유를 나타내는 표현이다.

16 감각동사의 보어 자리에는 형용사를 쓴다. sweetly → sweet

17 'hear'의 목적격보어는 동사원형 또는 현재분사가 온다. fell → fall/falling

18 'look' 뒤에는 형용사가 오지만 'look like' 뒤에는 명사가 온다.

19 ① 'find'의 목적격보어는 형용사이다. interest → interesting
④ 'advise'의 목적격보어는 to부정사이다. jog → to jog
⑤ 사역동사 'let'의 목적격보어는 동사원형을 써야 한다.
to introduce → introduce

20 ② an angry → angry, ③ busily → busy,
④ sadly → sad

21 ③ 4형식 문장, ①,②,④,⑤ 5형식 문장

22 ①,③④,⑤ 3형식 문장이다. ② 4형식 문장이다.

23 첫 번째 문장: '~에게'의 뜻으로 쓰인 전치사 to
두 번째 문장: 'ask'의 목적격보어를 이끄는 to부정사

24 4형식에서 3형식 문장으로 전환할 때 수여동사 'buy, get'에 알맞은 전치사는 'for'이다.

25 4형식에서 3형식 문장으로 전환할 때 'tell, give'에 알맞은 전치사는 'to'이다.

26 〈보기, ②〉 목적격보어, ① 목적어, ③ 주격보어, ④ 직접목적어, ⑤ 간접목적어

27 〈보기, ③〉 그리워하다, ① 지나치다, ②,④,⑤ 놓치다

28 ③ 보기의 문장은 4형식 문장으로, 3형식으로 전환할 때 필요한 전치사는 'to'이다.

29 보기의 문장은 3형식으로, 3형식에서 4형식으로 전환할 때 'ask'의 전치사인 'of'를 없애고, 직접목적어와 간접목적어의 위치를 바꿔준다.

30 감각동사 뒤에는 형용사가 와야 한다. gratefully–grateful

31 (1) 너는 그 조개들을 어떻게 얻었니? – 해변에서 주웠어.
(2) 그녀는 어디에서 시험을 봤니? – Green 초등학교에서.
(3) 그들은 점심에 무얼 먹었니? – 크림 스파게티
(4) 너는 누구를 좋아하니? – Jerry.

32 ① clean – to clean, ③ to enjoy – enjoy,
⑤ comes – to come

33 ① I – me, ③ draw – to draw

34 3형식 문장에서 'show'의 전치사는 'to', 'cook'의 전치사는 'for'이다.

35 주절은 긍정, 동사는 과거형(were)이므로 부가의문문에는 '과거형의 부정'을 나타내는 부가의문문이 온다.

36 ③ 4형식 문장 '주어+동사+간접목적어+직접목적어'
⑤ 3형식 문장 '주어+동사+직접목적어+전치사+간접목적어'

37 〈보기, ②, ④〉5형식 문장, ①,③ 3형식 문장, ⑤ 4형식 문장

〈서술형 평가〉

38 'advise'의 목적격보어로 to부정사를 써야 한다.

39 감각동사 'look' 뒤에는 형용사가 와야 한다.

40 부가의문문의 질문에 부정어가 있어 대답에 'not'이 포함된다면
'No, 주어+not'으로 답한다.

41 (1) 주절이 긍정이므로 부가의문문은 부정으로 묻는다.
(2) 주절의 동사가 완료형일 경우 완료형으로 묻는다.
(3) 'Let's' 명령문의 부가의문문은 긍정/부정에 관계없이
'shall we'를 사용한다.

42 의문사가 없는 간접의문문의 경우 'if'를 넣어준다.

43 생각을 나타내는 단어 'think'가 있을 경우, 의문사는 문장의 맨
앞으로 위치한다.

44 타동사 'deny'의 목적어로 동명사가 온다.

45 3형식의 문장에서 동사 'dislike'의 목적어로는 동명사가 온다.

46 5형식 '동사+목적어+목적격보어'의 순서로 써 준다.

47 간접의문문에 의문사가 없을 때는 그 자리에 'if'가 들어간다.

Chapter

02 동사의 시제

Lesson 2-1 현재형

p. 052

A
1 is
2 gets
3 boils
4 orders
5 enjoys
6 cries
7 travels
8 goes
9 starts
10 arrives

B
1 will snow → snows
2 leave → leaves
3 is baking → bakes
4 will arrive → arrives
5 becomes → will become
6 don't → won't
7 fix → will fix

Lesson 2-2 현재형과 현재진행형

p. 053~054

A
1 is playing
2 are dancing
3 is lying
4 is taking
5 am eating
6 are talking
7 is sleeping
8 is writing
9 is going
10 Are / studying

B
1 'm loving → love
2 is owning → owns
3 go → going
4 are hating → hate
5 is rising → rises
6 is remembering → remembers
7 are belonging → belong
8 ate(now) → am eating(X)
9 thinking → thinks
10 are understanding → understand

Lesson 2-3 과거형

p. 057~058

A
1 told – told
2 thought – thought
3 began – begun
4 mistook – mistaken
5 wound – wound
6 proved – proved (proven)
7 blew – blown
8 flew – flown
9 ate – eaten
10 brought – brought
11 left – left
12 won – won
13 rode – ridden
14 saw – seen
15 chose – chosen
16 forgot – forgotten
17 shook – shaken
18 lost – lost
19 cut – cut
20 caught – caught
21 cast – cast
22 bent – bent
23 drove – driven
24 did – done
25 fed – fed
26 showed – showed(shown)
27 tore – torn
28 bled – bled
29 bore – born
30 dug – dug
31 built – built
32 hung – hung
33 grew – grown
34 knew – known
35 felt – felt
36 hid – hidden
37 laid – laid
38 made – made
39 met – met
40 wrote – written
41 read – read
42 kept – kept

43	shot – shot
44	stood – stood
45	taught – taught
46	paid – paid
47	swept – swept
48	sold – sold
49	let – let
50	overcame – overcome

B
1	danced	2	built
3	taught	4	met
5	caught	6	born
7	thought	8	flew
9	sat	10	forgot

Lesson 2-4 과거형과 과거진행형

★Check up! p. 059

A
1	was jogging	2	was taking
3	was eating	4	was cleaning
5	was reading		

Lesson 2-5 미래형

★Check up! p. 060

A
1	arrive	2	will do
3	is going to	4	return
5	will visit	6	don't
7	is going to travel	8	will buy
9	will	10	going to play

Practice More I p. 061~062

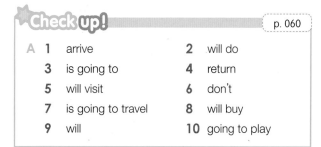

A
1	starts	2	came
3	made	4	go
5	fought	6	born
7	want	8	is leaving
9	rises	10	is

B
1	is	2	arrives
3	was taking	4	gets up
5	finishes	6	was watching

| 7 | broke out | 8 | is raining |
| 9 | equals | 10 | are / do |

C
1	be → is
2	come → comes
3	is smelling → smells
4	am thinking → think
5	will want → want
6	is belonging → belongs
7	will finish → finish
8	having → have(are having)
9	freeze → freezes

D
1	am playing the piano now.
2	wrote a novel three years ago.
3	will go to the concert with Olivia next week.
4	were preparing for the party last night.
5	is drawing a portrait for her now.
6	wash my dog every evening.
7	went hiking to enjoy the mountain.

Lesson 2-6 현재완료의 쓰임과 형태

★Check up! p. 064

A
1	Have / been	2	has forgotten
3	has lived	4	have lost
5	has studied	6	has / finished
7	has / eaten	8	has / seen
9	Has / met		

Lesson 2-7 현재완료_완료

p. 065

A 1 I have just finished my homework.
2 James has not arrived at school yet.
3 The bus has already left.
4 She has just sent me an email.
5 Has Linda eaten yet?
6 He has just finished doing the dishes.
7 They have already climbed the mountain.
8 Jeju Island has already become a famous tourist attraction.
9 Has Bread already cleaned his room?
10 She has just planted fifty sun flowers.

Lesson 2-8 현재완료_결과

p. 066

A 1 나는 내 키를 잃어버렸다.
2 Jane은 로마에 다녀왔다.
3 그녀는 이 차를 샀다.
4 나는 다리가 부러졌다.
5 아버지는 집으로 가버렸다.

B 1 has taken　　2 have washed
3 has told　　4 has forgotten
5 has gone to

Lesson 2-9 현재완료_경험

p. 067

A 1 has never been　　2 has never seen
3 Have/ever been　　4 has never eaten
5 has met once　　6 has never heard
7 have seen/before　　8 have been/twice
9 has never read

Lesson 2-10 현재완료_계속

p. 068

A 1 for　　2 since
3 for　　4 since
5 for　　6 since
7 since　　8 for
9 for　　10 since
11 for　　12 since
13 for　　14 since
15 since

Lesson 2-11 현재완료의 부정문과 의문문

p. 069

A 1 finished not → not finished
2 Do you have → Have you
3 not → X
4 Have you not → Have you / Haven't you
5 Hasn't → Have
6 not have → have not
7 ever John → John ever
8 meet → met
9 driven you → you driven
10 hasn't → haven't

Lesson 2-12 현재완료와 과거형

☆Check up!   p. 070

A
1	visited	2	has lived
3	bought	4	have/seen
5	has played	6	had
7	has taught	8	rang
9	has/gone	10	cleaned

Lesson 2-13 과거완료

☆Check up!   p. 071

A
1	had lost	2	had ended
3	had lived	4	had gotten
5	had met	6	had gone
7	had bought	8	had made
9	had forgotten	10	had/gone
11	had finished	12	had waited

Practice More Ⅱ   p. 072~074

A
1	visited	2	bought
3	has lost	4	ran
5	haven't eaten	6	was
7	have lived	8	finished
9	went	10	have heard

B
1 for → since
2 have → has
3 since → for
4 have seen → saw
5 had → X
6 studied → has studied
7 have lost → lost
8 never heard → have never heard
9 has rained → rained
10 has finished → finished
11 already has → has already
12 Has he been → Was he
13 going → gone

C
1 Have you ever lived
2 has been broken
3 has gone to Japan

4 Have you done
5 did you buy
6 went to school
7 has never seen
8 have had the TV since 2001
9 has known
10 has used/for seven years
11 have studied/for ten years
12 has painted/for five hours
13 have used
14 has been angry

D
1 She has had the bag for three years.
2 They have stayed at my grandmother's house since Thursday.
3 They have worked here for two months.
4 My mom has had the dress since last year.
5 I have taught students for thirty years.
6 Yujin has played soccer since 2011.
7 He has been friends with Linda since last May.
8 My dad has had the shirt for twenty years.
9 Tim has lived in Gwangju for two years.
10 James has left Korea.

중간 기말고사 예상문제

내신 최다 출제 유형   p. 075

01 ⑤   02 ③   03 ④   04 ⓐ fell, ⓑ was
05 the escalator   06 ⑤   07 ③

해설

01 'when'은 구체적인 과거시점을 나타내므로 단순 과거형을 사용하고, 'for'는 현재완료 계속적 용법으로 현재완료형을 사용한다.

02 〈보기, ③〉 현재완료 – 계속, ①,② 현재완료 – 경험, ④ 현재완료 – 결과, ⑤ 현재완료 – 완료

03 과거의 경험을 묻는 현재완료 의문문: Have+주어+과거분사~?
'yesterday'라는 확실한 과거의 시점: 과거형

04 fall – fell – fallen, is – was – been

05 앞에 나온 단어의 반복을 피하기 위해 'it'을 사용했다.

06　① is hating – hates

　② am not believing – don't believe

　③ knows – knew, ④ are liking – like

07　'last year'는 확실한 과거 시점이기 때문에 현재완료에 쓸 수 없다. hasn't worked – didn't work

p. 076~081

01 ③	02 ④	03 ⑤	04 ②	05 ③
06 ②	07 ⑤	08 ③	09 ③	10 ③
11 ③	12 ④	13 ②	14 ③	15 ④
16 ①,③	17 ②,⑤	18 ①,③	19 ③,④	20 ②
21 ⑤	22 ③	23 ③	24 ④	25 ①
26 ④	27 ③,④	28 ③	29 ③	30 ①,④

〈서술형 평가〉

31　are going to

32　finished, went

33　written

34　Have you / heard

35　was watching

36　Danny has visited the orphanage for a month.

37　They have been in Thailand for three weeks.

38　Judy saw her friends at the concert a month ago.

39　They have played soccer for ten years.

40　has broken

41　has lived / for two years

42　Ron lived in London five years ago.

　　He moved to Korea three years ago.

　　He has lived in Korea for three years.

해설

01　send – sent – sent

02　do – did – done

03　come – came – come

04　write – wrote – written

05　enjoy – enjoyed – enjoyed

06　already: '이미, 벌써' 돈을 다 써버렸다는 의미를 나타내므로 과거분사형이 나와야 한다.

07　'ever'는 현재완료의 경험을 나타낼 때 함께 쓰이는 표현으로 앞의 단어는 'have'가 알맞다.

08　어떤 장소에 다녀왔다는 의미의 현재완료형은 'gone'을 쓰지 않고 'been'을 써 준다.

　→ 'gone'을 쓰면 그 장소에서 돌아오지 않은 것을 뜻한다.

09　〈보기, ③〉 계속적 용법. ①,② 경험, ④,⑤ 결과

10　〈보기, ③〉 경험, ①,⑤ 계속, ② 완료 ④ 결과

11　became → become

12　for → since

13　has+과거분사: has been

14　'Have you heard~?' '~에 대해 들어봤니?'

15　현재완료의 강한 부정을 나타낼 경우 'have never+과거분사'

16　② have took – have taken, ④ yesterday – X,

　⑤ has watch – watched

17　① have gone – went, ③ have you taught – did you teach, ④ have been – were

18　① hear → heard, ③ have visited → visited

19　③ since → for, ④ saw → seen

20　〈보기, ②〉 현재완료 경험, ① 현재완료 결과, ③ 현재완료 완료, ④,⑤ 현재완료 계속

21　be going to는 미래형을 나타낸다.

22　Have you~?에 대한 대답은 Yes, I have. / No, I haven't.로 해야 한다.

23　be going to+장소: ~에 가고 있는 중이다 – 현재진행형 문장.

24　과거의 일이 현재까지 이어져온다. 현재완료의 계속적 용법 'have+과거분사'

25　과거 시점부터 쭉 이어져 오는 일: 현재완료 have+과거분사

26　과거 시점부터 쭉 이어져 오는 일: 현재완료 have+과거분사

27　③ try → tried, ④ grow and grow → grew and grew

28　'~해본 적 있니?'는 과거의 경험을 묻는 표현이다. 'have+과거분사'

29　미래를 표현하는 방법으로 'will/be going to'를 사용하며, 모두 뒤에 동사원형이 온다.

30　'every+요일/on+요일+-s: 매 ~요일마다 (on 뒤에 's'를 붙이는 것을 잊어서는 안 된다.)

〈서술형 평가〉

31　미래형의 조동사 will 대신에 be going to를 대신하여 쓸 수 있다.

32　첫 번째 문장은 현재완료형으로 'have+과거분사'의 형태를 사용한다.

　두 번째 문장은 단순 과거형이므로 go의 과거형인 went를 써 준다.

33　현재완료의 완료 형태이므로 'have+과거분사'를 사용한다. write의 과거분사형은 written이다.

34　have+과거분사: '듣다'의 과거분사형은 heard이다.

35　'~하고 있던 중이었다'는 과거진행형이다.

36　한 달 전에 행했던 일이 지금까지 이어져 오고 있다. 현재완료의 계속적 용법이며, 'have+과거분사+for'의 순서에 맞춰 문장을 완성한다.

37　3주 전에 태국으로 갔다가 오늘 왔다고 했으니 3주 동안 그곳에 머물렀던 것을 알 수 있다.

38 단순 과거시제이다.

39 과거부터 해온 일이 현재까지 이어져오고 있는 것이므로 현재완료의 계속적 용법이다. 주어＋have＋과거분사의 순서로 문장을 완성한다.

40 어제부터 오늘까지 깨진 창문이 수리되지 않은 상태로 이어져오고 있다. have／has＋과거분사: break의 과거분사형은 broken이다.

41 2년 전 미국에서 살고 있는 가족이 현재에도 살고 있는 깃으로 '현재완료의 계속'인 것을 알 수 있다.

42 'Ron이 5년 전 런던에서 살았다'와 '3년 전에 한국으로 이사를 왔다'는 과거형을 사용한다.
마지막 문장에서 그 후로 지금까지 한국에 살고 있다는 것을 의미하므로 현재완료형을 써준다.

Chapter

03 조동사

Lesson 3-1 조동사의 종류

p. 086

A 1 will lose weight
2 may go to America for the fashion show
3 Can/keep a diary
4 must get off
5 should go to bed early
6 Would/a favor
7 may not like
8 must be hasty
9 will go to Canada
10 must wash your hands

Lesson 3-2 would / would like (to)

p. 087

A 1 would like
2 Would you like
3 would like to
4 Would you like to
5 would like to
6 Would
7 to play

Lesson 3-3 can (1)

p. 088

A 1 is able to sing
2 was able to solve
3 couldn't stop
4 were able to win
5 could/drive
6 can swim
7 can't go
8 was not able to read

Lesson 3-4 can (2)

p. 089

A 1 took → take
2 making → make
3 coming → come
4 being → be
5 can passed → could pass
6 to learn → learn
7 teaches → teach

Lesson 3-5 be able to

p. 091

A 1 He can speak English well.
2 We will be able to pick you up at the airport tomorrow.
3 She isn't able to drink more than three cups of coffee
4 Are they able to arrive on time?
5 She will be able to become a doctor
6 Is Andy able to teach himself Chinese?
7 She was not able to dance in front of the audience a few years ago.
8 I am still not able to ride a bike.
9 He won't be able to see her again.
10 They weren't able to go there.

Lesson 3-6 will / be going to

p. 092~093

A 1 am going to read
   2 are not going to go
   3 will knit
   4 Would/take pictures
   5 Will/study
   6 will eat
   7 is going to go
   8 Would/make
   9 am going to buy
   10 are going to eat
   11 are going to prepare
   12 Would/turn down the volume

Practice More I

p. 094~096

A 1 is able to fix   2 can't tell
   3 will travel   4 were able to stay
   5 is going to   6 is able to speak
   7 am going to visit   8 are not able to fly
   9 Are/going to   10 Are/able to
   11 Can   12 is going to
   13 won't   14 were not able to go

B 1 makes → make
   2 go → going
   3 bought → buy
   4 to raise → like to raise
   5 reading → read
   6 believe you → you believe
   7 able not → not able
   8 flying → fly
   9 Could → Would
   10 participated → to participate
   11 not will → will not
   12 enjoyed → enjoy
   13 going not → not going
   14 being → is

C 1 They are going to go to the soccer stadium.
   2 would like to meet you

   3 is not going to see
   4 will eat some sandwiches
   5 was going to jog
   6 Would you mind if I turn on
   7 He could(was able to) run faster
   8 Can the rumor be true?
   9 Daniel can (is able to) assemble the computer alone.
   10 we could not (couldn't) win the game

Lesson 3-7 may / migh

p. 98

A 1 허락   2 추측
   3 추측   4 허락
   5 추측   6 추측
   7 허락   8 추측
   9 허락   10 추측

Lesson 3-8 may have+과거분사 / might be

p. 99

A 1 may have missed
   2 may not have lied
   3 may have cried
   4 might be a chef.
   5 may have watched
   6 might not be an actor
   7 might not have passed the exam

Lesson 3-9 have to / must

A 1 의무　　　2 추측
　3 의무　　　4 추측
　5 의무　　　6 의무
　7 추측　　　8 의무

B 1 You don't have to get up early tomorrow.
　2 Do/have to wear
　3 didn't have to take the plane
　4 must not hit others
　5 Does/have to go to the party
　6 must not cheat
　7 must follow the rule of the game
　8 must be quiet

Lesson 3-10 should/had better

A 1 had better take a rest
　2 should do your best
　3 should read three books by next week
　4 had better go home early
　5 had better take a taxi
　6 should not put off our work
　7 should not go outside
　8 should stop watching TV
　9 had better cook five dishes
　10 should help the poor

B 1 has → had
　2 to get → get
　3 picking → pick
　4 not better → better not
　5 not should → should not
　6 have → had
　7 paying → pay
　8 eat better not → better not eat
　9 setting → set
　10 to take → take

Lesson 3-11 ought to

A 1 ought not to leave his brother alone at home
　2 ought not to be exposed to violent things
　3 ought to fix your broken car
　4 People ought not to drink and drive
　5 ought to be on time for the appointment
　6 ought not to take a picture here
　7 ought to write a book report

Lesson 3-12 would / used to

A 1 [과거의 상태]　　2 [과거의 습관]
　3 [과거의 상태]　　4 [과거의 습관]
　5 [과거의 상태]　　6 [과거의 상태]
　7 [과거의 습관]

B 1 used to　　　2 used to
　3 would　　　4 used to
　5 used to　　　6 would
　7 used to　　　8 would
　9 used to　　　10 would

Lesson 3-13 조동사 do

A 1 강조　　　2 대동사
　3 강조　　　4 대동사
　5 강조

B 1 did　　　2 Does
　3 do　　　4 does
　5 did　　　6 Do
　7 didn't　　　8 did

Practice More II

p. 108~110

A
1 can
2 has to
3 ought to
4 must
5 don't have to
6 Shall
7 should
8 must not
9 should not
10 Shall we

B
1 read → to read
2 starting → start
3 has to → have to
4 has to not → doesn't have to
5 be fix → fix
6 has to → had to
7 not better → better not
8 hitting → hit
9 oughts → ought
10 has → have

C
1 Would
2 have to
3 May
4 might
5 can/are going to
6 should
7 Can
8 don't have to
9 Can
10 May

D
1 I had better go shopping with Lina.
2 He must be Jim's English teacher.
3 Would you introduce yourself?
4 Returning home might take more than three weeks.
5 I used to have a fountain in the garden in my house.
6 Would you like to have dinner with us?
7 John would be a soccer player when he was young.

중간 기말고사 **예상문제**

내신 최다 출제 유형

p. 111

01 ③ 02 ② 03 ② 04 ① 05 ④
06 ⑤ 07 ④

해설
01 drinks – drink
02 ① doesn't has – doesn't have, ③ will buys – will buy
④ need – needs, ⑤ cann't – can't
03 ① pops – pop, ③ drinking – drink, ④ uses – use,
⑤ not may – may not
04 does – do
05 ④ 일반동사 do: ~하다, ①,②,③,⑤ 동사를 강조하기 위한 조동사 do
06 〈보기, ⑤〉 ~인 것이 틀림없다 – 강한 추측의 의미
①,④ ~해서는 안 돼 – 강한 금지, ②,③ ~해야만 한다 – 의무
07 ① a coffee – some coffee, ② drank – drink,
③ can able to – can (is able to), ⑤ taking – take

p. 112~117

01 ④ 02 ⑤ 03 ② 04 ③ 05 ①
06 ③ 07 ③ 08 ① 09 ⑤ 10 ②,④
11 ③ 12 ② 13 ④ 14 ③ 15 ④
16 ④ 17 ① 18 ①,③ 19 ③,④ 20 ②
21 ② 22 ① 23 ① 24 ① 25 ④
26 ③ 27 ③ 28 ④ 29 ⑤ 30 ③

〈서술형 평가〉
31 must be
32 used to go camping
33 don't have to (don't need to, need not)
34 are able to
35 shopping on the Internet
36 may (might)
37 had better find something interesting to do
38 You should wash your hands first
39 I like dogs.
40 need not
41 have to
42 We had better not go out tonight.
43 You must finish your homework before you read comic books.

01 can = may ～해도 될까요?

02 could not = was not able to ～할 수 없었다

03 must = should ～해야만 한다

04 강한 금지 ～하면 안 돼: must not

05 강한 추측 must be

06 〈보기, ③〉 ～임에 틀림없다

07 〈보기, ③〉 동사를 강조하는 'do'

08 〈보기, ②,③,④,⑤〉 ～해야 한다, ① ～임에 틀림없다

09 ① She'd not better → She'd better not, ② to ask → ask
   ③ to get → get, ④ washing → wash

10 ② didn't nothing → did nothing, ④ don't know →
   doesn't know (didn't know)

11 should not ～하지 않는 것이 낫다 '잠을 잘 잘 수 없기 때문에
   너무 많은 커피를 마시지 마라'라는 금지의 표현이다.

12 단순 현재형 문장이다.

13 must not ～하면 안 돼
   '빨간 불일 때 길을 건너서는 안 된다'라는 강한 금지의 표현이다.

14 '표정이 좋아 보이지 않는다'라는 앞의 내용을 뒷받침할 문장을
   찾는다.

15 need not ～할 필요가 없다
   '버스를 놓치지 않으려면 일찍 잠자리에 들어야만 한다'라는 의
   무를 나타내는 문장이므로 '불필요'를 뜻하는 'need not'은 빈칸
   에 알맞지 않다.

16 〈보기, ①,②,③,⑤〉 ～할지도 모른다, ④ ～해도 좋다

17 can 할 수 있다 = be able to

18 ①,③ would – used to 과거의 규칙적인 습관이나 상태를 나
   타낼 때는 used to를 사용한다.

19 ③ Yes, you can → Yes, you may. ④ No, you may. →
   No, you may not.

20 다음 문장에 '다른 이들도 줄을 섰으니 여기에 서면 안 된다'라는
   표현을 찾는다.

21 대동사 did는 앞의 내용을 포함하고 있다. 동사 'did'의 목적어
   를 찾는다.

22 ① ～하면 안 돼: must not

23 첫 번째 문장은 '비가 올 것 같으니 우산을 가져가는 것이
   좋겠다'라는 충고의 내용이다.
   두 번째 문장은 과거형이므로 must의 과거형인 had to를
   사용하는 것이 알맞다.

24 'I don't know exactly(정확히는 몰라)'라는 말과 연결했을 때,
   추측을 나타내는 문장이다.

25 첫 번째 문장: 너는 운전을 그렇게 빨리 하면 안 돼.
   두 번째 문장: 너는 운전을 그렇게 빨리 할 필요가 없다

26 〈보기, ③〉 ～해도 된다(될까요), ①,②,④,⑤ ～할 수 있다

27 지켜야 하는 의무를 표현할 때 'have to'를 사용한다.

28 '～하면 안 돼'의 강한 금지는 'must not'을 사용한다.

29 과거에는 했던 일이나 지금은 하지 않은 일에 대해서 표현할 때
   'used to'를 사용한다.

30 had better not ～하지 않을 것이 좋겠다

〈서술형 평가〉

31 be sure (that) '～을 확신하다'의 의미로 강한 추측을 나타낸다.

32 과거에는 했지만 현재는 하지 않은 것을 표현할 때 used to를
   사용한다.

33 'but'은 앞의 말에 대한 반대를 뜻하므로, 앞 문장이 무엇인가를
   사기 위해 밖으로 나갔다면 지금은 그럴 필요가 없다는 것을 뜻
   하는 말이 온다.

34 'can' ～할 수 있다는 의미로 쓰였다(= be able to)

35 'It'은 앞 문장에 있는 목적어의 반복을 피하기 위해 사용되었다.

36 '～할지도 모른다'라는 추측의 의미를 가지고 있는 단어는 'may'
   이다.

37 'had better'는 '～하면 좋겠다'라는 권유의 의미다.

38 '집에 돌아오면 제일 먼저 손을 씻어야 한다'라는 약한 강조의 의
   미를 갖고 있다.

39 '개를 좋아하지 않았으나 어린 여동생으로 인해 지금은 그렇다'
   라는 것을 말하고 있다. '그렇다'는 것은 문맥상 개들을 좋아한다
   는 것으로 이해할 수 있다.

40 don't have to (～할 필요가 없다) → don't need to 또는
   need not으로 바꿔 쓸 수 있다.

41 강조를 뜻하는 must와 같은 뜻으로는 have to를 사용할 수 있다.

42 had better not ～하지 않는 것이 낫겠다

43 must ～해야만 한다, before ～전에

Chapter

04 명사, 관사와 대명사

Lesson 4-1 명사의 종류

Check up!

p. 121~122

A
1 cups
2 bread
3 painters
4 is
5 is
6 people
7 likes
8 baby
9 salt
10 is

B
1 are → is
2 papers → paper
3 fishes → fish
4 are → is
5 person → people
6 were → was
7 live → lives
8 much → many
9 is → are
10 many → much

Lesson 4-2 명사의 복수형

Check up!

p. 124

A
1 man
2 tomatoes
3 pictures
4 foxes
5 boy
6 companies
7 mice
8 toys
9 leaves

B
1 monkeies → monkeys
2 child → children
3 photoes → photos
4 person → people
5 teeths → teeth
6 knifes → knives
7 cup → cups
8 gooses → geese
9 potatos → potatoes

Lesson 4-3 관사의 쓰임

Check up!

p. 126

A
1 an
2 the
3 a
4 The
5 an
6 the
7 an
8 Thc
9 a
10 The

B
1 the her → her
2 the → X
3 A → The
4 the bus → bus
5 a → the
6 a → X
7 church → the church
8 a → the
9 a → X
10 An → The

Lesson 4-4 셀 수 없는 명사의 양 표현

Check up!

p. 128

A
1 a pound of
2 two cups of
3 bowls
4 bottle
5 slices
6 pounds of
7 a spoonful of
8 a sheet of
9 a bar of

B
1 coffees → coffee
2 bottle → bottles
3 cup → bowl
4 sheets → pieces
5 spoonfuls → spoonful
6 pounds → bars
7 bunches → glasses (bottles)
8 bars → bottles (glasses)

Lesson 4-5 주의해야 할 명사의 단수/복수

p. 129

A

1	is	2	glasses
3	fish	4	think
5	cattle	6	is
7	is	8	is
9	pants	10	gloves

Lesson 4-6 명사의 소유격

p. 131

A
1. Sam's white cat
2. Mira's English book
3. butterfly's wings
4. the owner of this house
5. Helen's beautiful smile
6. the dog's black tail
7. the top of the bottle
8. the women's bathroom
9. yesterday's weather
10. the shape of the ball

B
1. daughter → daughter's
2. parents's → parents'
3. test's result → test result
4. The blanket of Tim → Tim's blanket
5. The news of today → Today's news
6. Dickens's → Dickens'
7. a → X
8. Poems of Kate → Kate's poems
9. friends's → friends'

Lesson 4-7 명사의 동격

p. 132

A

1	that	2	, / ,
3	of	4	that
5	of	6	that
7	,	8	of

Practice More I

p. 133~135

A

1	companies	2	children
3	teeth	4	deer
5	cities	6	leaves
7	mice	8	oxen
9	geese	10	men

B

1	are	2	the flute
3	bread	4	were
5	airplane	6	a
7	children's smile	8	has
9	the school	10	meters

C

1	the	2	X
3	a	4	X
5	an	6	the
7	's	8	The / X
9	's	10	the

D
1. pieces of cake
2. bars of chocolate
3. loaf of bread
4. bottles(glasses, cartons) of milk
5. bowls of soup
6. pound(loaf) of meat
7. spoonful of salt / slices(pieces) of cheese
8. sheets(pieces) of paper
9. bars of soap

E

1	many → much	2	deers → deer
3	Toms' → Tom's	4	moneys → money
5	cookie → cookies	6	fishes → fish
7	this pant → these pants	8	a → the
9	economy → economics		
10	womans → women		

11 the → X

12 heros → heroes

F **1** grandparents'(house).

2 Hellen's dress and Nami's dress

3 bird's wings

4 Physics is

5 three glasses of ice water

6 five spoonfuls of sugar

Lesson 4-8 대명사의 종류

Check up! p. 138

A	1	his	2	Both
	3	Our	4	her
	5	myself	6	yours
	7	Which	8	Either
	9	What	10	who

B	1	I → me	2	of she → of herself
	3	nor → or	4	him → his
	5	It's → Its	6	ours → ourselves
	7	some → any	8	she → herself
	9	herself → himself	10	There → Those

Lesson 4-9 재귀대명사

Check up! p. 140

A	1	X	2	himself
	3	X	4	himself
	5	X	6	herself
	7	themselves	8	X
	9	X	10	yourself
B	1	herself	2	myself
	3	himself	4	itself
	5	themselves	6	yourself
	7	herself	8	yourself
	9	herself	10	yourself

Lesson 4-10 지시대명사

Check up! p. 142

A	1	It	2	These
	3	who	4	this
	5	that	6	This
	7	These	8	Those
	9	that	10	They

B **1** That vase was broken by Ted.

2 That guy is handsome.

3 This is my favorite annimated movie, 'Magic Kaito.'

4 This girl is my friend, Linda.

5 Look at those cute babies!

6 The length of a winter night is longer than that of a summer night.

7 They are wearing school uniforms.

Lesson 4-11 의문대명사

Check up! p. 144

A	1	Who	2	What
	3	Whose	4	whom
	5	Who	6	What
	7	Which	8	Whom
	9	Whose	10	Which

B **1** Which flavor do they want?

2 Which city do you want to visit, London or Manchester?

3 What patterns does she like?

4 Who is he talking with?

5 Whose picture is more beautiful?

Lesson 4-12 'it'의 여러 가지 쓰임

p. 146

A
1 that → it
2 This → It
3 What → Which
4 Which → What
5 that → it
6 are → was
7 that's → it's
8 them → it

B
1 It is certain that she will come back in winter.
2 It is going to rain next week.
3 made it possible to achieve our goal
4 It was the bag that I bought last week.
5 What classes does Jenny have this afternoon?

Practice More Ⅱ

p. 147~148

A
1 our → their
2 your → yourself
3 This → It
4 herself → her
5 it → itself
6 That → Those
7 these → it
8 you → yourself
9 Which → Whose

B
1 yourself
2 both
3 Some
4 they
5 one
6 her
7 mine
8 her
9 our

C
1 yourself
2 it
3 herself
4 herself
5 That
6 this
7 It

D
1 couldn't fix the car by herself.
2 It was hard for her to watch the movie all night.
3 They were proud of themselves.
4 Those boxes are not mine.
5 It is hot and humid in paris.
6 I don't like the shirt, but my daughter likes it.

7 It was a streetlamp that I saw last night.
8 John's help made it possible for us to hold the seminar successfully.

Lesson 4-13 부정대명사_one / some / any

p. 151

A
1 it
2 some
3 some
4 one
5 Some
6 any
7 Some
8 anything
9 One
10 one

B
1 anyone
2 something
3 Anyone
4 something
5 anything
6 anyone
7 Something

Lesson 4-14 부정대명사_another / other (1)

p. 152

A
1 another
2 another
3 other
4 the other
5 other
6 others
7 other
8 another
9 others
10 others
11 the other

Lesson 4-15 부정대명사_another / other (2)

★ Check up!

p. 154

A
1	the others	2	others
3	the other	4	Some
5	other	6	the other
7	others	8	the others
9	another / the others		

B
1 three / one / another / the other
2 One / and / the other
3 One / so / the others

Lesson 4-16 부정대명사_both / all

★ Check up!

p. 156

A
1	All	2	is
3	both	4	get
5	are	6	All of
7	Not all	8	is
9	Both	10	All

B
1	but → and	2	are → is
3	were → was	4	is → are
5	was → were	6	both → both of
7	or → and	8	of food → of the food
9	gets → get	10	All not → Not all

Lesson 4-17 부정대명사_each / every

★ Check up!

p. 157

A
1	Each of	2	each of
3	Every	4	Not everyone
5	Each	6	was
7	actors	8	every
9	buys	10	student

Lesson 4-18 부정대명사_either / neither

★ Check up!

p. 159

A
1	have	2	or
3	eat	4	either
5	either	6	nor
7	was	8	make
9	nor	10	is

B
1	Either / or	2	neither can
3	doesn't like / either	4	Neither / nor
5	either of them	6	either of

Practice More Ⅲ

p. 160~162

A
1 it → one
2 questions → question
3 other → the other
4 movie → movies
5 sweet anything → anything sweet
6 are → is
7 any → some
8 girl → girls
9 are → is
10 nothing → anything
11 are → is
12 one → it
13 some → any

B
1	anything	2	One / the other
3	Some	4	any
5	another	6	Some / other
7	each	8	Every
9	Neither	10	something
11	neither	12	something
13	Both	14	one
15	it		

C
1	ones	2	were
3	are	4	other
5	Both	6	or
7	will my sister	8	nothing

D
1 Neither Tim nor James has arrived yet.

2 I can win either of the two.

3 Neither of Sam's stories was amazing.

4 Some are jogging and others are playing badminton.

5 She doesn't have any problems these days.

6 I want to know what other people think.

7 I lost my bike on the way home, so I should buy new one.

중간 기말고사 **예상문제**

내신 **최다 출제** 유형   p. 163

01 ③   02 ⑤   03 ②   04 ③   05 ⑤

해설

01 all of+복수명사, all+복수명사

02 〈보기, ①,②,③,④〉 강조용법으로 쓰였다.
⑤ 동사의 목적어 역할을 하는 재귀용법으로 쓰였다.

03 대상이 셋일 때 'one~, another..., the other−'
(하나는 ~이고, 다른 하나는 ...이고, 나머지 하나는−)이라고
표현한다.

04 주어를 강조하는 강조적용법의 재귀대명사이다. 강조용법의 재
귀대명사는 생략이 가능하다.

05 two pairs of jeans

p. 164~169

01 ②	02 ④	03 ③	04 ③	05 ②
06 ③	07 ④	08 ③	09 ②	10 ⑤
11 ①	12 ②	13 ④	14 ①	15 ③
16 ④	17 ①	18 ③	19 ④	20 ②
21 ③	22 ⑤	23 ①	24 ③,⑤	25 ①,②
26 ⑤	27 ②	28 ③	29 ②,④	30 ④
31 ③	32 ②	33 ④	34 ③	

〈서술형 평가〉

35 childs → children

36 student → students

37 (1) glasses of, (2) cup of, (3) pairs of

38 (1) Which, (2) Whose

39 myself

40 whom / 누구와 함께 그를 위해 무엇을 할지 의논해야 할까?

41 Which / 오늘 밤 빨간색과 분홍색 중 넌 어떤 드레스를 입을 거야?

42 (비인칭 주어 it) It's Wednesday.

43 (강조적 용법) We have to finish them ourselves this time.

44 He put in a spoonful of salt and two spoonfuls of sugar.

45 There is no food of eating full with him.

해설

01 ① hero – heroes, ③ roof – roofs, ④ tomato – tomatoes, ⑤ piano – pianos

02 ① kangaroo – kangaroos, ② dish – dishes, ③ city – cities, ⑤ leaf – leaves

03 do one's best 최선을 다하다

04 ① benchs – benches, ② mouses – mice ④ monkies – monkeys, ⑤ pigges – pigs

05 ② 사물을 가리키는 it ①,③,④,⑤ 비인칭 주어 it

06 〈보기, ③〉 재귀적 용법, ①,②,④,⑤ 강조적 용법

07 〈보기, ④〉 비인칭 주어 it, ①,②,③,⑤ 사물을 가리키는 it

08 a pairs – a pair

09 have – has

10 That is Kate's watch.

11 ② She has three cats. ③ My uncle is very tall. ④ Is that your bag? ⑤ Can you play the flute?

12 ① Is Jinsu sad? ③ Today is the first day of school. ④ She looked very smart. ⑤ Our teacher was a homeroom teacher.

13 ① peppers – pepper, ② a bottles – a bottle, ③ meats – meat, ⑤ coffees – coffee

14 첫 번째 문장: 'to drink' 마실, 두 번째 문장: 'to learn' 배울

15 • what kind of dress do you want to buy?
• what do you think of Mr. Brown?

16 ④ 강조적 용법의 재귀대명사는 생략이 가능하다. ①,②,③,⑤ 재귀적용법

17 can 뒤에는 동사 원형이 온다.

18 noisy – noise

19 most of 대부분의, some of 몇몇의

20 one~ the other... (둘 중에) 하나는 ~이고, 다른 하나는...

21 one~, another... the other− (셋 중에) 하나는 ~이고, 다른 하나는 ...이고, 나머지 하나는 −

22 〈보기, ⑤〉 동격, ①,④ 지시대명사, ② 관계대명사, ③ 명사절을 이끄는 접속사

23 〈보기, ①〉 가주어 it, ②,④,⑤ 비인칭 주어 it,
　　③ 사물을 가리키는 주어 it

24 ③ is – are, ⑤ have – has

25 ③ this – that, ④ These – This, ⑤ those – these

26 ⑤ 'news'와 'they won a car race'는 동격이며,
　　이를 표현하기 위해 'that'을 사용하였다.

27 ② either: 둘 중 하나는, 'either of+복수명사+단수동사'

28 유일한 것을 나타낼 때 'the'를 붙인다.

29 ① were – was (단수취급) ③ didn't – did (neither 자체가
　　부정의 뜻을 가짐), ⑤ pictures – picture (every+단수명사)

30 'Not+every+단수명사' 모든 단수명사가 ～하는 것은 아니다
　　→ 부분부정

31 for oneself 혼자 힘으로

32 ① his → he, ③ her's → her, ④ does → do,
　　⑤ herself → her

33 ones → one

34 ③ 종족의 대표를 표현 ①,②,④,⑤ '하나의' 의미

〈서술형 평가〉

35 'child'의 복수형은 'children'이다.

36 one of+복수명사

37 셀 수 없는 명사를 숫자로 표현할 때는 수량을 나타내는 단위에
　　'-s/-es'를 붙여 복수를 표현한다.

38 (1) 어느 컴퓨터가 더 좋으니? (2) 나는 이 보고가 마음에 들어.
　　누구의 생각이지?

39 재귀적용법, 강조적용법

40 전치사 뒤에 의문대명사의 목적격을 쓴다.

41 선택의문문에는 'which'를 사용한다.

42 '비인칭 주어 it'의 쓰임: 날짜, 요일, 날씨, 명암, 시간, 거리 등
　　ex) • It is snowing now.
　　　　• It's October 31st.
　　　　• It takes an hour by bus.
　　　　• It's so dark.
　　　　• It's ten fifty.

43 생략이 가능한 조건의 재귀대명사를 생각하며 문장을
　　만들어 본다.
　　ex) • I don't blame myself.
　　　　• She herself usually cooks for her sister.
　　　　• They are watering the garden themselves.

44 셀 수 없는 명사의 수량의 단위 표현에 '-s/-es'를 붙여준다.

45 'There is no food (음식이 없다)' + of + 'eating full (배불리 먹을)'
　　→ 'of' 이하와 'food'는 동격이다.

Chapter 05 수동태

Lesson 5-1 수동태 문장 만들기

p. 174

A 1 was destroyed   2 invented
  3 was caught   4 were invited
  5 were caused   6 was released
  7 were made   8 danced
  9 was fixed   10 was directed

B 1 Her dog was washed by Susan.
  2 The book was written by Harry.
  3 The cave was found by her in 1989.
  4 Some pants and glasses are bought by Emma.
  5 The flower festival is held by Mr. Han every year.
  6 The picture was hung on the wall by me.
  7 Helen was invited by him to his graduation party.
  8 A letter is delivered by the postman.

Lesson 5-2 동명사 / 진행형의 수동태

p. 175

A 1 being bitten   2 being taken
  3 being invited   4 being ordered
  5 being treated

B 1 is being fixed   2 is being developed
  3 is being prepared   4 is being made
  5 is being exchanged   6 is being cleaned

Lesson 5-3 조동사 / to부정사의 수동태

p. 176~177

A 1 is going to be made
  2 to be blamed
  3 is expected to be seen
  4 are not allowed to take
  5 are ordered to follow
  6 to be burned
  7 has to be turned in
  8 was asked to protect
  9 were told to attend

B 1 The promise should not be forgotten by Alex.
  2 Her room has to be cleaned by Helen.
  3 The picture may be painted by him.
  4 The students should be praised by the teacher.
  5 Our house may be destroyed by the storm.
  6 Her book will be lent to me by Jane.
  7 The play will be performed by the actors.
  8 A new version of design has to be developed by the organization.
  9 The statue should not be touched by them.
  10 Other people's stuff must not be stolen.

Lesson 5-4 완료형의 수동태

p. 178~179

A 1 carried   2 opened
  3 have not been   4 has been burned
  5 been accpeted

B 1 has been used   2 had been cured
  3 have been helped   4 had been done
  5 have seriously polluted 6 has postponed
  7 had been thrown   8 has been built
  9 had not been bought 10 had not been given

Lesson 5-5 4형식 문장의 수동태

A 1 Some sandwiches are made for me by mommy.
2 A new bag was bought for me by Jeff.
3 A new shirt was sent to him by Karen.
4 Chinese is taught to us by Mr. Wang.

B 1 → An email is sent to Mina by him.
2 → I was shown his new movie by John.
→ His new movie was shown to me by John.
3 → A delicious pasta was cooked for me on our anniversary by Anna.
4 → She wasn't given a new shirt by Tim.
→ A new shirt wasn't given to her by Tim.
5 → Hana was taught how to make cookies by Mr. Smith.
→ How to make cookies was taught to Hana by Mr. Smith.
6 → I was told Sally's favorite movie by mom.
→ Sally's favorite movie was told to me by mom.
7 → Blue shoes were bought for his girlfriend yesterday by Sam.
8 → The students' answer sheets weren't returned by their teacher.
→ The answer sheets weren't returned to the students by their teacher.
9 → The rooms were lent to his friends by Thomas.
10 → The key wasn't brought to me by that boy.

Lesson 5-6 5형식 문장의 수동태

A 1 was advised   2 was named
3 was made   4 was taught

B 1 The dog was seen running down the street by me.
2 They were expected to pass the exam by their teacher.
3 Her clothes are always kept cleaned by Sue.
4 Their baby was called Jake by them.
5 I was allowed to go hiking with my friends by father.
6 Tina is thought a beautiful girl by people.
7 James was elected a chief coach by the team.
8 The medicine was found useless by me.
9 She was warned not to put anything on the table by them.
10 I was made to get a good grade by my teacher.

A 1 was disappeared → disappeared
2 is belonged → belongs
3 be → being
4 leave → left
5 collected → is collected (was collected)
6 be using → being used
7 blame → be blamed
8 being → be
9 was happened → happened
10 teaching → taught
11 publishing → published
12 visited → is visited
13 readed → read
14 using → used
15 elected → was elected

B 1 to   2 to
3 for   4 of
5 for   6 to
7 for

C 1 → My dogs were fed a delicious meal.
      → A delicious meal was fed to my dogs.
   2 → His baby was taken care of by him.
   3 → She was given a beautiful brooch.
      → A beautiful brooch was given to her.
   4 → John was heard singing(to sing) a song with his brother by me.
   5 → We were made to be quiet by the teacher.
   6 → The data was used to solve the problem by the researchers.
   7 → Jina is encouraged to become a musician by her father.
   8 → I was given the letter on our wedding anniversary by Linda.
      → The letter was given to me on our wedding anniversary by Linda.
   9 → His white shirt was made for her husband by Helen.
   10 → The poem is read to me by mom.
   11 → A subscription was sent to her by the doctor.

D 1 should be sold
   2 will be released
   3 was bought for me
   4 was recorded
   5 will be polluted
   6 were enticed to buy
   7 can be delivered to people
   8 was followed
   9 should not be put
   10 has been heard
   11 was not composed

Lesson 5-7 동사구의 수동태

Check up!

A 1 My clothes were laughed at by him.
   2 Tom couldn't be caught up with by his mother.
   3 The president is looked up to by many people.
   4 The radio was turned off at night by Brad.
   5 The dog was ran over on the street by the car.
   6 The orphans were taken care of by Harry.
   7 The park is made use of as a gym by some people.

Lesson 5-8 be used to의 수동태

Check up!

p. 189

A 1 is used to
   2 are used to exercising
   3 used to be
   4 is used to season
   5 used to study
   6 would stretch
   7 is used to studying
   8 used to go

Lesson 5-9 'by' 이외의 전치사를 사용하는 수동태

Check up!

p. 190

A	1	was surprised at	2	were shocked at
	3	was tired of	4	was interested in
	5	was covered with	6	was excited at
	7	was made of	8	was pleased with
	9	were made from	10	was filled with

Practice More Ⅱ

p. 191~193

A 1 in   2 at
3 with   4 of
5 of   6 at
7 to   8 with
9 from   10 with

B 1 keeping → to keep
2 was used → used
3 being → be
4 laughed up → laughed at
5 got → getting
6 was resembled → resembled
7 write → writing
8 don't use → am not used
9 was become → became
10 seeing → seen
11 getting → to get
12 for → to

C 1 is interested in   2 makes use of
3 making   4 to live
5 driving   6 to spread
7 caught up   8 looked at

D 1 The roof was covered with snow.
2 Children were excited at ice skating.
3 Namsan Tower is known for its night view.
4 He was married to a kind, beautiful woman.
5 Chemical weapons were used to attack the neighboring country.
6 The rule was made to teach traffic safety.
7 The players are welcomed by the crowd.
8 The director was satisfied with my acting.
9 Solar energy will be used to solve the problem.
10 Some difficult questions were asked of me by Helen.

E 1 were given to the students by Mrs. Dickens
2 was handed a bunch of files in his office by Jerry
3 was made to pay the fine yesterday (by them)
4 was allowed to go on a picnic yesterday by me
5 was heard to laugh (laughing) behind the door by me

중간 기말고사 예상문제

내신 최다 출제 유형

p. 194

01 ③   02 ②   03 ①   04 ⑤   05 ④

해설

01 was met → met
02 ① Jacy → by Jack, ③ invite → invited,
④ calling → called, ⑤ is invent → was invented
→ 유명한 발명품이나 글, 그림 등은 과거에 끝난 일이므로 수동태를 사용할 때 be동사는 과거형을 써주어야 한다.
03 막연한 일반인이거나 분명하지 않은 경우 'by+목적격(행위자)'는 생략이 가능하다.
04 의문사가 없는 수동태의 경우 'be동사 + 주어 + 과거분사 + by + 목적격'의 형태를 가진다.
05 조동사가 있는 수동태는 '조동사+be+과거분사'의 형태로 나타낸다.

p. 195~200

01 ②   02 ⑤   03 ③   04 ③   05 ②
06 ①,③   07 ②,④   08 ④   09 ②,⑤   10 ④
11 ②   12 ④   13 ②   14 ③   15 ②,④
16 ①,③   17 ④   18 ②   19 ②   20 ②
21 ⑤   22 ③   23 ①   24 ③   25 ⑤
26 ④   27 ⑤   28 ③   29 ③   30 ②

〈서술형 평가〉
31 made from
32 is filled with
33 are recycled
34 has been watered
35 (1) is used (2) are held
36 was sculpted
37 will be carried
38 My umbrella was broken by Jamie.
39 The bracelet was made of green and pink jade beads.
40 The garden was cleaned by me.
41 A postcard with sunflowers printed on it was not sent to me by Uncle Jack.
42 Does her mom prepare orange juice every morning?
43 A desk was made for me by my father when I was young.

01 질문이 현재형이므로 대답에 시제 일치를 시켜준다.

02 'be interested in' ~에 흥미를 가지다

03 겨울 기간 동안 문이 잠긴다는 의미의 수동태 문장이다.
'be+과거분사'

04 과거형이며 주어가 복수이다. 수동태 'were+과거분사'의 형태를 찾는다.

05 미래의 수동태 형태는 'will be+과거분사'이다.

06 ① teached → taught, ③ wrote → written

07 ② took → was taken, ④ was call → was called

08 was making → was made

09 ② were chose → were chosen,
⑤ is surround → is surrounded

10 ④ be interested in, ①,②,③,⑤ 수동태 목적어 'by+목적격'

11 be+과거분사: is cooked

12 be+과거분사: are brought

13 능동태 문장이 과거형으로 쓰였으므로 수동태의 동사는 be동사의 과거형인 'was' 또는 'were'를 사용한다.

14 능동태 문장이 현재형으로 쓰였으므로 수동태의 동사는 be동사의 현재형인 'am/are/is' 중 주어의 인칭에 맞게 골라 쓴다.

15 ① is belonged → belongs, ③ Hellen was bought a doll
→ A doll was bought for Hellen,
⑤ made with → made of

16 ② was keep → was kept, ④ was elect → was elected
⑤ painting → painted

17 'be interested in' ~에 흥미를 가지다

18 'be covered with' ~로 뒤덮이다

19 is sent − was sent

20 수동태의 be동사가 과거형이므로, 능동태의 본동사를 과거형 시제로 일치시킨다.
수동태 by+목적격: 능동태 목적어,
수동태 was bought: 능동태 bought,
수동태 주어: 능동태 목적어

21 수동태의 be동사가 과거형이므로, 능동태의 본동사를 과거형으로 시제를 일치시킨다.
수동태 by+목적격: 능동태 목적어,
수동태 was invented: 능동태 invented,
수동태 주어: 능동태 목적어

22 능동태 목적어: 수동태 주어,
능동태 동사: were raised.
능동태 주어: 수동태 by+목적격

23 능동태 목적어: 수동태 주어,
능동태 동사: is cleaned
능동태 주어: 수동태 by+목적격

24 be happy − happy

25 be satisfied to → be satisfied with

26 일반적인 사실이나 사람이 나오면 'by+목적격'을 생략할 수 있다.

27 직접목적어가 쓰인 4형식 문장의 수동태이다. 'give'와 함께 쓰이는 전치사 'to'를 써준다.

28 '많은 가난한 아이들이 Jenny와 그녀의 친구들에 의해 도움을 받는다'라는 수동태의 뜻으로 쓰였다. 주어가 복수이고 현재형 문장이므로 'are helped'가 알맞다.

29 'be composed of' ~로 구성되다.
'be made of' ~로 만들어지다

30 'be shocked at' ~에 충격을 받다,
'be disappointed at' ~에 실망을 하다

〈서술형 평가〉

31 화학적 반응이 일어나 물질의 성질이 바뀔 때는 'be made from'을 사용한다.

32 'be filled with' ~로 가득 차다

33 현재형의 수동태이므로 'be동사+과거분사'의 형태가 되어야 한다.

34 현재완료의 수동태이므로 'have(has)+been+과거분사'로 나타내야 한다.

35 (1) is used: 프랑스어는 캐나다에서 사용된다.
(2) are held: 올림픽은 4년마다 열린다.

36 '미켈란젤로에 의해 조각되었다'라는 의미의 수동태

37 미래를 나타내는 수동태: will be+과거분사

38 A: 누가 우산을 망가뜨렸니?
B: 나의 우산은 Jamie에 의해 망가졌어.

39 'be made of' ~로 만들어지다

40 cleaned (과거): was cleaned

41 4형식을 수동태로 전환하는 문장이다.
능동태의 동사가 과거형이므로 수동태에서는 'was sent'로 전환되고, 부정문이기 때문에 was 뒤에 not을 붙여준다.

42 능동태 문장으로 전환할 경우 'Her mom prepares the orange juice every morning.'이며, 이를 다시 의문문의 형태로 바꾼다.

43 4형식 문장의 수동태이다.
동사 'made'의 전치사로 'for'가 나왔다.

Chapter
06 부정사

Lesson 6-1 부정사의 형태와 역할

Check up! p. 203

A
1 To be
2 to go
3 to buy
4 to write
5 to play
6 to go
7 to meet
8 to live in
9 to do
10 to fly

Lesson 6-2 부정사의 명사적 용법 (1)_주어/보어 역할

Check up! p. 204~205

A
1 It is usually hard to get up early.
2 It is really fun to go hiking with friends.
3 It is dangerous to go out alone at night.
4 It is necessary to rest.
5 It is exciting to watch horror movies.

B
1 It is easy for me to understand this lecture.
2 It is difficult for Helen to learn French.
3 It was nice of him to visit his grandmother once a week.
4 It is necessary for me to talk with my family.
5 It is wise of you to make a priority list.
6 It is interesting for Mike to ride a bike along the river.
7 It is kind of them to help the poor.
8 It is useful for me to study Korean history.

Lesson 6-3 부정사의 명사적 용법 (2)_목적어 역할

Check up! p. 206

A
1 to be
2 to know
3 to study
4 to participate in
5 to buy (buying)
6 to know
7 to lose
8 to attend
9 to make

Lesson 6-4 의문사+to부정사

Check up! p. 207~208

A
1 where I should go
2 how he should make a chocolate cookie
3 how to protect the environment
4 who should teach us English
5 when she should leave
6 what she should buy
7 how to use the microwave
8 how to drive a car
9 what to do first
10 when I should start

B
1 what to do
2 how to distinguish
3 what to bring
4 how to attract
5 when to finish

Lesson 6-5 부정사의 형용사적 용법

Check up! p. 209~210

A
1 a chair to sit on
2 opportunities to practice
3 friends to play with
4 paper to write on
5 books to read
6 friend to live with
7 to buy a car
8 a house to live in

B 1 many friends to talk with
  2 three dogs to take care of
  3 it's time to get up
  4 enough time to help me
  5 something to drink
  6 no one to go fishing with me
  7 somebody to volunteer for the work
  8 to buy some bread
  9 much work to do
  10 something interesting to do to relieve her stress

Practice More I

p. 211~213

A 1 of   2 for
  3 to   4 for
  5 of   6 for
  7 for   8 of
  9 of   10 for

B 1 to write with   2 to live in
  3 to talk with(to)   4 to sit on
  5 to eat with   6 to turn to
  7 to write on   8 to write about

C 1 Tell → To tell   2 take → to take
  3 climbing → climb   4 of → for
  5 sitting → sit   6 doing → to do
  7 be → to be   8 study → to study
  9 for → of   10 with → in

D 1 to run away   2 how to assemble
  3 when I should stop   4 where to go
  5 makes me tired to study
  6 eating something spicy
  7 what he should do
  8 It is not easy to keep pets.
  9 started playing tennis

E 1 a project to
  2 to learn how to ski this winter vacation.
  3 It is helpful to drink a cup of warm milk
  4 The best way to achieve your goal
  5 It is very important to break your bad habit.
  6 The fastest way to go to school

7 to turn the TV volume up so high.
8 It is wrong for them to act like that.
9 decided not to have snacks anymore.
10 I have something important to tell her.

Lesson 6-6 부정사의 부사적 용법 (1)

Check up!

p. 215~216

A 1 to pack up to go hiking
  2 in order to meet
  3 to issue
  4 in order to watch
  5 to pass the exam.
  6 in order to buy

B 1 for   2 to
  3 for   4 to
  5 to   6 to
  7 for   8 to

Lesson 6-7 부정사의 부사적 용법 (2)

Check up!

p. 217~218

A 1 I am so tired to go to the party.
  2 Helen practiced soccer everyday to become a great soccer player.
  3 You must be diligent to arrive at the office early.
  4 She stopped eating junk food to lose weight.
  5 Mary was sad to fail the interview.
  6 I was frightened to see a black cat at midnight.
  7 We were hungry not to eat lunch.
  8 John was smart to solve the difficult problem easily.
  9 I was happy to get an A on the math test.
  10 Jennifer went to a shopping mall to buy new pants.

B 1 나는 해외봉사에 참여하게 돼서 너무 행복했다.
  2 살을 뺀다면, 너는 더 건강해질 거야.

3 그는 자라서 이탈리아에서 유명한 예술가가 되었다.

4 힘없이 걷는 것으로 보아 그는 피곤한 것이 틀림없다.

5 우리는 그 끔찍한 소식을 듣게 되어 유감이다.

6 이번 영어 시험의 중요성을 알게 된다면, 너는 열심히 공부 할 것이다.

Lesson 6-8 자주 쓰이는 부정사 표현

★Check up! p. 219~220

A 1 to weak → too weak

2 enough strong → strong enough

3 sold → sell

4 not order → order not

5 can → can't

6 tiring → tired

7 sadly → sad

B 1 too / to go   **2** so / that / can't

3 so / that / can join   **4** in order to buy

5 skillful enough to fix   **6** (so as) not to fail

7 so / that / can't knit   **8** fast enough to arrive

9 in order to study   **10** (so as) not to lose

Lesson 6-9 목적격보어로 쓰이는 부정사

★Check up! p. 221~222

A 1 to go   **2** clean

3 to decide   **4** sing

5 to go out   **6** to become

7 dance   **8** stay up

9 to fix   **10** stand

B 1 He expected me to meet John.

2 Jane asked her mom to buy a new car.

3 They allowed us to hold the party in their garden.

4 Mike noticed Ted wearing his shirt.

5 Please let me know when Eric will leave.

6 She helped her husband fix the light.

7 Tim made me check our summer vacation schedule.

Lesson 6-10 원형부정사

★Check up! p. 223

A 1 (to) do   **2** shake (shaking)

3 become   **4** (to) write

5 cry (crying)   **6** go

7 water (watering)   **8** (to) pass

9 run (running)   **10** (to) move

Practice More Ⅱ p. 224~226

A 1 ⓐ   **2** ⓓ

3 ⓑ   **4** ⓒ

B 1 cry   **2** clean

3 to buy   **4** too

5 to make   **6** smart enough

7 to succeed   **8** of

9 to lose   **10** do

C 1 It is too small to wear.

2 It is hot enough to swim in the sea.

3 I ran to catch the train.

4 went to the museum to do our homework.

5 let me know how to fix the watch.

6 They saw the boy dance

7 I saved money to buy John's album.

8 The letter made me cry when I read it.
(= When I read the letter, it made me cry.)

9 Joe was stupid enough to believe the rumor.

10 It was easy for Mina to remember his name.

D 1 come → to come

2 enough strong → strong enough

3 to late → too late

4 buying → to buy

5 doing → do

6 cried → cry (crying)

7 to know → know

8 of → for

9 sitting → to sit

10 listening → to listen

E 1 I'm old enough to travel alone.

2 It was difficult for Judy to understand the lecture.

3 She went to the store to buy the lamp.

4 The chair was too old to sit on.

5 Mom had me clean the room.

6 I wrote a note in order not to forget the appointment.

7 The movie is too violent for children to watch.

중간 기말고사 **예상문제**

내신 최다 출제 유형

p. 227

01 ④   02 ③   03 ④   04 ③,⑤   05 ③

06 ③

해설

01 live – live in
→ to부정사가 수식하는 house는 'live in'에서 'in'의 목적어이므로 생략할 수 없다.

02 첫 번째 문장: 사람의 성격을 나타내는 형용사가 왔기에 'of+목적격'의 형태를 취한다.
두 번째 문장: to부정사 의미상의 주어는 'for+목적격'이다.

03 ④ 명사적 용법의 목적어 역할, ①,②,③,⑤ 형용사적 용법

04 〈보기, ③,⑤〉 부사적 용법, ①,②,④ 명사적 용법

05 ③ 부사적 용법 ①,②,④,⑤ 형용사적 용법

06 〈보기, ③〉 부사적 용법 ① 형용사적용 법, ②,④,⑤ 명사적 용법

p. 228~233

01 ④   02 ①   03 ③   04 ④   05 ⑤
06 ④   07 ①   08 ④   09 ⑤   10 ③
11 ③   12 ①   13 ⑤   14 ②   15 ③
16 ④   17 ②   18 ①   19 ②,④   20 ②
21 ⑤   22 ①   23 ③   24 ②   25 ④
26 ②   27 ⑤   28 ②   29 ④   30 ②
31 ②,③   32 ⑤   33 ①,③   34 ③   35 ②

〈서술형 평가〉

36 It

37 to buy

38 too heavy for her to lift

39 would like to fly in the sky

40 told people to keep away

41 didn't mean to make you angry

42 The farmer allowed them to pick some blueberries.

43 I don't know what to say.

44 is too small for Alex to put on

45 is strong enough to lift the barbell

해설

01 'tell'의 목적격보어로는 to가 온다.

02 사역동사 'let'의 목적격보어는 원형부정사가 온다.

03 사역동사 'make'의 목적격보어로는 원형부정사가 온다.

04 ready to부정사: ~할 준비가 된

05 '선택하기 위하여' to부정사의 부사적 용법이다.

06 〈보기, ④〉 부사적 용법, ②,③,⑤ 명사적 용법, ① 형용사적 용법

07 〈보기, ①〉 형용사적 용법, ②,③,⑤ 명사적 용법, ④ 부사적 용법

08 〈보기, ④〉 형용사적 용법, ①,③,⑤ 명사적 용법 ② 부사적 용법

09 사람의 성격이나 성질 등을 나타내는 형용사 뒤에는 'of+목적격'을 사용한다.

10 would love+to부정사, expect+to부정사

11 sing – to sing

12 'too~ to...' 너무 ~해서...하지 못하다. (=so that cannot)

13 ⑤ 명사적 용법, ①,②,③,④ 부사적 용법

14 ② 형용사적 용법, ①,③,④,⑤ 명사적 용법

15 ③ 명사적 용법, ①,②,④,⑤ 부사적 용법

16 ④ of, ①,②,③,⑤ for

17 ② for, ①,③,④,⑤ of

18 ② staying → to stay, ③ be → to be, ④ he → him, ⑤ leaving → to leave

19 ①, ③, ⑤ – 'watch, listen, hear'등의 지각동사 뒤에는 목적격보어로 원형부정사 또는 현재분사가 와야 한다.

20 ① help (준사역동사) – 목적격보어로 동사원형 또는to부정사가 와야한다. ②,④,⑤ make, have, let (사역동사) – 목적격보어로 동사원형이 와야 한다.

21 ⑤ 가주어 it, ①,② 비인칭 주어 it, ③,④ 사물을 가리키는 it

22 That → It
It~to 구문 – It: 가주어, to~: 진주어

23 to memorizing– to memorize
It~to 구문 – It: 가주어, to~: 진주어

24 need+to부정사 (또는 명사)

25 '자원봉사를 하기 위해'는 to부정사의 부사적 용법이다.
–to do volunteer work

26 의문사+to부정사 = 의문사+주어+should+동사원형

27 의문사+to부정사 = 의문사+주어+should+동사원형

28 'so~ that 주어+can't' = too~ to..

29 so~that주어+can = ~enough for+목적격+to부정사

30 ② 형용사+enough to, ①,③,④,⑤ too~ to...

31 ② buy – to buy, ③ leaving – to leave

32 to부정사의 부정은 'not(never)+to+동사원형'이다.

33 '의문사+to부정사' – ② meet → to meet, ④ go → to go,
⑤ doing → do

34 what to+동사원형: 무엇을 ~할지

35 how to+동사원형: 어떻게 ~할지

〈서술형 평가〉

36 to부정사가 문장의 주어 역할을 할 때 'It~to' 용법으로 바꿀 수 있다.

37 to부정사의 부사적 용법 '~하기 위하여'로 바꿔 쓸 수 있다.

38 too~ to... ~하기엔 너무 ...한

39 would like to부정사 ~하고 싶어 하다

40 'tell' 뒤에 목적어+to부정사가 온다.

41 'mean'은 to부정사를 목적어로 한다.

42 'allow'뒤에는 '목적어+to부정사'가 온다.

43 what to say 무엇을 말해야 할지

44 too~ to... 너무~해서 ...하지 못한

45 형용사+enough to부정사 ~하기에 충분한

Chapter 07 동명사

Lesson 7-1 동명사의 쓰임

Check up!　　p. 237~238

A
1 Making
2 Exercising
3 believing
4 playing
5 speaking
6 relieves
7 being
8 making
9 solving
10 traveling

B
1 Ride → Riding
2 travel → traveling
3 to go → going
4 get → getting
5 be → being
6 knit → knitting
7 accepting not → not accepting
8 Exercising not → Not exercising
9 make → makes
10 act → acting
11 are → is
12 Play → Playing
13 get → getting

Lesson 7-2 동명사를 목적어로 쓰는 동사

Check up!　　p. 239

A
1 playing
2 being
3 changing
4 cleaning
5 eating
6 flying
7 going
8 littering
9 playing
10 going
11 living
12 taking

Lesson 7-3 동명사와 to부정사의 동사

Check up!　　p. 241

A
1 to make/making
2 visiting
3 talking
4 to jog/jogging
5 to lock
6 to get
7 to spend/spending
8 to buy
9 changing
10 to work/working

B
1 그들은 싸움을 멈췄다.
2 John은 떠나기 전에 창문을 닫는 것을 잊어버렸다.
3 Emma는 영어 시험을 감독해야 하는 것을 기억했다.
4 Helen은 시험 삼아 그에게 전화해봤다.
5 너는 최선을 다하려고 노력해야 한다.

Lesson 7-4 동명사의 의미상의 주어

Check up!　　p. 242

A
1 my(me)
2 Jimmy's
3 him
4 her

B
1 to ask → asking
2 he → his(him)
3 not come → not coming
4 danced → dancing

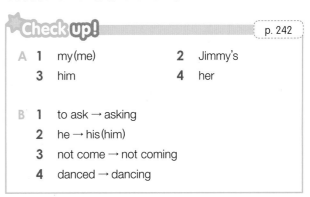

Practice More I
p. 243~245

A
1 Being
2 assembling
3 baking
4 telling
5 wearing
6 writing
7 Swimming
8 asking
9 preparing
10 participating

B 1 hearing   2 his having
   3 passing
   4 my(me) not attending
   5 my(me) opening   6 not turning in
   7 telling

C 1 dance → dancing   2 to go → going
   3 to buy → buying   4 study → studying
   5 she → of her   6 talk → talking (to talk)
   7 telling → to tell   8 I → me
   9 to go → going   10 make → making

서술형 연습

D 1 Her job is teaching math to students.
   2 Exercising regularly makes me healthy.
   3 I can't stand her acting like that.
   4 A man stopped walking to ask for directions.
   5 They are looking forward to Tim's passing the exam.
   6 His hobby is painting still-lifes.
   7 I had to put off making the movie.
   8 You can learn a lot just by watching.
   9 I tried buying a new oven.
   10 Do you mind us using this phone?

Lesson 7-5 동명사의 숙어 표현 (1)

Check up!   p. 248

A 1 about going   2 in cooking
   3 to studying   4 to attending
   5 about raining   6 at speaking
   7 for inviting   8 like eating
   9 from running   10 finishing
   11 at seeing   12 to showing
   13 for spending   14 to reading
   15 seeing

Lesson 7-6 동명사의 숙어 표현 (2)

Check up!   p. 249

A 1 repair → repairing
   2 to read → reading
   3 solved → solving
   4 passing → no passing
   5 to develop → developing

Practice More II   p. 250~252

A 1 to go → about going
   2 to study → of studying
   3 go → going
   4 buying → buy
   5 cleaning → cleaned
   6 jog → jogging
   7 not → no
   8 to eat → eating
   9 about → for
   10 see → seeing
   11 In → On
   12 buy → buying
   13 to → at
   14 broken → breaking
   15 take → taking

B 1 to be exchanged
   2 cannot but cry
   3 to knitting
   4 baking
   5 go to an amusement park / go to an amusement park / to going to an amusement park

서술형연습

C 1 People were busy swimming in the sea.
   2 It is no use selling this dress to her.
   3 We are looking forward to receiving a reply from her.
   4 On entering the room, I heard a baby crying.
   5 How about traveling to Europe during winter vacation?

6 It's no use trying to stop John.

7 People could not help laughing at him.

8 Mike is having trouble finding the book.

9 My family spent too much time talking about where to go on holiday.

10 Why did he objet to moving to this house?

D 1 On finishing my homework

2 How about writing a fairy tale for our child?

3 I had trouble remembering all the students' names.

4 kept me from going to the concert with my friends.

5 It is no use buying that house.

6 I objected to accepting her suggestion.

7 Her laziness prevented her from exercising regularly.

8 What do you say to making a party dress for Amy?

9 is not used to wearing a suit.

10 is worth being honored by everyone.

중간 기말고사 **예상문제**

내신 최다 출제 유형

p. 253

01 ⑤　　02 ⑤　　03 ③　　04 ②,④　　05 ②

06 ①,⑤

해설

01 Eat − Eating

02 ⑤ 진행형 문장이다. 〈보기, ①,②,③,④〉 동명사

03 동명사 관용표현: 'on+동명사 '~하자마자

04 ② 'look forward to −ing' ~하기를 학수고대하다: meet → meeting, ④ 'give up' −ing ~하는 것을 포기하다: exercise → exercising

05 ① give → giving, ③ eat → to eat (eating), ④ to remodeling → remodeling, ⑤ visiting → to visit

06 ② visiting → to visit, ③ travel → traveling, ④ to take → taking

p. 254~259

01 ③	02 ②	03 ⑤	04 ④,⑤	05 ②
06 ③	07 ②	08 ①	09 ③	10 ①
11 ④	12 ③,⑤	13 ④	14 ①	15 ②
16 ③	17 ②	18 ④	19 ⑤	20 ①
21 ③	22 ②	23 ④	24 ①	25 ⑤
26 ②	27 ②	28 ③	29 ①	30 ①
31 ③	32 ③			

〈서술형 평가〉

33 to answer

34 Getting

35 send − sending

36 take − taking

37 That kind of problem is worth discussing.

38 Walking alone at night can be dangerous.

39 I tried wearing the skirt, but it was too small.

40 Learning (To Learn) from your mistakes

41 to ask for Ellen's email address.

42 meeting him last year.

해설

01 'would you mind+동명사~?' ~해 주시겠어요?

02 'enjoy+동명사' ~하는 것을 즐기다

03 'be looking forward to+동명사' ~하기를 학수고대하다

04 ① to talk → talking, ② changing → to change, ③ taking → to take

05 ② 현재분사, ①,③,④,⑤ 동명사

06 'practice+동명사' ~하는 것을 연습하다

07 문장의 주어로 동명사(또는 to부정사)가 온다. 동명사나 to부정사가 주어로 쓰였을 경우 동사는 단수 취급 한다.

08 'keep a diary' 일기를 쓰다, 'in English' 영어로

09 ③ 문장의 주어로 쓰인 동명사는 단수 취급해 준다.

10 ① 동사가 주어의 위치에 오려면 동명사 또는 to부정사의 형태가 되어야 한다.

11 'be good at+동명사' ~을 잘 한다

12 ③ wake − waking ⑤ having − have

13 동명사 의미상의 주어는 소유격 또는 목적격을 써준다.

14 cannot help 동명사 ~하지 않을 수 없다

15 동명사의 부정은 부정어(not/never)를 동명사 앞에 쓴다.

16 현재 진행형, 〈보기, ①,②,④,⑤〉 동명사

17 ② 현재분사, 〈보기, ①,③,④,⑤〉 동명사

18 ④ 분사 (명사를 수식), 〈보기,①,②,③,⑤〉 동명사

19 hearing → to hear

20 What do you say to+동명사 ~하는 게 어때?

21 begin+동명사(또는 to부정사) cry → crying (to cry)

22 'be excited about+동명사' ～에 대해 흥분되다, 'enjoy+동명사' ～하는 것을 즐기다

23 전치사의 목적어로는 동명사가 온다.

24 '～을 하는것은'으로 시작하는 주어는 동명사 또는 to부정사가 올 수 있다. Playing basketball (= To play basketball)

25 'remember to부정사' ～하는 것을 기억하다

26 are → is (동명사가 주어일 경우 단수 취급한다.)

27 'thank ... for+동명사' ～에 대해 ...에게 감사하다

28 ① to be → being, ② read → reading, ④ to get → getting, ⑤ sings → singing

29 ② to leave → leaving, ③ hunt → hunting, ④ fix → fixing, ⑤ climb → climbing

30 〈보기, ①〉 동명사_목적어, ②,③ 동명사_보어, ④ 현재분사, ⑤ 동명사_주어

31 〈보기, ③〉 동명사_주어, ①,②,④,⑤ 동명사_목적어

32 'remember+to부정사' ～할 것을 기억하다, 'remember+동명사' ～한 것을 기억하다

〈서술형 평가〉

33 'forget to부정사' ～할 것을 잊다

34 문장의 주어로는 동명사나 to부정사가 올 수 있다. 지시어가 동명사이니 'getting'이 알맞다. get up-일어나다

35 전치사의 목적어로는 동명사가 온다.

36 'think of+동명사' ～하는 것에 대해 생각하다

37 'be worth –ing' ～할 가치가 있다

38 동명사+시간의 부사구+can+be

39 'try+동명사' (시험 삼아) ～해보다

40 It～to구문: 진주어 to 이하가 주어가 될 수 있도록 to부정사나 동명사로 고쳐 쓴다.

41 'forget to부정사' ～할 것을 잊다

42 'remember+동명사' ～한 것을 기억하다

Chapter 08 분사

Lesson 8-1 분사의 종류

p. 263~264

A
1	baking	2	broken
3	finished	4	dancing
5	depressed	6	rising
7	moved	8	filled
9	boring	10	disappointed

B
1	sleeping	2	left
3	excited	4	frightening
5	hung	6	studied
7	walking		

Lesson 8-2 명사를 꾸며주는 분사

p. 265

A
1	making	2	stolen
3	wearing	4	wounded
5	fallen	6	boiling
7	running (run)	8	abandoned
9	sitting	10	drawn
11	talking	12	used

Lesson 8-3 보어로 쓰이는 분사

p. 266

A
1	surprised / 주격보어	2	crying / 목적격보어
3	frightened / 주격보어	4	called / 목적격보어
5	exhausted / 주격보어	6	scared / 주격보어
7	waiting / 목적격보어	8	torn / 주격보어
9	jogging / 목적격보어	10	broken / 목적격보어
11	eating / 목적격보어	12	moved / 주격보어
13	running / 목적격보어		

Lesson 8-4 현재분사와 동명사

p. 267

A
1	(A)	2	(B)
3	(A)	4	(A)
5	(B)	6	(B)
7	(A)	8	(B)
9	(A)	10	(B)

Practice More I

p. 268~270

A
1	lost	2	walking
3	wounded	4	stolen
5	lying	6	wearing
7	tired	8	standing
9	finished	10	grazing

B
1	given	2	walk
3	missing	4	improved
5	purchased	6	damaged
7	interviewing	8	having
9	proposed	10	featured

C
1	②	2	①
3	④	4	⑤
5	③		

D
1 He bought a book written by James Brown.
2 We watched the shocking news.
3 I saw the man baking bread in the bakery.
4 There is a man called 'yes-man' in our company.
5 The studying students were sleepy.
6 The boys exercising in the gym are Aron and Jim.
7 I saw the smoke coming out of the window.
8 The roof covered with leaves looks dirty.
9 They know a woman cooking in the kitchen.
10 The injured soldiers were taken to a hospital.

E
1 The new song composed by John was great.
2 Let's get this cake wrapped.
3 My homework is reading a poem written in French.

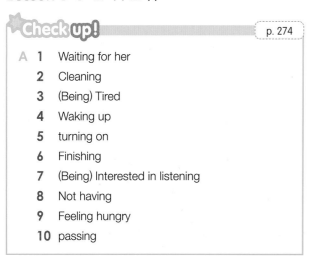

4 Jenny wants her room cleaned.
5 You should memorize the given sentences.
6 This bowl imported from India was broken.
7 I saw monkeys juggling at the zoo.
8 Tim saw her eyes fill with tears.
9 The policeman chased the robber running away down the street.
10 I heard my name called in the garden.

Lesson 8-5 감정을 나타내는 분사

p. 272

A 1 exhausted   2 satisfying
  3 confused   4 moved
  5 tiring   6 depressed
  7 amazing   8 surprised
  9 shocking

Lesson 8-6 분사구문 (1)

p. 274

A 1 Waiting for her
  2 Cleaning
  3 (Being) Tired
  4 Waking up
  5 turning on
  6 Finishing
  7 (Being) Interested in listening
  8 Not having
  9 Feeling hungry
  10 passing

Lesson 8-7 분사구문 (2)

p. 276

A 1 Not knowing
  2 Living in Paris
  3 Turning left
  4 Being too young
  5 Walking down
  6 Not having
  7 Getting up late
  8 Passing my brother
  9 Having too many clothes
  10 drinking coffee

Lesson 8-8 with＋명사＋분사

p. 277~278

A 1 bandaged   2 pointing
  3 turned   4 played
  5 waving

B 1 with his son watching TV
  2 with tears falling down her cheeks
  3 with their hands waved
  4 with Mike jogging
  5 with his cell phone ringing
  6 with his head nodded
  7 with the woman dancing in the street
  8 with his arms crossed
  9 with her baby sleeping
  10 with her hair flying

Practice More Ⅱ

A
1 boring / bored
2 exhausting / exhausted
3 interesting / interested
4 confusing / confused
5 amazing / amazed
6 moving / moved
7 puzzling / puzzled
8 satisfying / satisfied

B
1 She being → Being
2 Listened → Listening
3 Knowing not → Not knowing
4 boring → bored
5 Study →Studying
6 sing → singing
7 crossing → crossed
8 She arriving → Arriving
9 apologizing → apologized
10 sat → sitting

C
1 If you are satisfied with our restaurant's service
2 When Linda entered the room
3 as she called his name
4 Although he was rich
5 Since (As) I finished my speech
6 While they had dinner

D
1 Coming across Tom
2 Turning right at the corner
3 Checking the test results
4 Not knowing how to fix the car
5 Sleeping too much in the daytime
6 watching the movie

E
1 Passing the exam, you will be able to get anything you want.
2 Not knowing how to get to the station, I had to ask him.
3 Going to school in a foreign country, he has many friends in Korea.
4 Feeling tired and hungry, we could not do anything.
5 Falling from the tree, Cindy had broken her leg.
6 Having a lot of money, she doesn't want to help the poor.

중간 기말고사 예상문제

내신 최다 출제 유형

p. 282

01 ③   02 ②   03 ⑤   04 ②   05 ①
06 ④

해설

01 〈보기, ③〉 현재분사, ①,②,④,⑤ 동명사
02 exciting → excited 감정을 나타내는 주어가 사람일 경우 과거분사를 사용한다.
03 분사구문으로 바꿀 때 접속사와 주어를 생략하고 '동사+ing' 형태로 만든다. Cheap the shirt is nice. → Being cheap, the shirt is nice.
04 문맥상 '시골에 살기 때문에'라는 표현이 맞으며, 알맞은 접속사로 'because'가 들어간다.
05 ① 동명사, ②,③,④,⑤ 현재분사
06 첫 번째 문장: 개가 짖고 있는 주체이므로 능동의 의미인 현재분사가 알맞다. 두 번째 문장: 직업이 만족을 주는 주체이므로 현재분사가 알맞다.

p. 283~289

01 ①   02 ②   03 ③   04 ②   05 ⑤
06 ⑤   07 ④   08 ③   09 ③   10 ④
11 ③   12 ②   13 ④   14 ①   15 ⑤
16 ⑤   17 ②   18 ④   19 ③   20 ①
21 ⑤   22 ④   23 ②   24 ②   25 ③
26 ③,⑤   27 ②,④   28 ①,⑤   29 ③
30 exciting → excited   31 ③   32 ②   33 ②,③
34 ①,④   35 ②

〈서술형 평가〉

36 crying / shocked
37 waiting / moved
38 frightened
39 disappointed
40 satisfied
41 Being written in English
42 her sister reading comic books
43 While you study in class
44 and her crayon box is opened
45 After taking a short break, we started practicing.
46 Not being honest, you couldn't make any friends.

01 명사를 꾸며주는 과거분사(수동)이다.

02 감정을 나타내는 분사는 사람이 주어일 때 과거분사를 사용한다.

03 분사구문 Written in easy English → As the book is written in easy English

04 명사를 수식하는 분사로 수동의 관계이므로 'posted'라고 해야 한다.

05 감정을 나타내는 분사는 주어가 사물일 때 현재분사를 사용한다. bored → boring

06 ① disappointing → disappointed, ② confused → confusing, ③ moved → moving, ④ embarrassing → embarrassed

07 ① interested → interesting, ② shocking → shocked, ③ boring → bored, ⑤ depressing → depressed

08 ③ A: 분사구문 – When I sat by the camp fire
B: 5형식 문장

09 첫 번째 문장: 명사를 수식하는 현재분사 (능동)
두 번째 문장: 감정을 나타내는 분사는 사람이 주어일 경우 과거분사 사용

10 A, B 감정을 나타내는 주어가 사물일 경우 현재분사를 사용한다.

11 ③ 명사를 수식하는 현재분사 – 능동, ①,②,④,⑤ 동명사

12 ② 현재 진행을 나타내는 분사, ①,③,④,⑤ 동명사

13 ④ 동명사, ①,②,③,⑤ 분사

14 분사구문 만들기 – 접속사와 주어를 생략하고 동사를 현재분사의 형태로 만든다.

15 분사구문 만들기 – 접속사와 주어를 생략하고 be동사를 현재분사의 형태로 만든다.

16 분사구문의 동시 동작 'and it destroyed all the houses' → 접속사, 주어 생략, 동사+ing

17 'As he needed some money to buy a cell phone' → 접속사, 주어 생략, 동사+ing

18 동시동작을 나타내는 분사구문 동사로 현재분사가 나와야 한다.

19 'Because (As) he wanted to know what to do'를 분사구문으로 바꾼 것이다.

20 '속삭이고 있는'은 현재분사의 진행을 뜻한다.

21 분사구문의 형태로 바꿀 때 동사는 현재분사의 형태가 되어야 한다. Sat → Sitting

22 부사절과 주절의 주어가 다를 때 분사구문에 주어를 써 주어야 한다. Being rainy → It being rainy

23 부사절과 주절의 주어가 다를 때 분사구문에 주어를 써 주어야 한다. having no water to drink → others having no water to drink

24 부정문을 분사구문으로 바꿀 때 'Not'을 문장 맨 앞에 두고, 동사는 현재분사를 만든다.

25 painting – 'while she painted'의 분사구문이다.

26 ③ hiding – hidden, ⑤ wrote – written

27 ② shocking – shocked, ④ frightening – frightened

28 〈보기, ①,⑤〉 현재분사, ②,③,④ 동명사

29 감정의 주체가 사람일 경우는 과거분사를 쓴다.
exciting → excited

30 감정의 주체가 사람일 경우는 과거분사를 쓴다.

31 Not having enough money , Although he doesn't have enough money

32 첫 번째 문장은 이유, 두 번째 문장은 양보를 나타낸 문장이다.

33 ① embarrassing – embarrassed, ④ tiring – tired, ⑤ depressed – depressing

34 ② Wanting not – Not wanting, ③ Happy – Being happy, ⑤ Danced – Dancing

35 앞 문장에는 '이유'를 설명하는 접속사가 와야 맞다.

〈서술형 평가〉

36 첫 번째 문장: 명사를 수식하는 현재분사(능동)
두 번째 문장: 감정을 나타내는 분사가 사람일 경우 과거분사 사용

37 첫 번째 문장: 명사를 수식하는 현재분사(능동)
두 번째 문장: 감정을 나타내는 분사가 사람일 경우 과거분사를 사용한다.

38 수동을 나타내는 과거분사를 사용한다.

39 '실망되어진 얼굴'의 뜻에는 수동을 의미하는 과거분사를 사용한다.

40 감정을 느끼는 주체가 사람이기 때문에 과거분사를 사용한다.

41 부사절과 주절의 주어가 다르므로 분사구문에서 주어를 써 주어야 한다.

42 'with+명사+분사' 구문이다.

43 분사구문에 주어가 생략된 것은 주절의 주어와 같다는 의미이므로 주어는 'you'로 받는다.

44 명사와 분사의 관계가 수동인 경우이다. 전치사 'with' 대신에 'and'를 쓰고 생략된 be동사를 넣어준다.

45 분사구문의 부사절의 동사는 현재분사를 사용한다.

46 분사구문의 부정형은 'not'을 문장의 맨 앞으로 놓는다.

Chapter 09 형용사와 부사

Lesson 9-1 형용사의 역할과 쓰임

★Check up!
p. 294

A 1 awake 2 asleep
3 something sweet 4 negative thinking
5 alike 6 cheerful
7 an impressive movie 8 anyone friendly
9 awesome 10 older

B 1 all of the dogs are asleep
2 watch an exciting baseball game
3 someone smart for the job
4 anything expensive last weekend
5 nothing to tell me
6 have a chocolate ice cream
7 interesting books to read

Lesson 9-2 the＋형용사, 고유형용사

★Check up!
p. 296

A 1 Chinse 2 have
3 Englishman 4 The
5 The Italians 6 Germans
7 the weak 8 like
9 Japanese 10 learn
11 poor 12 English
13 the sick

Lesson 9-3 형용사의 어순

★Check up!
p. 297

A 1 a small white 2 the first two
3 all new blue wooden 4 those pretty young
5 my kind new English 6 the beautiful pink
7 two delicious large French
8 a comfortable large new green plastic
9 his four small white German
10 a new green Korean

Lesson 9-4 불완전자동사와 감각동사

★Check up!
p. 299

A 1 sweety → sweet 2 palely → pale
3 happily → happy 4 magical → magic
5 to eat → eating 6 wake → awake
7 familiarly → familiar 8 badly → bad
9 strangely → strange 10 leave → leaving

Practice More I
p. 300~301

A 1 something cold 2 moving
3 live 4 bad
5 sad 6 quiet
7 are 8 the sick
9 enjoy 10 pale
11 new car 12 asleep
13 beautiful things 14 important
15 comfortable

B 1 happily → happy
2 white small → small white
3 the both → both the
4 goes → go
5 cheerful someone → someone cheerful
6 the poors → the poor
7 funny something → something funny
8 nervously → nervous
9 live → alive

C 1 The blind
2 the rich
3 the young
4 the Chinese
5 the homeless
6 the disabled
7 positive
8 the poor
9 The old

D 1 was a great English teacher
2 Two Americans played with us
3 The French are usually romantic.
4 I like Korean movies very much.

5 your English will get better.

6 The young like to hang out

Lesson 9-5 수량 형용사_many / much / a lot of

★ Check up! p. 303

A **1** many **2** much
3 much **4** many
5 much **6** many
7 much **8** many
9 much **10** many

Lesson 9-6 수량형용사_(a) few / (a) little

★ Check up! p. 304~305

A **1** a little **2** a little
3 a little **4** a few
5 a little **6** a few
7 a little **8** a few
9 a few **10** a little
11 a little **12** a few
13 a little **14** A few
15 a little

B **1** a few → a little **2** a little → a few
3 few → some **4** a few → a little
5 little → few **6** few → little
7 a little → a few

Lesson 9-7 수량형용사_some / any

★ Check up! p. 306

A **1** some **2** some
3 some **4** any
5 any **6** some
7 any **8** some

B **1** any **2** Some
3 any **4** some
5 some **6** some
7 any

Lesson 9-8 수량 형용사_each / both / no

★ Check up! p. 307

A **1** both **2** students
3 most **4** no
5 was **6** are
7 times **8** country
9 the boys **10** person's

Lesson 9-9 기수와 서수를 사용한 숫자 표현

★ Check up! p. 308

A **1** two / the Second
2 seven / the seventh
3 the third
4 five / the fifth
5 three fourths
6 two and four sixths
7 nine thirteenths
8 five and eight tenths
9 fourteen / the fourteenth
10 two fifteenths

Lesson 9-10 배수사

★ Check up! p. 309

A **1** three times **2** four times
3 twice **4** once
5 twice **6** three times
7 five times **8** ten times
9 many times

Practice **More Ⅱ**

p. 310~312

A
1	much	2	few
3	much	4	some
5	any	6	has
7	any	8	any
9	a few	10	few

B
1 second → two
2 any → some
3 teacher → teachers
4 Japan → Japanese
5 child → children
6 want → wants
7 fourth → four
8 two → twice
9 visitor → visitors
10 few → little
11 many → much
12 much → many

C
1	a little	2	little
3	A few	4	a little
5	eight/the eighth	6	three sevenths
7	aren't any	8	some
9	any	10	a lot of(many)

D
1 three times in the fourth act.
2 John doesn't make any trouble any more.
3 Each of you is beautiful and special.
4 Mr. Lee visited Canada three times
5 you had better not eat any junk food.
6 Every boy practiced hard to win the soccer game.
7 We will arrive at the base camp in a few minutes.
8 Every day is the same. I want to go abroad.
9 There was some fruit in the truck.
10 this bridge is five times longer than that one.

Lesson 9-11 부사의 역할과 종류

★Check up!

p. 314~315

A
1	early	2	Fortunately
3	exactly / tomorrow	4	easily
5	so / seriously	6	endlessly
7	Unfortunately / already	8	fluently / quickly
9	well	10	completely

Lesson 9-12 형용사로 부사 만들기

★Check up!

p. 317

A
1	happily	2	really
3	quickly	4	wholly
5	truly	6	finally
7	gently	8	easily
9	politely	10	fully
11	madly	12	prettily
13	sadly	14	luckily
15	carefully	16	terribly
17	successfully	18	bravely
19	basically	20	simply
21	hard	22	differently
23	visibly	24	seriously
25	widely	26	busily
27	comfortably	28	dully
29	angrily	30	anxiously
31	clearly		
32	fully		
33	loudly		
34	suddenly		
35	reasonably		
36	slightly		
37	slowly		
38	nicely		
39	safely		
40	foolishly		

Lesson 9-13 뜻이 다른 두 가지 형태의 부사

Check up!
p. 318

A 1 late
2 hard
3 lately
4 near
5 highly
6 nearly
7 high
8 lately
9 hardly
10 high
11 late

Lesson 9-14 빈도부사

Check up!
p. 319

A 1 comes always → always comes
2 sometimes can → can sometimes
3 never think → never thinks
4 always is → is always
5 eats never → never eats
6 late seldom → seldom late
7 always are → are always

Practice More Ⅲ
p. 320~321

A 1 happily
2 basically
3 comfortably
4 fast
5 realistically
6 honestly
7 quickly
8 terribly
9 wholly
10 politely

B 1 hard
2 long
3 enough
4 Long
5 fast
6 high
7 hard
8 enough
9 high
10 late

C 1 hardly
2 often goes
3 lately
4 beautifully
5 high
6 near
7 exactly
8 hardly
9 carefully

D 1 Tim usually comes on time.
2 My son often likes to wear his red coat in winter.
3 I rarely see Helen these days.
4 I think they will never catch up with me.
5 When she is alone, she usually calls me.
6 he could hardly walk.
7 He always closes the window.
8 James and his mom sometimes go to the movies together.
9 I rarely buy luxurious things such as jewelry.
10 What do you usually do on holidays?

Lesson 9-15 already / yet / still

Check up!
p. 323~324

A 1 ① already, ② still, ③ yet
2 ① still, ② yet, ③ already
3 ① still, ② already, ③ yet
4 ① still ② yet ③ already
5 ① already ② still ③ yet

B 1 still
2 already
3 yet
4 already
5 yet
6 still
7 already
8 yet
9 still
10 already

Lesson 9-16 too / either

Check up!
p. 325

A 1 too
2 either
3 too
4 either
5 too
6 either
7 neither
8 either
9 either
10 neither

Lesson 9-17 So do I / Neither do I

p. 326

A
1	So am	2	So did
3	Neither did	4	Neither was
5	So does	6	Neither did
7	Neither did	8	Neither can

Lesson 9-18 very / much / else / even

p. 327

A
1	very	2	very
3	much	4	much
5	very	6	much
7	else	8	even
9	else		

Lesson 9-19 ago / before

p. 328

A
1	before	2	ago
3	before	4	ago
5	ago	6	before
7	before	8	ago
9	ago	10	before

Lesson 9-20 이어 동사_타동사+부사(+목적어)

p. 330

A
1. turn it off
2. looking for a dictionary
3. Look at the picture
4. give it up
5. pick you up
6. wake him up
7. waiting for her
8. take off your shoes / take your shoes off
9. agree with you
10. depend on their parents
11. put the hat on / put on the hat
12. throw garbage away / throw away garbage
13. check them out
14. listened to the radio
15. sitting on the chair

Practice More IV

p. 331~333

A
1	either	2	still hasn't
3	am	4	much
5	anywhere else	6	already
7	even realize	8	Neither
9	ago	10	can

B
1. too / too / have
2. either / neither/ Neither
3. too / too / did
4. either / neither / Neither
5. too / too / do
6. either / neither / Neither
7. too / too / do
8. too / too / does
9. too / too / do

C
1. You have to turn it in by tomorrow morning.
2. Jack will pick them up at the airport.
3. You should take it off when you enter a room.
4. Don't turn it off. I need to watch Amy's talk show tonight.

D
1. a map for → for a map
2. down it → it down
3. ago → before
4. already → still
5. yet → still
6. much → very
7. can else → else can
8. on them → them on
9. very → much
10. off it → it off

E
1. He is going to pick them up at the airport.

2 Don't throw garbage out the window.

3 Minji put it on in the room.

4 Don't give up. Do your best!

5 Would you turn off the light?

6 You shouldn't put it off. The due date is Friday.

중간 기말고사 예상문제

내신 **최다 출제** 유형

p. 334

01 ③　　02 ④　　03 ②　　04 ⑤　　05 ①,③

06 ③,④　07 ②

해설

01 첫 번째 문장: 긍정문에서는 'some'을 사용한다.
두 번째 문장: 'money'는 셀 수 없는 명사이므로 'a little'이 맞다.

02 ① warm something → something warm,
② interesting something → anything interesting
③ youngest → younger, ⑤ very funny man → a very
funny man

03 '타동사+부사'에서 대명사가 목적어로 올 때는 타동사와 부사 사이에 와야 한다.

04 Exciting something → Something exciting

05 권유문에는 'some'을 사용한다. ③ 부정문에는 'any'를 사용한다.

06 ① the fifteenth of May, ② nineteen fifty-eight,
⑤ the first of November

07 ① large strong → strong large, ③ an old big → a big old
④ white small → small white, ⑤ My all → All my

p. 335~340

01 ⑤	02 ③	03 ③	04 ④,⑤	05 ①
06 ③	07 ②	08 ④	09 ②	10 ⑤
11 ①	12 ②	13 ④	14 ③	15 ①
16 ③	17 ③	18 ④	19 ⑤	20 ④
21 ①	22 ③	23 ⑤	24 ②	25 ②,④
26 ③	27 ⑤	28 ①	29 ③	30 ③,④
31 ②,⑤	32 ④	33 ⑤	34 ②	

〈서술형 평가〉

35 successful → successfully

36 either

37 Neither am I.

38 four times

39 (1) $\frac{2}{5}$ - two fifths

(2) $\frac{6}{3}$ - six thirds

(3) $3\frac{5}{6}$ - three and five sixths

40 easy → easily

41 some

42 Emily is looking for something exciting.

43 The poor are not always unhappy.

44 How did you get to the Art Gallery?

45 So does Judy.

46 Neither can I.

해설

01 ①,②,③,④ 형용사 – 부사, ⑤ 명사 – 형용사

02 ③ 유의어 관계, ①,②,④,⑤ 반의어 관계

03 'a few minutes later' 몇 분 후에

04 'Why are you so upset (sad)?' 너 왜 그렇게 기분이 좋지 않니 (슬프니)?

05 'lots of people' – 많은 사람들
'much, a little, little'은 셀 수 없는 명사와 쓰이며, 'any'는 부정문에 쓰인다.

06 took과 out 사이에 대명사가 위치해야 하며, 'looked at'의 목적어는 전치사 뒤에 위치하기 때문에 뒤에 나오는 것이 알맞다.

07 한 문장에 여러 개의 형용사가 있을 경우 순서는 '성질-크기-신구-색깔-국적-재료'의 순서이다.

08 ① many → much, ② 7-years-old → 7-year-old,
③ happily → happy,
⑤ a photo interesting → an interesting photo

09 ① already → yet, ③ very → much, ④ too → either,
⑤ stopping → stop

10 good something → something good

11 usually is → is usually

12 well → good

13 like → alike

14 a number of 많은

15 부정문에서 '또한'은 'either'를 쓴다.

16 ① a few → many, ② a few → a little, ④ some → much,
⑤ little → some

17 interesting something → something interesting

18 명사를 수식하는 형용사가 와야 한다. carefully → careful

19 분자는 기수, 분모는 서수이다. 분자가 복수일 경우 분모에 's'를 붙여준다.

20 We have never seen such a graceful woman.

21 '아직'이라는 뜻을 가진 부정문에는 'yet'을 사용한다.

22 Why not 왜 안 돼?

23 How often~? 얼마나 자주~?

24 ② 많이, 〈보기, ①,③,④,⑤〉 훨씬

25 ② fastly → fast, ④ late → lately

26 health → healthy

27 else nothing → nothing else

28 '조동사+빈도부사'의 형태이다.

29 anything+형용사

30 ③ a few 약간, 조금, ④ plenty of 많은

31 ① professional someone → someone professional,
③ wrapped up them → wrapped them up,
④ took out it → took it out,

32 'some = a few' 조금, 약간

33 'How far~?' 얼마나 멀리~? – 거리를 물어보는 표현이므로 그에 맞는 대답을 찾는다.

34 부정에 대한 동의의 답으로 'Me, neither'를 쓸 수 있다.

〈서술형 평가〉

35 일반동사 뒤에는 주로 부사가 온다. successfully 성공적으로

36 부정문에서 동의 표현은 'either'를 사용한다.

37 부정문에 대한 부정의 대답으로는 'Neither 동사+주어'로 답할 수 있다.

38 배수를 나타낼 때 한 배는 once, 두 배는 twice, 그 이상부터는 '숫자+times'로 한다.

39 분수를 영어로 표현할 때는 분자는 기수, 분모는 서수로 표현한다. 분자가 2 이상일 경우 분모에 's'를 붙여준다. '$3\frac{5}{6}$'과 같은 분수를 표현할 때는 앞의 숫자와 분자는 기수, 분모는 서수이다.

40 'find'를 수식하는 부사의 형태를 사용한다.

41 (A) 약간의 물을 마시고 싶다. → some,
(B) 약간의 돈이 남았다. → some

42 'look for' ~을 찾다, something+형용사

43 'the+형용사(~한 사람들)'은 복수로 취급한다.

44 How 어떻게, get to ~에 도착하다

45 'So+동사+주어'는 긍정문에 동의할 때 쓰는 표현이다.

46 'Neither+동사+주어'는 부정문에 동의할 때 사용한다.

Chapter 10 비교구문

Lesson 10-1 비교급과 최상급 만들기_규칙변화

Check up! p. 344

A
1 harder → hardest
2 hotter → hottest
3 colder → coldest
4 faster → fastest
5 easier → easiest
6 happier → happiest
7 larger → largest
8 longer → longest
9 higher → highest
10 lower → lowest
11 closer → closest
12 earlier → earliest
13 heavier → heaviest
14 prettie → prettiest
15 dirtier → dirtiest
16 fresher → freshest
17 thinner → thinnest
18 thicker → thickest
19 deeper → deepest
20 bigger → biggest
21 more exactly → most exactly
22 milder → mildest
23 poorer → poorest
24 colder → coldest
25 more useful → most useful
26 more fluent → most fluent
27 more tired → most tired
28 fatter → fattest
29 kinder → kindest

Lesson 10-2 비교급과 최상급 만들기_불규칙변화

Check up! p. 346

A
1 worse → worst
2 later → latest
3 more → most
4 less → least
5 worse → worst
6 better → best
7 elder → eldest
8 fewer → fewest
9 farther → farthest
10 further → furthest

B
1 more
2 better
3 older
4 latter
5 worse
6 more
7 farther

Lesson 10-3 as 원급 as

Check up! p. 348

A
1 possible
2 as
3 many
4 new
5 long
6 as
7 could
8 early
9 yours
10 quickly

Lesson 10-4 비교급의 비교

Check up! p. 349

A
1 earlier
2 better
3 farther
4 worse
5 bigger
6 more nervous
7 later
8 more
9 neater

Lesson 10-5 비교급 and 비교급

Check up! p. 350

A
1 The more / the smarter
2 higher and higher
3 paler and paler
4 The more / the wider
5 The angrier / the more
6 lower and lower
7 The more / the shier
8 The more / the happier
9 taller and taller

Practice More I

p. 351~353

A
1 further → furthest
2 more → most
3 fewer → fewest
4 cheaper → cheapest
5 smaller → smallest
6 latter → last
7 worse → worst
8 younger → youngest
9 less → least
10 more useless → most useless
11 happier → happiest
12 more convenient → most convenient
13 greater → greatest
14 more easily → most easily
15 lonelier → loneliest

B
1 older
2 farther
3 later
4 dark
5 those of a dog
6 so
7 hard

C
1 as old as
2 as fast as he could
3 as much / as
4 as soon as
5 as early as

D
1 The higher / the smaller
2 The warmer / the more
3 hungrier and hungrier
4 The higher / the fresher
5 The more tired / the more
6 The brighter / the more
7 The hotter / the angrier

E
1 listen as carefully as possible.
2 helped the injured soldiers as much as possible.
3 his name as soon as possible.
4 is taller than his brother.
5 as fast as she could.
6 has to arrive as early as he can.
7 as hard as we can.
8 climbs mountains as often as possible.

Lesson 10-6 원급 / 비교급의 강조

Check up!

p. 355

A
1	X	2	O
3	O	4	X
5	O	6	X
7	O	8	X
9	X	10	O

Lesson 10-7 최상급의 비교

Check up!

p. 356

A
1 the smartest
2 the most beautiful
3 the most handsome
4 the most interesting
5 the best
6 the funniest
7 the easiest
8 the oldest
9 the most foolish

Lesson 10-8 최상급의 다른 표현

Check up!

p. 357~358

A
1 → No other / as tall as
  → No other / taller than
  → taller than any other
  → taller than all the other
2 → No other / as fun as
  → No other / funnier than
  → funnier than any other
  → funnier than all the other
3 → No other / as heavy as
  → No other / heavier than
  → heavier than any other
  → heavier than all the other
4 → No other / as famous as
  → No other / more famous than
  → more famous than any other
  → more famous than all the other

5 → No other / as smart as

→ No other / smarter than

→ smarter than any other

→ smarter than all the other

6 → No other / as short as

→ No other / shorter than

→ shorter than any other

→ shorter than all the other

7 → No other / as useful as

→ No other / more useful than

→ more useful than any other

→ more useful than all the other

8 → No other / as graceful as

→ No other / more graceful than

→ more graceful than any other

→ more graceful than all the other

Practice More Ⅱ

p. 359~360

A 1 most   **2** all the other

3 much   **4** students

5 more   **6** of

7 No other   **8** more tired

9 the most   **10** the fastest

B 1 long and long → longer and longer

2 smarter → smartest

3 of → in

4 very → X

5 boy → boys

6 still → more

7 very → X

8 most → the

9 students → X

10 more → X

C 1 the fastest animal

2 the most important day

3 the most difficult question

4 the hardest time

5 the most interesting book

6 the scariest movie

7 the hottest day

8 fancier than

9 greater / any other

10 the best project

중간 기말고사 예상문제

내신 **최다 출제** 유형   p. 361

01 ①   **02** ③   **03** ②   **04** ②   **05** ④

06 ①

해설

01 one of the 최상급+복수명사: student → students

02 ① math → than math, ② best → better,

④ heavier → heaviest, ⑤ more → the most

03 not as~as A – A만큼~하지 않은 = less than A

– A보다 덜 ~한

04 ~보다 몇 배 ....한 – 배수사+as 원급 as

05 Christine is not smarter than Kelly.

06 'very'는 '매우'의 뜻으로 원급을 강조할 때 사용한다.

p. 362~368

01 ①   **02** ④   **03** ③   **04** ⑤   **05** ③

06 ②   **07** ③   **08** ⑤   **09** ①   **10** ②

11 ③   **12** ⑤   **13** ②   **14** ⑤   **15** ③

16 ①   **17** ①   **18** ②   **19** ③   **20** ⑤

21 ③   **22** ②   **23** ⑤   **24** ④   **25** ③

26 ③   **27** ④   **28** ③   **29** ③   **30** ③,⑤

〈서술형 평가〉

31 city – cities

32 more difficult / easiest

33 (A) not as (so) / as

(B) taller than

(C) the tallest

34 more fun (funnier)

35 (1) fun as

(2) more fun than any other

36 The camera is the most expensive thing.

37 The umbrella is the cheapest thing.

38 An umbrella is not as(so) expensive as sneakers.

(= Sneakers are more expensive than an umbrella.)

39 The condition is getting better and better.

40 The Nile is the longest river in the world.

41 Louvre is one of the most popular museums in the world.

42 There is nothing more exciting than playing tennis.

01 slim – slimmer – slimmest

02 much – more – most

03 good – better – best

04 the+최상급: the most popular 가장 인기 있는

05 비교급을 만들 때 2음절 이상의 형용사는 'er' 대신에 'more'을 붙여준다.

06 'very'는 원급을 강조할 때 쓰인다

07 'pretty'는 원급을 강조할 때 쓰인다.

08 'very'는 원급을 수식한다.

09 'much'는 비교급의 강조에 쓰인다. much → very, so, pretty 중 하나와 바꿔 쓴다.

10 'the+최상급' = 비교급+than all the other+복수명사

11 'the+최상급' = There is nothing~ 비교급+than

12 동사에서 파생된 형용사의 최상급은 단어 앞에 'most'를 붙여준다.

13 거리를 나타낼 경우 'far'의 변화는 'far – farther – farthest'이다.

14 more shorter → shorter

15 앞의 문장을 보면, Jinny가 키가 더 작다는 의미가 되므로, 두 번째 문장에서는 'taller than' 으로 표현해 준다.

16 비교할 대상이 동일하게 나와야 한다. Nothing → No other city

17 비교급을 강조할 때 쓰이는 부사로는 'much, still, a lot, even'등이 있다. 'very'는 원급을 강조할 때 사용한다.

18 비교급+than / 비교급+than

19 비교급+than / 비교급

20 No other 단수명사+as 원급 as A: A만큼 ~한 다른 것은 없다

21 There is nothing~, 비교급+than... : ~보다 더 ...한 것은 없다

22 ① more money as → more money than,
③ smaller as → smaller than ④ good than → good as,
⑤ more older → much older

23 ① hotter as → hotter than, ② the happyest → the happiest
③ good than → better than, ④ as taller as → as tall as

24 비교급+than: ~보다 더 ~한

25 as 원급 as: ~만큼 ...한

26 Molly가 '6th grade', 6학년으로 나이가 제일 많다는 것을 알 수 있다.

27 No other+복수명사~, 비교급+than A: A보다 ~한 다른 것은 없다

28 the+비교급, the+비교급: ~할수록 ...하다 – won't be → will be

29 ① sounds → sounds like, ② the smaller → smaller, ④ tallest → the tallest, ⑤ hottest → the hottest

30 ③ seriousest → most serious, ⑤ most thinnest → thinnest

〈서술형 평가〉

31 one of the 최상급+복수명사

32 비교급+than, the+최상급+of 집단

33 (A) 진수가 민호보다 작지 않다. not as~as

(B) 강호가 민호보다 크다. 비교급+than

(C) 진수가 제일 키가 크다. the+최상급

34 뒤에 'than'이 나오는 것으로 '비교급+than' 구문임을 알 수 있다.

35 the+최상급
= No other+복수명사~, as 원급 as A: A만큼 ~한(다른) 것은 없다.
= 비교급+than any other+단수명사: ~는 다른 어떤 (단수명사) 보다 ~하다.

36 가장 비싼 물건이 무엇인지 물었고, 답은 카메라이다.

37 가장 싼 물건이 무엇인지 물었고, 답은 우산이다.

38 원급 비교: not as A as B: B만큼 A 하지 않는,
비교급 비교: 형용사+than : ~보다 더 ~한

39 비교급+and+비교급: 점점 더 ~하다

40 the+최상급+in 장소: ...에서 가장 ~한

41 one of the 최상급+복수명사: 가장 ~한 것들 중 하나

42 There is nothing, 비교급+than: ~만큼 ..한 것은 없다.

Chapter 11 가정법

Lesson 11-1 가정법의 종류

Check up!
p. 372

A
1 he studied / could pass
2 he were
3 James had read / would have been
4 I wish / played the piano
5 as if she had been
6 comes / will go
7 practice / will go
8 as if / were interesting
9 had enough time / could help
10 I wish / had lived
11 I were / could sleep
12 I wish / had understood
13 as if he had known
14 I were not short / could be
15 had been wise / could not have acted

Lesson 11-2 가정법 과거

Check up!
p. 374

A
1 If my father were not short, I would not be short.
2 If she didn't have a telescope, she could not see the star.
3 If John didn't work hard, he could not earn a lot of money.
4 If my test result were good, I would not be disappointed.
5 If the MP3 player were mine, I could lend it to her.
6 If she knew the answer, she could solve the problem.
7 If Sam didn't practice the piano hard, he could not win the competition.
8 If Steve didn't have enough money, he could not buy a new car.

9 If the weather were not fine, we could not go on a picnic with our family.
10 If my brother were older, he could understand the lecture.

B
1 As she doesn't know the fact, she can't tell it to me.
2 It doesn't snow a lot, so we can go to the festival.
3 As she doesn't like him, she may not write a letter to him.
4 I do my best, so I can get an A on the final test.
5 He doesn't have enough time, so he can't meet her again.

Lesson 11-3 가정법 과거완료

Check up!
p. 375~376

A
1 had read
2 could have traveled
3 had had
4 could have passed
5 could have enjoyed
6 had been rich
7 would have stayed
8 had been
9 would not have said
10 could have answered

B
1 If Linda had not been busy, she could have visited her grandparents.
2 If I had had a car, I could have picked up Jane at the airport.
3 If he had not been so busy, he would not have forgotten Sally's party.
4 If she had kept her promise, they would not have been disappointed.
5 If I had cleaned my room, my mom would not have been really angry.

Lesson 11-4 조건절 if

A 1 will meet → meet
   2 took → take
   3 like → likes
   4 go → will go
   5 was → is
   6 could → can
   7 win → will win
   8 will read → reads
   9 help → will help

Lesson 11-5 I wish 가정법

A 1 weren't   2 didn't pass
   3 weren't   4 had remembered
   5 am not   6 had studied
   7 aren't   8 were
   9 had attended   10 had visited

B 1 had talked   2 bought
   3 spoke   4 hadn't been
   5 knew   6 were
   7 hadn't played

Lesson 11-6 as if 가정법

A 1 as if he liked eating chocolate cake.
   2 as if she had been a singer.
   3 as if he had not slept well last night.
   4 as if she did not sing very well.
   5 as if she could have played the piano.
   6 as if they had liked to go fishing.
   7 as if she had a cold.
   8 as if it had been her idea.
   9 as if I had hidden something from him.
   10 as if he had been good at dancing.

B 1 as if / had met   2 as if / were
   3 as if / hadn't washed   4 as if / knew
   5 as if / were   6 as if / had been

Practice More Ⅰ

A 1 will go   2 have enjoyed
   3 had had   4 have played
   5 could have eaten   6 had had / have picked
   7 had accepted   8 could fix
   9 have to   10 will be

B 1 am not a bird / can't fly
   2 had been / wouldn't have made
   3 were not in trouble
   4 had not agreed with
   5 had enough time / could
   6 doesn't trust
   7 I am not / can't solve
   8 had an appointment / couldn't come
   9 had talked / wouldn't have made
   10 had not been / could have attended
   11 is busy
   12 wasnt' good at / couldn't become
   13 isn't popular

C 1 그는 직업이 없는 것처럼 행동한다.
   2 내가 너라면, 나는 시험을 통과하기 위해 최선을 다할 것이다.
   3 그가 그녀를 믿었었더라면, 그녀는 테니스 시합에서 이겼을 것이다.
   4 나의 아들이 시간을 낭비하지 않았더라면 좋을 텐데.
   5 그가 일찍 일어난다면, 그는 산을 오를 수 있을 텐데.
   6 그는 마치 그녀를 다시 만난 것처럼 말한다.
   7 그녀는 뚱뚱한 척 한다.

D 1 I didn't visit the festival, so I couldn't eat many delicious foods.
   2 In fact, he wasn't poor in his youth.
   3 As you littered, you paid a fine.
   4 Mr. Kim exercises regularly, so he doesn't become fat.

5 I'm sorry she didn't win the contest.

6 As she has much work, she can't sleep more.

7 You live in Seoul, so you can see the night view.

8 As they didn't learn how to make cookies, they couldn't help Sean.

E 1 I wish he had read many books.

2 He talks as if he had never met her before.

3 If John had sung well, he could have been the lead singer of the band.

중간 기말고사 **예상문제**

내신 **최다 출제** 유형

p. 385

01 ② 　 02 ② 　 03 ②,③ 　 04 ⑤ 　 05 ⑤

해설

01 (A)(B) 가정법 과거 문장이며, 가정법에서 be동사는 인칭에 상관없이 'were'를 사용한다.

02 직설법이 과거형의 부정문이므로 긍정의 'I wish+가정법 과거완료'가 와야 한다.

03 ① will come → come, ④ could made → could make, ⑤ not see → didn't see

04 I wish+주어+동사 과거형: have → had

05 가정법 과거완료 형태이다.

p. 386~393

01 ①	02 ②	03 ④	04 ③	05 ⑤
06 ②	07 ⑤	08 ③	09 ②	10 ③,⑤
11 ②	12 ⑤	13 ②	14 ②,③	15 ④
16 ②	17 ③	18 ②	19 ⑤	20 ②
21 ①,④	22 ①,②,⑤	23 ⑤	24 ②	25 ③
26 ③	27 ③	28 ②	29 ④	30 ①

〈서술형 평가〉

31 had been

32 had traveled

33 had got up (gotten up) / have climbed

34 were an Italian restaurant

35 If, won't (will not)

36 as if

37 had worked

38 were not

39 you would have

40 today is not

41 William talks as if he were very silly.

42 If I prepared a tent, I wouldn't come back home tonight.

43 If he doesn't mind it, we can go to the festival together.

44 had more money / he could buy the new bike

45 had practiced hard / they could have won the game

해설

01 조건을 나타내는 if절의 동사는 현재형을 사용한다.

02 과거 사실의 반대의 상황은 가정법 과거완료 'If+주어+had p.p, 주어+would have p.p'를 사용한다.

03 will be sunny → is sunny : 조건을 나타내는 if절의 동사는 현재형을 사용한다.

04 didn't tell → hadn't told

05 him was → he were

06 현재사실에 반대되는 일을 가정할 때는 가정법 과거로 바꾸어 쓸 수 있다.

07 직설법 과거는 'as if+had p.p'의 반대 상황이다.

08 보기: 그녀가 충분한 돈이 있다면 그 모든 책들을 살 수 있을 텐데.
→ 그녀가 충분한 돈이 없기 때문에 그 모든 책들을 살 수 없다.

09 가정법 과거는 직설법 현재형이고, 반대되는 상황이다.

10 ① may → may not, ② 'll have → won't have, ④ may → won't

11 두 번째 문장: didn't know → knew

12 두 번째 문장: 가정법 과거완료 – If+주어+had p.p+, 주어+would+have p.p

13 went → go

14 ② had visited → have visited, ③ wasn't → weren't (가정법에서 be동사 과거형은 인칭에 상관없이 모두 'were'을 사용한다.)

15 현재사실과 반대되는 구문은 가정법 과거이다. [If+주어+과거동사, 주어+would+동사원형]

16 실현 가능성이 있는 단순 조건문이다.
[If+주어+현재형, 주어+can+동사원형]

17 명령문+or~: ~해라, 그렇지 않으면

18 ① will grow → grows, ③ will arrive → arrive,
④ have had → have, ⑤ would → will
→ 실현 가능성이 있는 단순 조건문이다. 조건문에서 If절은 미래 표현을 현재형으로 한다.

19 직설법 문장을 가정법으로 전환한 것이다.

20 I wish 가정법 과거완료 형태이다.

21 ② would have → would have had, ③ bought → would buy,
⑤ could have played → could play

22 ① hadn't enjoy → hadn't enjoyed, ② helped → had helped
⑤ had clever → had been clever

23 I wish+과거: 현재와 반대되는 상황, I wish+과거분사: 과거와 반대되는 상황

24 가정법 과거완료_과거사실과 반대
[If+주어+had+과거분사..., 주어+would, could, should...
+have +과거분사~] 만약 ...했었다면, ~이었을텐데

25 가정법 과거완료_과거사실과 반대
[If+주어+had+과거분사..., 주어+would+have+과거분사~]
만약 ...했었다면, ~이었을 텐데

26 if절의 동사가 과거형으로 가정법 과거형의 문장이다. if절 다음에는 'would+동사원형'이 와야 한다.

27 직설법이 현재형 부정이면, 가정법은 과거형의 긍정이 되고, 긍정이면 부정이 된다.

28 첫 번째 문장: 과거 사실과 반대되는 소망을 나타내므로, 'I wish+had p.p'를 사용한다.
두 번째 문장: 가정법 과거 문장이므로 if절의 동사는 단순 과거형이 알맞다.

29 'as if+과거시제'는 현재 사실의 반대를 뜻하고, 'as if+had p.p'는 과거 사실의 반대를 뜻한다.

30 첫 번째 문장: 가정법 과거완료
'If+주어+had p.p, 주어+could have p.p'
두 번째 문장: 'I wish 과거' 또는 'I wish 과거완료'를 사용한다.
(→ 위 문장에 때를 나타내는 부사가 없기 때문이다.)

〈서술형 평가〉

31 'I wish, had p.p: ~했었더라면 좋을 텐데' 구문이다.

32 과거의 사실과 반대되는 일을 소망하는 표현이다.
'I wish+가정법 과거완료'

33 과거사실의 반대 상황이다_가정법 과거완료

34 현재사실에 대한 소망 _ I wish+가정법 과거

35 '명령문, and...' ~해라, 그러면... 의 뜻을 가진 명령문은 조건절 'if' 문장과 바꿔 쓸 수 있다.

36 'in fact'구문은 'as if'구문으로 바꿔 쓸 수 있다.

37 가정법 과거완료 형태이다.

38 가정법 과거 형태이다. be동사는 인칭에 상관없이 'were'를 사용한다.

39 가정법 과거_현재 사실과 반대되는 일을 나타낸다.

40 'as if' 과거형_현재 사실과 반대되는 상황을 나타낸다.

41 현재의 사실과 반대되는 일을 나타낸다. 'as if' 구문을 'in fact' 구문으로 바꿔 쓸 수 있다.

42 현재사실에 반대되는 일을 이야기할 때 가정법 과거를 사용한다.

43 Unless = If~not: ~하지 않는다면

44 때를 나타내는 부사 'now'로 인해 가정법 과거를 사용한다.

45 때를 나타내는 부사 'last year'로 인해 과거 사실과 반대되는 가정법 과거완료를 사용한다.

12 관계사

Lesson 12-1 관계대명사의 역할과 종류

Check up!

p. 398

A
1 the book / which
2 the bag / whose
3 what
4 The baby / who
5 the house / whose
6 a boy / who
7 a friend / whose
8 some tea / which
9 what
10 the table / which

B
1 which my father composed
2 whose color is red
3 whom I met last week
4 that we visited last winter
5 that have super heroes who save the world
6 which she took yesterday
7 which I lived in for seventeen years
8 whose topic was how to live a successful life
9 who lives in Busan
10 that attracts many people to our performance

Lesson 12-2 관계대명사 who

Check up!

p. 399~400

A
1 I know the girl who jogs every morning.
2 Tim and Jane are singers whom I love.
3 Do you remember Jane who was our class president?
4 I have a sister who has a long blond hair.
5 There is a man whom I want to talk with.
6 She met a boy whose brother is a dentist.
7 I saw a man and a bird that were sitting on the bench.
8 Mary is a student who got the first prize in English speaking contest.
9 He remembered Jane who was sitting next to Linda.
10 They respect James who has a lot of wisdom.

B
1 who was sitting next to Sam
2 who is running down the street
3 who can answer all the difficult questions
4 whom I wanted to meet
5 whose coat is green is our grandmother
6 who used to clean the street
7 who was looking for a dog
8 who work in the hotel
9 whose hair is blond
10 whom I invited to my birthday party

Lesson 12-3 관계대명사 which

Check up!

p. 401~402

A
1 which   2 whose
3 are   4 whose
5 which   6 which
7 which   8 which
9 which   10 which

B
1 This is a desk which father made for me.
2 I have a cat which has black and white fur.
3 This is the car which I fixed by myself.
4 Jane likes to read the book whose cover is black.
5 The song is good which Harry made for his wife.
6 Edward made some food which I liked.
7 This is my daughter's room whose walls are green.
8 This letter which Jim wrote to me was so moving.
9 Tim should clean his car which is too dirty.
10 I want to buy the camera which many people like.

Lesson 12-4 관계대명사 that

p. 403

Check up!

A
1 that / whom
2 that
3 that
4 that / which
5 that
6 which / that
7 that
8 that
9 who / that
10 that

Lesson 12-5 관계대명사 what

p. 405

Check up!

A
1 What
2 what
3 what
4 what
5 That / what
6 what
7 What
8 that
9 what
10 what

B
1 I don't believe what you said to Tim.
2 Mother bought what I wanted for my graduation present.
3 What you prepared for your son's birthday party will make him happy.
4 That movie is not what I want to watch.
5 I think Jane has to do what is best for her.
6 What Lisa needed was paper and pencils for her study.
7 They wanted to know what Helen wanted to have for New Year's day.

Lesson 12-6 관계대명사의 생략

p. 406

Check up!

A
1 (which)
2 (X)
3 (that)
4 (X)
5 (which was)
6 (that)
7 (which)

Practice More I

p. 407~408

A
1 who
2 whom
3 which
4 whose
5 which
6 that
7 that
8 whose
9 whom
10 whose

B
1 whose → which(that)
2 which → who(that)
3 which → whose
4 whose → which(that)
5 whose → whom
6 that → what
7 which → who(that)
8 whom → who
9 what → whom
10 whose → who

C
1 which is
2 who are
3 which was
4 which is
5 which are
6 that
7 whom
8 who is

D
1 This is a school which my daughter will attend next year.
2 The boy is a famous dancer who has lived in this city for five years.
3 She was going to the tower whose night view was awesome.
4 The woman who is wearing a red raincoat is running down the street.
   (= The woman who is running down the street is wearing a red raincoat.)
5 I have a friend whom I can depend on.
6 This is the last thing that he had in his pocket.
7 There is a restaurant which(that) opens early in the morning.
8 The man is our math teacher who said we should study hard for the final exam.

Lesson 12-7 관계부사

Check up!
p. 410

A
1 where　　2 when
3 how　　　4 when
5 how　　　6 where
7 why　　　8 where
9 when

Lesson 12-8 관계부사 when, where

Check up!
p. 411~412

A
1 where　　2 when
3 where　　4 the day
5 the place

B
1 I remember the day when my son gained his feet for the first time.
2 Tokyo is the city where I want to go.
3 She went to America when she was an elementary school student.
4 This is the place where I lost my bike.
5 He doesn't forget the day when he bought his first car.
6 Busan is a big city where my best friend lives.
7 Sam still remembers the day when he first met his girlfriend.
8 April first is the day when people can be forgiven for their lies.
9 This is the building where they have built for five years.
10 Kate told me the day when she left for China.
11 Nick waited for her in the park where they usually exercise.
12 We will go hiking this Saturday when our parents celebrate wedding anniversary.

Lesson 12-9 관계부사 why, how

Check up!
p. 413~414

A
1 Tim didn't know the reason why his mom was angry.
2 I can't understand the reason why she cries.
3 → I'll teach you how you can write a good novel.
   → I'll teach you the way you can write a good novel.
4 They didn't know the reason why she left suddenly.
5 → She'll tell me how I can fix my oven by myself.
   → She'll tell me the way I can fix my oven by myself.
6 Tell me the reason why she gave up the competition.
7 → Can you tell me how you solved all the problems?
   → Can you tell me the way you solved all the problems?
8 I didn't know the reason why he didn't come to the party last night.
9 → John learned how the chef made the pasta.
   → John learned the way the chef made the pasta.
10 Does he tell the reason why he has to get up early tomorrow?

B
1 how (the way) you folded the paper crane
2 how (the way) I draw pictures
3 the reason
4 how (the way) she got first prize
5 why I should do

Lesson 12-10 관계부사의 생략

Check up!
p. 416

A
1 → I can remember the day when we first met.
   → I can remember when we first met.
2 → Tell me the reason why they were late.
   → Tell me why they were late.
3 → We remember the city where my son was

born.

→ We remember where my son was born.

4 → Do they know the time when our performance will begin?

→ Do they know when our performance will begin?

5 → I can't remember the way (that) Koreans make kimchi.

→ I can't remember how Koreans make kimchi.

6 → We are going to the place where we got married.

→ We are going to where we got married.

7 → Helen got up at that time when the alarm went off.

→ Helen got up when the alarm went off.

8 → I know the reason why she resigned from her position.

→ I know why she resigned from her position.

9 → We want to know the day when she will graduate.

→ We want to know when she will graduate.

Lesson 12-11 관계사의 계속적 용법

Check up!

p. 418

A **1** John made a new movie, which was really exciting.

2 This is my friend, who majored in English education.

3 Mr. Park, who was my professor, recieved an honor last week.

4 We went to the store, where there were many beautiful flowers.

5 I have three sons, who are actors.

6 Amy took me to the seminar, where we could taste a variety of food.

7 I want to introduce my husband, Jack, who likes to play soccer.

8 My mother, who got a new job last month, was really happy.

9 He read about the person, who invented the washing machine.

10 I watched the drama, which was really boring.

Practice More II

p. 419~421

A **1** that (which) **2** (X)
3 which (that) **4** when
5 (X) **6** what
7 where **8** why

B **1** which
2 where (at which)
3 what
4 the way (how)
5 what
6 where (in which)
7 which (where / that)
8 that (which)

C **1** Do you know (the place) where Jade and Amy will get married?

2 → This is the cafe where Jane sometimes drinks juice.

→ This is the cafe in which Jane sometimes drinks juice.

3 My uncle, who is a businessman, is working in China for a month.

4 → Can you remember (the place) where we lived for fifty years?

→ Can you remember the place in which we lived for fifty years?

5 → We liked the way my mother scolded us.

→ We liked how my mother scolded us.

6 I often go to Namsan Tower, where I can see squirrels.

7 Do you know the reason why she didn't come to the party?

8 He watched the TV talk show, which I watched at Linda's house.

D **1** What the teacher wants us is to do our best.

2 I found an old radio in the house where they lived.

3 We remember the day when you first met us.

4 The young boy, who is thirteen years old, can speak English fluently.

5 Look at the amusement park where the children are playing.

6 He goes back home next week, when the test ends.

7 I made a new friend in America, who was a musical actor.

8 Mr. Park, who was my old English teacher, went to America to study English literature.

9 I didn't remember the day of my parents' 50th wedding anniversary.

10 I don't understand what he means.

중간 기말고사 **예상문제**

p. 422

내신 **최다 출제** 유형

01 ①   02 ③   03 ②   04 ④   05 ③
06 ②

해설

01 ① whose, ②,③,④,⑤ that
02 '주격 관계대명사'만 생략할 수 없다. 생략하려면 'which are'까지 해야 한다.
03 선행사 'the way'와 관계부사 'how'는 같이 사용할 수 없다.
04 소유격 관계대명사 'whose'가 오며, 'that'은 소유격의 형태가 없다
05 'the thing that'은 선행사를 포함하는 관계대명사 'what'으로 바꿔 쓸 수 있다.
06 선행사를 포함하고 있는 관계대명사 'what'이 알맞다.

p. 423~429

01 ②   02 ①   03 ①   04 ③   05 ⑤
06 ④   07 ②   08 ④   09 ②   10 ③
11 ①   12 ③   13 ③   14 ②,③   15 ①,④
16 ①   17 ②   18 ②   19 ④   20 ⑤
21 ⑤   22 ②   23 ②,③   24 ④,⑤   25 ②
26 ②   27 ④   28 ②   29 ①,②   30 ②
31 ⑤   32 ②   33 ③   34 ①   35 ③

〈서술형 평가〉

36 when
37 what
38 that
39 단어: which are
이유: '주격 관계대명사+be동사+분사'에서 '관계대명사+be동사'는 생략이 가능하다.

---

40 Saturday is the day when I play tennis.

41 We should respect the way others think.

42 Let's find other people who live in this town.

43 We know the boy who(m) (that) everyone loves so much.

44 These are the CDs of English grammar which (that) my brother bought for me.

45 This is the biggest bookstore where I usually buy books.

해설

01 사람이 선행사일 경우 'who' 또는 'that'을 사용하고, 사물이 선행사일 경우 'which' 또는 'that'을 사용한다.
02 사물이 선행사일 경우 'which' 또는 'that'을 사용하고, 사람이 선행사일 경우 'who' 또는 'that'을 사용한다.
03 선행사가 사람이므로 'who', 선행사가 사물이므로 'that'이 알맞다.
04 주격관계대명사 'who'를 사용하는 것이 알맞다.
05 'is'가 'she' 뒤로 가야 한다. → Can you tell me the reason why she is angry?
06 선행사 'prince'가 사람이므로 'who'가 온다.
07 선행사가 사물이지만, 소유를 나타내고 있다. 'whose'가 알맞다.
08 선행사가 장소를 나타내는 'the place'이므로 관계부사 'where'가 오는 것이 알맞다.
09 ② 관계대명사 who, ①,③,④,⑤ 의문사 who
10 ③ 'day'를 수식하는 의문형용사, ①,②,④,⑤ 선행사를 포함한 관계대명사
11 사물을 선행사로 하는 주격 관계대명사 'which'는 'that'과 바꿔 쓸 수 있다.
12 'the way'는 관계부사 'how'의 선행사로 바꿔 쓸 수 있다.
13 선행사 'leaves'가 목적어 역할을 하며, 이에 따라 바꿔 쓸 수 있는 것은 'which'이다.
14 〈보기, ②,③〉 관계대명사, ①,④,⑤ 의문대명사
15 〈보기, ①,④〉 관계대명사, ②,③,⑤ 의문대명사
16 목적격 관계대명사는 생략할 수 있다.
He baked some bread with the blueberries (that) he grew.
17 선행사가 사물이므로 관계대명사 'which'가 온다.
18 주격 관계대명사와 그 동사는 생략할 수 없다.
19 주격관계대명사는 생략할 수 없다.
20 ⑤ 주격 관계대명사, ①,②,③,④ 목적격 관계대명사
21 ⑤ 관계대명사, ①,②,③,④ 접속사
22 '주격 관계대명사+be동사+분사'에서 '관계대명사+be동사'는 생략할 수 있다.
23 ② which – whose, ③ which – who (that)

24 ④ what – which (that) ⑤ who – which (that)

25 'that'이 들어간다.

26 선행사가 사람과 사물일 때 모두 사용할 수 있는 관계대명사는 'that'이다.

27 〈보기, ④〉 접속사, ①,②,③,⑤ 관계대명사

28 ② whom → who

29 ③ whose → who, ④ whom → whose, ⑤ student arrived → student that arrived

30 선행사가 'the reason'일 경우 관계부사는 'why'가 온다.

31 분사나 전치사구를 동반한 '관계대명사+be동사'는 생략이 가능하다.

32 'who'는 전치사 'of'의 목적어이다. 목적격 관계대명사는 생략이 가능하다.

33 ③ whose ①,②,④,⑤ who

34 ① who, ②,③,④,⑤ which

35 ① which → when, ② what → why, ④ how → X, ⑤ how → why

〈서술형 평가〉

36 선행사 'the month'가 날짜를 가리키는 말이기 때문에 관계부사 'when'을 써 준다.

37 선행사가 없고, 내용상 '~하는 것'이 나와야 하므로 'what'이 알맞다.

38 선행사가 '사람+동물'일 경우 관계대명사 'that'을 써주는 것이 알맞다.

39 이유는 ['관계대명사+be동사' 생략이 가능] 이라는 말이 들어가면 맞음

40 the day+관계부사 when

41 'the way' 방법을 나타내는 선행사

42 선행사가 '사람'이므로 관계대명사는 'who'가 나오는 것이 맞다.

43 'who'의 목적격을 사용하거나 'that'을 사용하여 두 문장을 연결한다.

44 선행사가 사물이므로 목적격 관계대명사 'which' 또는 'that'을 사용한다.

45 선행사가 장소를 뜻하는 'book store'이므로 관계부사 'where'가 필요하다.

Chapter 13 접속사

Lesson 13-1 등위접속사

☆Check up!

p. 434

A	1	so	2	but
	3	or	4	but
	5	or	6	so
	7	for	8	or
	9	but	10	and

Lesson 13-2 명령문과 and / or

☆Check up!

p. 435

A	1	and	2	or
	3	and	4	or
	5	and		

Lesson 13-3 상관접속사

☆Check up!

p. 436~437

A	1	both	2	or
	3	neither	4	not only
	5	well	6	nor
	7	but also		

B	1	has →have	2	nor → or
	3	either (nor) → neither (or)	4	and → or
	5	don't like → likes	6	go → goes
	7	is → are	8	like → likes
	9	are → is	10	buy → buys

Lesson 13-4 종속접속사_that

☆Check up!

p. 438~439

A	1	보어	2	목적어
	3	보어	4	주어
	5	목적어	6	주어
	7	보어	8	목적어
	9	주어		

B	1	명사절	2	명사절
	3	명사절	4	명사절
	5	동격절	6	동격절
	7	명사절		

Lesson 13-5 종속접속사_whether / If

☆Check up!

p. 440

A	1	Whether	2	whether
	3	if	4	whether
	5	if	6	whether
	7	whether	8	if
	9	whether	10	if
	11	Whether	12	whether

Lesson 13-6 종속 접속사_시간이나 때를 나타내는 접속사

☆Check up!

p. 442

A	1	After	2	since
	3	Every time	4	When
	5	while	6	since
	7	until	8	before
	9	until	10	when
	11	since	12	since
	13	read	14	When
	15	since	16	As
	17	while		

Practice More I

p. 443~445

A
1 or
2 but
3 so
4 and
5 for
6 so
7 and
8 but
9 or
10 for
11 or
12 and

B
1 for
2 reading
3 or
4 if (whether)
5 is
6 go
7 whether
8 neither
9 they said
10 that

C
1 that
2 if, whether, that
3 That
4 whether
5 that
6 if, whether
7 that
8 whether
9 that, whether
10 whether
11 that
12 if, whether
13 whether

D
1 Both Helen and her father watch the nine o'clock news every night.
2 Either Yumi(Sumi) or Sumi(Yumi) should serve as the class president.
3 Tom doesn't like not only playing computer games but also doing a puzzle.
4 I wonder whether or not he will leave now.
   (= I wonder whether he will leave now or not)
5 I want to eat neither pasta nor pizza now.
6 She likes to listen to music while she reads books.
7 My brother hurts his leg every time he plays soccer.

Lesson 13-7 if / unless / because

p. 447

A
1 If
2 Unless
3 If
4 Unless
5 unless
6 If
7 unless

Lesson 13-8 so that / so~that

p. 448~449

A
1 I am saving money so that I can study abroad next year.
2 They practiced hard so that they could get the gold medal.
3 Please turn off the light so that my baby can sleep now.
4 I registered the baking class so that I could learn how to bake bread.
5 He took photos of her so that he could keep memories of her.
6 Mina quit her job so that she could start her own company.
7 He called me so that he could make an appointment.

B
1 so long that / couldn't
2 so sweet that / doesn't
3 so nervous that / didn't
4 so smart that / can
5 so busy that / couldn't
6 so tired that / couldn't
7 so hard that / couldn't

Lesson 13-9 though / although / even though

p. 450

A
1 Although he is Korean
2 though I got first place in the English speaking contest
3 Even though she was sick
4 Although he didn't get the best actor award
5 though I want to go to bed.
6 Even though she seemed sad.
7 although his goal was to lose weight.
8 although there was a small chance of being a member of the national soccer team.
9 although he doesn't come back home.
10 Though she is five.

Lesson 13-10 접속부사

p. 451

Check up!

A 1 However   2 Therefore
  3 In addition   4 For example
  5 However(But)   6 Finally

Practice More II

p. 452~454

A 1 since (because / as)
  2 if (whether)
  3 unless
  4 surprised that
  5 so that
  6 as (because)
  7 that
  8 since (because / as)
  9 Even if (Even though)
  10 because of

B 1 whenever   2 After
  3 until   4 so / that
  5 although   6 since
  7 so that   8 While
  9 as soon as   10 before

C 1 I must sleep now so that I can go to the mountain in the morning.
  2 I was so scared that I couldn't enjoy the horror movie.
  3 Although the service was very bad, the food was delicious.
  4 The zoo is so small that we can see it in a day.
  5 Though the traffic was very heavy, we could arrive on time.
  6 We should save money in order to go to America next year.
  7 Today was so hot that I had to reapply sunscreen all day.
  8 I worked so hard that I got a promotion faster than any other employee.
  9 He turned down the light so that his baby could sleep well.
  10 The pizza was so large that all of our family could eat it.

D 1 (C)   2 (A)
  3 (B)   4 (G)
  5 (H)   6 (D)
  7 (I)   8 (J)
  9 (E)   10 (F)

중간 기말고사 예상문제

내신 최다 출제 유형

p. 455

01 ①   02 ④   03 ⑤   04 ②   05 ①
06 ③,⑤

해설

01 listen to → listening to
→ 상관접속사: 문법적으로 대등한 관계의 것을 사용해야 한다.
02 ④ 목적격 관계대명사, ①,②,③,⑤ 접속사
03 After I get up. → After I got up, – 동사를 과거형으로 바꾸고, 콤마를 넣어준다.
04 한 문장 안에 원인과 결과를 표현할 때는 접속사 'so (그래서)'를 사용한다.
05 'if∼not' = unless 만약 ∼하지 않는다면
06 ① and → if, ② which → when, ④ will meet → meet

p. 456~462

01 ④	02 ①	03 ⑤	04 ②	05 ③
06 ②	07 ③	08 ①	09 ④	10 ②
11 ③	12 ②	13 ⑤	14 ②	15 ⑤
16 ③	17 ④	18 ①	19 ④	20 ⑤
21 ②	22 ①	23 ⑤	24 ③	25 ②
26 ③	27 ①	28 ⑤	29 ②	30 ④
31 ③	32 ①	33 ③	34 ②	35 ⑤
36 ⑤	37 ④	38 ③	39 ④,⑤	40 ①,②

〈서술형 평가〉

41 so that   42 In addition
43 but   44 Though
45 For example   46 After
47 When   48 and
49 both / and

01 'if' ~한다면

02 'because' ~ 때문에 – 뒤에 문장이 온다.

03 'while' ~하는 동안

04 'that'은 목적어 역할을 하는 명사절을 이끈다.

05 'unless' ~하지 않는다면 – 문맥상 뒤의 부정적 의미의 문장으로 보아, 앞 문장 역시 부정적 의미가 포함된다.

06 ② 지시 형용사, ①,③,④,⑤ 접속사

07 ③ 'However' 하지만, 그렇지만 – 앞뒤 문장이 서로 대조되는 의미를 가질 때 사용한다.

08 ① 의문부사, ②,③,④,⑤ 접속사

09 ④ that은 보어 역할을 하는 명사절을 이끈다.

10 〈보기, ②〉~하고 있을 때, ① ~ 때문에, ③ ~함에 따라, ④ ~만큼, ⑤ ~로서

11 'both A and B' A와 B 둘 다

12 'when' ~할 때

13 앞뒤 문장이 서로 대조될 때는 'however'를 사용한다.

14 'when' ~할 때, 'with' ~와

15 'because' ~때문에, 'unless' ~하지 않는다면

16 because+문장, because of+명사(구)

17 'in the end' = 'finally' 결국엔

18 〈보기, ①〉접속사, ②,③,④,⑤ 의문부사

19 'neither A nor B' A와 B 둘 다 아닌

20 'so ~ that...' 너무 ~해서 ...한

21 'so ~ that...' 너무 ~해서 ...한

22 '명령문, and' ~해라, 그러면.. – 정기적으로 운동을 해라, 그러면 너는 살이 빠질 것이다.

23 '명령문, or' ~해라, 그렇지 않으면 – 이 약을 먹어라, 그렇지 않으면 낫지 않을 거야.

24 문맥 상 앞뒤의 내용이 대조가 되어야 알맞다.
Miranda는 모자가 많지만, 그녀 스스로 디자인해서 만든다고 했으니, 많은 돈을 쓰지 않는다는 표현이 와야 한다.

25 〈보기, ②〉~하면서, ①,⑤ ~때문에, ③,④ ~로서

26 'whether' ~인지 아닌지

27 'while' ~하면서, ~하는 동안

28 'every time' ~할 때마다

29 'because' ~때문에 – because+문장

30 'however' 그러나, 하지만 – 앞뒤 문장의 내용이 대조일 때 사용한다.

31 'although' 비록 ~일지라도

32 'so' 그래서 – so 이하에 앞의 원인에 대한 결과가 나온다.

33 'when' ~할 때

34 'for example' 예를 들면

35 'so' 그래서

36 'however = but' 그러나, 하지만

37 'in addition = moreover' 게다가

38 'if~not = unless' 만약 ~하지 않는다면

39 because → because of ⑤ will come → come

40 ③ dances well → a good dancer,
④ be loved → being loved,
→ 상관접속사의 경우 문법상 대등한 관계에 있는 것들이 온다.
⑤ I → me – 전치사 with의 목적어 Harrison처럼 대명사 'I'도 목적격 인칭대명사가 된다.

〈서술형 평가〉

41 'so that' ~하기 위해서

42 'in addition' 게다가

43 'but' 하지만

44 'though' ~임에도 불구하고

45 'for example' 예를 들면

46 'after' ~한 후에

47 'when' ~할 때 – 시간을 나타내는 접속사

48 '명령문, and' ~해라, 그러면

49 'both A and B' A와 B 둘 다

Chapter 14 전치사

Lesson 14-1 전치사의 역할

p. 465

A
1 to / the hotel
2 on / the table
3 about / the accident
4 along / the street
5 at / the news
6 about / the star
7 of / preparing
8 on / the grass
9 since / last month
10 for / my mother

Lesson 14-2 시간, 때를 나타내는 전치사 (1)

p. 466

A
1 on
2 at
3 on
4 in
5 At
6 on
7 on
8 on
9 in
10 in

Lesson 14-3 시간, 때를 나타내는 전치사 (2)

p. 467

A
1 for
2 after
3 during
4 from
5 since
6 from
7 until
8 after
9 during
10 since

Lesson 14-4 장소를 나타내는 전치사

p. 468

A
1 in
2 on
3 at
4 in
5 at
6 in
7 in
8 At
9 at
10 in

Lesson 14-5 위치를 나타내는 전치사

p. 470

A
1 behind
2 across from
3 next to (by / beside)
4 in front of
5 next to (by / beside)
6 between / and
7 across from
8 between / and
9 behind
10 in front of

Practice More I

p. 471~473

A
1 among
2 next to
3 under
4 for
5 over
6 behind
7 at
8 between
9 among
10 in

B
1 at
2 by
3 Before
4 from
5 after
6 for
7 for
8 by
9 From
10 during

C
1 on the street
2 in Minhyuk's car
3 down the stairs
4 throughout the forest
5 in university
6 in the box
7 in front of many people
8 the Internet
9 at the meeting
10 under the tree

D
1 He lived with five dogs on the mountain.
2 I am going to visit grandmother on Sunday.

3 The department store is in front of the perfume store.

4 You had better watch out for pickpockets on the subway.

5 Helen should send this letter to her father by October 3rd.

6 Many beautiful pictures are hung on the wall.

7 Jane is leaving for America on Sunday.

8 My sister doesn't even drink water at night.

9 There is a big crowd in the plaza.

10 We are going to have lunch with Mr. Park tomorrow afternoon.

Lesson 14-6 방향을 나타내는 전치사

Check up! p. 475

A
1 through		**2** up
3 across		**4** around
5 into		**6** out of
7 through		**8** in
9 along		**10** to
11 into		**12** around

Lesson 14-7 도구, 수단을 나타내는 전치사

Check up! p. 476

A
1 with		**2** by
3 with		**4** by
5 with		**6** by
7 with		**8** with
9 by		

Lesson 14-8 형용사와 함께 쓰는 전치사

Check up! p. 478

A
1 of		**2** from
3 for		**4** for
5 about		**6** at
7 in		**8** from
9 for		**10** of
11 for (about)		**12** for
13 of		**14** for
15 of		

Lesson 14-9 동사와 함께 쓰는 전치사

Check up! p. 479

A
1 for		**2** at
3 for		**4** with
5 about		**6** for
7 on		**8** of
9 for		**10** to

Lesson 14-10 기타 전치사

Check up! p. 480

A
1 to		**2** about
3 like		**4** by
5 without		**6** of
7 like		**8** as
9 to		**10** for
11 about		**12** of
13 with		**14** as
15 about		

Practice More Ⅱ p. 481~483

A
1 for		**2** as
3 by		**4** to
5 As		**6** of
7 like		**8** with
9 to		**10** by

B
1 for		**2** up
3 into		**4** along
5 through		**6** out of
7 From		**8** across
9 around		**10** to

C
1 looking for		**2** buy / for
3 absent from		**4** Thank / for
5 interested in		**6** different from
7 is good at		**8** are ready for
9 listen to		**10** is famous for

D **1** She will travel by ship.

2 He piked her up with a new car.

3 John doesn't write a letter without his pen.

4   I practiced playing the piano with a new piano.
5   She was looking for her cat.
6   Harry was afraid of thunder.
7   Jim and Sora were raised by their grandmother.
8   We did our homework on Tim's computer.
9   Mom always goes shopping by taxi.
10 I'm waiting for the airplane from Seoul.

중간 기말고사 예상문제

p. 484

내신 최다 출제 유형

01 ④   02 ③   03 ①   04 ⑤   05 ②

06 He doesn't wash the dishes without gloves.

해설

01 'be different from' ~와 다르다. 'in English' 영어로
02 'be curious about' ~에 호기심이 있다
03 ① at → of – 'be tired of' ~에 싫증 내다
04 탁자와 침대 사이, 또는 각각 탁자, 침대 옆의 표현을 사용할 수 있다.
05 ① by → as, ③ waiting of → waiting for, ④ at → for, ⑤ at → in
06 'without' ~없이

p. 485~490

01 ②   02 ④   03 ③   04 ③   05 ②
06 ⑤   07 ③   08 ②   09 ②   10 ⑤
11 ③   12 ④   13 ④   14 ①   15 ②
16 ⑤   17 ③   18 ⑤   19 ②   20 ②,③
21 ③   22 ②   23 ⑤   24 ①   25 ①
26 ③   27 ②   28 ⑤   29 ①,④   30 ②,③

〈서술형 평가〉

31 by / to   32 to / for
33 for / in   34 on / of
35 after / with   36 down
37 along   38 through
39 My family and I get up at 10 o'clock every Sunday.
40 I looked at the pictures on the wall.
41 We've waited for him for two hours.
42 Many boys are around Jessie and they are laughing.
43 without
44 like
45 put up

해설

01 날짜나 요일 앞에는 'on'을 붙인다.
02 표면에 접촉해 있는 것을 나타낼 때는 'on'을 쓴다.
03 'be full of' ~로 가득 차다
04 'prefer A to B' B보다 A를 더 좋아하다
05 'in the kitchen' 주방에
06 ① because → because of, ② at → in, ③ to dance → dancing, ④ next → next to
07 'until' ~까지
08 'out of' ~밖으로
09 'by' ~함으로써
10 〈보기, ⑤〉 ~을 입고, ①,④ ~안에, ②,③ 시간을 나타내는 'in'
11 'into' ~안으로
12 'by' ~에 의해
13 'with' ~을 가진, ~와 함께
14 'from now on' 지금부터, 'on Friday evening' 금요일 저녁에
15 in → as (~로서)
16 'be good at' ~을 잘하다, 'in' – 공간을 나타내는 전치사로 사용되었다.
17 'breathe in' 숨을 들이마시다 'play with' ~을 가지고 놀다
18 'wrong with' ~이 잘못된, 'about' ~에 대한
19 첫 번째 문장: 빈 칸 뒤에는 절이 있으므로 'while'을 써준다.
    두 번째 문장: 특정한 기간 앞에는 'during'을 써준다.
20 ① for → of, ④ in → on, ⑤ of → on
21 'for' ~동안 (시간을 나타내는 숫자 표현)
22 'like' ~처럼
23 ① of → on, ② in → on ③ at → on, ④ in → up
24 on → over
25 'in' ~의 (크기)로
26 'pay ~ for...' ...에 대해 ~을 지불하다
27 'in + 월', 'on + 월, 일'
28 'believe in' ~을 믿다
29 ② for → since, ③ while → for, ⑤ every Saturdays → every Saturday (on Saturdays)
30 ② in the → at, ③ clean → cleaning

〈서술형 평가〉

31 첫 번째 문장: 방법을 나타낼 때 by,
    두 번째 문장: 도착지를 나타낼 때 to

32 첫 번째 문장: 'to' ~에게,
두 번째 문장: 'for' 방향을 나타내는 전치사

33 첫 번째 문장: 시간의 길이를 나타내는 숫자 표현은
'for'를 사용한다.
두 번째 문장: 'in English' 영어로

34 첫 번째 문장: 'on' ~위에
두 번째 문장: 'tired of' ~에 싫증난, 지겨운

35 첫 번째 문장: 'after school' 방과 후에
두 번째 문장: 'wrong with' ~이 잘못된

36 'down' ~아래로

37 'along' ~을 따라

38 'through' ~을 통과하여

39 'ever' 매~, ~마다, 'at' – 시간 앞에 쓰인다.

40 'look at' ~을 바라보다, 'on' – 표면상 맞닿은 것의 위를 말할 때
사용한다.

41 'wait for' ~를 기다리다, 'for'–시간의 길이를 나타내는 숫자 표현
과 함께 쓰인다.

42 'around' ~주위에, laugh 웃다

43 'without' ~없이

44 첫 번째 문장: 'like' ~처럼, 두 번째 문장: 'look like' ~와 닮은

45 'put up with' ~을 참다

Chapter 15 화법과 속담

Lesson 15-1 평서문의 화법 전환

Check up! p. 494~495

A
1. Minji told him that she knew how to play the game.
2. My mother told me that I should be polite to everybody.
3. Jane told us that it was rainy that day, so we should change the plans.
4. Mom told my brother that he should study hard.
5. Tom said that he would be back next month.
6. He said that he couldn't believe the rumor then.
7. Father told me that he was going to go to Japan the next day.
8. Jim told her that he would love her forever.
9. Jane told us that she would attend the metting in Busan
10. Tim told me that he had bought a new car the previous week.

B
1. My little sister said, "I broke Tim's window."
2. My friend told me that he(she) was going to quit his job.
3. The girl said that she didn't want to go hiking.
4. Jenny said to her friends, "I invite you to my birthday party."
5. Tim said to his son, "You have to save money."
6. Jina told him that she would make some food for the picnic.
7. Mike said, "I will go to Jeju Island next week."

Lesson 15-2 의문문의 화법전환

Check up! p. 497

A
1. Kate asked me if she could borrow my car.
2. Father asked where his key was.
3. Amy asked her who was calling.
4. The lady asked me if I enjoyed the party.
5. The man asked her if she could say that again.
6. She asked if I was for or against her opinion.
7. Andy asked me if I was looking for the book.
8. He asked her what made her cry.
9. I asked Jack where I could get the ticket.
10. The gentleman asked her where the conference center was.

Lesson 15-3 명령문의 화법전환

Check up! p. 498~499

A
1. She told me to tell her why I cried.
2. The teacher advised her to study hard to pass the exam.
3. Mom told my brother to get up early in the morning.
4. Jim told her to exercise regularly.
5. Mom advised me to quit playing right then.
6. Mr. Kim ordered us not to be late the next day.
7. She told her son to pass her the salt.
8. John ordered her to turn in her paper by five.
9. Mrs. Anderson advised me to stop copying novels.
10. Tina told me not to play the piano at night.

Lesson 15-4 속담표현 익히기

Check up! p. 501~502

A
1	②	2	⑥
3	③	4	④
5	⑤	6	⑫
7	⑩	8	⑬
9	⑪	10	⑦
11	⑨	12	①
13	⑧		

B
1. make light work
2. thicker than water
3. Where there is a will
4. A watched pot

5 Necessity / invention

6 Teaching / learning

7 no moss

8 A little / none

9 laughs last

10 before they hatch

Practice **More** I

p. 503~505

A 1 told me that he didn't forget my birthday.

2 me if I could go to the concert with him that night.

3 her to send those letters that day.

4 him that she couldn't understand what he was saying.

5 John what he was looking for then.

6 James if she could borrow his car.

7 her not to throw garbage away there.

8 me to put on my raincoat because it was rainy that day.

9 him that she couldn't remember his name.

10 his son to be careful when he drove a car.

B 1 went

2 said

3 it was

4 not to

5 who was

6 the next day

7 she was

8 to speak

9 if

10 to wait

C 1 He who laughs best laughs last.

2 Necessity is the mother of invention.

3 A watched pot never boils.

4 A friend in need is a friend indeed.

5 After a storm comes the calm.

6 Where there is a will, there is a way.

7 Rome was not built in a day.

8 Strike while the iron is hot.

9 Out of the frying pan into the fire.

10 A rolling stone gathers no moss.

중간 기말고사 **예상문제**

내신 **최다 출제** 유형

p. 506

01 ③ **02** ② **03** ① **04** told, not to be

05 ④,⑤

해설

01 전달동사가 과거형이기 때문에 종속절의 시제는 과거 또는 과거완료가 와야 한다.

02 의문사가 없는 의문문의 간접화법– 전달동사는 'asked'로 바꾸고, 'if'로 문장을 연결한다.

03 명령문을 간접화법으로 바꿀 때 'to'를 사용하여 문장을 연결한다.

04 부정 명령문을 간접화법으로 바꿀 때 'not to+동사원형'의 형태가 된다. 직접의문문의 전달동사는 'told, advised, ordered' 등으로 바꿀 수 있다.

05 ① who was I → who I was – '의문사+주어+동사'의 어순이 된다. ② that pay attention → to pay attention – 명령문의 간접화법은 'to'를 사용하여 문장을 연결한다.
③ I will move → I would move

p. 507~511

01 ③ **02** ③ **03** ② **04** ⑤ **05** ④

06 ② **07** ④ **08** ① **09** ② **10** ④

11 ⑤ **12** ④ **13** ② **14** ③ **15** ⑤

16 ③ **17** ③ **18** ② **19** ① **20** ④

21 ④

〈서술형 평가〉

22 Phillip said to me, "I am pleased with the magic show."

23 Ian said, "My mom makes aprons well."

24 Kelly told us that she was so happy then.

25 Nicole asked a woman if (whether) the post office was near there.

26 Robin asked Jennifer what she was doing.

27 could

28 takes

29 said that she didn't like spaghetti with cream sauce

30 asked me if I had watched that movie

31 He asked me why I liked old music.

해설

01 doesn't → didn't
→ 주절의 동사가 과거이기 때문에 종속절의 동사 역시 시제를 일치시켜 줘야 하므로 과거형으로 고쳐 써야 한다.

02 의문문의 화법을 전환할 때 'said to → asked'로 바꾸고, 종속절의 동사 역시 과거형으로 바꾼다.

03 주절이 과거형이기 때문에 'will'의 과거형을 써서 'would'로 표현한다.

04 의문사가 있는 의문문의 화법을 전환할 때 의문사가 주어인 경우에는 '의문사＋동사'의 어순을 그대로 사용한다. 직접의문의 동사가 과거형일 경우, 간접의문문의 동사는 한 시제 더 앞선 'had＋과거분사'로 나타낸다.

05 전달동사가 과거이므로, 종속절의 시제도 이에 따라 일치시켜준다.

06 말 한마디에 천 냥 빚을 갚는다.
　　－ A soft answer turns away wrath.

07 명령문의 간접화법의 부정은 not to부정사로 표현한다.
　　→ The teacher said to us, "Don't run in the hallway."

08 일반적인 사실은 주절의 시제와 관계없이 항상 현재형으로 나타낸다.

09 명령문의 간접화법에서 부정표현은 'not＋to 동사원형'의 형태가 되어야 한다.

10 의문사가 있는 의문문의 간접화법에서 'said to'는 'asked'로 바뀌고, 전달문은 '의문사＋주어＋동사'의 어순이 된다.

11 의문사가 없는 직접화법의 의문문이다.

12 처음 전학 왔을 때는 키도 작고 말도 없어서 바보가 아닐까 생각했는데 학기가 끝나고 나서 모든 과목에 있어서 전교에서 가장 높은 점수를 받는 것을 보고 놀랐다는 내용이다. 이 글은 겉만 보고 판단해서는 안된다는 교훈을 준다.

13 남학생이 다리를 다쳐서 학교를 가지 못하는 사이 친구가 매일 숙제와 학교 진도사항을 가지고 와서 알려주었다. 힘들 때 도와주는 친구가 진정한 친구라는 속담이 알맞은 대화다.

14 평서문의 간접화법은 문장을 연결하는 접속사 'that'이 온다.

15 전달 동사 'told'가 과거형이므로, that 이하의 동사 역시 과거형으로 바꿔야 한다. will pick → would pick

16 의문사가 없는 의문문을 간접화법으로 전환할 때 'if' 또는 'whether'로 연결하며, 전달동사가 과거이므로, 'can' 역시 과거형으로 바꿔야 한다.

17 평서문의 간접화법 전환은 'said to'를 'told'로 바꾼 후 'that'으로 문장을 연결한다. 전달 동사가 과거형이기 때문에 'that'이하의 동사 역시 과거형으로 바꿔야 한다.

18 전달 동사의 시제가 과거형이므로, 현재진행형을 과거진행형으로 바꿔 준다.

19 아는 것이 힘이다. → Knowledge is power

20 ④ 하늘은 스스로 돕는 자를 돕는다. → Heaven helps those who help themselves.
　　⑤ 속담은 과거형으로 표현하지 않는다.

21 'asked'를 'said to'로 바꾸고 콤마와 따옴표로 전달자를 구별한다.

〈서술형 평가〉

22 'tell → say to' ～에게 말하다

23 간접화법에서의 동사가 과거형일 경우, 직접화법의 동사는 현재형이다.

24 동사의 시제를 일치시켜 준 후, 부사 역시 시제에 맞게 바꿔 준다.

25 의문사가 없는 의문문을 간접화법으로 전환할 때 'if (whether)'를 사용하여 두 절을 연결해 준다.

26 의문사가 있는 의문문을 간접화법으로 전환할 때, '의문사＋동사'의 순서로 한다.

27 주절의 시제가 과거이기 때문에 'that' 이하의 동사 역시 시제를 일치시켜줘야 한다.

28 현재의 습관에 관한 것이기 때문에 현재형을 써도 된다.

29 동사 'said'와 문장을 연결하는 'that'이 온다.－ 평서문의 간접화법

30 동사 'asked'와 문장을 연결하는 'if'가 온다.
　　－ 의문사가 없는 의문문의 간접화법

31 동사 'asked'와 문장을 연결하는 의문사가 온다.
　　－ 의문사가 있는 의문문의 간접화법

GRAMMAR
MASTER

Level 1	**Level 2**	Level 3

http://www.wcbooks.co.kr